Lukács and Brecht

DAVID PIKE

Lukács and Brecht

The University of North Carolina Press

Chapel Hill and London

©1985 The University of North Carolina Press

All rights reserved

Manufactured in the United States of America

Library of Congress Cataloging in Publication Data

Pike, David, 1950–

Lukács and Brecht.

Bibliography: p.

Includes index.

1. Lukács, György, 1885–1971. 2. Philosophers—Hungary
—Biography. 3. Brecht, Bertolt, 1898–1956—Political
and social views. 4. Brecht, Bertolt, 1898–1956—
Aesthetics. I. Title.

B4815.L84P5 1985 199'.439 84-17406

ISBN 0-8078-1640-x

To the memory of Franz Fühmann

CONTENTS

. . . .

PREFACE

. . . .

We met in Moscow, and in a coffee house Brecht said to me
at the time: "You see, there is a crowd of people who are
determined to incite me against you, and there are certainly
just as many who wish to incite you against me. Let's not
engage in that sort of thing." —Lukács, *Gelebtes Denken*

These two portraits deal with variations of what Czeslaw
Milosz described as "the undefinable menace of total rationalism"[1]—the nature of intellectual life in countries where a rational but lifeless orthodoxy restricts thought to narrowly prescribed lines of reasoning and whose representatives retaliate
against anyone trying to break the bonds of that decreed orthodoxy. The specific variation considered here is a *self-imposed*
form of that menace, namely, an intellectualism undermined
by the very system of rationality supposedly capable of expanding the potentialities of the human mind to its greatest limits.
In a word, this volume inquires into the workings of a dominant and dominating form of logical reasoning upon the minds
of two men, Georg Lukács and Bertolt Brecht, who embraced a
dogma and allowed it to take over their life and work. When
treated as a pair, Brecht and Lukács are usually thought of in
terms of their irreconcilable views on art, but the purpose of
the following portraits is not to reexamine the history of their
well-known aesthetic differences, which culminated in the so-
called expressionism debate of 1937 and 1938. That controversy, which always comes to mind when Brecht and Lukács are
mentioned in the same context, is only of peripheral interest to
the following two studies. For one, the subject has been dealt
with elsewhere,[2] and, for another, the chief concern of this
book, the intellectual obsession with a rational dogma, is really
a matter somewhat separate from that particular exchange of
opinions over aesthetic theories, with all the political intrigues
behind it.

Not that the two problems are in any sense divorced from
each other. The incompatability of Brecht's notions of epic the-

ater and Lukács' convictions about literary realism was paradoxically engendered by an almost identical aesthetic pursuit
that had its roots in the political dogma. Both writers were un-
relentingly hostile to the creation of artistic illusions supposedly representing the reality of life. Brecht intended his theater productions to be a reversal of stage depictions of a static,
unchanging world, and he designed his dramas to show that
immediate reality was not historically fixed and unchangeable.
He wished to present human beings on stage in a social and
political setting that nudged the theatergoers into asking prob-
ing questions about the reality reenacted in front of their eyes,
instead of regarding it as an entertaining diversion. However
much his ideas may have crossed with Brecht's in every other
respect, Lukács likewise promoted styles of writing that he
thought went beyond the representation of a naturalistic, surface reality to reveal the essence of socio-historical phenomena
and their effect upon the consciousness and actions of fictional
but true-to-life characters.

The conflict between the two men inevitably arose because
experimental forms for Brecht were an aesthetic requisite to
the accomplishment of revolutionary goals, whereas Lukács
took "subjective" avant-garde experimentation for literary decadence in the age of capitalist decline—regardless of Brecht's actual intentions—and advocated traditional forms of nineteenth-
century realism instead. In Lukács' mind, this style was the
only adequate aesthetic medium for writers aspiring to objective literary representation. But the point is that each of the
two aesthetics assumed a knowable, preexisting reality; and for
both writers, this reality or perception of reality sprang from a
dogma that led to the suppression of inconvenient facts and to
the virtual mythologization of concrete historical circumstances when applied back to the explicit reality of the ob-
served world. This intellectual trap produced a mounting discrepancy between the thought that flowed from a politicized
aesthetic originally conceived as a means of realistic literary
creation and the actual reality understood as the necessary target of literary or dramatic realism.

In Lukács' case, his imagined reality became part of the
general political mythology that he assisted nolens volens in
constructing, and in frequent instances he argued in favor of

fictional representation that was inherently incapable of defictionalizing the original dogma by balancing it against the world of empirical reality. Lukács' aesthetic of realism could scarcely have been more anti-realistic. As for Brecht, his understanding of realism and the means of achieving it conflicted, ironically, with the prescriptions on art imposed and enforced by the prime defenders of the political dogma to which he otherwise subscribed with relatively few reservations. Fortunately for him, he did not choose Soviet exile when he fled from Germany, and so the breach between reality and its fictionalized representation never really assumed the hypertrophied proportions that it inevitably took on in much of Lukács' theoretical writing. Another reason for that, too, was simply Brecht's general avoidance of Soviet reality as the subject of direct literary portrayal, a reality that he had otherwise enveloped with a number of quintessentially Stalinist myths.

For both men, however, their commitment to a dogmatized and dogmatic political credo was the prime source of their artistic and philosophical inspiration; the dogma inspired them in their quest for aesthetic solutions appropriate to the contemporary political age, the transition from capitalism to socialism, and they both used it to claim exclusivity for their respective theoretical approaches. But the dogma likewise produced a view of the two antithetic political systems that often failed to correspond with the real world and yielded depictions of a social reality that only existed in their own minds. The dogma functioned, then, to form an interrelated understanding of fascism in Germany and socialism under Stalin. These two political and social realities were viewed by Brecht and Lukács in a related light not in spite of their basic theoretical antinomy but because of it—fascism and socialism were both, each in its own way, products of knowable historical laws.

Lukács and Brecht both regarded German fascism as the historically lawful, undisguised manifestation of the "most chauvinistic, most aggressive, most nationalist elements of finance capital," as the Comintern designated it, and this exclusively rationalistic, economistic view of fascism led both men to precise analyses of some sides of fascism and features of life in a fascist state. But these observations often remained in the realm of partial truths, and, however accurate some of them may have been, they never added up to a broad perspective of the whole. Rather, Brecht and Lukács habitually arranged these half-truths so that the emerging totality matched a preconceived notion of how they thought the whole ought to appear, defining any facts and circumstances that failed to mesh perfectly out of existence. The overall consequence for both writers was in many instances a vulgarization of the intricacy of National Socialism as a social, historical, and human phenomenon.

The writing of both men can be examined for traces of the damage done to their work by a dogma that caused frequently oversimplified and ultimately inaccurate or one-sided representations of National Socialism.[3] Examinations of this sort would show, however, that Lukács' writing suffered to a far greater extent than Brecht's. After all, Lukács went into Soviet exile and had little chance to modify the original dogma—as it pertained to fascism—when new information came to light. He could not have modified it if he had wanted to and even then, in the interest of his own survival, could only have done so in his private thoughts. Outside information that tended to go against the dogma was simply not available to him in the USSR. Brecht, on the other hand, was not nearly as constricted by external circumstances in forming his opinion of National Socialism. Though the dogma caused his critical faculties to atrophy and often deprived his political philosophy of any real sophistication, in his artistic work he was accustomed to abstracting his settings and characters to such an extent that his unmediated political views and stubborn illusions rarely resulted in creative work that contained offensively hackneyed or unacceptably simplistic, one-dimensional depictions of reality. Besides which, Brecht was simply a man of countless contradictions, and these also show up in his creative writing. Of course, another obvious factor entered in. Unlike Lukács, whose very life was threatened, Brecht was able to practice and refine his art without fear of an arrest by the Soviet political police in the early hours of the morning. He had no such external inducement to violate his own artistic impulses and bring his creative writing into close proximity to or absolute conformity with the doctrine.

But the dogma also impelled both men in another direction.

"Consistent reasoning which orders one to by-pass a fact when a concept comes into conflict with reality must eventually lead to costly errors,"[4] wrote Milosz. These errors are conspicuous in the writing of Brecht and Lukács, whose prefashioned understanding of fascism trapped them into an assessment of the Soviet Union, the antithesis of fascism. This assessment matched reality even less than their judgment of Hitler's National Socialism. Their essentially Stalinist interpretation of fascism worked to nullify most perceptions of the USSR that departed from the standard, authoritative presentation of "Soviet reality." In the process of defining the dynamics of political and intellectual life under Stalin, they fictionalized basic features of that existence by accepting, largely unchallenged, many of Stalin's most fundamental, self-serving myths.

Lukács, living in the USSR, should have been far better informed than Brecht about Soviet realities and the gap between them and Stalin's complex of fictionalizations. Lukács, it would seem, ought to have had the opportunity to modify the dogma at least slightly, if only in his mind. He was on the spot and presumably capable of observing the actual workings of Soviet reality, much as Brecht was somewhat less susceptible to the rigid Stalinist dogma about fascism because he could alter the doctrine as new information came to his attention, as long as the new facts were still at least roughly compatible with the original dogma. The difference between the experiences of the two men, of course, was that many facts never got through to Lukács or any other ordinary Soviet citizen, facts and arguments perhaps available to Brecht; and when they did, Lukács simply did not have the liberty to reshape a doctrine, even if he had been capable of assimilating contradictory information without distorting it to fit the "dialectic." Given the circumstances of life under Stalin, Lukács could conceivably have led a schizophrenic intellectual existence, sporting one political philosophy for external appearances and cultivating another for his own private purposes. After 1953 he expended a great deal of energy constructing this very legend about his intellectual life in Stalin's time. But Lukács, as the following portrait tries to show, became far more caught up in the hyperrational perversions and syllogisms of intellectual Stalinism than he ever cared later to admit.

If only because of the ready access to information, Brecht ought to have been better able than Lukács to revise the dogma when certain developments in Soviet Russia leaked out to the West and suggested strongly that reality had outpaced the doctrine. In Western European exile throughout the thirties, Brecht was certainly exposed to facts and arguments withheld from Lukács in his shielded existence in Moscow, which is not to say that Lukács could not deal effectively with circumstances that ran counter to his own preexisting dialectic by ignoring them or rationalizing them out of an objective existence. Paradoxically, then, Brecht in certain respects had a greater opportunity than Lukács to acquaint himself with views of events in Stalin's Russia that contradicted his own political philosophy, but he proved just as adroit as Lukács at dismissing many of them; and what he was told about the Soviet Union in conformity with Stalin's various fictions he accepted by and large on blind faith, occasionally mixing in a small measure of operationally meaningless skepticism.

Their "dialectical thinking" turned both Brecht and Lukács into tyrannophiles. This is no doubt a harsh judgment, but one that is not unjustified in a specific context. In Brecht's mind, Stalin's "immense services," his general "usefulness," consistently outweighed his possible misconduct, "mistakes" and crimes that, as far as Brecht was concerned, were mostly never confirmed anyway. Lukács' similar brand of tyrannophilia pervades many of his writings in the thirties. As late as 1969 and presumably until his death in 1971, Lukács' basic political judgment of the dead tyrant remained, "Without Stalin, things would have been impossible,"[5] and Lukács achieved a near-perfect unity of political theory and philosophical or literary-critical practice. The irony in Brecht's case was that his political theory was usually suitably orthodox from a Stalinist perspective in matters pertaining to the Soviet Union but that he had gotten off on the wrong track in his artistic practice. The conflict between political theory and literary practice in Brecht's case explains his treatment at the hands of the Stalinists before 1933 (the polemics against him in the *Die Linkskurve*), during the exile years (the expressionism debate), and after the war in East Germany (the various antiformalism campaigns). In the mid-thirties especially, from a distance of a few thousand kilometers, the German and Soviet Stalinists tried unsuccessfully to impose their special aesthetic canon upon Brecht, which they called socialist realism. But he stood his ground then and later in the GDR and retained his artistic integrity, however one cares to criticize certain distinct features of his work. Lukács, by contrast, was victimized by the Stalinists only in the sense that his own politics, combined with the experience of thirteen years under Stalin, caused him to participate in the operationalization of the very dogma that turned against him and perverted much of his work by melding theory and practice. (The extent to which that participation was voluntary or under duress is the subject of the first portrait.) In any case, Lukács paid a high price for the benefits that his orthodoxy afforded him. There is also good reason to believe that he recognized the toll, if only intuitively, and envied Brecht for his independence at the same time he chastised him for it: "Brecht always wanted, in the most fantastic way, . . . to reserve a secure and kosher place for himself within the party, on the one hand, and maintain complete freedom on the other hand."[6] Lukács certainly had Brecht's artistic freedom in mind, too; and though he opposed Brecht's literary practice and would have had no qualms about helping to place restrictions upon him had he lived in the USSR, Lukács may have been subliminally envious of Brecht because he, Lukács, had been unable to locate a similarly secure, kosher, and, above all else, at least limitedly independent niche for himself in the party. Unlike Brecht, Lukács sought his political and intellectual security directly *in* the party, which Brecht never officially joined, and the "kosher" niche that Lukács undoubtedly hollowed out for himself there exacted a high intellectual and moral price, even though it did offer him at the same time a modest measure of security, at least as much as could be expected under the circumstances.

Whatever conclusions one draws about the lasting artistic significance of the aesthetic theories that Brecht and Lukács evolved from the political dogma and whatever correspondences and contradictions between political theory and literary critical or creative practice one may identify in their writings, both men seem to have died generally guilt-free with respect to their moral complicity in the advocacy of a doctrine whose practical side killed millions and whose theoretical rationalizations both Brecht and Lukács assisted, to varying degrees, in formulating. Lukács made a practice of analyzing the essence of Stalinism in the USSR after 1953, working hard on the legend of his own opposition to it even while constantly backtracking by explaining how indispensable Stalin had been; whereas Brecht generally kept silent until, "angered" and "embittered"[7] by Khrushchev's revelations at the twentieth party congress, which largely only confirmed what was already known in the West, he wrote several poems about Stalin—for his desk drawer. But in at least two of these, Brecht still clung to notions of Stalin's historical "usefulness." Perhaps this almost pathetic unwillingness to sever their final judgment of one of history's greatest mass murderers from ultimately apologetic rhetoric about "historical accomplishments" was the means by which Brecht and Lukács—maybe even subliminally—assuaged their own consciences and achieved some peace of mind about their role in it all. If so, the following utterance made later by one of Stalin's surviving victims in reference to the de-Stalinization campaign in 1962 is perhaps not altogether irrelevant and certainly raises a question that has been ignored for too long: "They are afraid that an unqualified exposure of Stalin would turn its cutting edge against them. These people are dancing cravenly around his image, sometimes playfully sticking their tongues out at it, sometimes, on the contrary, bowing and scraping before it, recalling his past 'services.' I think that this 'balancing act' on questions of the personality cult will end in political and ideological bankruptcy for these people."[8]

ACKNOWLEDGMENTS

This volume originated in two phases. The first two chapters of the Brecht portrait were written in winter 1982 for publication in the *Brecht Yearbook*. During the second half of 1983 I revised this version and wrote a third chapter for it, together with the entire Lukács portrait. This latter work was done with the support of the Alexander von Humboldt-Stiftung. All translations from the German and Russian are mine throughout unless otherwise indicated.

David Pike
Bad Godesberg
December 1983

. . . .

PART ONE

Lukács

CHAPTER I

Introduction

The demands made by the German Communist party (KPD) upon its intellectuals underwent a sweeping revision during the bolshevization of the party in the twenties. The KPD had no compelling reason any more to call upon the intellectuals for theoretical analyses of current events because ideology and its translation into political action was no longer the preponderant issue by the end of the decade. Policies having increasingly little to do with pristine doctrine were prescribed to the KPD by the Communist International in accordance with Soviet state interests as Stalin defined them, and the German Communists now counted upon their intellectuals to come up with the ideological rationalization for these largely imposed political programs. Theoretical discussion and inner-party criticism degenerated largely into haggling over comparatively irrelevant doctrinal fine points already so constricted by calcified obsessions with "right" and "left" deviations that meaningful debate was out of the question. Conflicts and scandals within the party went on, but this kind of discord, though those involved invariably couched their arguments in doctrinal terms, often arose only because select political functionaries had already been marked as targets after having lost a behind-the-scenes fight over some strategical-tactical issue. To add to the confusion, disagreements of this sort were often so snarled in private animosities that it was impossible to tell quarrels based on genuine policy differences from controversies originating in personal feuds and rivalries.

In this entire process, most of the party's original intellectuals lost any hope of influencing policy based on their notion of correct theory. Now they were expected to slip into a new role as apologists responsible for thinking up the ideological phrases legitimizing the current line. In the face of this challenge to the qualities that made them intellectuals in the first place, many capitulated altogether and went along with what was demanded of them, some perhaps reluctantly, others with no apparent misgivings; a few turned their backs to a role that they quickly spotted as an utter perversion, either severing their ties with the party or being eventually expelled; and a small number presumably convinced themselves that they could compromise enough to stay in the party while still resisting the pressure to conform completely.

LUKÁCS AND STALINISM

Late in his life Georg Lukács singled out this precise subordination of theory to practice as the essence of Stalinism. Under Stalin the labor movement retained the practical character of Marxism in theory, but in practice revolutionary activity was no longer planned with any real concern for a correct theoretical understanding of the complex issues involved. Rather, that "understanding" was affixed after the fact to a specific tactical course of action. Whereas the basic course of social development proceeded according to Marx and Lenin in an essentially predetermined direction, with specific questions of strategy and tactics arising from time to time within the context of this general historical trend, Stalin had reversed this sequence. "He regarded the tactical problem as being primary and derived the theoretical generalizations from it."[1] This is Lukács' characterization of a state of affairs typical of a monolithic Communist party that claims to act in accord with a specific ideology mandating a certain course of revolutionary action but that generally designs tactics and strategy first and reserves only an ancillary role for theory. Once a party reaches this stage, theoretical judgments arrived at independently and without taking note of the preeminence of political questions may easily conflict with the party's current line and become an outright hindrance to the pursuit of a particular policy. By no means is the doctrine that brought the movement to power abandoned; it contains, after all, the party's surface raison d'être—its historical legitimization and the ideological validation of its exclusive claim to rightful power. But reduced to an appendage of politics, the theory is corrupted.

Lukács never had any disagreement with the basic theory. His problems with the party, where they genuinely existed, stemmed from the difficulty of keeping the relationship between theory and practice in an alignment proper from the perspective of the political leadership. By the late twenties, he had lost the opportunity to articulate and refine the theory without outside interference and was obliged to pursue his vocation just like other party intellectuals charged with rationalizing tactics. The trouble was that the party kept changing its line, and on each occasion the intellectuals naturally had to revamp the theory and do it fast. Otherwise, the theoretical ground on which their feet were firmly planted would soon begin to shake underneath them, regardless of whether the party had been standing by their side just a short time before. When that happened in Lukács' case, even if he had been convinced of the truth of "his" theories when he entrusted them to paper, resistance was always the furthest thing from his mind, at least until after Stalin's death. He yielded to the party presumably because "party discipline is . . . a higher, more abstract stage of loyalty. The loyalty of a person in public is to take an ideological stance with regard to some historically given direction, and it remains loyalty even when there is not complete unity in one concrete issue or another with this historical tendency."[2]

Lukács claimed that he never solved this kind of dilemma by a total capitulation of principles; he spent the better part of a lifetime, and certainly the Stalin years, in search of ways to make correct theoretical pronouncements without being overly obvious about it. In other words, he was constrained to promote his version of theoretical truth while concealing as best he could possible related strategic and tactic inferences that clashed with official policy. If Lukács' version of events is accurate, he had to have made his points in terms sufficiently vague and indirect to prevent the party's chief ideologues from uncovering or, if it suited their purposes, contriving some deviation. No matter how covertly or attenuatedly these ideas were expressed, the risk would still have been substantial, especially during Soviet exile, and on several occasions during his lifetime Lukács was in fact "discovered." These discoveries sometimes had a basis in fact; just as often, personal or political considerations unrelated to the actual substance of Lukács' position on a given issue produced the essentially meaningless charges of "idealism" or "revisionism" that echoed and reechoed down through the years. In any case, the self-criticism that Lukács practiced on these occasions was, he claimed, absolutely cynical and served a single ultimate objective.[3] His insincere renunciations functioned as an "admission ticket" enabling him to pursue the activity that outweighed in importance any other: using his intellectual abilities to further the working-class cause or, by the late twenties, fighting fascism. Neither enterprise would have been possible, he contended, had he not played his cards carefully and ended up outside of the party.[4]

The moral dilemma sprang from the fact that the struggle with fascism coincided with the worst years of Stalinism, and Lukács fought his battles as a member of Stalinized Communist parties, first the Hungarian, then the Soviet, the German, and, finally, the Hungarian again. Using Lukács' own definition of Stalinism, the period in which he produced his most highly regarded work were years when the chasm between theory and practice was widest. That circumstance alone, it seems, ought to have presented Lukács with an insurmountable obstacle to the evolution of his ideas. But in 1969 Lukács claimed that all of his literary theoretical essays written in the Soviet Union had in fact contained elements in opposition to Stalinism, from "Erzählen und Beschreiben" to "Die intellektuelle Physiognomie des künstlerischen Gestaltens" and including the article about the application of Lenin's teachings to literature.[5] That particular piece, he said, was aimed directly at Stalinism. Not that he had come out openly against the regime, of course; but when Johannes R. Becher complained to him in Soviet exile that writing was impossible nowadays because anything sincere was prohibited and what was of poor quality ought not to be committed to paper in the first place, Lukács answered that this was simply not so. Granted, criticizing Stalin for being a poor Marxist was out of the question. But Lukács could point to a regional party secretary and describe his faulty understanding of Marxism in terms that came close to the "good" Marxism of the central party organs. Of course one took a certain risk, Lukács admitted, and Becher wished to know how to establish the limitations of one's criticism. Lukács answered that it was all very simple. "When I bang my head against the wall, I know I cannot go on and have to turn around."[6]

If Lukács' rendition of his past attitudes is accurate, he apparently pressed his views to the limit under the singularly restrictive conditions of Stalinism, constantly risking the danger that the wall marking the perimeters of a position still defensible even when gauged against Stalinist standards would be used to put him up against. How credible is Lukács' version of his oppositional posture in Soviet exile? An answer to the question is hard to come by because on those occasions when his principles may have had an unorthodox kernel to them, if only by implication, Lukács would still have been compelled to weave them together so tightly with Stalinist thought that the two sets of ideas virtually merged. Reading Lukács today, it is a painstaking process to distinguish between remarks made out of expedience or opportunism and utterances of a Stalinist tenor that may have mirrored genuine conviction at the time Lukács made them.[7] By arguing as Lukács later did, he established a built-in rationalization for any embarrassing passage— it was merely "tactical." In this fashion, of course, entire books could be dismissed as grand camouflage. If it is true, on the other hand, that he smuggled opposition into his major writings published in Stalin's time and in Stalin's Russia, his methods are definitely worth examining because Lukács must have constructed a cohesive body of thought, containing a distinct though covert anti-Stalinist core, during the bloodiest, most paranoid years of Stalinism. This intellectual coup would have to have succeeded against the backdrop of a mercurial Stalinist political line that was equally unified or "cohesive" in the sense that precipitous shifts in tactics called for the immediate synchronization of theory in all areas of ideology, historiography, philosophy, and literary theory. Did Lukács really contrive to blend his work into the pattern of theoretical Stalinism in the Soviet Union while maintaining the inner integrity of an anti-Stalinist nucleus?

Just before he died, Lukács spoke of all his "Moscow heresies"[8] and contended that his opposition to Stalinism in Soviet exile was not just confined to the realm of aesthetics but was "universal."[9] How did he fool the ideologues? "You had to quote Stalin in some way; an article in which Stalin's name did not appear could scarcely be published. But that could be solved by my writing to the effect that, as Stalin expresses it so well, history is a struggle between the old and the new. Having done that, the matter was taken care of as far as I was concerned."[10] But was it really all that simple or is there something to Leszek Kołakowski's argument that Lukács' profound erudition and intellectual power guaranteed the superiority of his ideas to the best brain storms of "run-of-the-mill ideologues of Stalinism, who were all ignoramusus,"[11] but that the end result was still quintessentially Stalinist—at its highest level of theoretical, aesthetic, and philosophical articulateness, but the progeny of Stalinism nevertheless?

THE BLUM THESES

Lukács' account of his work and its relationship to Stalinism hinges to a large extent on his later claims about the Blum theses of 1928 and their importance for the evolution of his thought. These theses represented a radical turnabout in his political outlook, he said;[12] his career as a party politician came to an abrupt halt when the Comintern denounced the theses, but at the same time, they opened the door to his pioneering work in the field of Marxist philosophy and aesthetics. He summed up this curious dialectic in his autobiographical notes: "Politically: a devastating defeat. Expulsion from CI [Communist International] a danger. Korsch's fate. Powerlessness during the crisis caused by fascism. On the other hand, the impetus to a higher level of development and greater effectiveness of the theory. This duality: to give up the first [political activity] and to expand the second [ideological activity]."[13]

As Lukács viewed his own intellectual development, then, he built upon the foundation of the theses in all of his subsequent work, and his ideas evolved with logical consistency. Everything in his thought was therefore the continuation of something previous, and he was personally unaware of any inorganic elements.[14] In particular, the theses reflected his passage from a sectarian to a more pragmatic view of revolution and revolutionary development. Prior to them, Lukács explained, he and others in the party had all acted like messianic sectarians, convinced that revolution would take place the following day.[15] But the practical considerations of daily party work in Hungary under the conditions of illegality had forced the Landler faction, of which Lukács was a member, to view prospects for revolution in Hungary more realistically, even though this realism impinged upon the sectarianism still standard in Béla Kun's faction of the party and, of course, in the Communist International. Lukács' Blum theses and its central idea of "democratic dictatorship," an ostensibly broader appeal to the masses than proletarian dictatorship, therefore witnessed to the "triumph of Hungarian realism"[16] and marked the beginning for him personally of a straight line of continuity in his thought. This is Lukács' reading of events.

The Blum theses, it is true, ended in one of Lukács' most serious confrontations with the party, and his detractors were still holding up his arguments in them as an illustration of Lukács' long-standing practice of deviationism more than a quarter of a century later, though the precise political epithets changed somewhat over the years. On the eve of the Comintern's most emphatic and inflexible ultra-extremist phase, Lukács' advocacy of a more moderate sounding political program—"democratic dictatorship"—as the strategy best suited for Hungary was bound to collide head-on with all the congealed notions of proletarian revolution and proletarian dictatorship. Their revision, tactical or otherwise, struck Stalinist Marxist-Leninists as utterly inconceivable. The Comintern, after all, had recently held its sixth world congress, and by the time it met in summer 1928, its organizational structure and operating principles matched Lukács' own later characterization of Stalinism as the reduction of theory to the status of an appurtenance to an already set program of political action. In line with the Comintern's basic function, one of the primary purposes of the sixth congress was to define the ideological rationale for Stalin's reversion to radical policies symbolized by the replacement of the New Economic Policy with the First Five-Year Plan, a switch in policy motivated to a significant degree not by ideological or economic considerations at all but by the inner-party power struggle.

By the late twenties changes in Soviet domestic policy routinely affected the setting of Comintern principles mandatory for all Communist parties. Thus, class warfare outside the Soviet Union was said to have taken a turn similar in intensity to that in the USSR. The relative stabilization of capitalism in existence since 1924 was over, ran the usual argument, and the Comintern had entered its "third period" of activity since the end of the war. The political and economic affairs of industrialized capitalist states around the world were soon to be wracked by profound crises. The requirements of self-defense now impelled the bourgeoisie in the direction of an economic offensive against the proletariat, both as a means of recouping its financial losses and of surviving the proletariat's renewed readiness to engage in revolutionary action. "Wars and revolutions" were imminent, and the major earmarks of these years were the emergence of "fascism," on the one hand (a synonym for the most violent form of the capitalist offensive), and, on the other hand, the increasingly militant posture of the revolutionary proletariat.

In this overwrought atmosphere Lukács' mention of "democratic" rather than proletarian dictatorship, even if he envisaged it at the time only for Hungary, was soon taken as a bid of open defiance by the Comintern. The program itself was expressed in vague terms; today, especially with the hindsight of Stalinist tactics like those practiced during the popular front era of the thirties and in the postwar popular democracies in Eastern Europe, the program comes across as little more than a roundabout way of arriving at the same political objective. It was characterized only by a bit more rhetorical flexibility. "Democratic dictatorship, then, as a more perfect realization of bourgeois democracy, is in the strict sense of the word a battleground—the location of the all-important battle between the bourgeoisie and the proletariat."[17] But the democratic dictatorship was fundamentally incompatible with the economic and social power of the bourgeoisie, Lukács added, even though the "class content" of its specific objectives and immediate demands did not transcend the bounds of bourgeois society or, rather, was the ultimate realization of bourgeois democracy. As such, it brought society to a crossroads. Democratic dictatorship was thus a dialectical form of transition, either to proletarian revolution or to counterrevolution. Because history could not stand still, democratic dictatorship needed to be understood, then, as an expression of this concrete transition, one in which the bourgeois revolution evolved into a revolution of the proletariat.[18]

One of the major threats to genuine democracy in Germany came in the form of Social Democracy, said Lukács, and, like Stalin, he traduced "opportunism" as nothing but a brand of fascism: The Social Democrats pretended to offer the workers a choice between democracy and fascism, but by acting as if democracy as it then existed in Germany was distinct from fascism, they threw sand in the eyes of the proletariat. Social Democracy backed suppression of the class struggle, blocked the fight for better wages, and allowed itself and the trade-union bureaucracy to be drawn into and swallowed up by the fascist state apparatus.[19] Therefore, the thought uppermost in the minds of the Communists ought to be the unmasking of the fraudulent Social Democratic option "democracy or fascism." The current stirrings of a democratic development in Hungary as well as in the "Western democracies," charged Lukács, represented in reality only a strain of fascistization contingent upon cooperation between the big bourgeoisie and the Social Democratic labor bureaucracy. That was why the solution democracy or fascism needed to be countered with a different solution: "'class against class,' . . . the struggle for democratic dictatorship."[20]

In the Comintern's third-period rhetoric, the slogan "class against class" implied that the present revolutionary crisis had stripped Social Democracy of its working-class facade and laid bare its congenital allegiance to the bourgeoisie. It was incumbent upon the Communist party to assist the proletariat in ridding itself of Social Democratic illusions about "democracy" in a bourgeois state as the most direct means of inspiring the working class in its struggle against the imperialist or fascist bourgeoisie—thus, class against class.[21] Though Lukács himself refrained from using expressions like "social fascism," "moderate wing of fascism," "third party of the bourgeoisie," "main social prop of the bourgeoisie," or "twin of fascism," the substance of his remarks about Social Democracy coincides with Stalinist thinking with regard to the "twins" of fascism. Symptomatically, the Blum theses contained no reference to Hitler.

Whether Lukács anticipated the reaction in the Comintern to his idea of democratic dictatorship when he wrote the theses or even intended the slogan to be taken as a possible strategy not just for Hungary but for the industrialized European nations as well remains a subject of speculation. In any event, the Comintern reacted to the theses quickly. Lukács' talk of a "bourgeois democratic" as opposed to a proletarian dictatorship or a democratic dictatorship of workers and peasants in place of the standard dictatorship of the proletariat was "liquidationism" in the Hungarian Communist party. What Lukács had really done was to plant his feet firmly upon Social Democratic soil by suggesting that bourgeois democracy was the best battlefield for the struggle between bourgeoisie and proletariat. "He denies thereby the growth of the bourgeoisie's form of democracy into fascism; he disregards the entire third period." His theses had nothing in common with bolshevism.[22]

Lukács recanted. Years later he explained that he had exchanged his repudiation of the theses for a figurative "admission ticket"—the chance to remain in the party and continue fighting fascism. But Lukács' retrospective account of his actions does not hold up very well under closer examination. On numerous occasions after 1945, Lukács made the point that his emphasis on democracy in the Blum theses represented the first tentative expression of ideas to which the party returned seven or eight years later during the popular front, when Stalin inaugurated a political program distinguished by an apparent renunciation of proletarian revolution and dictatorship in favor of democracy. Lukács' rendition implies that he, and not the party, had correctly defined the political tactics supposedly best geared to European circumstances; he, rather than the party, had recognized early on that the tide of revolution in Europe had crested and that the forces of reaction were gathering momentum, twin developments that placed the tactics of a united and popular front on the agenda. But precisely under these ominous circumstances, with Hitlerism on the rise, leadership was no longer forthcoming from the Comintern. The organization was falling increasingly under the sway of Stalin's tactics.

The Comintern vacillated between right and left, and Stalin himself, Lukács explained, intervened calamitously in this vacillation around 1928 by calling Social Democracy the twin brother of fascism,[23] thus slamming the door shut to any united front with the left. Though he, Lukács, supported Stalin against the opposition in Soviet internal affairs, particularly against Trotsky, this particular action of Stalin's was personally repugnant to him.[24]

This claim is the cornerstone of Lukács' retrospective efforts to detach himself from Stalin's policies, in this instance from the disastrous party obsession with "social fascism." Though he later insisted that the seventh world congress in 1935 and the resultant new political line completely affirmed his Blum theses,[25] Lukács never pointed out that the Communists in the mid-thirties, however halfheartedly, also repudiated one of the key ideas of the theses: the seventh world congress finally rejected the standard Comintern identification of Social Democracy with a form of fascism. In 1967 Lukács also chose to say nothing about his own support of Stalin's epithet with respect to the "twin brothers of fascism," support lasting well into 1933; nor did he mention his continuing abuse of Social Democracy as a form of fascism as late as 1934.[26] The popular front policy "vindicated" Lukács' theses, then, only in the limited sense that there were some rudimentary similarities between his "democratic dictatorship" and the "genuine" democratic republic that the Communists advocated for Germany during the popular front years. Beyond that, there was no particular pioneering quality to the theses, neither in terms of a later Communist reassessment of policy, nor with respect to Lukács' own intellectual development.

In any event, Lukács' mythmaking about his own personal evolution begins with the theses and proceeds to his first extended stay in the Soviet Union. His direct involvement in party politics in 1928–29, the Blum theses, and the blistering criticism to which they were subjected made it clear to him that his future lay in areas less strewn with pitfalls than the formulation of party policy in day-to-day tactical issues. For if he had been so obviously right in the theses about matters of tactics and still suffered such a devastating defeat at the hands of the party, his "practical political" abilities in the future had to become profoundly problematical. For that reason, he had a clear conscience about withdrawing from his political career and concentrating on theoretical concerns.[27] As disastrous as the theses had been for him in the realm of politics, then, they initiated a change in his entire philosophical outlook,[28] and with fundamentally altered views he started work in 1930 in the Marx-Engels Institute in Moscow. As Lukács told the story in 1967, two fortunate occurrences combined there with the "political-theoretical significance" of the Blum theses to give even greater meaning to the new direction of his thought. One event was his reading of Marx' "Ökonomisch-philosophische Manuskripte," the other was his friendship with Mikhail Lifshitz. While reading Marx, all the "ideological biases" of *Geschichte und Klassenbewusstsein*, his influential volume of 1923, collapsed. He soon came to understand that he would have to begin his work entirely anew if he wished to realize his theoretical ideas as he now envisaged them. With his feet on Soviet soil, he found himself exhilarated by prospects for a new beginning.[29]

Excursus
The Philosophy Debate

The single greatest factor influencing Lukács' political and theoretical thought after 1930 was not really the Marx manuscripts or the Blum theses at all. In fact, the change in his basic outlook to which Lukács was later so fond of referring was occasioned less by his own theoretical insights than by his general acceptance of opinions voiced by the winning side in the "philosophy discussion" that took place in the Soviet Union in 1930 and 1931. In June 1934 Lukács addressed the Institute of Philosophy of the Communist Academy and noted that the idealistic foundations of his own world view had begun to crumble in the course of his own "practical party work" and in direct proportion to his familiarity with the writings of Lenin and Stalin. "However," Lukács added, "it was my stay in the Soviet Union in 1930 and 1931, especially the philosophical discussion taking place at the time, that brought me to a point of complete clarification of philosophical questions."[1]

The irony about Lukács' expression of indebtedness to this particular discussion is that this very debate betokened Stalin's first heavy-handed interference in theoretical disputes. A milestone in the process that transformed Marxism-Leninism into a "science of legitimation,"[2] the debate spelled the end of any quest for philosophical or ideological insights in the USSR that had merit independent of their usefulness to Stalin as a theoretical endorsement of his policies. From now on, the Stalinists understood "Leninist party-mindedness," as they and no one else defined it, to be the sine qua non not just of Soviet philosophy but of all "theoretical fronts," especially Soviet historiography and literary criticism. The debate was a graphic illustration of the essential dynamics of intellectual Stalinism as Lukács himself later characterized them: Stalin took the scientific and theoretical principles of social development established by Marx and Engels, canceled them out as determining factors in setting strategical or tactical policy, and thus reversed the "hierarchy: principle-strategy-tactics."[3] Ideology reverted accordingly to a rhetorical affirmation of Stalin's politics—a system of appended principles that required fresh doctoring every time Stalin switched his tactics.

This was Lukács' assessment of Stalinism in 1967; but things had appeared differently to him at the time of the very debate that turned his "hierarchy" around. It was on the eve of this discussion that Lukács arrived in the Soviet Union, "Cominterned," he said, to Moscow.[4]

MECHANISTS, DIALECTICIANS, AND MENSHEVIZING IDEALISTS

The debate was not a sudden occurrence. Throughout much of the twenties, Soviet philosophy had been the battleground for a controversy between two camps made up of "dialecticians" and "mechanists,"[5] the difference between the two schools of thought being a more or less honest disagreement over whether the natural sciences or philosophy deserved priority in a materialist view of the world. The mechanists were professing Marxists, but they held that the natural sciences and the quest for scientific laws in nature should be unencumbered by philosophical interference; the dialecticians, whose primary exponent was Avram Deborin, took the opposite tack and gave philosophy a higher order of precedence. The party eventually intervened and condemned both camps, creating a "dialectical synthesis of both forms of ignorance,"[6] as Kołakowski summed up the intrinsic philosophical significance of their programs. But these disagreements had still reflected fairly normal intellectual processes, at least until the very end. Servility, to cite Kołakowski again, had not yet become the whole raison d'être of Soviet philosophy.[7]

It did when Stalin intervened in Soviet philosophical disputes. He spoke at the Conference of Marxist Agricultural Workers in December 1929, where his key note—one that he repeated ad infinitum in the coming years—was that theory had "lagged" behind the practice of socialist construction;[8] and one year later, an interview with the party executive of the Institute of Red Professors was staged at which Stalin coined the infamous expression "menshevizing idealism" to characterize the Deborin group. Finally, he sent an open letter to the journal *Proletarskaja revoljutsija* in October 1931 that added even sharper political accents to the debate.

In the remarks made on these three occasions, Stalin established the guidelines and set the tone for a debate that intermingled ideological and political considerations, reducing theory to the status of a handmaiden of politics, domestic and foreign: the ideology was articulated and manipulated to justify the excommunication of the widest array of Marxist Russian and Western European political figures and to anathematize as many of these non-Stalinist viewpoints as possible by lumping them all together under a few choice labels. "The true explication and development of Marxist theory is taking place only in the Soviet Union," said Mark Mitin, one of the young Stalinist philosophers who launched their long careers in the philosophy debate; "a genuine science of society is possible only in our country. Our party and the Comintern are, today, the only representatives and exponents of Marxist theory."[9] Stalin's three talks were said to have forged the "links in a single chain of measures" taken to "pull together" those sections of the "theoretical front" that had lagged behind and thus to close the gap between theory and practice. That gap was to be stopped by erecting the theoretical underpinning to a politically motivated crusade against real and potential opponents of Stalinist policies at the crucial midpoint of the First Five-year Plan and by contrasting multiple forms of "revisionism" with the only true Marxism of the day, Stalinist Leninism. For instance, it was charged that representatives of the "mechanistic revision of dialectical materialism" provided the theoretical basis for the opportunistic right deviation ("the agency of kulakism in the party"), whereas the "idealistic revision of materialist dialectics" practiced by the "menshevizing idealists" was directly related to deviations stretching from menshevism and the Second International to more recent Social Democratic "revisionists," including an entire band of contemporary political apostates or "falsifiers" of Marxism like Alfred Adler,

Karl Kautsky, Heinrich Brandler, August Thalheimer, Rosa Luxemburg, and, of course, Trotsky, whom Stalin had recently banished to Prinkipo.[10]

Leninism, characterized in Stalin's original words as the Marxism of the epoch of imperialism and proletarian revolution, was elevated to the level of a qualitatively new stage of development in all areas of Marxist theory. The canonization of Leninism as the only true Marxism in the current era was, of course, a transparent attempt to legitimize Stalin's rule, and this particular motive, though the cult of Stalin's personality was still in its infancy, occasionally shone through the rhetoric. As one commentator put it, the party answered Deborin's "Menshevist slander" with Stalin's "classical appraisal" (in *Problems of Leninism*) of the role played by Lenin in the development of Marxist philosophy. This definitive elaboration by the present leader (*vozhd*) of the Leninist party remained unshaken by all the efforts of the pathetic little creatures of defunct menshevism, menshevizing idealism, and, outside the USSR, the Second International (the "International of Social Fascists").[11] But their efforts did pose a certain threat to the construction of socialism in the USSR because the praxis of the proletariat, actively involved in the construction of socialism and forced to ward off ideological subversives, called for a solid theoretical shield; advanced theoretical work that stood in the service of socialist construction, unveiled the perspectives of the future, and articulated the tasks of the forward march toward communism was indispensable. Unfortunately, antiphilosophical deviations had surfaced within certain vacillating circles of the party. These circles had "failed to understand" sufficiently the essence of the doctrine developed by Marx, Engels, and Lenin and had "not grasped" the best traditions of bolshevism.[12] But the party was uncovering all that was putrid and opportunistic, all that was non-Bolshevist and anti-Leninist in the theory—everything that in one form or another expressed a bourgeois or petty bourgeois influence on the ideology of the proletariat, no matter how well such contaminating influences disguised and hid themselves.[13]

On the one hand, then, the mechanists were "liquidators" who ignored the Leninist phase in the evolution of dialectical materialism and "openly" denied the theory of materialist dialectics. The "menshevizing idealists," on the other hand, had become caught up in the debilitating mysticism of Hegelian philosophy and were equally blind to the Leninist stage of Marxist philosophy.[14] Thus, of the "two brands of revisionism of Marxism," the mechanistic kind was "openly Menshevist" in character, whereas the other, cleverly disguised menshevizing idealism, basically sailed "under the flag of Hegelianism (Deborin)."[15] In fact, the Stalinist philosophers made the entire question of Marx' relationship to Hegel and the Hegelian dialectic the touchstone for any kind of "revisionist renunciation" of Marxist philosophy. In this respect, wrote Mitin, the entire "pleiad" of revisionists, from Bernstein, Cunow, and Kautsky up to and including the mechanists and Bukharin, was a characteristic phenomenon. If this "pleiad of revisionism" failed to grasp revolutionary materialist dialectics, if it negated or distorted materialist dialectics, the original source of these misguided views was the notion that Hegelian idealism cast a dark shadow on the writings of Marx and Engels.[16] Lenin's seminal accomplishment, by way of contrast, had been to reestablish the correct relationship between Marx, Engels, and Hegel after all the misrepresentations produced during the era of the Second International. As for the onetime Menshevist Deborin and his present followers, they had mixed elements of materialism with Hegel's "idealistic dialectic."

Along with its "Hegelism," there was a second, equally important philosophical dimension to "Deborinism." Deborin and his followers favored the Menshevik Plechanov over the Bolshevik Lenin.[17] The writings of the Deborinites contained "a complete obfuscation of the new stage in the development of dialectical materialism. At best they represented the attempt to "'dress up' Lenin à la Plechanov, to obscure the Plechanovist errors, and so on and so forth."[18] The Deborinite argument that Marxism evolved from Marx and Engels by way of Plechanov to Lenin, turning Lenin into a mere pupil or successor of Plechanovist Marxism, was an outrage; the succession ran from Marx-Engels directly to Lenin, and not by way of Plechanov. Lenin was the only, the most consistent, the most orthodox independent Marxist after Marx and Engels,[19] whereas Plechanov had never developed beyond the perimeters of Marxism in the era of the Second International. His political and theoretical ideas accordingly mirrored the typical gap between theory and practice existing in the tradition of the Second International. The chasm between putting theoretical words about dialectical material- ism on paper and the inability to apply dialectical materialism, charged Mitin, was crassly expressed in Plechanov's work.

THE CLASS STRUGGLE INTENSIFIES

These quasi-theoretical matters were said to have a direct prac- tical bearing upon the development of communism. Though the alignment of class forces in the Soviet Union itself assured the "victory of socialism," the party's "concentrated attack" all along the home front was associated with a sharpening of the class struggle that represented just "one of the links of a gen- eral intensification of class warfare on a worldwide scale."[20] In- ternationally it was critical to remember—in light of the "gi- gantic struggle between capitalism and socialism"—that the Second International, "the International of Social Fascism," was the most important mainstay of imperialism and the great- est pillar of capitalism in the current era. "The intensification of the class struggle between two systems in the international arena, the intensification of the class struggle in connection with the successes of socialist competition here in the USSR, cannot be designated in any other terms than as a sharpening of the struggle between bolshevism and menshevism; it must be designated as a step-up in the struggle between the Comintern and the Second International."[21]

Whether menshevism sailed "under the flag of idealism or mechanism," Mitin added, Marxism-Leninism was compelled to "exterminate" definitively all such views,[22] and Stalin's letter to the journal *Proletarskaja revoljutsija* in October 1931 helped identify some further prime targets: Rosa Luxem- burg and Leon Trotsky. Luxemburg, one of the leaders of the prewar left Social Democrats in Germany, had openly opposed the Bolsheviks, Stalin explained. Whereas the Mensheviks in Russia had preferred a policy of accord with the liberal bour- geoisie, the Bolsheviks advocated a program of alliance with the working class and the peasantry. In these disputes Parvus and Rosa Luxemburg "combined the utopian and semi-Menshevist scheme of permanent revolution," which was inspired by the Menshevist denial of a policy of alliance between the working class and the peasantry, and "set it in opposition to the Bolshevist idea of a revolutionary democratic dictatorship of the proletariat and peasantry." This "semi-Menshevist scheme of permanent revolution" was later taken over by Trotsky and turned into a weapon in the struggle against Leninism.[23] As it was primarily intended to do, Stalin's attack upon Luxemburg cast an ominous shadow upon a host of Stalin's political enemies. *"In light of Comrade Stalin's letter,"* one of the primary tasks along the "philosophical segment" of the theoretical front was now

> *to intensify the struggle with the social fascist ideology of the Second International, especially with the ideology of "left-wing" social fascism (Adler, Trotsky, Brandler, Thalheimer, and others); to shake up the theoretical principles of prewar centrism (Kautsky, Trotsky), which are incompatible with dialectical materialism and which evolved into social fascism; to do the same with the semi-centrist, semi-Menshevist, Luxemburgian theories and those wavering compromisers in the ranks of the Bolsheviks who made accommodations with these theories during the time of the imperialist war (Bukharin, Pjatakov, and others), etc.; to unmask the antiscientific, anti-Marxist, anti-Leninist character of the methodology of those smuggling Trotskyist or any other kind of contraband; and, in a truly Bolshevist fashion, to lay bare the rotten "philosophical foundations" of those engaged in smuggling Trotskyist contraband.[24]*

The lesson was clear: the original sin of all these renegades was their insufficient attention to the relation between theory and practice. To drive a wedge between philosophy and politics, between philosophy and the topical tasks of socialist construction, was to restore one of the Second International's most pernicious traditions and dogmas.[25]

Under Stalin "honest" theoretical deviations would never really occur again after the philosophy debate as the result of judgments suggested by inherent logic and free from political considerations or shifting allegiances. Rather, infidelity to the principles of dialectical materialism, which· revealed themselves only to genuine Marxist-Leninists anyway, came about as a natural consequence of political shortcomings and "sins," a failure to identify unreservedly with the only true Leninist party and its present leader, Stalin. Mitin asked whether the "sins" committed by the Deborinites in their philosophical writing ought then to be regarded in connection with the political errors of this group and whether the essence of these theoretical errors was not really of a Social Democratic nature.[26] They were, of course, according to Mitin, whose rhetoric aped Stalin's habit of posing questions that listeners could only answer in one way without self-incrimination; and Mitin's linkage of theoretical error with political "sin" helped in the general establishment during the debate of a menacing precedent for the future. Beginning with the philosophy debate, it became standard practice in the Soviet Union to link any real or supposed theoretical insufficiency to a political cause, even if the "deviation," as in the case of Deborin's original menshevism, lay years or even decades in the past. The philosophy debate, which was never a genuine discussion of theoretical issues at all, ended philosophy debates in the Soviet Union under Stalin. What followed were almost exclusively political vendettas and crusades disguised as legitimate theoretical discussion and differences of opinion. These were sometimes started by cliques whose members all had careers in need of advancement; and sometimes they were incited by Stalin himself, whenever he gave the signal, for whatever reason or whim he might have had, that changes on a theoretical level were in order,[27] whereupon a host of party scriblers promptly reached for their pens.

This was the world of Stalinism just emerging when Lukács arrived in Moscow in early 1930. He was about to enter a realm of political arbitrariness and theoretical artificiality. In the coming years Stalin would continue to make changes in the ideological "line" and manipulate the theory perhaps as much as anything to institutionalize fear and uncertainty in Soviet society. The intellectuals, whose responsibility it was to supply the theoretical adjustments to each new ideological program and to spend long hours guessing at the next, were especially dispirited by Stalin's "artificial dialectic"[28] and turned into a thoroughly intimidated social stratum that largely policed itself. Once the various shifts and switches of the ideological line had reached the point where for many these fluctuations had become impervious to rational analysis and therefore wholly unpredictable, and once the application of terror became absolutely arbitrary, the intellectuals grew even more acutely sensitive to the tiniest of ideological inflections and the slightest hint of new accents; at the same time they were overwhelmed by the seeming hopelessness of complying unwaveringly—in spite of their best efforts—with the ever-changing law laid down by the deified General Secretary in the Kremlin. Trembling in fear of siding with a potentially wrong opinion, failing to uncover an alien idea, or advocating an outlook that could possibly be canonically denounced before the day was out, and often assuming that people had actually done something to cause their arrest (a comforting notion implying that one's own arrest was avoidable if one exercised the proper caution), many intellectuals became even more spontaneously servile and instinctively, unthinkingly compliant. The "consistent elimination of conviction as a motive for action"[29] was frequently the outcome in all areas of social intercourse and especially for the various forms of intellectual activity.

Reading Lukács' essays today, it is easy to lose sight of the nightmarish atmosphere of universal horror and gnawing fear in which many of them were written. Or was Lukács spiritually and humanly immune to this political and intellectual malignancy? If so, he was peerless in this respect. But if there is at least some truth to the argument that "the aim of totalitarian education has never been to instill convictions but to destroy the capacity to form any,"[30] and if Lukács' long years in Soviet exile may be regarded as a form of "totalitarian education," then the main implication of this insight for an evaluation of his theories developed in these years is self-evident.

Moscow, 1930–1931

The philosophy debate had repercussions in virtually every branch of Soviet intellectual life, and the *"struggle for Leninism,"* for the "Leninist principle of party-mindedness," ended up as the highest priority for literature, too.[1] This battle for a "Marxist-Leninist world view" in literature, fought concurrently with the war "on the philosophical front," lasted until the relative pluralism in literary styles of the twenties gave way to what Lukács himself referred to many years later as an "arid naturalism garnished with so-called revolutionary romanticism."[2] Literary theory and criticism likewise degenerated into pointless debates and jejune disputes over the true meaning of an inherently meaningless socialist realism, with everything theoretical that Stalin and his protégés touched turning to mediocrity or worse, and the quality of criticism plummeting to a level matched only by the postwar *Zhdanovshchina.*

ACCOMMODATION OR AUTONOMY?

Assuming that Lukács was not immune to the Stalin touch, at what stage in the development of his literary theories did the tremendous pressure to bring his ideas into basic conformity with the predominent intellectual trends of Stalinism prove too much for him to withstand? Lukács later answered these questions with his usual insistence that his ideas were actually an unspoken protest against Stalinist habits of thought,[3] but he in fact did not manage to exempt his work from Stalin's encroachment into the realm of philosophy and art; as a matter of fact, much of Lukács' inspiration in these early years came to him directly from the triumphant battles on the "theoretical fronts" of ascendant Stalinism.

Lukács' essays, those written in Moscow in 1930 and 1931,

in Berlin from 1931 to 1933, and the ones published through the end of the decade in Soviet exile, divulge an evolving pattern of adjustment and accommodation to establishmentarian trends in Soviet literary theory. That Lukács might have been an ordinary opportunist, that his ideas meant nothing to him outside the immediate context of the situation in which he found himself, or that he merely reacted to intellectual and political trends around him—this conclusion does not necessarily follow from Lukács' act of tuning his work to harmonize with the theoretical strains of Stalinism. He surely had his baser motives, though many of these were probably repressed or sublimated at the time or later and quickly transformed into elaborate historical and then personal rationalizations soothing to his conscience. Lukács was, in any event, a consummate dogmatist who defended his ideas with a zealousness bordering on sectarian and self-righteous fanaticism. But the important point in his case, it seems, is that his dogmatism, for all its Stalinist overtones, was not absolutely identical with the unalloyed form of totally corrupt cynicism common among many intellectuals living under Stalinism. Rather, it took on shades more redolent of a reconciliation of the Orwellian opposites "cynicism with fanaticism."[4] In other words, a fanaticized certitude about the historical infallibility of the special dogma that invested his writings with what he assumed to be a universal validity mingled in Lukács with various manifestations of unadulterated cynicism.

Lukács arrived at this state of mind not at the beginning but at the end of the thirties, and, in his case, this unusual spiritual transformation—for which he had been predisposed well before the thirties—reflected a process of intellectual and moral degeneration in which far more than mere personality defects and character flaws were involved. Rather, the experience seems to have been a universal one for many intellectuals and artists living in Stalin's Russia,[5] and in it the quotidian factor first of fear and then of sheer terror should never be overlooked as a formative and deformative force in their lives.[6] Though he later chose to dispute the similarities, Lukács' views on theoretical matters almost always corresponded closely to official Soviet notions on like or related subjects. Yet precisely in those years in which intellectual pursuits counted among the most hazar-

dous forms of earning a living in the USSR, no known spokes-
man of Stalin's literary policy ever challenged Lukács on specific issues strongly enough to force him to repudiate any
major feature of his literary theory.[7] Lukács' various rounds of
cynical self-criticism date back to the years before high Stalinism, to the eve of it, or to the years just after the war.

Now Lukács' knack at charting a course between various
heresies, many of which had been previously accepted as orthodox viewpoints, may well bespeak a special cunning on his part
at getting ideas across in an anti-intellectual atmosphere. This
reading of his activity in Soviet exile would most closely approach Lukács' own rendition. But it simply cannot be demonstrated that his work merely slipped by the censors and that his
ideas were only tolerated, not understood enough to cause him
any serious trouble. To the contrary, these ideas *prospered* in
Soviet exile, at least until 1939, and this circumstance alone
suggests strongly the basic theoretical compatability of Lukács'
views with the orthodoxy of the day. Certainly no thinker expressing opinions seriously at odds with Stalinist viewpoints
in the thirties, least of all Lukács, even if the protest was "unspoken," stood much of a chance of survival in the long run,
especially considering that even the most orthodox among the
intellectuals in the USSR had no assurance whatever under
Stalin of protection from the terror. The Stalinists were anti-
intellectual, period, and feared convictions of any kind, even
the orthodox sort, indeed, these perhaps most of all; but being
themselves intellectual mediocrities of the worst kind by no
means obstructed their uncanny sense of smell, in fact enhanced it with respect to sniffing out ideas that were inimical
to their orthodoxy or could be branded as such through some
form of casuistry.

This is not meant as a suggestion, on the other hand, that
Lukács' accommodation to the intellectual mainstream of Stalinist Russia did not coexist in his writing with a concerted
effort to define a cohesive Marxian theory of literature. It
did, and this latter enterprise definitely ran a risk of falling
out of step with that orthodoxy, or being denounced as incompatible with it, precisely because his was a serious undertaking and because the Stalinists had a congenitally suspicious
nature when it came to earnest intellectual inquiry, "Marxist-

Leninist" or not. Lukács' work needs to be looked at from both these angles—conformity as well as limitedly autonomous thinking—if any sense is to be made of the correlation between his writing and authoritative Soviet literary theories in the thirties. The book reviews that Lukács published in 1930 and 1931 in the *Moskauer Rundschau*, his first writings on literature following the Blum theses, show clearly if still imperfectly how Soviet debates fashioned Lukács' opinions from the very beginning of what he called his theoretical activity.

The Russian Association of Proletarian Writers (RAPP) exerted perhaps the strongest influence on Lukács from 1930 to 1932, and his essays in the *Moskauer Rundschau* need to be understood as at least a partial expression of the RAPP canon and, therefore, the first significant step in Lukács' process of adaptation to the developing mainstream of Stalinist thought. When he arrived in Moscow in mid-1930, RAPP had reached the pinnacle of its power in Soviet literary life and was exploiting to the fullest its status as the literary organization whose political and theoretical program brandished the party's stamp of approval. RAPP's preeminence among Soviet literary groups and associations began to erode quickly in mid-1931 and the party then disbanded the organization altogether with the famous central committee resolution of April 1932. But RAPP ideas and concepts still dominated a major sector of Soviet literary life for the duration of Lukács' first stay in Moscow. Summing up the substance of RAPP's program, the prevailing issue in political matters was the problem of fellow traveler writers in the USSR. RAPP considered them simply "class enemies in literature" and coined appropriately belligerent slogans like "For the Hegemony of Proletarian Literature" or "Ally or Enemy." Whatever happened to be said about the organization later (the central committee used RAPP's bellicose attitude toward non-Communist writers as a pretext for disbanding the organization), RAPP's posture was completely in step with the times. Party spokesmen never reproached RAPP prior to 1932 for its treatment of the fellow travelers; in fact, RAPP's "ally-or-enemy" dealings with non-Communist writers had a direct analogy in Stalin's own "attitude toward the old [bourgeois] intelligentsia, . . . mainly expressed by the policy of routing them," and his call for the development of "Red specialists" to take their place.[8]

In literary questions RAPP spokesmen blended antagonism toward any form of writing that smacked of innovation and experimentation or tended toward open political agitation and unequivocal rejection of psychologically unsophisticated, politically serviceable proletarian literature. RAPP advocated instead a form of psychological realism based on the author's grasp of dialectical materialism. This basic RAPP attitude toward literary creation translated into the celebrated but later denigrated slogan "For the Living Man,"[9] a phrase that expressed "the necessity of struggle with stereotypes, with schematic portrayal, with 'bare poster art,' and of development in the direction of showing forth the complex human psyche, with all its contradictions, elements of the past and seeds of the future, both conscious and subconscious."[10] The related injunction to proletarian writers practicing RAPP's "dialectical materialist creative method" was an adaptation of Lenin's paraphrase of Tolstoy, "to tear off the masks" or "for the removal of any and all masks."[11] This obliged writers to explore the psychology of all their fictional characters, whether kulaks, former bourgeois, or Communist party functionaries, by removing their "masks." "The Leninist characterization of Tolstoy's creation, 'the tearing off of all masks,' has a tremendous significance for writers who are working out their own creative method," read one RAPP resolution; "[s]uch a slogan opposes the tendency to 'varnish' reality . . . and is directed at a Bolshevik *cognition* of that reality. . . . For, 'Since when do Bolsheviks fear the truth?' says Comrade Stalin."[12]

Lukács later made highly disputable claims about this period of his life and work, insisting that he had always opposed RAPP. His essays, however, reveal unmistakable theoretical and political similarities with the organization's position. One example will suffice at this point: RAPP and Lukács shared a mutual hostility toward experimental and agitational forms of art. When Lukács arrived in Moscow, RAPP had just been subjected to heavy criticism from a group of writers and critics whose theoretical platform was also at variance with Lukács' evolving theory. RAPP defended itself with arguments to which Lukács would have subscribed. The head of RAPP, Leopold Averbakh, charged that the group antagonistic to RAPP, Litfront, "had its basic nourishment in the moods of petty-bourgeois revolutionism" and went on to explain that the art theory of "Litfront" was one of liquidation with respect to proletarian art. Its founders proposed to substitute for art literature the chronicling of facts, newspaper and publicistic writing, and so on. "Denying the need for any psychological delineation in literature ('one may manage without psychology'), the 'Litfront' people rolled down to speculative schematism in the solving of creative questions, to the varnishing of the realities [sic], acting in the last case against the Leninist slogan of RAPP which called for the 'tearing off of all and any masks.'" The entire activity of "Litfront" had been condemned by *Pravda* and by proletarian literary opinion as Menshevik and antiproletarian.[13]

Lukács was naturally receptive to any organization fighting "the chronicling of facts" and pleading for psychological delineation in literature. That the party itself sided with RAPP against Litfront only made it easier for Lukács to identify himself politically with an organization whose program accorded with the essentials of his own outlook anyway.

THE *MOSKAUER RUNDSCHAU*

Not all of these issues are readily apparent in Lukács' early writings in the *Moskauer Rundschau*; some are evident just beneath the surface, but others appear only in a rudimentary form. These essays lack the sharp edges, in particular the abrasiveness and aggressive polemics, characteristic of Lukács' later work. But bearing in mind that he had just narrowly escaped serious party sanctions on account of the Blum theses, Lukács' comparative timorousness may betoken his hesitation at this time to commit himself beyond the point where he could still back away from his positions quickly if necessary. This explanation may help account for the degree of equivocation that these early essays exhibit. Whether his ultimate purpose was to praise or to criticize a specific author, Lukács usually went in for some variation of an on-the-one-hand-on-the-other-hand analysis. This approach, in fact, may be a mark of Lukács' early realization that authors in the Soviet Union whose work was singled out for official approbation one day could fall into disfavor the next, almost as hastily as political expedience could propel an author whose writing had been previously unrecognized or even considered unfit into sudden and unexpected prominence because he supposedly displayed traits exemplary for Soviet literature in some hitherto undiscovered way. Lukács thus may have grasped rapidly that literary trends in the USSR at the time were susceptible to largely unpredictable political whims; that he could not bank on the literary policies and official preferences of the day necessarily existing several days hence; and that his pronouncements as a literary critic needed to take these dangers into account.

In his review of Anna Karavajeva's novel *The Factory in the Forest*[14] Lukács voiced his objections right at the beginning. The stormy tempo of socialist development in the USSR allowed for a reading of Soviet novels unique to literature. Works of fiction treating topical issues at the time these books were conceived or put on paper came out in print as "historical novels" because they mirrored a way of life or modes of thinking already part of past history. The reader could easily ascertain the extent to which an author had duly considered certain developing trends that later turned out to be decisive factors while these transformations were still in their most incipient stage. But fairness and "historical tact" were called for anyway on the part of the reader as a "prophet with hindsight" because these trends could later take qualitatively new turns of such a magnitude that the early anticipation or accurate prediction of future development was all but impossible. (Besides, Lukács warned, under some circumstances premature anticipation of a coming change could actually be a crude mistake.)

But Lukács promptly ignored his own plea for "historical tact" and analyzed Karavajeva's depiction of the "reconstruction of a dilapidated factory" out in some remote Soviet village to determine "how many of the tendencies that have now led and are leading to a radical turnabout in the fate of the village and to the rapid advance of the village toward socialism were already evident then, if only in an embryonic form." The results were disappointing; there was no hint at all in the novel of the collectivization of agriculture, neither as a plan, a project, nor even as a distant possibility.[15] It would never occur to him, said Lukács, to reproach Karavajeva for this shortcoming were it not for Fedor Panferov's novel, *Brusski* (the name of a commune), where these trends had already been represented in literature in a form entirely consonant with the prevailing stage of development.[16]

These reservations notwithstanding, Lukács spoke in glowing terms of specific qualities that set Karavajeva's novel apart from other Soviet novels with similar thematic concerns, especially Boris Pilnjak's *The Volga Flows into the Caspian Sea* and Leonid Leonov's *Construction*. Unlike Pilnjak's and Leonov's handling of the village, Karavajeva brought the class structure of her village to life because she avoided a psychologically inert portrait of class relations that suspended all motion by treating the characters who incarnated these relations as fixed personalities set in their ways for the duration of the time encompassed by the novel. Lukács' distinction between schematism and dialectics, or agitation as opposed to "creative representation" (*dichterische Gestaltung*)[17] in character portrayal, divulges a clear similarity between Lukács' terminology and that employed by RAPP critics.

In this essay especially, Lukács supplied a précis of his literary theory in his insistence that the individuality and personal fates of fictional characters must be woven into the treatment of their social or class being if the characters are to be compelling as individuals and not degenerate into schematic representations of an immutable class outlook or allegiance. Lukács made no mention here of the RAPP slogan "For the Living Man" or "For the Removal of Any and All Masks"; instead, he used his own corresponding phrases that show up time and again in his later essays—"individual physiognomy," for instance, or the all-embracing notion of creative representation, that is, *Gestaltung*. But the particular quality that Lukács had in mind was directly analogous to basic RAPP aesthetic criteria, and both RAPP and Lukács crusaded against forms of writing in which "this interlacing [of social being, individual character, and personal destiny] is in part totally absent (the figures have no individual physiognomy) and in part not creatively rep-

resented, causing then the lack of an organic connection between the individuality of the figures and their class destiny,
especially with their life as a member of the party."[18]

The quality of representation, by which Lukács understood
the portrayal of characters in a mix of their individuality and
their behavior as class beings, also headed his list of requirements for realistic literature in his reviews of books by Mikhail
Sholokhov, Ilja Ehrenburg, and Leonid Leonov. But in these essays he set out to show how other circumstances, preeminently
a writer's choice of "style" and the factors that determined or,
in the case of the author's world view, essentially predetermined this choice, complicated creative representation and
often blocked the path leading to realistic writing as Lukács
defined it. An inherent class bias—more simply put, his world
view—was not the cause of Sholokhov's difficulties in the second volume of *The Quiet Don,* said Lukács. Because Sholokhov
was thought of as a Marxist-Leninist writer, a deficient dialectical materialist grasp of his subject matter could not be blamed
for the failure of the novel. In Lukács' view, the faults of the
second volume were, rather, congenital defects of a style that
made literary representation structurally impossible. These defects were not yet conspicuous in the first volume. There Cossack villages, families, individual Cossacks, their relations,
daily life, joys, sufferings, passions—"everything emerges with
natural organic persuasive power from this foundation; everything functions as a slice of nature from the Don region." As a
consequence, an extremely suggestive poetic appearance came
about.[19]

The sequel, on the other hand, disintegrated entirely into
episodes that were not "organically" connected because Sholokhov had omitted the "social aspect," the class conditions of
the Don Cossacks. He had not treated Cossack daily life in relation to the special economic and political circumstances of
czarism responsible for the pattern of settlement and the division of soil in the Cossack region. This omission had not
proven critical as long as daily life was the focus of the novel, as
it had been in the first volume; but in the sequel, the war and
the revolutionary events that followed convulsed the villages,
bringing the "driving forces" behind the social upheaval to the
surface. Military conflict, the disintegration of the front, civil

war, the breakdown of society according to class, the vacillation of the intermediate classes between revolution and counterrevolution—this concatenation of events together comprised
the extended process of revolution that Sholokhov should have
used to show his characters' development "from the *elementary to the conscious.*"[20]

As a realistic writer, Sholokhov bore the responsibility of
showing with poetic images, and not merely with unem-
bellished intellectual, analytical methods, how these events re-
fashioned an isolated group of Cossacks, imparting to them a
greater sense of awareness or consciousness and politicizing
them. Sholokhov ought to have revealed how the Cossacks left
their previous "elemental" (that is, spontaneous or natural) life
and how this "elementariness" engendered by their original social circumstances lived on in the Cossacks' "conscious" period, decisively affecting their conscious behavior and decisions. But just when the novel's key structural difficulties
called for an adequate aesthetic resolution, the work broke
down: "The place of that which is creatively represented is
taken more and more by what is nakedly intellectual, raw agitation. The turns occur without any developmental preparation." Whereas the first portion of the novel had been almost
exaggeratedly "organic," now everything occurred "suddenly,"
by way of intellectual persuasion. "Arguments are advanced
and take effect. But there is no *creative representation* to
demonstrate why the arguments function so convincingly."[21]

These points are all familiar from Lukács' essays of the mid-
thirties and later. The issue here is not the early stage at which
Lukács first began to articulate ideas that he later expanded
upon (though this is noteworthy in itself) but rather the mixture in his early writing of concepts enunciated as an identifiable expression of his unspoken but knowing participation in
ongoing Soviet literary theoretical discussions and ideas that
might better be regarded as originally Lukács'.[22] Separating the
two dimensions is a painstaking process, but Lukács' unvoiced
plaidoyer "for the living man" in his criticism of Sholokhov
was in clear keeping with RAPP's theoretical demands, and the
same is true of his point that intellectualized explanations and
politically tendencious arguments, to say nothing of "raw agitation," were anathema to realistic writing.

The Sholokhov review did include one point that was not a stated part of the RAPP program, though it tied in to both RAPP's and Lukács' understanding of realism. Lukács hinted that an author's intentions, even if he was a Marxist, offered no assurance in themselves that the events he portrayed would be realistic if he did not employ a correct "style." RAPP's theory carried a similar implication, except that RAPP critics outstripped Lukács in their imperiousness. For them the very idea that honest Marxist intentions could ever lead to artistic results inconsistent with RAPP's interpretation of dialectical materialism in literature was unthinkable. If a writer produced work that violated RAPP concepts, the fault lay in his ideology. The consequence of RAPP's claim to be in possession of exclusive theoretical truth was its fulsome habit of passing sentence on any departure from its theoretical standards as conscious and purposeful opposition to the Soviet regime. Lukács saved that kind of censoriousness for his later essays, but even now there was a rudimentary similarity between his opinions and RAPP's inasmuch as RAPP's linkage of groups like the Pereverzev school, the Left Front of Art (LEF), or Litfront to political deviations presupposed that "true" Marxist-Leninist writers were historically bound to employ RAPP's dialectical materialist creative method and none other. The difference between RAPP and Lukács at this juncture was merely one of degree. RAPP equated theoretical with deliberate political malfeasance, whereas Lukács was just developing the tendency to deny the status of Marxist-Leninist to writing that did not correspond to his theoretical injunctions. But he did not yet tie theoretical shortcomings to any sort of willful political wrongdoing.

Lukács would soon expand his ideas into a full-blown theory that was incorporated into official Soviet socialist realism following RAPP's dissolution. In the form that it assumed in Lukács' later work and as a key component of socialist realism in the thirties, the question of authorial intention evolved in two directions. Lukács later relied upon his argument that a historically improper style did away with any chance for realistic representation to upbraid even writers close or actually belonging to the Communist party, like Bertolt Brecht and Ernst Ottwalt, for formalism and decadence. Having opted for what Lukács stigmatized as "subjective" art forms (montage, reportage, or experimental theater), the Marxist or Marxist-Leninist intentions of these writers were immaterial. This same attitude prospered in the Soviet Union after 1933 and was behind the official Soviet antagonism toward the avant-garde or experimental in general and toward Brecht in particular.

The other side to the problem of authorial intention entered into Lukács' theory under Engels' notation of Balzac's "triumph of realism." Certain classical writers created realistic literature capturing the "driving forces" of history in spite of a world view severely impaired by their class background and inborn biases. This accounted for what Lukács called the "natural materialism"[23] of the past masters: their inherent ability to write realistically in spite of conflicting political or class-engendered intentions, as long as they made use of an objective form. Soviet literary theoretical spokesmen used the identical line of reasoning to help embellish a reputation tarnished by the widespread assumption outside the USSR that Soviet cultural policy had little respect for the cultural heritage. After the turn to the popular front in 1935, the acknowledgment that some contemporary bourgeois writers wrote or could write realistic literature in spite of their "faulty consciousness" then became a pillar of the popular front in Soviet cultural policy as it was pursued outside the USSR.[24]

This theory is evident in embryonic form in Lukács' review of Sholokhov, which is especially surprising because Lukács had presumably not yet read the letter that Engels wrote Margaret Harkness mentioning Balzac's "triumph of realism" and later cited by Lukács repeatedly as incontrovertible proof that his theory was "Marxist."[25] But as early as 1930 Lukács tried to demonstrate that, even in the case of a Communist author, intentions were insufficient by themselves to overcome the impediments to realism brought about by use of an incorrect, subjective method. Even though Sholokhov intended to depict "the awakening of consciousness in a social stratum that previously acted in keeping with elemental and unconscious impulses," he fell short of his goal because his style was not equal to the task. He understood the Cossacks in terms of their daily life, and he had a Marxist-Leninist grasp of the relevant historical issues. But his use of inadequate stylistic or structural devices, the substitution of subjective intellectual discussions for the artistic representation of the political and ideological development of his characters, was an insurmountable obstacle to the realistic figuration of the social issues involved.

Lukács picked out similar faults in Ilja Ehrenburg's work, though he added an additional factor to all those frustrating any hope for realism, one not at issue with Sholokhov: the author's class background or world view. Sholokhov failed in the sequel to *The Quiet Don* not because he misunderstood the interplay of historical forces but because he substituted naked intellectuality and raw agitation for creative representation. With Ehrenburg's work the issue was clouded from the outset by his "world view." Ehrenburg belonged to the petty bourgeois intelligentsia, explained Lukács, an intermediate class not organically connected with either of the two classes—bourgeoisie or proletariat—contending with each other for power. This class bias explained Ehrenburg's limitations as a writer. He had firsthand knowledge of revolutionary events "in the land of the victorious proletariat" and was therefore less predisposed to the inconstancy of Western European literati who vacillated "between abstract utopia and abstract hatred for the Bolshevist 'hell.'"[26] In the course of the revolution, Ehrenburg had been able to observe the impuissance of intellectuals in a period marked by the most intense class conflict, and this recognition brought him to the point of criticizing the very class to which he belonged. But his specific "plight," as Lukács defined it, was his failure to advance one more step; his self-criticism came to a halt right at the entrance way and failed to result in an association with one of the powerful competing classes. He remained mired in his own outlook, his own emotions, his own world view.

Ehrenburg had tried his hand at depicting character types belonging to different classes; in one specific case, Lukács noted that he had truly wanted to portray and contrast a simple Communist with a common hood. "However," said Lukács, "the essence of a poet is not a function of his desires but his *representation*. The most trustworthy gauge for evaluating a writer is therefore always the question of what he produces in the way of creative representation." Whereas Sholokhov's intentions had been crossed up by an incorrect style, Ehrenburg's problem was less easily correctable, regardless of his intentions. His admittedly considerable literary talents proved wholly inadequate when a portrayal of revolutionaries was called for instead of a description of small-time hoods or helpless victims of the capitalist machine, men who let themselves be carried along by circumstances. The failure of Ehrenburg's representational powers was thus the logical outgrowth of his own social or class background and colored even the most artistically successful passages in his writing. The passages all bore the stamp of the lyric or ironic outsider and were depicted from the perspective of a literati's writing. In the description of capitalism this perspective stood out less, but the dissonance became "piercingly sharp"[27] in the depiction of the proletarian revolution.

Lukács focused on similar limitations in Leonid Leonov's *Construction,* in which the best intentions were spoiled by a class-engendered style. In this novel, said Lukács, the author was generally at pains to grasp the nature of socialist construction and portray it as it truly was. But Lukács identified major problems, and his specific objections were again redolent of standard RAPP complaints. The figures in the novel dissolved into nebulous, bloodless schemata. The construction of socialism in a distant northern region of the country failed to come alive and was not depicted in persuasive human terms. The most essential elements came across, rather, as inert and lifeless, as a merely programmatic surface reality that never penetrated to the essence of things. "The better, the more artistically and consistently he endeavors to represent immediately perceptible reality," said Lukács, "the more he is bound to *remain at the level* of this form of surface reality, the less he can go beyond it to get at the deeper, not directly evident, but real driving forces of the action." The more consistently he captured and evoked the spirit of separate moments, the more the objective coherence of the whole was lost in the process.[28]

The consequences of Leonov's representational techniques came out in a particularly crass fashion in his use of psychology. Psychology should never be employed in a manner that obscured what was "essential," said Lukács; by way of example, he brought up Leonov's handling of a conversation between a "counterrevolutionary officer" and a former Red partisan.

Leonov had used the opportunity to delve into the officer's "confused, feverish fantasy," but in so doing he threw no additional light either upon the figures or their relationship to each other. Rather, "the simple fact of *class-generated necessity* that governs the actions of the officer becomes mysterious, romantic, unpersuasive." In his criticism Lukács may have felt compelled to come out strongly against certain misuses of psychology in literature because RAPP itself had recently been upbraided by its critics for the twin slogans "For the Living Man" and "For the Removal of Any and All Masks."[29] Moreover, at just about this time, RAPP's heavy emphasis on psychology was gradually becoming the target of more officially inspired objections voiced by Stalinist philosophers such as Mark Mitin and Pavel Judin. But Lukács still used the opportunity to draw a clear distinction between Leonov's psychological portrait with the type of psychology that figured prominently in Lukács' understanding of realistic literature, and on this point Lukács was in essential agreement with RAPP's idea of "the living man." In his review of Leonov, Lukács referred to this "living man" in a more roundabout way as "the concrete, imaginable, and represented unity of individual and class," a quality that, in Lukács' mind, had grown increasingly rarer since Fielding and Goethe, Balzac and Tolstoy. The means of literary expression, he charged, had grown increasingly subjective; the overall context, the totality of society, drowned in a raging sea of direct, momentary images.

Here Lukács injected an abbreviated form of his theory of the objectivity of art forms. Describing the historical origin of Leonov's style, he explained: "In the age of parasite capitalism, this style is therefore the most consistent expression for the feelings of broad segments of the upper classes. However one chooses to assess the value of this style historically and aesthetically, it is (or was) in any case in total harmony with the content that it came into being to depict." A glaring contradiction could not help but arise, however (the title of Lukács' article underscored his point), as a result of Leonov's amalgam of a new content or subject matter with the deficiencies of an old form. Leonov employed an historically superseded style to treat the construction of socialism, the obdurate resistance of the backward and benighted peasant masses in the countryside, and the triumph of proletarian "purposeful awareness" (*Ziel-bewusstheit*) over this resistance. Under these circumstances, the style interfered with representation; the psychology concealed the larger picture, the class context, and the atmospherics produced chaos rather than order—"the content contradicts the form. It passes judgment on and destroys the form." Why did Leonov employ such a style instead of searching for one more adequate to the tasks of a Soviet writer? "Le stil c'est l'homme. But the man is a product of his class circumstances."[30] Leonov, a highly gifted writer, belonged to that caste of intellectuals who had emerged from the villages. Though inwardly still a part of village life, these writers had nonetheless become intellectuals, and this "'inconclusive' situation" conditioned and determined his style.

LUKÁCS AND RAPP

While in Moscow in 1930 and 1931, Lukács began work on a theory that combined elements very nearly like and at times identical with RAPP's theoretical canon with features more distinctly his own. He shared certain broad notions with RAPP about styles of writing supposedly contrary to the historically "objective" and conscious creative method most in keeping with dialectical materialism. RAPP called its theory the "dialectical materialist creative method," which ruled out any expression of individuality or spontaneity in form or content and implied that those not practicing this method were not dialectical materialists, not Marxist-Leninists, and therefore suspect, alien elements in Soviet literature. The correlative reasoning ran as follows: as conscious revolutionaries, the avant-garde of the proletariat, Marxist-Leninists refused to admit that spontaneity in effecting social and political change played more than an ancillary role in a revolutionary situation. Successful revolutions never sprang solely from spontaneous mass uprisings; rather, a proletarian revolution presupposed the leadership of a Marxist-Leninist party responsible for at least a partial transformation in the thinking of the masses from their previously inarticulate and spontaneous rejection of the old system to a level of class consciousness and "purposeful awareness" that enabled them to follow the party's lead. Marxist-Leninist writers, in a similar fashion, created realistic litera-ture depicting men in society on the strength of a mature awareness of the historical laws that underlay social develop-ment. These artists had to put themselves in a position to understand the transformation "from the elemental to the con-scious" and portray it dialectically—realistically—in litera-ture. This task required a degree of consciousness on their part made possible only by an adequate grasp of dialectical materi-alism. Without it, RAPP contended, writers could never repre-sent Soviet reality truthfully.

Lukács argued along the same general lines, though he also analyzed the interplay of other factors that interested the RAPP critics less. The point of the Sholokhov review was to show that this writer's particular problem arose less out of his unawareness of the "driving forces" of history than because of technique. But Sholokhov's incorrect style also reflected a faulty consciousness inasmuch as it betrayed an inadequate ap-preciation of how dialectical materialism combined with artis-tic representation to yield realistic literature. Sholokhov needed to heed Lukács' advice in the future in order to trace the path of his Cossacks "from the elemental to the conscious." Other-wise he would remain shackled by his special form of "spon-taneity," his own natural inclinations as a writer, and his work would drift further away from a dialectical materialist portrayal of reality into the realm of raw agitation. Lukács made the question of consciousness less a direct issue in his discussion of Ehrenburg and Leonov, concentrating mainly on the manner in which world view and class background combined to pro-duce a style that hindered realism. He did not make it clear at this point whether he regarded such writers as victims perma-nently scarred by their class background; nor, however, did he explicitly exclude the possibility that they could acquire the consciousness, the knowledge and experience, necessary for the creation of realistic literature. Later essays in Berlin and the Soviet Union attempted to resolve that question.

Like RAPP, then, Lukács distinguished sharply between the conscious application of dialectical materialism to literary cre-ation and a sort of spontaneous capitulation to uncontrolled, "natural," pseudo-artistic impulses and inclinations. Lukács' more specific personal contribution to the theory was his concern with authorial intention, especially as it pertained to past writers. On this point he differed in emphasis from RAPP. Though RAPP by no means discounted the cultural heritage and set up Tolstoy as at least a partial model for Soviet writers, the RAPP critics were simply more concerned in their theory with present-day Soviet reality. Lukács, on the other hand, began thinking in terms of the applicability of his theory to past literature during his first stay in Moscow, but for the most part he did not pursue the issue systematically until after 1933.[31]

As he related the question of intention to contemporary Soviet writers, Lukács refused to admit that realism could "triumph" over an inadequate consciousness, arguing along two lines: no realism was possible without a correct style, and Soviet writers had an obligation to turn themselves into Marxist-Leninists—their use of a correct style was an integral part of this transformation—if they hoped to depict Soviet life. Lukács was not yet willing to follow RAPP's lead and criminalize literary theoretical "errors," but certainly not because his theoretical principles were intrinsically more liberal. Although his basic principles changed little when he arrived in Berlin, the relative tolerance in the Moscow essays for those who in some way failed to live up to his standards or discounted his advice altogether vanished from his later writings with hardly a trace. Why? Lukács seemed to act later as if he had somehow been granted a personal exemption from the Stalin touch, but he actually was very sensitive to outside political pressures in developing his theory. His less dogmatic posture in 1930 and 1931 in Moscow perhaps reflects a lingering uncertainty about his standing in the party following the scandal surrounding the Blum theses, and he may have been determined to keep as low a profile as possible without, of course, falling silent entirely. Added to this insecurity was the general hesitation about just what the party approved of in literature or would choose to approve tomorrow. That hesitation had faded entirely by the time he began to write for *Die Linkskurve* in Berlin.

Interlude

RAPP's power to influence Soviet literary theoretical and political affairs began to erode the same year that Lukács left for Berlin. It is difficult to pinpoint exactly when the official process of erosion started, however, because the challenges to RAPP's preeminence did not emanate at first just from official quarters, and the complaints about the organization published in the Soviet press were spread throughout most of 1931 and 1932.[1] With the benefit of hindsight, the temptation is to suggest that the decision to dissolve RAPP was reached only after the organization had fulfilled a task set aside for it by the party: prior to its dissolution, RAPP was given a free hand to crusade against a variety of other Soviet literary groups, a role in which it clearly reveled as a self-constituted enforcement agency of Soviet literary standards. RAPP was brutal, for instance, in its treatment of groups like Litfront, the Pereverzev school of criticism, and the alliance known as Pereval. These organizations were naturally pilloried for their theoretical orientation, which failed to square with RAPP's; but the campaign against them was especially unsavory because RAPP could not resist the urge to couple its theoretical inquisition with the new emphasis on "Leninism" and "Leninist party-mindedness in literary criticism" introduced in the philosophy debate. Equating any divergence from its policy with outlooks stigmatized by the Stalinist philosophers as political aberrations, RAPP tried to make it an ideological delict to oppose its own organization.

Leopold Averbakh, for example, was not content just to repudiate Litfront's art theory. He rounded out his quasi-theoretical remonstrations with the charge that Litfront was Menshevist, antiproletarian, and an asylum for "anti-Party elements, for supporters of the right-'left' political bloc of Syrtsov-Lominadze."[2] Other RAPP critics singled out Pereverzev's literary theory for criticism and charged that it was a reflection of "menshevizing idealism and mechanism,"[3] following up that senselessness with another absurdity—Pereverzev had much in common with the ideology of the Second International, ergo, he had engaged in Menshevist subversion.[4] Pereval was the victim of a similar defamation campaign. Averbakh characterized its ideological basis as a representation of "the kulak ideology in Soviet literature,"[5] and other RAPP critics referred to Pereval as a rallying point for reactionary forces among writers. It had unfurled "anew the banner of Trotsky's and Voronskij's theory."[6]

RAPP AND THE STALINIST PHILOSOPHERS

RAPP's passion for assaulting other groups after the fashion of the Stalinist philosophers won their applause, even if their basic approval was intermingled with the first tentative expressions of dissatisfaction with the organization. RAPP was *"pursuing essentially a correct literary political line,"* said Mitin in early 1931,[7] but the literary segment of the theoretical front had been just as susceptible to the deleterious influence of the Deborinites as the other spheres of theoretical activity. The necessity of an unwavering struggle for a "Marxist-Leninist world view and for the dialectical method in literary theory" remained the most urgent task confronting literary scholars and proletarian literature.[8] In a word, RAPP's theoretical work had not kept pace with the "current tempo" of socialist construction, and this theoretical "lag" was blamed in general terms on the organization's insufficient grasp of Leninism "as a new and higher stage in the development of the dialectical materialist world view."[9] In RAPP's case, its slogan "For Plechanovist Orthodoxy" was said to be entirely contrary to Leninism,[10] a natural objection for the Stalinists considering that Plechanov was one of the primary philosophical targets of the debate. Mitin conceded that much could be learned from Plechanov's writings on literary theory and aesthetics, but it was a grievous error to isolate Plechanov's thinking in this area from his incorrect philosophical or, much worse, political views. These views, by and large, had later been taken over by menshevism. This lack of theoretical clarity was responsible for RAPP's advocacy of abstract, easily misunderstood slogans such as "For the Living Man" and "For the Removal of Any and All Masks," as well as for its heavy emphasis on "psychologism." Still, in March 1931 Mitin left his criticism of RAPP at that, dropping the subject with the general words of advice that Lenin's work represented a "colossal theoretical wealth." The time was now at hand to draw upon these riches in developing a Leninist literary criticism.

The Stalinist philosophers thus had differences with RAPP over specific theoretical questions that struck them as a potential threat to "Leninism" in literary criticism. But at this stage these disputes were still comparatively minor, perhaps just an expression of the natural Stalinist inclination to universalize theoretical points of contention by applying them indiscriminately, even to allied groups, and they by no means threatened the more-or-less tacit understanding that RAPP represented the party's viewpoint in literature. Certainly neither Lukács nor anyone else had any reason at the time to suspect that in several months RAPP would lose its favored status with the party completely; in fact, positive assessments of RAPP's activity abounded in the Soviet press in the meantime, easily outweighing any critical notes. In August 1931 *Pravda* published an article entitled "For the Hegemony of Proletarian Literature." Under RAPP's banner "Voronskiism, LEFism, Pereverzevism, and 'Litfront'" had been routed, an outcome that exemplified the correctness of RAPP's "basic orientation" in literary political matters. In particular, *Pravda* singled out for special praise another RAPP slogan, "For the Great Art of Bolshevism," calling it a valuable weapon to be used in "mobilizing millions" for the construction of a socialist society. For this and other reasons, despite some irritating imperfections, RAPP was and always had been a "militant organization of the working class on the literary front" and was rightly acknowledged as the "foremost organization carrying out the party line on the literary front."[11]

Even later in the year and just a few months before the central committee disbanded RAPP altogether, official and semi-official articles in *Pravda* still gave only an inkling of the party's growing unhappiness with the organization's unwilling-ness to fulfill certain expectations. Mitin, Judin, and several other critics, for instance, coauthored an article in *Pravda* al-luding to problems that had come up with RAPP. The RAPP leadership had evidently started to balk at the attempts origi-nating in the philosophy debate to turn RAPP into a mere re-ceptacle of party instructions and apparently felt that it had every right to pursue its own literary theory, which it took to be the proper reflection of dialectical materialism in literature. Mitin and Judin wrote that the need for "Bolshevist party-mindedness" was one of the preeminent lessons learned in the recent discussions along the "theoretical front," and "party-mindedness in theory" had tremendous practical significance.[12] "For us, therefore, it is unacceptable to speak in any terms other than of one general line to be followed in the various spe-cific sections of the front involving theory or practice: in phi-losophy, literature, history, and so on." Under the "party's leadership," RAPP had achieved considerable success in work-ing toward the hegemony of proletarian literature and against "unconcealed as well as camouflaged antiproletarian trends from Voronskiiism to Litfrontism," but the struggle was far from over; direct and disguised forms of resistance to Marxism-Leninism had not yet been "liquidated," and the utmost vigi-lance was still imperative in all areas of socialist construction, as "Comrade Stalin's recent article" dealing with the applica-tion of Leninist principles of party-mindedness to politics and theory had underscored. Moreover, Stalin's letter to *Proletar-skaja revoljutsija* was said to be directly relevant to the prob-lems with RAPP. "Comrades from RAPP" had been heard talk-ing about some special "general line of RAPP," but anyone who spoke like that underestimated "the political damage of this sort of outlook, which *objectively* creates the opportunity to discuss the RAPP line as being independent of the general line of the party."[13]

Mitin and Judin then added these complaints to their list of grievances: "Closely related to the faulty understanding of Leninist party-mindedness in philosophy is the attempt to rep-resent the sphere of creative literature and criticism as the sole domain of 'specialists.'" Averbakh, for instance, had recently spoken harshly of those party workers who he felt had no particular expertise in the area of literature but had undertaken—on the strength of the party's understanding of Marxist-Leninist theory—to assist proletarian literature in achieving a higher level of theoretical maturity. Averbakh had turned away such offers of assistance, overlooking the point that, without a profound understanding of dialectical materialism, all talk of the need to raise proletarian literature to a higher level lost its credibility. Besides which, Mitin and Judin went on, "even after meaningful work has been done in the sphere of philosophy toward exposing the mechanistic and Deborinist revision of dialectical materialism, a number of comrades from RAPP continue to tolerate serious theoretical errors, principally in the matter of menshevizing idealism."[14]

Mitin and Judin next set their sights on RAPP's slogan "For the Removal of Any and All Masks." The political point behind their theoretical reservations was especially conspicuous: "We have already noted that this slogan is too general and is in need of greater precision. *Mechanistically* transferring it to the conditions of the dictatorship of the proletariat, the comrades [from RAPP] tolerate a profound theoretical and political error." In this particular instance, happily, RAPP had been receptive to the objections to its appeal, practiced self-criticism, and clarified the meaning of the slogan by adding to the words "For the Removal of Any and All Masks" the phrase "from the class enemy, bureaucrats, wreckers, and so on."[15] It hardly needed to be pointed out that Bolsheviks eschewed disguises and masks.

In spite of these complaints about certain features of RAPP's program, however, those in the central committee with enough high-level backing to arrive at a consensus in favor of RAPP's abolition were at this point apparently not yet planning to abandon the organization and by no means regarded the friction that they were experiencing with RAPP as a major problem. Even though one of Stalin's right-hand men, Lev Mekhlis, called for a "Bolshevist reorganization" of RAPP in an article that came out just a few days after the one signed by Mitin and Judin, he still made a point of lauding RAPP for its role in "unmasking Voronskiism, Pereverzevism, Litfrontism, and other recidivists."[16]

IN THE SERVICE OF THE COMINTERN?

For the better part of 1930 and 1931, Soviet literature and literary criticism passed through a turbulent phase marked by blistering criticism of all kinds of literary alliances and associations and by their degradation as Menshevist and Trotskyist havens whose outlook in literary affairs hampered and sometimes even openly subverted the *"struggle for Leninism in literary criticism and in proletarian literature."* [17] Almost to the day of its dissolution, RAPP was virtually the only organization spared the brand of political denunciation in the guise of theoretical disagreements flung at its competitors, presumably because RAPP had assisted so eagerly in the liquidation of the other "nonproletarian" groups and had been thought of by the party, at least until late 1931, as its own commissar in literary matters. But when RAPP balked at relinquishing its right to formulate theory according to its understanding of dialectical materialism in literature, the party dissolved it. [18]

By the time the criticism of RAPP first started to appear in journals and newspapers influential enough to arouse any suspicion about the future of the organization, Georg Lukács was no longer in the Soviet Union. Why had he left? Simple, he said decades later: "I wanted to leave Moscow." [19] This writer has suggested elsewhere that things were not quite as simple as Lukács' remark makes them out to be, that he was sent to Berlin, and that his activity in the League of Proletarian Revolutionary Writers (BPRS), RAPP's sister organization in Germany, was in some way associated with policy within the KPD central committee influenced by Heinz Neumann, Willi Münzenberg, and Leo Flieg. [20] But this point should not be taken to mean that Lukács' work in Berlin was a direct *party* assignment. It could scarcely have been one because the KPD in those years never got around to setting an unambiguous policy in literary political and literary theoretical matters. Factions existed in the central committee, of which the group around Neumann and Münzenberg was just one (and then only until spring 1932). [21] Throughout the entire existence of the BPRS, when the KPD central committee or politburo was not studiously ignoring the organization, the group's leadership was by and large left to its own devices in policy matters. [22] The

BPRS' inability to settle on an official theoretical platform was one of the results.

László Sziklai remarks also that Lukács was sent to Berlin; he writes that Lukács left Moscow for Germany "on a political mission,"[23] and it is of course preposterous to imagine that Lukács could merely have packed his suitcase on a whim and caught the next train to Berlin, the more so if his initial stay in Moscow had been a form of "Cominternment." Moreover, Lukács received a new party card upon departure. Whereas he had belonged to the Soviet Communist party in Moscow, he left for Berlin as a member of the KPD, a switch that scarcely falls into the domain of private preference. The point is simply this: It is one thing to contend that Lukács needed and had high-level approval to move to Berlin and that some influential KPD or Comintern leaders, Münzenberg perhaps, had an interest in his departure and perhaps even ideas about the nature of his Berlin stay. But it is a different matter altogether to argue that he was sent "by the CI" with the express assignment of assisting those writers in the BPRS executive grouped around Johannes R. Becher, Andor Gábor, and Otto Biha, who were experiencing difficulties with the left-wing opposition in the organization.[24]

This latter argument presumes that Lukács was dispatched to Berlin to carry out a hard-and-fast cultural policy, knowing precisely what "the party" or "the CI" expected of him. The suggestion that he was not acting on his own in Berlin but must have been sure of the full support of the party may seem perfectly reasonable,[25] but it is a vastly oversimplified explanation for the imperiousness and self-assurance that Lukács displayed in Berlin. It again infers that a party cultural policy existed, whereas Lukács himself referred later to the "opinions fluctuating back and forth" in the central committee, whose secretariat sometimes sided with and sometimes against him and Becher;[26] and it rules out the possibility that Lukács might have had reasons of his own for behaving as he did.

Lukács' work in Berlin more likely consisted less in adhering to strict official guidelines than in trying to adapt to the situation in Germany his personal theoretical blend of the "insights" gained in the philosophy discussions, various RAPP principles, and his own original ideas. This explanation can account for Lukács' new ruthlessness in theoretical questions that some scholars have otherwise interpreted as a reflection of a distinctly articulated party assignment. By the time Lukács arrived in Berlin, he evidently had a growing sense of confidence about his role as interpreter of dialectical materialism in literature, though, paradoxically, this mounting assertiveness may well have sprung from yet another scare that Lukács had recently experienced and that may have prompted his departure from Moscow in the first place. There is every reason to believe that the controversy surrounding the Blum theses had frightened Lukács badly—being the single target of a Comintern campaign of political abuse was not a pleasant experience under any circumstances; and it seems reasonable to assume that this confrontation with the party had left Lukács with the visceral feeling that his theories should be developed in the future with as accurate a sense as possible of the current political constellation in the party and with at least some thought given to those ideological trends likely to emerge in the coming weeks or months. This interpretation does not mean that Lukács' theory was exclusively a reflection of the changing political and ideological circumstances of the time, but his conscious and subconscious adaptation of his theory to party policy had to be a significant factor in the formulation of his ideas after the Blum theses taught him what it meant to stick his neck out too far on controversial issues.

Add to that the fact that Lukács narrowly escaped being drawn into another dangerous political controversy in 1931, a scant two years after the Blum theses (or only one if they were discussed in February-March 1930). Then the image of a frightened Lukács getting out of Moscow in 1931 and arriving in Berlin, not with specific orders to carry out but with the private determination to demonstrate his political reliability to the party, comes gradually into focus. What scared him this time? Lukács' name had appeared in the philosophy debate in two different contexts; both were politically compromising, though one was a more direct attack upon the "idealism" of *Geschichte und Klassenbewusstsein*.

Lukács was first mentioned in the resolution published by the "party cell" of the Institute for Red Professors in *Pravda* on 26 January 1931. According to this resolution, Deborin's 1924

criticism of Lukács' *Geschichte und Klassenbewusstsein* was
a classic example of the Deborinites knack for "camouflaging"
their own idealistic revision of Marxism by attacking Lukács':
"This is a remarkably clever form of the idealistic revision of
Marxism; taking great pains to hide behind a protective materialist and Marxist phraseology and often dressed in Marxist-
Leninist raiments, it frequently expresses its own sharp opposition not just to the open, clerical counterrevolutionary
idealism championed by a Losev, but also to Hegelian idealists
of Lukács' type."[27] Mark Mitin utilized virtually identical
phrases in one of his articles,[28] but he still placed more emphasis on Deborin's "revisionism" than on Lukács' "idealism." A
second reference, however, had far more serious overtones.
Mitin wrote that Lenin's writings underscored the need for a
struggle against a revisionist attitude "toward the dialectic in
general and the Hegelian dialectic in particular," which, "beginning with Bernstein and ending with Bukharin," ran "like a
red thread" through revisionist writing. But a battle was to be
"waged simultaneously with works of the kind dealing with
the Hegelian categories and dialectic that we find among representatives of an idealistic revision of Marxism, beginning with
Lukács and ending with Deborin."[29]

Why was Lukács suddenly targeted for criticism along with
Deborin and Bukharin? Were the attacks precipitated solely by
the Stalinists' regular penchant for dredging up past controversies and "deviations" or was Lukács perhaps caught up in the
debate because he was then working in the Marx-Engels Institute, for whose director, David Rjazanov, Stalin had a particular animus?[30] The articles mentioning Lukács never associated
him directly with Rjazanov, but it is entirely in the realm of
possibility that the Stalinists linked the pair in unpublished
debates and discussions simply because Lukács worked under
Rjazanov and definitely had a questionable party reputation at
the time. The *Pravda* resolution of January 1931, after all, complained about those who downplayed Lenin's significance as a
theoretician and philosopher and expressed its conviction that
this was no doubt connected with the objectives of the schol-
arly work being done by the Marx-Engels Institute.[31] Rjazanov
himself was slandered with references to his "Menshevist conception"[32] of Marx' philosophical evolution and with com-

ments about his "Menshevist distortions."[33] Mark Mitin reviled Rjazanov first because he had supposedly denied that
Leninism constituted a "new stage in the development of dialectical materialism"[34] and from that charge went over to political denunciation. Rjazanov's views on Leninism and philosophy ran (again, "like a red thread") through the writings of
Deborin and his group, whose ideas were shared by "'such theoreticians'" as Trotsky, Zinoviev, Preobrazhenskij, Bukharin,
and "whoever else belongs among them." Even more damaging
was Mitin's accusation that Rjazanov sought a practical outlet
for his theoretical views: "Events of the immediate past have
shown that [Rjazanov] has fallen to the point of giving direct
assistance to the counterrevolutionary Menshevist organization. For that he was expelled from the party."[35]

No blood was shed at the time, but most of the philosophers
associated with Deborin and berated in the philosophy debate
disappeared after 1936, though Deborin himself, by some
strange quirk of fate, died a natural death in 1968.[36] Rjazanov
met with a familiar end, though there is a good reason for letting Lukács tell the story: "Rjazanov was the director of the
Marx-Engels Institute. He was a famous Marxist who had been
responsible for the large Marx-Engels edition many years ago.
He was an eccentric person, but extraordinarily learned and a
real Marxist scholar. He had already experienced some sort of
unpleasantries during my first stay, was sent off to the prov-
inces, and during the great trials, then, he finally disappeared.
No one knows the details."[37]

The gaps in these remarks may reflect the deterioration of
Lukács' mind by 1971; he was eighty-five, dying of cancer, no
longer in full possession of his faculties. He was speaking about
events that had happened forty years before, and his forgetfulness might be understandable. In 1945, on the other hand,
Lukács would have remembered the events of 1930 and 1931
well. He had worked then as a scholar at the Marx-Engels Institute (IMEL), he said, primarily involved in working out his own
definitive standpoint in philosophical questions. "I fought
against Deborin and Rjazanov," he added, "as a member of the
Russian Communist party (B) in the [party] organization of
IMEL, in accordance with the party line."[38] So in 1945 there
was evidently little mystery in Lukács' mind after all about the

nature of Rjazanov's "unpleasantries" in 1931; his name had been mentioned all too prominently in the press in connection with the philosophy debate, occasionally in the same articles as Lukács', and he was implicated publicly in the Menshevik trial, too. It seems highly unlikely that Lukács could have been at all ignorant of these events at the time they happened. Whether the state of his health in 1971 accounts for his memory lapses or whether his tight-lipped reference to vague "unpleasantries" hid a personal sore spot in the recesses of his mind is impossible to say. In any event, it is hard to imagine that Lukács took no action in 1931 to protect himself—fighting against Deborin and Rjazanov "in accordance with the party line"—when it appeared that he might be swept into the same political vortex into which other prominent victims of the philosophy debate were disappearing.

. . . .

CHAPTER 5

Berlin, 1931 – 1933

If one assumes that Lukács was leading an imperiled existence when he left for Berlin, his departure should probably be seen as an attempt to avoid a political confrontation from which he had little chance of emerging unscathed, a way of removing himself from trouble with the help of friends in the KPD or the Comintern who could influence the issuing of travel papers and hustle him out of Moscow under the pretext of a "political mission" of the Comintern. If so, Lukács' theoretical writings published in Berlin ought to be regarded, at least to some degree, as a purposeful exhibition of political reliability. His domineering treatment of other writers, combined with his zealotry in politicizing and virtually criminalizing contradictory viewpoints through the use of defamatory innuendos based on idioms from the philosophy debate, may well have been a bid to get back in the good graces of the Stalinist powers that be after his second brush with disaster in 1930 and 1931. However, this reconstruction of Lukács' motives, if it is accurate, does not necessarily imply that he was cynical about espousing a blend of his own ideas on literature, RAPP's theoretical standards, and the various views of the Stalinist philosophers. Lukács' highly developed instinct for survival may well have been functioning so reflexively by now that he himself was no longer entirely conscious of the gradual forfeiture of his theoretical autonomy; and it is entirely possible that he took the Stalinist motifs in his writing for his own original discovery of certain theoretical truths.

REHABILITATION?

When Lukács arrived in Berlin in 1931, RAPP's theoretical and political authority was still completely unchallenged in the eyes of those in charge of the BPRS; and, in fact, most of the articles written by Lukács and Johannes R. Becher for *Die Linkskurve,* the journal brought out by the BPRS, intermingle basic RAPP propositions with the general principles put forward by the Stalinists in the philosophy debate. Becher, for instance, drew upon the *Pravda* editorial "For the Hegemony of Proletarian Literature" for his own article dealing with a "turning point" in the work of the BPRS. *Pravda* had complained about the inadequacy of RAPP's "theoretical work" in apprehending the tasks confronting the proletarian literary movement; the top priority for an upcoming RAPP plenum needed to be the search for new ways of "liquidating the ever-persistent lag in literature behind the demands of the period of socialist construction." The "militant" RAPP slogan "For a Great Art of Bolshevism," which contrasted with the "banality" and "varnishing of reality" advocated by Litfront, was a meaningful attempt to meet this challenge.[1]

Becher reiterated the salient points of the *Pravda* commentary in his analysis of the German proletarian literary movement, echoing the standard lament about the gap between theory and the practical demands of the day. "Our literature's backwardness with respect to revolutionary development," Becher said, "is likewise a sign that our comrades have not kept pace in their understanding of things compared with the revolutionary knowledge contained in Marxism-Leninism."[2] To catch up with revolutionary development, proletarian revolutionary writers had to commit themselves to becoming schooled Marxists, which implied that the BPRS had no intention of sitting back and waiting "until the writers whom we need come to us 'of their own volition' [*von selbst*]. It is our responsibility to create our writers and our literature."[3] In the sense that the leading proletarian writers in Germany consciously defined and actively pursued ends in literature that would finally bridge the gap between theory (the "backwardness" of proletarian literature) and the revolutionary reality of the day, Becher, using RAPP vocabulary, called these literary avant-gardists "the pioneers of a great Bolshevist art."[4] This was the true Leninist avant-garde in literature, and Becher relied upon the authority of the *Pravda* attack upon radical left-wing forms of art in the USSR to contrast "the great art of bolshevism" with his version of the radical "nonsense" disseminated recently by so-called avant-gardists like Sergej Tretjakov, who was visiting Berlin at the time.[5] "In this category belong the overemphasis upon experimentation, arrogance in matters of form, and playing agitation and propaganda off against each other," said Becher; "in this category belongs the nonsense about the 'end of literature' or the view of the writer's function as that of a specialist, a literary engineer who practices his vocation up in his studio and who looks upon the revolutionary movement as a training ground."[6]

Becher's next major programmatic article was a similar restatement of RAPP positions mingled with criticism and demands influenced by the current status of the philosophy debate, which had just received added impetus from Stalin's letter to *Proletarskaja revoljutsija*. In this particular article Becher launched another attack upon radical Communist literature that practiced a brand of political agitation at variance with RAPP's less blatantly utilitarian "creative method." Among the "left-wing" errors were an exuberantly proletarian disposition, an unwillingness to learn, an overemphasis on content at the price of formal refinement, a disregard for the literary heritage, the notion that literary tasks consisted exclusively of supplying the daily Communist press with reportage and publicism, and a "pure, unprincipled spontaneity and praxis-oriented activity (*Praktizität*)."[7]

Becher's concern with "spontaneity" in literature is a gauge of the impact that Stalin's letter to *Proletarskaja revoljutsija* and his criticism of "Luxemburgism" (spontaneity) as opposed to Leninism (consciousness) had upon the KPD and upon the BPRS.[8] Becher, in fact, enjoined members of the BPRS to study this letter for its application to literature and to take to heart also the similar lessons contained in the first published KPD response to Stalin's letter, Ernst Thälmann's article in *Die Internationale* entitled "Einige Fehler und Schwächen in unserer theoretischen Arbeit und der Weg zu ihrer Überwindung." But Stalin's cannonades at Social Democracy, menshevism, and Rosa Luxemburg also toughened an already unswerving antagonism toward "social fascism." The corresponding phenomenon in the BPRS was a hardening of the organization's already unyielding line with respect to non-Communist writers. The

BPRS, said Becher, would welcome any writer willing to fight against fascism in any form (against Hitler fascism and social fascism), against imperialist war and white terror, and any writer willing to participate in the struggle for socialist construction and for the defense of the Soviet Union. This supposed openmindedness is what Becher was thinking of when he invoked the quality of the BPRS' "nonpartisanship." This nonalignment by no means suggested, on the other hand, that the BPRS failed to recognize the leading role of the party or did anything to weaken it; it did not mean, he cautioned, that the BPRS neglected to regard the Communist party as "the proletariat's supreme form of consciousness and organization."[9] Moreover, said Becher, "We in the Bund make no secret of our opinion that a proletarian revolutionary writer must be a Marxist-Leninist, as well as a writer, in his work, if he wishes to satisfy the demands placed upon him by proletarian revolutionary literature."[10] As for other writers, neither Gerhart Hauptmann, nor Heinrich Mann, nor any other "Untertan" or subject, regardless of his pompous name, were worthy of fighting side by side with proletarian writers;[11] exemplars were Marx and Lenin, or a Gorki, and above all else the revolutionary labor movement itself.[12]

LUKÁCS, RAPP, AND THE FELLOW TRAVELERS

Lukács' articles in *Die Linkskurve* should be read as a similar cross between RAPP principles and various ideas centering on the lag between theory and practice deplored by the Stalinist philosophers. In the case of RAPP, Lukács' retrospective reconstruction of his own attitude toward the organization at the time is important because it illustrates his inability to recognize or admit the extent of his own involvement in the articulation and administration of an authoritative and authoritarian literary policy backed by Stalin's various lieutenants. As a literary critic he had participated in the battles against RAPP while he was still in Germany, Lukács claimed in 1945, and this opposition in 1931 and 1932 (as well as his later activity in the USSR against naturalism, formalism and vulgar sociology) coincided with the line set by the party.[13] In 1957 Lukács elaborated further and spoke of the hopes awakened in him by the very debate that heralded the gradual end of a still somewhat unfettered intellectual and literary life in the USSR. The philosophy debate, he explained, led him to hope for a clarification of the relationship between Hegel and Marx, Feuerbach and Marx, and Marx and Lenin, and for release from the "so-called" Plechanovist orthodoxy. But Lukács emphasized that the dissolution of RAPP in 1932, an organization that he had always opposed, especially prepared the way for a flowering of socialist literature, as well as Marxist literary theory and criticism, unhampered by any form of bureaucratism.[14]

Lukács never associated the political purpose of the philosophy debate, at least not publicly, with the destruction not just of RAPP but of all autonomous and semi-autonomous literary alliances and associations in the USSR. In fact, Lukács claimed later to have welcomed the end of an organization that he described as being itself a bureaucratic obstacle to the unhindered progress of socialist literature, betraying no awareness whatever that his later interpretation actually matched the very rationale given by the Stalinists at the time for doing away with an outfit that they came to see by late 1931 as a growing hindrance to *their* objectives. In 1971 Lukács added further confusion to the picture of his past attitudes. He did not return to the Marx-Engels Institute when he arrived back in Moscow in 1933 because in the meantime a campaign had begun on Stalin's initiative that definitely had its positive sides, notably in the struggle against RAPP.[15] Without explaining just what his failure to return to the Marx-Engels Institute had to do with Stalin's campaign against RAPP,[16] Lukács gave the following rendition. The campaign against RAPP had actually served the good purpose of putting a stop to the Trotskyist Averbakh, Averbakh *unmöglich zu machen* was Lukács' choice of words. This was supposedly Stalin's exclusive interest in this matter. But Judin and above all Usievich had also been involved in this campaign. They attacked the aristocracy of RAPP functionaries and called for a general Russian writers' union to replace the "narrow-minded RAPP," which only accepted Communist writers into its ranks. "In a general writers' union," Lukács explained, "every Russian writer in the Soviet Union would be welcome, and the union would then take care of the affairs of the Russian writers. I also joined up with this movement."[17]

Lukács' talk about the "Trotskyist" Averbakh and his further account of RAPP's abolition was a Stalinist invention. No longer in complete control of his mind by 1971, it is tempting to suggest that Lukács reverted late in his life to the party version of events given at the time they occurred and that in his old age he had lost whatever ability he might once have had to discriminate between the political reality of an ordinary defamation campaign and the ideologically colored fabrications and lies dredged up by the Stalinists to give their activity the stamp of legitimacy. Perhaps some of the contortions in Lukács' autobiography and his almost pathetic inability to hide his essential agreement with repressive administrative measures was the price that he paid in his old age for having led a schizophrenic life for so many decades. By calling Averbakh a Trotskyist, for instance, Lukács indicates his acceptance of all the lies about Averbakh that Judin and other Stalin protégés concocted to destroy Averbakh after RAPP's abolition.[18]

Lukács' remark that Stalin was primarily concerned in the anti-RAPP campaign with ridding the organization of "the Trotskyist" Averbakh points, moreover, to a surprisingly naive understanding of Stalin's motives; and it is topped only by Lukács' line that Judin and Elena Usievich, one of Lukács' closest friends in the USSR, were somehow motivated in their opposition to RAPP by their anger with its intolerance toward other writers and that they were guided by their own magnanimity in wishing to replace RAPP with a liberal writers' union open to all Soviet writers. Just like his interpretation of the Averbakh affair, Lukács' story of the prelude to the creation of a single, "nondiscriminating" Soviet writers' union with room for all coincides with the prescribed explanations given at the time.

During his eighteen months in Berlin Lukács wrote about two kinds of writers: authors and intellectuals who, without being Communists, were highly critical of capitalism and frequently sympathetic to the Soviet Union; and Communist writers whose work clashed with Lukács' formal standards. In later years Lukács often contrasted Communist "sectarianism" toward politically nonaligned intellectuals who sympathized with communism with his own broadmindedness. In 1969, for instance, he remarked that in joint undertakings in which Communist writers cooperated with the "bourgeois opposition" the official party line in 1931 and 1932 had been too left-wing to suit him. Closer relations with left-wing intellectuals had been called for.[19] But there is the usual discrepancy in these remarks between the nature of Lukács' actions and his retrospective account of his conduct.

It may be true, as Lukács also suggested, that Becher had a "more left-wing radical outlook" in BPRS matters than Lukács. Becher's articles in *Die Linkskurve* abound with derogatory allusions to fellow traveler writers—utter failures, he complained, in any serious class conflict.[20] But Lukács' suggestion that his approach was somehow free of such prejudices is simply not true and would hardly have been possible under the circumstances anyway. The ideological dynamics of the philosophy debate virtually mandated rigidity, for Lukács as well as for Becher and the other principle spokesmen of the BPRS. When Becher employed the misnomer "nonpartisanship" to describe the BPRS' approach to other writers, listed the conditions under which a non-Communist intellectual would be welcomed as a partner in the struggle against the system, and enjoined BPRS members to learn from Thälmann's article in *Die Internationale* and Stalin's letter to *Proletarskaja revoljutsija*, his conceit reflected a literary political policy constricted by the philosophy debate. Additionally, his demands merely restated Soviet thinking at the time on the subject of RAPP's approach to fellow travelers. The *Pravda* article "For the Hegemony of Proletarian Literature" had praised RAPP for expanding its "influence" among fellow travelers, the result being that they had "joined the ranks of literary allies of the working class."[21]

Lukács likewise expected "sincere" non-Communist writers and intellectuals who opposed capitalism to come over to the Marxist-Leninist side. He never budged from this position in Berlin and very little afterwards, not even during the halcyon days of the popular front. Speaking of a new era in the attitude of the Western European intelligentsia to the building of socialism, Lukács was full of praise for Bernard Shaw's "enthusiastic utterances" about conditions in the Soviet Union following his journey to the USSR.[22] But there was an undeniable arrogance to Lukács' attitude that Shaw had basically acknowledged plain facts anyway, obvious to any intellectual who was capable of being honest with himself, and that Shaw, whose world view still evinced tendencies pointing in the direction of fascism no less, now ought to take the next logical step toward communism. He needed only to be properly encouraged by the right kind of propaganda. Shaw represented an increasingly broad segment of left-wing intellectuals who, however belatedly, were profoundly impressed by the results of socialist construction, said Lukács. These intellectuals had liberated themselves sufficiently from the ideological bonds of capitalism to appreciate the facts of socialist construction as facts, but they had "thus far" managed to draw only tactical, not Marxist, ideological conclusions from them. A clear recognition of both the positive significance of such "conversions" as well as a realistic awareness of their limitations, said Lukács, had to result in an intensification of "our propaganda" among this group of intellectuals in order to secure their detachment from the ideology of capitalism.[23]

Lukács' handling of Gerhart Hauptmann also witnesses to the limits of his understanding for socially critical non-Communist writers. Lukács categorized Hauptmann's type of class-determined criticism as "subjective idealism." During the bourgeois revolutionary period, the intellectuals representing the liberal bourgeoisie had freed themselves from the morality handed down to them, but their own helpless morality broke down completely when faced with the facts posed by the epoch of imperialism.[24] One could choose to pity Hauptmann as a victim of the ideological decline of his class, Lukács concluded; "but he went along with everything associated with this decline without resistance, thereby prostituting and passing final sentence upon himself as a poet—voluntarily, honestly, but completely."[25]

Lukács' later allusions to "the narrow-minded RAPP"[26] perhaps ought to be read, then, in the context of his own schoolmasterish criticism of non-Stalinist intellectuals. It really differed little from RAPP's position, which exhibited the same pharisaic condescension toward any intellectual who was something less than an unabashed "Bolshevik," as RAPP interpreted that quality. Averbakh, for instance, talked of "educating and re-educating the fellow travelers," insisting: "We must see to it that each fellow-traveler within our ranks shall grow as speedily as possible into a genuine proletarian writer."[27] To his plea for an "attitude of comradeship contributing to their quickest bolshevization and to their ideological artistic growth," Averbakh added: "There are those [fellow travelers] who come to us, but have not yet become completely identified with us. There are others who waver today, under stress of the current situation, while even yesterday they were quite consistent proletarian writers. It would be quite foolish to cast aside such people. It would be 'communist pride' of the most vulgar character. It would mean the encouragement of the line of least resistance; for, it is easy to expel, but hard to reform. We must find the sympathetic attitude for each writer, the specific approach in each individual case." What did this sympathetic attitude imply? It meant, said Averbakh, criticism in matters of principle. Whereas some thought that one had to exercise tolerance and liberalism with respect to a writer's defects in order to be sympathetic, he believed that real sympathy consisted in "frankly and honestly criticizing a writer in the light of principles, thereby helping him in the improvement of his creative methods."[28]

AGAINST THE THEORY OF SPONTANEITY IN LITERATURE

Lukács' treatment of Shaw and Hauptmann might be characterized likewise as "frankly and honestly criticizing" in the light of principles, toward the goal of their "quickest bolshevization"; and, in his articles about writers who belonged to the BPRS or identified with it, Lukács was just as unbending in his insistence that the only unobjectionable world view was "Marxism-Leninism" as it was currently being defined by the Stalinists and by Lukács himself. In his articles on Willi Bredel and Ernst Ottwalt, Lukács demonstrated what he thought it meant for a proletarian revolutionary writer to be a Marxist-Leninist, "as well as a writer, in his work," as Becher had phrased it.[29] The RAPP or RAPP-like diction stands out unmistakably in Lukács' criticism of Bredel: the absence of "living men and vibrant, changing, fluid relationships between human beings," "application of the dialectic," "absence of dialectics in literary representation," and so on.[30]

But it is especially important not to overlook Lukács' penchant for intermingling these RAPP principles with the political-ideological views set down as law in the philosophy debate. Most of Lukács' theoretical utterances in *Die Linkskurve* represent an exercise in utilizing the ideological injunctions and political abuse customary in the debate to lend his personal verdict on these writers the quality of incontrovertible doctrine. "Proletarian revolutionary writers must not be permitted now, at a time when the tasks *along the entire front* of the class struggle are being set ever higher, to lag behind the *general movement*,"[31] read Lukács' rendering of the jargon common in the philosophy debate. Proletarian revolutionary writers were to use relentless self-criticism, the merciless exposure of the lag and its causes, and the establishment of specific tasks that matched the general high plateau of the revolutionary class struggle to acknowledge the gap between theory and the current status of revolutionary practice. Once acknowledged, this gap needed to be liquidated "as quickly as possible through tough, goal-oriented work and by *mastering* the application of materialist dialectics in literary creation."[32] It was an entirely justifiable expectation that proletarian revolutionary writers, "in their manner of representation," should attain the level of the day-to-day class struggle, and Lukács claimed the right to demand still more—"that the top achievements of our literature with respect to applying the dialectic should be measured against the top achievements of the revolutionary practice and theory of the KPD and the Comintern."[33]

Lukács' combination of RAPP language with the political atmospherics of the philosophy debate came across still more clearly in his next article, in which he undertook less to pinpoint and analyze theoretical positions than to defame the author. Following publication of Lukács' essay on Bredel, Otto Gotsche responded in *Die Linkskurve* with a defense of Bredel. Writers ought to listen more carefully to the "masses," said Gotsche, and proletarian revolutionary literature needed to be exposed to mass criticism because the literary backwardness sprang precisely from the fact that the writers were insufficiently under the control of the people.[34]

Gotsche's argument was an open challenge to Lukács' stress on the conscious acquisition of Marxism-Leninism as a world view, in the writer's work as well; and, answering Gotsche, Lukács echoed Becher's comments about "consciousness" versus "pure, unprincipled spontaneity" in proletarian revolutionary literature and in literary criticism. Lukács wished that writers could pursue their work with a Marxist consciousness sufficiently advanced to enable them concurrently to scrutinize their own "creative method" critically. Such was unfortunately not the case because proletarian revolutionary writers were rarely also practicing Marxist critics. It was thus incumbent upon the critics, not the writers, to apply materialist dialectics to the area of literature, thereby uncovering and elucidating that creative method which accorded with the problems of the class struggle.[35]

Then came the derogatory political insinuations inspired by Stalin's letter to *Proletarskaja revoljutsija*. Lukács likened Gotsche's opinion that literature should acquire its bearings from the masses to the "standpoint of spontaneity, one of the numerous Luxemburgian remnants in the German labor movement."[36] Progress in Marxist-Leninist literature would continue to come slowly as long as writers had complete freedom to develop their own styles of writing and failed to grasp the fact that a Marxist-Leninist creative method even existed or, from the opposite angle, that certain methods were anything but Marxist-Leninist, regardless of the writer's own honest intentions. A clear understanding of the goals and the difficulties that stood in the way of achieving them was absolutely necessary, but possible only "if we set out to liquidate this backwardness *consciously, by way of our activity* (and not by resting our hopes in the spontaneity of the movement as a whole)."[37] The result otherwise would be the use of inadmissible styles and forms of writing incapable of representing the world from a Marxist-Leninist point of view. As for Bredel, he had mistaken a mixture of reportage and minutes for "representation," *Gestaltung*. The problem was one of the creative method, and the question read, "can *a report or reportage replace literary repre-*

sentation? Is reportage, say, . . . the correct, 'timely' method for our literature? Or is it a lower-grade creative method that has been superseded in the Soviet Union but still needs to be overcome here?"[38]

Gotsche's point of view was a concession to spontaneity, Lukács went on. Giving in to spontaneity meant reconciling oneself to the "backwardness" of proletarian literature, rendering oneself susceptible to the influence of petty bourgeois "ideological residues" still present among both proletarian readers and writers. Lukács saw his task and the task of other Marxist-Leninist critics to be the struggle against the ideological legacy of the Second International, in the realm of literature as well as politics. The workers ought not to be confirmed in their incorrect views and in their stubborn unwillingness to discard the theory of spontaneity.[39] Lukács buttressed his conclusion by citing the importance of "Comrade Stalin's" remarks in *Proletarskaja revoljutsija* and the significance for the entire German labor movement of "Comrade Thälmann's" essays and speeches.

This particular article is a graphic illustration of Lukács' development into a contentious dogmatist informed with a sense of his own importance and determined to mediate—on his terms—between politics and literature. Lukács' indirect but obvious stress on his own role in the party as a Marxist-Leninist literary critic, his growing resolve to prescribe to writers a single kind of style that he sanctioned as Marxist-Leninist because of his knowledge of philosophical, ideological, and literary theoretical developments in the USSR, and his refusal to believe that writers might, by natural inclination, "spontaneously" chance upon acceptable and novel creative methods betoken, it seems, his determination to carve a meaningful niche for himself in the party. In the aftermath of the Blum theses, Lukács had been kicked out of the central committee of the Hungarian Communist party; his most significant book in the twenties, *Geschichte und Klassenbewusstsein*, had been ridiculed as idealistic in *Pravda*; and his name had appeared in influential articles along with tainted names like Deborin, Bukharin, Rjazanov, and Trotsky. Where in the party, he may have been asking, could he ever hope to find a sphere of activity commensurate with his intellectual abilities and ambitions?

Lukács may have answered the question in his attack on Gotsche, when he lept at the opportunity to present himself as the judge of that creative method which was to be regarded as dialectical materialist and therefore Marxist-Leninist. Much like the Stalinist philosophers in the Soviet Union, Lukács busied himself in Berlin with ferreting out all kinds of deviations and leftover traces of deleterious ideological legacies: spontaneity (the remnants of Luxemburgism and the Second International in literature and literary criticism), Trotskyism, idealism, Machism, mechanism, and so on. At the same time, however, he persisted in his efforts to expand his own literary theory that contained some of his answers to questions concerning the relationship between world view and style in works of the past and present as well as the works of Marxist-Leninist and non-Communist contemporary writers.

In June 1932 Lukács raised an issue that he had only touched upon briefly in the *Moskauer Rundschau*: the realistic literature of past writers and the connection between their patently false world view (their "false consciousness") and their realistic creative method. In his articles on Tolstoy and Dostoevski written during his first stay in Moscow, Lukács had just begun toying with the idea that realism in past great literature was in some way a surmounting of the class limitations imposed upon a writer by his world view, though he was not yet able to ground his theory officially in Engels' "triumph of realism." In early 1932, however, with the "friendly assistance of our Soviet Russian comrades,"[40] *Die Linkskurve* had acquired a copy of Engels' letter to Margaret Harkness and published it with introductory comments. Engels' analysis of Balzac illustrated perfectly the use of dialectics and needed to be taken as a warning against a mechanistic simplification of "our view of literature, which revolves around questions of class."[41] Lukács used Engels' letter to declare that great bourgeois writers, without being aware of it or without any clear intention, and sometimes even in spite of their intentions, under certain circumstances overcame the limitations of their "false consciousness" to get at the essential motive forces behind social development. Engels had pointed out that Balzac's conscious purpose had been the celebration of the declining class of the French ancien regime but that he had been "forced" to go against his own class sympathies and political biases to give a correct picture of contemporary society.[42]

The same was true, said Lukács, of Tolstoy and many other leading bourgeois writers; but Lukács' dilemma in 1932 was that his line of reasoning with regard to such realism, often accomplished "contrary to . . . consciousness," had the ring of a theory of spontaneity to it. If a false consciousness had not blocked the path to a "spontaneous" representation of reality in the case of the classics, why was a class bias or, to put it differently, the lack of an immaculate dialectical materialist world view, an insurmountable obstacle to realism for contemporary bourgeois or even for proletarian revolutionary writers? The revolutionary labor movement, Lukács explained, had attained a stage of historical maturity that it had not reached in Balzac's time; consequently, the "ideological barrier" that past writers had to overcome to achieve a triumph of realism simply no longer existed. Before, its social being had rendered it impossible for the proletariat (and thus for the proletarian writer) to go "beyond this barrier and to perceive class relationships and the development of the class struggle clearly behind the fetishized forms of capitalist society."[43] Not that this recognition and understanding was nowadays a direct, mechanical product of his social existence, an understanding that came to him automatically, Lukács added; it had to be attained through conscious work. But compared with times past, this understanding was now within the writer's grasp.

Earlier Lukács had used the antipodes "spontaneity" and "consciousness" to dismiss Gotsche's defense of Bredel; now, also taking at least a partial cue from the philosophy debate, Lukács' antinomies were "party-mindedness" versus "tendentiousness." The latter Lukács treated as a substandard style of writing that was also "spontaneous" for Lukács in the sense that a writer arbitrarily imposed a surface political tendentiousness upon his writing rather than allowing his "partisanship" to express itself naturally through the characters and situations. Lukács had a ready reserve of political innuendos to hurl at tendentious, as opposed to party-minded, writing, and they all came straight from the philosophy debate. "Today," he said, "when in our own theory and practice we are reexamining in all areas the ideological legacy of the Second International, we must be keenly aware in our literary theory and praxis too that we do not go on dragging along bourgeois luggage that came to us by way of the Second International." The method that exposed the errors and that lay bare their roots—the "non-liquidated" legacy of the Second International—was likewise the method providing the necessary assistance to overcome these errors: materialist dialectics, Marxism-Leninism.[44]

The key point for Lukács' application of his theory to proletarian revolutionary literature and to those practitioners of it who had once been bourgeois was a form of quasi-Leninist voluntarism. For example, the techniques of montage and reportage utilized by Ernst Ottwalt were an unacceptable "substitute"[45] for an objective art form capable of realistic representation. To acquire the "proletarian revolutionary creative method," a former bourgeois writer like Ottwalt, who had joined forces with the proletariat, had to make a complete break with his own class. Joining the Communist party or, even worse, merely sympathizing with it, was not enough; rather, a writer had to sever *all* of his ideological ties with the bourgeoisie. This "ideological" break was especially crucial for Lukács because he understood the use of a particular "creative method" to be the litmus test of the writer's ideological maturity. "Whereas the proletarian revolutionary poet, by making dialectical materialism the basis of his creative method, always has a clear view of the driving forces of the total process, the writer who stands in petty bourgeois opposition to capitalist society cannot use the total process and its driving forces, which he does not comprehend, as his point of departure."[46]

The expected outcome in such cases was a style, such as montage or reportage, that was structurally unequal to the task of capturing reality in all of its multiple dimensions, that is, "dialectically"; and this aesthetic defect was concomitant with the writer's faulty grasp of reality. Lukács was arguing in circles. The creative method reflected class background, class background determined creative method. In Ottwalt's case, Lukács first established the presence of an impaired depiction of reality. Working backwards, he then declared that these faults were "a necessary consequence of his creative method"[47] and deduced from Ottwalt's deficient method that identifiable ideological and political shortcomings had to be at the heart of it—an incomplete break with his former class and an attendant underdeveloped acceptance of dialectical materialism. It seemed to Lukács that these political consequences of Ottwalt's creative method merely reflected the social cause of his selection of this method to begin with. It was a reconciliation with the revolutionary proletariat that had originated from within bourgeois society, a reconciliation, however, that had thus far only developed into a criticism of the bourgeoisie and not to a complete coalescence with the revolutionary class. The criticism of bourgeois society generated from such an imperfect social standpoint therefore broke down at the halfway mark; it was mechanical and not dialectical.[48]

No sooner had Lukács arrived in Berlin than he appointed himself chairman of a one-man party tribunal meeting regularly to pass judgment on a writer's political and ideological orthodoxy. In his investigations, Lukács based his verdict almost exclusively on style, from which he deduced any additional evidence relevant to the case. A writer like Ottwalt or Brecht may have been as unqualifiedly loyal to the party as Lukács and subscribed without reservation to dialectical materialism as Stalin chose to have it defined. But when Lukács took issue with a creative method, he promptly combined his formalistic disapproval with a political inquisition to get at the class cause of the writer's defects. By making his social background the source of all a writer's formal flaws, Lukács seems, in fact, to have reverted to a form of fatalism akin in a way to the determinism of the literary sociologists in the Soviet Union, whom Lukács held in utter contempt after 1933.[49] But the prime difference is that Lukács never shut the door entirely to writers with nonproletarian backgrounds.

For great realistic writers of the past and evidently—though he was never very clear on this point—for certain contemporary bourgeois writers who met with his approval, Lukács invoked the principle of a triumph of realism, which was possible as long as a writer "represented" in his writing: "The *representation* of the total context [is] the *precondition for a correct composition* in the novel. That may happen on the basis of a 'false consciousness'; that is, in such a way that the author passes judgment on the times in which he lives and which he depicts and consciously advocates a past, declining society or a utopia only present in his imagination." But at the same time, he might recognize in his representation the driving forces in their proper relation, trace, and depict them. Precisely this, said Lukács, was what Engels regarded as "one of the greatest triumphs of realism." [50] For writers such as Bredel or Ottwalt, on the other hand, there could be no inadvertent or intuitive (spontaneous) triumph of realism, for they did not "represent." What was needed in their case was a voluntaristic act to purge themselves of all the ideological residues of their original class background; once these natural biases were eliminated, the underlying cause of a creative method out of harmony with Lukács' understanding of the only true Marxist-Leninist or dialectical materialist style of writing would be eradicated. These writers would begin "representing" in literature, and realism would be the result.

Lukács' literary theory automatically enhanced his own stature as a preeminent arbiter of Marxism-Leninism in literature, and he ensured the durability of his own authority by tying his principles to their official political, ideological, or philosophical equivalents taken from the philosophy debate. For instance, Lukács said that Ottwalt's "mechanistic and one-sided overemphasis" on the content of his work, regardless of whatever revolutionary quality it might lay claim to, drove a wedge between form and content; [51] "in this process, mechanical materialism evolves *into idealism*, which is what always happens when it undertakes to come to terms with the overall process. Applied to literature, formal experimentation is the result." [52]

Intentions were beside the point; in the case of an Upton Sinclair or Ottwalt, Lukács acknowledged that he was dealing with sincere intellectuals from the bourgeoisie—writers who were determined to use their literature to help destroy the class to which they had once belonged and who recognized that this was only possible by becoming one with the proletariat. [53] All the same, they had "thus far" failed to appreciate that their break with their class had to be complete, in the realm of ideology too; they had "not yet" realized that only such a total breach created the preconditions for merging themselves with the working class and for appropriating the world view of the revolutionary proletariat, dialectical materialism, for acquiring the ability to apply it.[54] It was all up to them.

In his last essay in *Die Linkskurve*, Lukács was just as combative as he had been in denouncing Otto Gotsche. Lukács disliked being contradicted, and when Ottwalt ventured to dispute his findings,[55] Lukács sharpened his language even further and spoke of the compendium of false views that formed the ideological substructure of Ottwalt's creative method.[56] Ottwalt had tried to make the point that a specific creative method was not the most urgent issue at all, arguing that a book's function in a specific political context mattered far more.[57] Such an outlook, which stressed the *"immediate"* reality of the day, reduced literature to agitation and formed the basis of an "anti-representation theory."[58]

Ottwalt had summarized his arguments in these words (which Lukács quoted): "'It is not the task of our literature to *stabilize* the consciousness of the reader, rather it wishes to *change* it.'" Lukács countered, "Brecht, too, sets the 'unchangeable man' of the old theater in opposition to the 'changeable and changing man' of the new,"[59] and he went on to contrive a dichotomy in Ottwalt's views between theory (interpretation) and practice (change), a conflict that obviously dovetailed with the basic categories of the philosophy debate. Ottwalt's theory, Lukács went on, apparently based itself on Marx's Feuerbach theses, which used the antinomies of interpreting reality as opposed to changing it to distinguish between past philosophical thought and present philosophy in the form of dialectical materialism.

Lukács rejected the notion, which he attributed to Ottwalt, that philosophers and thinkers only interpreted prior to Marx, whereas after him they changed or altered reality. This superficial vulgarization of Marx's views led to the loss of both the dialectical and the materialist content of Marxism. "Of course there was a '*changing*' of reality and thereby necessarily of consciousness, too; there was a praxis prior to Marx, too," said Lukács. "But—and this is the most important point—on the basis of a 'false consciousness' (Engels)."[60] Lukács was then able to contrast the activity of the proletariat in the past—with its "false consciousness"—and its conscious activity nowadays. The point, of course, was to discredit any stress on spontaneity in the current revolutionary labor movement at the expense of the theoretical and political leadership of the Communist party, the bearer of the class consciousness necessary for a successful revolutionary "practice." Lukács explained: "The fundamental change that Marx worked out here is thus not his replacement of 'non-praxis' with 'praxis'—that would be outdoing Hegel in idealism; rather, it is his recognition of the possibility granted objectively by the class circumstances of the proletariat to transform the previously 'unconscious' or 'falsely conscious' praxis into a conscious one, into a praxis with the proper consciousness."[61] Whether they realized it or not, said Lukács, the rigid distinction between the two periods, which underlay the views of Ottwalt and those who thought like him, had to lead to both mechanistic and idealistic consequences if thought through to the end.

Lukács protested so strongly against "mistakes" of this sort, he stressed, because these had played a similar role in his own work, *Geschichte und Klassenbewusstsein*, and his incorrect views at that time came about as a result of the same social cause responsible now for Ottwalt's errors: "an imperfect oneness with the revolutionary labor movement and *therefore* rigidity of method: slipping out of materialist dialectics into idealism or mechanism (or both)."[62] But there was still a glimmer of hope for all the Ottwalts, Bredels, and Brechts; he, Lukács, was living proof, after all, that what had not happened in their particular cases "yet" or "thus far" could still take place. Except that the writers involved would have to follow his example in severing all past class affiliations. Only then could they cleanse their minds and consciousness of the ideological pollutants left over from their former class affiliation and begin to master dialectical materialism as a creative method. Lukács may not have been consciously aware of it at the time, and he certainly never admitted it later, but the demands that he made upon these writers and upon intellectuals sympathetic to the Communist cause was essentially a call for their political and intellectual self-Stalinization: a process that he himself—perhaps inadvertently, unintentionally, spontaneously—had put well behind him even before fleeing back into Soviet exile to spend the next thirteen years.

Lukács' Theory of Fascism, Part I

Why did Lukács have trouble understanding Stalin's motives for staging the philosophy debate? Mitin, Judin, and intellectual impostors like them repeated the litany time and again that any Communist who accepted Marxism-Leninism in deed as well as in word had to accede to the principle of the unity of revolutionary theory and practice and that that unity, "as defined by Leninism," would automatically ensure *"an even steadier advance toward communism."*[1] This kind of rhetoric was plainly meant to establish the validity of the succession from Marx to Stalin (by way of Lenin), legitimize historically Stalin's five-year-plan policies, and stifle all criticism that might dispute the timeliness of Stalin's policies or even his fitness to lead the country. The German Communists had no trouble making the proper associations: encircled by capitalism, Soviet power—with the Leninist central committee at the head of the Bolshevik party—would not deviate from the course of the triumphant construction of socialism. "This course, Stalin's [*die Stalinsche*] general line of the CPUSSR, is the continuation of the historical role of Leninism."[2]

THEORETICAL MASQUERADE

The real link between "theory and practice" should probably have been apparent to anyone still able to approach Soviet matters with a skeptical mind. But Lukács, notwithstanding his later references to the "absorption of principles, perspectives, and strategy by tactics" under Stalin,[3] sided with Stalin's spokesmen in philosophical and theoretical questions—the very men now articulating the "system of principles" that performed as an appurtenance to political action. Not until 1930, during the philosophy discussion in the Soviet Union, had he managed to clarify completely his views on philosophy, Lukács said in 1945,[4] repeating the substance of his remarks to the Institute of Philosophy of the Communist Academy in June 1934;[5] and in the last months of his life, Lukács felt obliged to defend Stalin against "biased" criticism. The contention that Stalin had expressed only incorrect or anti-Marxist ideas in his lifetime was prejudiced. During his first lengthy stay in the Soviet Union, Lukács explained, the philosophy debate that Stalin had sparked against Deborin and his school took place; and, though many later Stalinist traits had naturally showed up in it, Stalin nevertheless backed an extraordinarily important standpoint that had played a positive role in Lukács' own development—Stalin had attacked the so-called Plekhanov orthodoxy.[6]

Lukács' comments illustrate the supreme importance that he attached to philosophical or ideological "truths" as he understood them, explain his readiness to participate in political crusades in which these supposed principles became dogmas to bludgeon the exponents of ideas allegedly alien to Stalinist Marxism-Leninism, and highlight his failure to date the corruption of theory under Stalin back to the debate of 1930 and 1931. What did Lukács mean, for instance, that Stalin had thrown his support behind an extraordinarily important theoretical principle? Did Lukács imagine in 1971 that Stalin had ever really been concerned with theoretical issues for the sake of their own intrinsic worth? If not, how could Lukács stress the theoretical "validity" of ideas articulated for the express point of police-state repression? The answer is that Lukács had little choice late in his life: he had in fact supported both Stalinist theory and Stalinist practice (as the following chapters try to show more clearly), and he probably realized it before he died. But by ignoring the actual "unity" of theory and practice under Stalin, that is, Stalin's manipulation of ideology to rationalize the terror, Lukács was able cautiously and circumspectly to concede his identification with at least some features of theoretical Stalinism without accepting any moral responsibility for all its practical side effects.

This mental process of self-exculpation was not, it seems, a conscious one in every respect. Some of the serious defects that Lukács' reasoning discloses were simply blind spots unique to him personally, and some may have been caused in the last few years of his life by his terminal illness.[7] Other misrenderings, on the other hand, serve a useful purpose and appear very much to have been patterned to rationalize Lukács' own past behavior. Insisting that he had established a private sphere of intellectual autonomy within the mainstream of conventional Stalinist thought became one of Lukács' passions beginning in the fifties. Certainly the roots of Stalinism as a complex of dogmas and myths extended further back than 1930 and 1931, but the general ideological offensive of those years was the first broad systematization of intellectual Stalinism, and it inflicted damage upon Soviet philosophy, historiography, and art from which Soviet intellectual life did not even begin to recover until after Stalin's death. Yet Lukács acknowledged precisely this ideological offensive to be the inspiration for much of his ensuing work, without conceding, of course, that there was a direct connection between the philosophy debate and the first steps taken toward the vassalization of Soviet literature. Whether Lukács ever really grasped this link can be debated; perhaps he repressed it early on because of the devastating implications that such an admission would have had for his own work. Be that as it may, for all his intelligence, Lukács' writing in Berlin and afterwards in Soviet exile was an integral part of Stalin's debasement of theory begun in the philosophy debate, and Lukács custom tailored the "lessons" of that debate to literature. He formulated a prescriptive aesthetic that politicized all interpretive categories and decreed violations of his aesthetic norms to be transgressions against the objective laws of Stalinist Marxism-Leninism.

After Stalin's death, then, Lukács pictured himself as a victim of the very political dynamic that had carried him along in the general flow of Stalinization sweeping over Soviet intellectual life. If one assumes that this process of spiritual corruption was in fact automatic, or at least semi-automatic, and that Lukács was not fully aware of what was happening to him, he probably began losing touch with the reality of political intrusions into theoretical matters during the RAPP affair. He apparently never understood why the party disbanded the organization. Neither in 1932 nor many years later did he grasp that RAPP had been politically victimized, for all its own belligerence and intolerance; and he failed to appreciate that fact presumably because the proper questions about the political reasons for the dissolution simply could not have occurred to him in 1932. Stalin's inversion of the "hierarchy of principle-strategy-tactics" seems not to have been a transformation that Lukács spotted clearly at the time, and even after he came to understand that particular dynamic, he was never able later to reassess events of the past that fit into it, either in the case of the philosophy debate or the dissolution of RAPP.

He simply failed to comprehend that the party aimed at something more in disbanding RAPP than ridding Soviet writers of a bureaucratic encumbrance to the unfettered development of a Communist literature. In his retrospective account of 1957, Lukács said he had welcomed the dissolution because he had expected the end of RAPP to usher in a new era of bureaucratically unhampered literary creativity, theory, and criticism; and when the bureaucratic intrusions into literary matters continued even after RAPP was broken up, Lukács claimed that he had been perplexed.[8] His first inclination at the time had been to blame the interference on still active RAPP partisans—"vestiges of a past not yet fully overcome . . . ('RAPPists,' vulgar sociologists, etc.)."[9] After a while, however, the presence of entrenched bureaucratic strongholds responsible for the obstruction to theoretical progress became impossible for him to overlook any longer. For a time he still tended to regard the rigidity and dogmatism in literary theory as a transitory phenomenon, even sighing on occasion when Stalin came to mind, "Ah, si le roi le savait." But before long, it dawned on him that the source of the contradictions between forward-moving currents enriching Marxist culture and the dogmatic, bureaucratic-tyrannical repression of independent thought lay in Stalin's regime and, consequently, in his person.[10]

This is Lukács' later account, but it is highly unlikely that he was completely aware of what Stalinism denoted in the early thirties, especially considering that he was living in Stalin's phantasmagorical world. Lukács' world must have been, at least to a certain extent, a make-believe society peopled, on the one hand, by superhuman Stachanovites exceeding their work

norms by hundreds of times and by Bolsheviks inspired by only
the loftiest of principles, and, on the other hand, by scheming
and conniving *vragi narodov*, enemies of the people, Trotskyists and such, acting on the orders of foreign capitalists or fascists and bent on wrecking socialism from within. In a word,
after 1933 Lukács was completely cut off from outside reality
and had to form his opinion of events beyond the Soviet borders
on the basis of information available or supplied to him within
the USSR. To make matters worse, he was equally handicapped
in attempting to arrive at an accurate image of life inside the
Soviet Union, both because he believed or wanted to believe
the official view of things anyway and because he had few opportunities to compare the validity of official claims about Soviet reality with outside information. As for his later attribu-
tion to himself of a fairly mature understanding of Stalinism
while it was in the process of unfolding, the obvious point is
that, after Stalin's death, Lukács could scarcely make a convincing case for his oppositional posture during Soviet exile
without imputing to himself a keen awareness of Stalinism at
the time. He thus projected his belated insights back into the
past. Having seen through Stalinism from its very inception, as
he claimed to have done, what was Lukács' course of action?
Every thinking person in those years, he said, had to keep the
"global historical" situation uppermost in his mind—the rise
of Hitler and his preparations for a war of annihilation against
socialism. He never doubted for a moment, Lukács said, that
all decisions arising out of this situation had to be uncondi-
tionally subordinated to it, "even if it was that which was most
dear to me personally, even if it was my own life's work."[11]

This is a queer admission, one that almost reads as if Lukács
had a bad conscience and felt obliged to explain himself and his
motives. What does he mean, for instance, that he willingly
assigned his own work a lower priority because the existence of
the only socialist state and therefore socialism itself was at
stake? This is evidently Lukács' roundabout way of justifying
his overall collaboration with the Stalinist establishment. Of
course physical opposition was out of the question, Lukács said
(though he later faulted the Germans for not having resisted
Hitler under similarly suicidal police-state conditions); but the

point for Lukács was that any criticism of Stalin would have willy-nilly meant moral support for the mortal enemy, "for the annihilator of any and all culture."[12] Under these circumstances, a willingness to compromise was called for; a Marxist author had to make certain compromises in order to publish and have any influence on things at all, Lukács explained, though his personal concessions never went beyond "quoting Stalin 'in keeping with protocol,'" and he was always concerned to keep even these citations to a bare minimum, reproducing only those pronouncements by Stalin that were "correct," though known long before him.[13] But Lukács made it a point to stress strongly that essentially "meaningless" concessions of this sort ought not to be taken as any kind of "capitulation to all of those ideological tendencies that arose in the course of the struggle, were propagated, and then vanished."[14] Forced to live with these constraints, Lukács employed the tactics of a "partisan" to fight for his ideas, as he put it. He used occasional Stalin quotes to get his writing into print and then expressed his deviating views, taking the necessary precautions, as openly as the historical leeway allowed.[15] Why was he never caught? He regarded himself as lucky, Lukács said, that his theoretical masquerade, driven by necessity, succeeded and that his hidden criticism was never uncovered.[16]

Did Lukács outwit the Stalinists with this "theoretical masquerade" or did his stay in the Soviet Union perhaps end favorably for him—leaving aside the role of sheer good fortune—because his assimilation into intellectual life under Stalin was largely complete? Lukács' earlier writings in Moscow and Berlin divulge a process of accommodation that placed him in the middle of Soviet intellectual currents. Though Lukács later claimed that the Blum theses provided the impetus and general tenor for all his subsequent "theoretical and practical activity,"[17] when he returned to Moscow in 1933, he picked up right where he had left off in Berlin: on the side of Stalinists like Mitin and Judin. In questions of theory and tactics with regard to fascism, as well as in matters of literary theory and literary politics, Lukács' views from 1933 to 1939 were never incompatible and often virtually indistinguishable from the prevailing authoritative outlook in all related questions.

THEORIES OF FASCISM

Lukács put his impressions of fascism on paper in "just a few weeks" after his arrival in Moscow in April 1933.[18] The manuscript, *Wie ist die faschistische Philosophie in Deutschland entstanden?*, is a compendium of conclusions by an ideologue who drew all his inferences from the aggregate of presumptions and dogmas that had been inviolable in the Comintern for years. Lukács' systematization of these assumptions is accordingly characteristic of the state of affairs in the KPD by early 1933. Hitler's rise to power had coincided with the final stages of the KPD's bolshevization and Stalinization; the party had been reduced to a state of intellectual impotence that left it ill-equipped to design flexible and imaginative policies for dealing with Hitler when such action was needed the most. Crippled by dogmas that the party could not reconsider when worsening circumstances called for a quick and flexible response, the party leadership reacted to Hitler's growing strength with claims of its own electoral victories and with persistent rhetoric about the "twin brothers" of social fascism and Hitler fascism.

Stalin's letter to *Proletarskaja revoljutsija* only exacerbated a situation substantially irretrievable already by expanding the Comintern's index of deviations. "Luxemburgism" now joined the other brands of invidious counterrevolutionary opportunism that reached from menshevism and Trotskyism to the unadulterated social fascism of the present day. The *Rote Fahne* editorialized, for instance, that Stalin's letter had even greater relevance for the KPD than for the Soviet Communist party. Throughout the development of German communism, from its beginnings as the radical left wing of Social Democracy to the wartime Spartacists and up to its current status as the Comintern's second largest party, "Leninist" clarification of party history had gone hand in hand with the topical tasks of the revolutionary movement, with the bolshevization of the party, and with the elimination of persistent Social Democratic, Centrist, and Luxemburgian survivals in the party.[19] The policies of the bourgeoisie, together with social fascist intrigues, made it especially urgent that the KPD and the masses clearly understand all questions relating to the party's "class line" and revolutionary strategy and tactics. "Every Communist and every class conscious worker must understand," the paper said, "that the major blow of a revolutionary policy has to be aimed at the main social pillar of the bourgeoisie, Social Democracy and its 'left' subsidiary in order to gather its own class, the revolutionary proletariat, in the camp of the revolutionary class struggle. In the absence of clarity on this point, a successful struggle by party and proletariat against the dictatorship of the bourgeoisie and fascistization is unthinkable."[20]

The German Communists echoed this formula over and over again in the months leading up to Hitler's assumption of power, and in October 1932 Ernst Thälmann again underscored the correctness of Stalin's conception of "fascism and social fascism" as twins rather than adversaries. Social Democracy remained the principal social prop of the bourgeoisie, he reaffirmed, and the bourgeoisie, the primary class enemy of the proletariat, could only be dealt with effectively if the Communists concentrated their main efforts on defeating Social Democracy.[21]

This vision of "social fascism" became a neurotic obsession with the party leadership.[22] It can be used, in fact, as at least a partial explanation for the rarity of any official or even semi-official treatment of National Socialism and its ideology that went beyond versions of fascism in the party press, versions that merely repeated sterile slogans about the "terror arm of the bourgeoisie," its radical wing, and its national and social demagogy. Ernst Ottwalt's *Deutschland erwache!* was an irregularity in the otherwise patterned Communist response to the rise of Hitler. Published in early 1932, Ottwalt used the book for a detailed exploration of the Nazi appeal to the lower middle class. Little in his study clashed directly with Marxism-Leninism, least of all his main contention that Nazism diverted potentially dangerous anticapitalist mass hostility away from the system and against the proletariat by playing upon the baser petty bourgeois instincts of nationalism and anti-Semitism. But various other considerations soon led to the quasi-official pronouncement in the *Rote Fahne* that the book had actually turned out to be "non-Marxist."[23] A year later, with Hitler in power, the KPD and Comintern were still without a study that treated National Socialism with the seriousness appropriate to the changed circumstances. *Deutschland erwache!* did come out that year in Russian with a foreword by I. Dvorkin that tried to compensate for the book's "failings" on certain points. The publication of this "non-Marxist" study was at least a sign that there was now some concern in the Comintern about the absence of a party history of National Socialism and that someone was trying to rectify the situation.[24]

Konrad Heiden's *Geschichte des Nationalsozialismus* was published two years later in Russian translation, but this volume was even less "Marxist" than Ottwalt's and required certain unspecified (but easily traceable and predictable) "deletions."[25] Dvorkin also wrote the "introduction" to this study, setting the record straight wherever Heiden's analysis conflicted with the Comintern's. From the party's point of view, though, both *Deutschland erwache!* and *Geschichte des Nationalsozialismus* must have been regarded at best as temporary solutions. In mid-1935, however, Hans Günther came out with his book, *Der Herren eigener Geist*, which took a comprehensive look at nineteenth- and early twentieth-century German philosophy in order to connect various philosophers and philosophical schools of the recent past with fascistic or National Socialist philosophers, ideologues, and thinkers. *Der Herren eigener Geist* was the first elaborate investigation by a member of the party into the superstructure-basis relationships that were said to exist between fascist ideology and monopoly capitalism in its ultimate imperialist or fascist form. The book was the first fully developed Marxist-Leninist-Stalinist rendition of National Socialist ideology and politics, and, though it explored new territory that had previously been ignored as long as the party looked at National Socialism as a peripheral threat in comparison with social fascism, the book arrived at no unconventional findings. *Der Herren eigener Geist* did present some persuasive arguments that might have counteracted the dogged illusion in the party that Hitler's success actually cast the die for an imminent unpreventable and inevitable mass uprising against the fascist bourgeoisie and its band of Nazi mercenaries. But scarcely a year passed before Günther disappeared as one of the first prominent German victims of Stalin's purges.[26] The usefulness of his book in party circles, of course, diminished accordingly. The KPD lost its only satisfactory account of National Socialism and remained without a replacement for the duration of the Third Reich.

Why Lukács' manuscript, *Wie ist die faschistische Philosophie in Deutschland entstanden?*, was not published at the time has never been clarified.[27] His commentary on the lawful social and historical "regularities" that brought Hitler to power, his correlation of these events with the real "class" substance of fascist philosophy, his incorrigible optimism that the imminent collapse of fascism would coincide with a proletarian revolution—none of these assumptions and arguments were politically errant in the slightest. His theory of fascism was comprised of all the usual third-period arguments that the Stalinists only toned down or relinquished when they switched to the strategy of the popular front late in 1935. The objective economic and social situation had set a tandem process in motion on a historic scale, namely, an economic crisis of capitalism so severe that the survival of the entire system was at stake and a proletarian ground swell of antisystemic frustration and anger. History had arrived at a fork in the road. One path lead in the direction of a "sharpened dictatorship of the bourgeoisie," the other toward a dictatorship of the proletariat. "Fascism or communism," Lukács insisted, there was no other alternative (72).[28]

"To be or not to be" (29) was Lukács' reading of the historical question as it pertained to the capitalist system, and the bourgeoisie quickly discovered in its search for a solution to the crisis that the options were now strictly limited; in the past, the ruling class had always managed to use the state form of bourgeois democracy to guard its interests against the proletariat, but the unprecedented severity of the economic crisis had now even radicalized the intermediate classes. Lukács' commentary: "The crisis, the mass unemployment and part-time work caused by it, the unprecedented drop in the workers' standard of living, the terrible devastation that the crisis brought about in the urban petty bourgeoisie and the peasantry, led unavoidably to a profound crisis of confidence in the capitalist system, a crisis also shared by the most backward masses, . . . and produced *a mass sense of outrage against capitalism"* (66). But rudimentary mass anticapitalism was one thing, the class consciousness necessary to concentrate it effectively for revolutionary purposes yet another. The disaffected masses, said Lukács, were backward and confused, and their under-developed awareness of the cause of their plight left these "frightened and berserk petty bourgeois" (67) wide open to demagogy. The masses demanded immediate action to improve their lives, and the bourgeoisie exploited their alienation to de-flect it away from the system and against the revolutionary pro-letariat. The bourgeoisie had to choose "either to look on help-lessly while the masses were gradually seized by Communist propaganda, regardless of their backwardness, while their mass outrage at capitalism evolved from confusion into a clear, militant posture against the capitalist system"; or to stage a *"pseudorevolutionary movement* that gathers up the still backward masses under the demagogic pretense of a 'radical up-heaval,' an immediate 'act of salvation,' and exploits the tempo-rary confusion of the masses' anticapitalist outrage in order to consolidate the tottering monopoly capitalist system" (68).

Such was Lukács' reading of bourgeois strategy, one that en-tailed a definite element of risk for the ruling class. Fomenting a mass movement by inciting anticapitalist emotions against the archenemy of capitalism, the revolutionary proletariat, was fraught with danger because the entire venture could so easily backfire if the mobilized masses ever saw through the ruse. But the worsening economic crisis, the increasing rest-lessness of the people, and the KPD's expanding influence left the bourgeoisie no choice; if action had not been taken quickly, the masses might have become *"really* anticapitalist, *con-sciously* anticapitalist, backers of *communism"* (30), and this threat overrode any anxiety about the bold experiment of exor-cising the devil (the growing hatred of the working masses against capitalism) by enlisting the aid of Beelzebub (by throw-ing this confusion into turmoil) (30).

Lukács contends time and again that things were fated to un-fold as they did and could have evolved no differently. Conse-quently, "the uniformity and necessity" (20) with which his-tory ushered in fascism also applied—"had" to apply—to philosophical currents that were precursors of fascism or to fascist philosophy itself. Tracing socioeconomic and political trends over many decades to illustrate how they wound up as monopoly capitalism and establishing the reciprocal relation between these developments and their superstructure reflection in philosophy and art constituted one of Lukács' greatest ambitions. Nor was there anything especially unique in Stalinist circles about this kind of cultural reductionism; the vast oversimplifications about sociopolitical evolution and its logical and "necessary" ideological, philosophical, and cultural spin-offs were the stock in trade of Soviet intellectuals in Stalin's time. Ironically, Lukács, however belatedly, eventually spotted this dimension of Stalinism. Hyperrationalism predominated philosophically in Stalinism, he said in 1971; "with Stalin, rationalism acquired a form in which it passes over into a certain absurdity."[29]

In his better writings, of course, there was simply no comparison between Lukács' articulateness and the standard vulgarizations of run-of-the-mill Stalinist intellectuals in their rationalizing of history. Lukács was undoubtedly more persuasive in postulating direct correspondences between basis and superstructure manifestations and their correlation over many years. But in *Wie ist die faschistische Philosophie in Deutschland entstanden?*, Lukács also went in for a brand of Stalinist teleology that bordered on the absurd, for instance in his division of the world into two camps, communism and fascism, and his ex cathedra pronouncement that every intellectual who did not choose Stalin over Hitler was a fascist or a dupe of fascism. This, too, should probably be regarded as a form of "hyperrationalism." For if National Socialism was the "necessary fruit of the development of the German bourgeoisie in imperialism" (20), it followed logically that fascist philosophy ought to be seen likewise as "the world view of the German bourgeoisie in the current epoch of decline" (76). Lukács thus declared National Socialist ideology to be the "organically bred, necessarily produced fruit of the *ideological development of the German bourgeoisie in the age of imperialism*" (41–42), the last and therefore highest stage of this development. This being the case, the political and ideological sides of fascism worked in harness toward the same end. The essential ideological contradictions of fascism, said Lukács of bourgeois strategy, was manipulation of anticapitalist sentiments among the masses "in order to instate the rule of monopoly capitalism with unprecedented harshness, in order to repress the revolutionary working class and the disaffected, rebellious toilers with equally unrivalled terror" (69).

Just how did ideology cause "millions" to act at cross purposes to their own interests? Answering this question was the point of Lukács' theory of fascism. But to prove his basic contention, Lukács had to touch on a matter still largely passed over in silence in the Comintern and KPD because it was embarrassing to admit that Hitler had succeeded so effortlessly where the Communists had failed so miserably. The Nazis had won the masses, and an explanation had to be found to account for the circumstance that millions somehow found it easier to believe in Hitler than in Thälmann or Stalin. Rather than explore the reason why the masses had fallen for the "utter nonsense" (74) of Nazi ideology instead of grasping the plain truth of Marxism-Leninism, however, the Communists, including Lukács, developed their vision of the ignorant and gullible masses who fell for Hitler simply because they believed his false promises. Of course Nazi ideology and the fascists' promises were "nonsensical," said Lukács, but only on the surface; underneath there hid very "real social problems, albeit problems unsolvable from the perspective of the bourgeoisie" (74–75), and these the bourgeoisie hoped in vain to surmount by promising the masses "the 'dissolution' of capitalism." They were to be persuaded that fascism betokened a new economic order—actual socialism, the right kind of socialism— and that exploitation would die out because classes no longer existed (69).

Lukács devoted over two hundred pages to an exploration of these issues. He purported to expose the fascist underpinnings of all non-Communist political programs and parties and argued that exponents of ideological, philosophical, and artistic views not explicitly "Marxist-Leninist" were responsible for misleading the people. These intellectuals were consequently either voluntary or coincidental bedfellows of fascism; either way, no intellectual outside the Stalinist camp could free himself of this accountability; all were infected by fascist philosophy as the summit of the protracted development of bourgeois thought in the age of decline (74). "All the thinkers of this period . . . who did not join the camp of the revolutionary proletariat or move in that direction, regardless of whether it was their intention or whether they knew it, [unavoidably] thought and acted in more or less fascist terms. The global historical dilemma of the period, fascism or communism, renders it unavoidable that fascist ideology become the generally prevalent tendency of the bourgeoisie" (72). These thinkers had been caught up in a historical process that they usually did not understand. Had they grasped it, Lukács said, many would have recoiled in shock and dismay. But their subjective morality, their personal political likes and dislikes, were irrelevant anyway. They were pioneers of fascism as a consequence of the objective historical situation and because of their class circumstances. "They are unaware of it, but they do it," wrote Marx (73).

RATIONALISM OR HYPERRATIONALISM?

Several years later, Lukács wrote over seven hundred pages to illustrate this "objectivized expression of ideas" and its "historically necessary range of influence."[30] In this particular book, the much-maligned *Die Zerstörung der Vernunft*,[31] he expanded upon many of the concepts first worked out in 1933 and designed to prove the responsibility of bourgeois philosophers and German philosophical trends of the recent past for present-day fascism. Lukács pursued all traces of prefascism with a relentlessness that can definitely be said to lend *Die Zerstörung der Vernunft* the quality of a "challenging indictment."[32] Many of his arguments, most of which are already present in an abbreviated form in the 1933 manuscript, are unsettling and by no means always readily refutable. Regardless, there is a zealotry to Lukács' single-minded distribution of all thought into the two categories of rationalism and irrationalism that Leszek Kołakowski called an almost total "assimilation to Stalinism." Lukács' tremendous erudition certainly set him apart from other Stalinist ideologues, and he wrote in a style that distin-

guished his work from that of ordinary intellectuals who published under Stalin. In this respect, Lukács was an imperfect
Stalinist, "but he made up for it in many others."[33]

According to Kołakowski, the essentially Stalinist feature of
Die Zerstörung der Vernunft (and this can be applied equally to
*Wie ist die faschistische Philosophie in Deutschland ent-
standen?*) is the "contention that since Marxism came on the
scene, all non-Marxist philosophy has been reactionary and ir-
rationalistic. In this way the whole of German philosophical
culture outside Marxism is condemned as an intellectual apparatus preparing the way for Hitler's assumption of power in
1933. Everybody was a herald of Nazism in one way or another." For Lukács, everyone was an irrationalist "who was not
an orthodox Marxist"; everyone who believed that elements or
aspects of being existed outside the range of discursive knowledge, who pointed to irrational forces governing the aggregate
behavior of human beings, who refused to accept the postula-
tion of historical laws and professed subjective idealism, who
denied that the meaning of the "totality" of history could be
scientifically ascertained, and who questioned the "'dialectical
reason' that Lukács took over from Hegel," a view of the world
regarding reason as being capable of understanding "the whole
of history and human society, including its Communist future"—all these thinkers were irrationalists and therefore allies of nazism. It would be hard, Kołakowski concludes, "to find
a more striking example of anti-rationalism than that afforded
by Lukács' own philosophy of blind faith, in which nothing is
proved but everything asserted *ex cathedra*, and whatever does
not fit the Marxian schemata is dismissed as reactionary
rubbish."[34]

Lukács must have known that his work was vulnerable to
criticism from this angle,[35] and, as he often did in cases where
there appeared to be an all too conspicuous similarity with certain features of Stalinist thought, he tried to defend his reputation by taking the offensive: his line of reasoning in *Die
Zerstörung der Vernunft* was not Stalinist at all but just the
opposite, anti-Stalinist. Following his return to Moscow in
1933, Lukács said, he began work on his philosophical writings
"and took up a position in total opposition to the line set down
by Stalin."[36] Perhaps by 1971 Lukács actually believed his own

myth, which he had been cultivating since the mid-fifties; he was definitely capable of focusing on abstract principles and excluding from his mind all the practical and political affinities that existed between his work and Stalinist thought. To prove his point, he explained that *Der junge Hegel* had been written at a time when Andrej Zhdanov had already denigrated the philosopher as an ideologue of feudalistic reaction against the French Revolution.[37] Whereas Zhdanov, "together with Stalin," had classified the entire history of philosophy as a struggle between materialism and idealism, Lukács had made an entirely different pair of opposites the center of his attention in *Die Zerstörung der Vernunft*—the struggle between rationalist and irrationalist philosophy.

This comment is a perfect illustration of Lukács' helplessness at reconstructing the nature of his past ideas as they related to mainstream Stalinism in philosophy, aesthetics, or political tactics. It is an incontrovertible fact that, after they were through dealing with him, Lukács sided with "dialecticians" such as Mitin and Judin in their attacks on all "isms" contrary to Stalinism, criticized the "idealistic" inclinations in his own work, and drew upon the lessons of the philosophy debate in working out features of his own literary theory. István Eörsi, whose taped conversations with Lukács in the last few months of his life were reworked to produce the "autobiography" *Gelebtes Denken*, tried to call Lukács' attention to some of these contradictions. Eörsi asked Lukács whether his principle that "innocent" philosophers did not exist and that earlier irrationalist tendencies in philosophy were responsible for fascism could not perhaps be turned around to hold Marx accountable for Stalinism. Lukács responded by arguing that the evaluation of a philosopher's work depended on whether specific theories were actually adhered to later and consistently applied. Historical accountability, he said, was a matter of the actual continuation of ideas.[38] Lukács' answer was not unreasonable; philosophers were not historically responsible for the later misuse of their work, only for the undistorted application of their ideas. But the real issue was whether Lukács' own teleological approach to philosophy, his exaggeration of necessity in dealing with supposed forerunners of fascist ideology, might not be akin to the "hyperrationalism" or "overemphasized necessity"[39] that he himself later classified as a major characteristic of Stalinist philosophy.

Lukács never conceded the slightest similarity between his basic concepts and the set of dogmas that constituted the core of Stalinism. He rejected entirely any insinuation that he might share some moral responsibility for Stalinism just as "irrationalist" philosophers were historically accountable in his mind for National Socialist ideology, regardless of their own subjective outlook or intentions. Every thinker was responsible to history for the objective content of his thought, Lukács said in the foreword to *Die Zerstörung der Vernunft*,[40] but this judgment evidently applied only to the irrationalists. Nietzsche was not distorted and misused by the Nazis; rather, his thinking was consistently and accurately applied. Any use to which Lukács' writing was put in Stalin's time, on the other hand, could only have involved the misrepresentation or perversion of his ideas, or so Lukács implied.

Lukács' specific points in his treatment of bourgeois philosophy in the 1933 manuscript are of less significance here. What is important is the overall reductionist approach to the work of various philosophers; his explication of schools of thought such as Philosophy of Life, various antiscientific trends in philosophy,[41] and the "new mythology" of the age of imperialism;[42] and his emphasis on the feature common to all—criticism of the present in ways that amounted to an indirect or "critical" apology of capitalism. His remarks all fit the following summary of the changeover from past subtle and indirect forms of mass control through manipulative uses of bourgeois ideology to the new monopoly capitalist strategy that brought fascism to power as an ostensibly anticapitalist political movement. Whereas the prefascist or at least not yet consciously fascist apologists of monopoly capitalism had applied this new form of apologia, criticism of the present, in order to hold back the people whom they could influence from coming out against the capitalist system and in order to steer the people's anticapitalist emotions into the false channel of nonaction and resigned acceptance of "fate," fascism used this method of apologia in order to incite the masses to a form of action whose social content was a more profound subjugation of the rebelling masses themselves. "That monopoly capitalism could be saved with the help of a mobilization of the masses' anticapitalist instincts and that millions rise up, fanatasized, in order to forge their own chains more strongly and repressively—that is the novel quality of fascist ideology" (108–9).[43]

PSEUDO-OPPOSITION

Lukács' exploration of National Socialism as a philosophical or ideological phenomenon lends his theory of fascism a dimension that the usual Comintern and KPD assessments of fascism lacked. These treatments fixed their attention largely on fascism as the "open" dictatorship of the bourgeoisie, as opposed to the cloaked or concealed dictatorship of bourgeois democracy, and rarely took ideological factors into consideration. This was a natural omission as long as the Communists treated fascism as nothing but a desperate bid of the most reactionary, most chauvinistic, most imperialist elements of finance capital to stay in power. From that vantage point, the party had little cause to concern itself with peripheral ideological issues that were of no particular political use to them in fighting the bourgeoisie.

Lukács' underlying premise that fascism was the "basic trend of the bourgeoisie in the 'Third Period' of the post-war crisis" (35) accords in its essentials with the Comintern view, but Lukács' theory contains a slight modification. Whereas the Comintern tended to emphasize the unambiguous master-servant relationship between bourgeoisie and Nazi party,[44] Lukács pointed to conflicts of interest within the bourgeoisie itself and to the absence of an overall consensus in the ruling class with respect to the fascist solution. His inference was that National Socialism enjoyed at least some independence from the bourgeoisie. Not all branches of industry were as thrilled "with the radical and hundred-percent form of fascism" (25)[45] as was heavy industry or the large capitalist agrarian concerns, he explained, because the fascist dictatorship denoted more than just a regime of terror for all workers (to that feature none of the industrialists objected); rather, the new system represented at the same time an unprecedented dictatorship of heavy industry *within* the factional variances in capitalism itself. The basic operation of capitalism, true, remained unaffected by such differences because the collective class interest took priority. Lukács explained his views: "The concrete question is being posed with increasing insistency in line with the deepening of the crisis, the mobilization not only of the proletariat but also the petty bourgeois masses, and the unrelenting upsurge in the anticapitalist feelings of the masses: *'To be or not to be for the capitalist system'*" (27–28). Particular factional interests naturally paled in significance to the greater danger threatening the entire class, he went on, and these interests had to yield to the general class interest of the bourgeoisie. The imperatives of the collective interest gained the upper hand in the oppositional segments of the ruling class also, and these elements—unenthusiastically and, at times, enraged and embittered—finally submitted to the unavoidable requirements of the age.

Lukács utilized this notion of divergent bourgeois interests to explain the presence of a non-Communist opposition to National Socialism that he disqualified as a form of pseudo-opposition (*Scheinopposition*): one that never transcended systemic bounds and thus helped prop up the regime by criticizing the establishment with what amounted only to an indirect apologia. Lukács' whole concept of a pseudo-opposition is, of course, just a reflection of Stalinist conceit in the question of antifascism. Opposition to Hitler that was not unreservedly Stalinist was condemned as fascist in one respect or another. In fact, Lukács charged these groups—pseudo-opponents—with having helped bring Hitler to power in the first place. They may have "opposed" National Socialism, but only for fear of their own individual or collective security as members of bourgeois factions bound to be less advantaged under a fascist dictatorship than before. Prior to 1933 all such opposition had resided in groups, organizations, or political parties sponsoring attempts to contain fascism within the existing bourgeois democratic system, but the mass hostility to the very democracy that had produced the devastating economic crisis now undermining the stability of the system soon dashed all hopes of a "democratic" solution. After all efforts to bring the mass movement under the control of the old bourgeois parties failed (had to fail, said Lukács, because the National Socialist method of misleading the masses demanded categorically sole rule as an outward manifestation and the pretense of a radical transformation of the entire system), the so-called opponents of fascism then had to "set aside their reservations and submit themselves to the National Socialist dictatorship" (30–31).

Lukács' contention that some bourgeois factions gave in to the necessity of a National Socialist dictatorship less enthusiastically than others was not a complete novelty at the time. From 1930 to 1932, for instance, Leon Trotsky came out with numerous articles and pamphlets in which he argued, not entirely unlike Lukács, that the bourgeoisie incurred a substantial risk in its decision to nurture an independent political movement such as National Socialism because there was no prior assurance that fascism would prevail in the end. It was an all-or-nothing gamble on the part of the ruling class to retain its hold on power in the face of a grave threat by a militant proletariat and the radicalized lower middle class. If the fascist movement, which was not subject to the direct orders of the bourgeoisie, failed to subdue the labor movement and then smash it altogether, the capitalist offensive could easily stall and the tide would turn. The working class would then go on to destroy not just fascism, but, with the petty bourgeoisie now on the side of the proletariat, would not stop until the entire capitalist system lay in shambles.

Whether Lukács read Trotsky's articles on National Socialism and incorporated particular features from them into his theory of fascism is impossible to tell; though he might have, the likeness of their theories in the matter of National Socialist autonomy does not necessarily prove that he accepted parts of Trotsky's argument because the idea that the bourgeoisie did not have complete control of National Socialism had also cropped up in the Comintern and KPD, where, however, it was eventually outlawed. Heinz Neumann and Hermann Remmele, who headed the KPD along with Thälmann, apparently awakened to the fact that nazism was more of a menace to the KPD than either they or the party had been prepared to admit earlier and that the continued militant Communist posture toward Social Democracy needed to be combined with urgent action to meet the Nazi threat.[46] For a variety of reasons, many of them resulting from personal rivalries in the party leadership, Neumann and Remmele were charged with "group activity" in 1932, and both were deprived of their party posts.[47] Later, following the Nazi takeover, Remmele actually classified the victory of fascism as a "change of systems"; the new regime was not fascist rule by the bourgeoisie, as the KPD contended, but a "dictatorship of the lumpenproletariat." In fact, the whole of bourgeois society was descending to the level of the lumpenproletariat, which embraced a "portion of the petty bourgeoisie."[48]

In June 1933 the KPD denounced these ideas as a "blatant mixture of naked opportunism, perfidious Trotskyism, and sheer putschism."[49] Six months later, Wilhelm Pieck expanded upon the charges and reiterated the Comintern position that bourgeois democracy and National Socialist dictatorship were identical. The "Neumann-Remmele group" had developed the theory of the "change of systems," of the "replacement of the rule of the bourgeoisie by the rule of bourgeois society sinking down into the lumpenproletariat," said Pieck. "This theory denies the fact that in the fascist dictatorship the content of the class rule of the bourgeoisie has remained the same as in the 'Weimar democracy,' and consequently leads to putting the form of rule of bourgeois democracy in opposition to the fascist dictatorship. It signifies a justification of the class collaboration policy of Social Democracy and denies the fact that the fascist dictatorship grows out of bourgeois democracy."[50]

Was Lukács influenced by Heinz Neumann and those in the party who, like Leo Flieg and perhaps Willi Münzenberg, subscribed to his views? Lukács knew the arguments, and he had personal contacts in Berlin with Neumann and the men around him, at least before Neumann was quarantined in Moscow in May 1932.[51] Once Neumann had been ousted from the party leadership, of course, he promptly became a pariah, and in Lukács' theory of fascism he expressed no sympathy for the "ultra radical point of view" that depicted National Socialism as "a banditlike encroachment of a small minority of riffraff —lumpenbourgeoisie and lumpenproletariat—. . . who have usurped control over the *entire* society, that is to say *over the bourgeoisie, too*" (40). Lukács did not, however, mention Neumann or anyone else by name.

Now it is true that in his manuscript Lukács stopped far short of the positions apparently held by Neumann and Rem-

mele, or by Trotsky, for that matter; all three discriminated between bourgeois and fascist dictatorship to a greater extent
than Lukács, who stuck closer to the Stalinist position and enhanced it only slightly by pointing to modest differences within
the bourgeoisie. The distinction was a crucial one for Lukács,
however, not because it made any real difference in his political
and economic assessment of National Socialism but because
his entire treatment of fascist philosophy and the "critical apologists" hinged on the notion of a pseudo-opposition to nazism
within the ruling and intermediate classes. Still, even if Lukács'
theory was more compatible with the Comintern's than with
the views that referred to a "change of systems," a certain similarity in his position and the standpoint of Neumann and Remmele cannot be ignored altogether. Lukács' criticism of their
analysis of fascism at the same time that he took a somewhat
similar view may be just another example of Lukács' adroit-
ness at playing both ends against the middle.

There remains a third possibility that might account for
Lukács' conception of the semi-autonomy of National Socialism. What appears to be a similarity with change-of-systems
theories in Lukács' book might denote little more than the
party's own "progress" by 1933—the expropriation of the very
point of view so recently discredited in the process of purging
Neumann and Remmele—in its impressions of a now ruling
form of fascism. Neumann had contended that the dynamics of
petty bourgeois mobilization by the fascists would ultimately
work to the disadvantage of the bourgeoisie; the very act of
radicalizing the masses with anticapitalist demagogy meant
that the petty bourgeoisie would presently abandon the Nazis
as soon as the anticapitalist promises were broken and consti-
tute a rear guard engaging in common action with the avant-
garde of the proletariat against the bourgeoisie.[52]

In 1932 the Thälmann leadership used Neumann's "optimism" about the underlying weakness of fascism and the related certainty of proletarian revolution to accuse him of "underrating fascism."[53] But after 1933 the situation appeared
differently to the party. The Comintern and KPD declined to
acknowledge that fascism had dealt the "revolutionary proletariat" a defeat and pronounced the catastrophe to be a strategic retreat, not a setback. With Hitler in power, the circum-

stances for the bourgeoisie could only worsen, which meant that proletarian revolution was drawing near. "The establishment of an open Fascist dictatorship, which destroys all democratic illusions among the masses, and frees them from the influence of the social-democrats, will hasten Germany's progress towards the proletarian revolution," read a Comintern resolution in April 1933.[54] Several months later Pieck voiced a similar confidence in terms that sounded much like Neumann's "underrating" of fascism and his theory of the lower-middle-class "rear guard." The Hitler dictatorship was a temporary hindrance that could not "put a stop to the development of the revolutionary forces."[55] Everywhere "dissatisfaction and indignation against the fascist regime" was growing, "among the workers, among the petty bourgeoisie and in the villages." The fascist mass basis was beginning to "shrink more and more and the deceptive social-demagogy begins to lose its force of attraction. On the other hand, the force of attraction of the Communists is growing."[56]

Lukács was equally confident that Hitler's days were numbered, and the same teleological penchant that stressed the historical necessity of fascism also served as the spark to his optimism. Fascism and all its attendant phenomena arose "by necessity from the objective overall situation created by the acute crisis of the capitalist system" (72). The prevailing economic and social conditions of the day, generated by objective historical laws, permitted no way out other than a hardened dictatorship of the bourgeoisie or dictatorship of the proletariat. The worldwide historical dilemma of the times, fascism or communism, made it necessary that fascist ideology become the general predominant ideological tendency of the bourgeoisie (72). In the face of the workings of these ironclad historical regularities, what exactly justified the optimism in Lukács' mind?

THE MATURATION OF PROLETARIAN REVOLUTION

Lukács' fetish for historical necessity, his compulsion to account for every political, ideological, and cultural feature of German life by theorizing within the narrowly prescribed parameters of inexorable historical laws, engendered ideas in his theory of fascism that threatened to lead directly to the sensitive subject of the unavoidability of fascism. Even before 1933 the Comintern and KPD had been confronted with fatalistic views of fascism that cropped up quite regularly as a natural consequence of the party's mandated revolutionary optimism and the consistent application of its own theory. The force of logic simply suggested to many that fascism ought to be allowed into power in order to hasten the progress of history and bring about a proletarian revolution; and, to counter the argument, Thälmann had been compelled to insist that fascist dictatorship was *not* "the 'last' stage of bourgeois class rule . . . , after which *only* the establishment of *proletarian dictatorship* can follow,"[57] and that fascism was not *"the father of revolution."*[58] In 1931 the idea of letting the Nazis into power so that they would discredit themselves politically and economically had been widespread in the party, both in the rank and file and in the leadership.[59] Late that year Thälmann charged the Social Democratic Party of Germany (SPD) with responsibility for the original idea. The Social Democratic concept of the "lesser evil" advocated a coalition of Heinrich Brüning and Hitler as preferable to a government run exclusively by Hitler, he said, and this policy expressed the idea that the Nazis should be allowed into power so that they might fail politically all the sooner. Similar notions, Thälmann warned, had also surfaced in the KPD; tolerating them meant knuckling under to the new "deceptive maneuver of Social Democracy," underestimating fascism, and teaching the masses passivity in the face of fascism.[60] Later, in October 1932, Heinz Neumann was rebuked for his "false, pseudorevolutionary" assessment of future prospects that stressed the internal crises of both the Nazi party and the SPD. These illusions encouraged "speculations centering around spontaneity and fatalistic attitudes" in the KPD.[61]

Lukács likewise voiced his aversion to the SPD's concept of the lesser evil, but the criticism had a disingenuous ring to it because the fatalistic tendency to regard fascism as inescapable or inevitable, which Thälmann and now Lukács imputed to the SPD, was a dominant characteristic of Lukács' own theory, if only by implication. He said of Social Democracy: "The infamous theory of the 'lesser evil' is buttressed by this fatalistic impression of the unavoidability of fascism: Brüning is a small evil compared with Papen, Schleicher compared with Hitler, tomorrow perhaps Hitler compared with 'National Socialist extremists,' and so on ad infinitum" (23). But the irony is that Lukács' own emphasis on the dynamics of historical necessity lent his ideas on fascism an unmistakable sense of determinism. To get around the fatalistic dimension of predetermination that infused his own theory, Lukács introduced the factor of Social Democracy.

Under certain conditions fascism was unavoidable, said Lukács, "*as long as* those forces are not untethered that are capable in and of themselves of putting an end to it: namely, the forces of the revolutionary united proletariat" (23). In a variation of the theory of gullibility that he applied to the masses in general, Lukács went on to explain how Social Democracy deluded its own rank and file into steering clear of the KPD and thereby provided Hitler with the kind of indirect mass support that he needed.

The demagogic key was Social Democracy's advocacy of "reason" as a political platform. In Lukács' view, the concept served a dual purpose. On the one hand, it concocted a conflict with the irrationalism of National Socialism where none existed; the workers were simply misled into thinking that Social Democracy was actually hostile to fascism, and the fact that "reason" for Social Democracy really meant "*capitalism that could function undisturbed and develop smoothly, without any contradictions*" (150) was hidden from their view. On the other hand, "reason" as a political program called for the systematic dissemination of falsehoods about communism. Leading Social Democrats were indefatigable campaigners, Lukács charged, when it came to using "reason" to counterbalance Communist appeals to the "base" rebellious instincts of "unenlightened" rabble who engaged in thoughtless actions like wildcat strikes and mass uprisings. "The 'unconscionable demagogues' who speculated on these 'baser instincts,' who induced the masses to commit such 'unreasonable,' irrational, purely instinctive acts, were for the social fascists precisely the *communists*" (150), said Lukács. Social Democracy sought to disparage these "unreasonable" and "irrational" appeals to revolutionary action with lies about a gradual, evolutionary "growing into socialism." But behind this strategy—the expansion and consolidation of the social basis of imperialism under the banner of a "new form" of socialism—lurked objectives that were entirely contrary to socialism: to cause the erstwhile revolutionary workers' party, the SPD, gradually to become one with the system of imperialist capitalism (156).

Preaching this "reason," said Lukács, disorganized the ranks of the proletariat, tore apart the proletarian revolutionary united front, broke active working-class resistance to fascism, and made Hitler fascism possible (188). Therein lay the true nature of Social Democratic "reason," and to understand its real essence was to grasp the profound inner relation between the "'hostile brothers,' fascists and social fascists" (150). "Reason" was no more than a ruse, a slightly roundabout way of achieving the same goal as fascist "irrationalism." "Reason" restrained the masses from storming the institutions of capitalism by passifying and reasoning with people. Fascism set out to accomplish the same goal by inciting the masses and redirecting the disgust that they felt for capitalism back at the proletariat, though the identity of goals between fascism and social fascism, Lukács concluded, could not obscure the fact that fascist demagogy had to outstrip its "social fascist 'twin brother' (Stalin)" (159–60) in competition for the support of the masses.

As usual, there is a lifeless, intellectualized logic—hyperrationalism is perhaps the better word—to many of Lukács' elaborations. Looking at the correlation of forces in Germany from his viewpoint, which stigmatized every form of political expression not exclusively Stalinist as knowingly or unknowingly fascist, Lukács reached a seemingly rational conclusion. A party operating within a system already internally fascistized nourished all the currents leading to an open, unconcealed brand of fascism. But Lukács' theory slipped out of his control when he took the next logical step and declared Social Democracy to be no different than any other bourgeois party. In spite of its circuitous route from "revisionism" to "social fascism," said Lukács, one feature remained constant all along the way: Social Democracy's transformation into a bourgeois party with a proletarian following. This process of bourgeoisization, because it went hand in hand with the fascistization of all other bourgeois parties, was thus equally a process of fascistization (185).

At this point in Lukács' elaborations, however, the contradictions set in, not in spite of his logic but because of it. Lukács always treated the fascistization of bourgeois democracy and the bourgeois parties as a predetermined historical process put in motion by the unavoidable crises of capitalism. By making Social Democracy a part of this development, Lukács implied willy-nilly that the split in the proletariat and the victory of fascism caused by it were just as inevitable as the general fascistization of the state and the rest of its political superstructure. A key passage in Lukács' theory reads: "A part of bourgeois politics is bourgeois thinking; the bourgeoisization of thought leads unremittingly in the direction of bourgeois politics; and the development of the bourgeoisie inclines inexorably in the direction of fascism. The common path that revisionism trod together with the imperialist bourgeoisie led inexorably to social fascism as an indispensable component, as an important motive force of the general process of fascistization. Leaving this path was and is *only* possible by taking steps in the direction of proletarian revolution" (187).

Lukács evidently melded the notion of a Social Democratic class betrayal begun many years earlier together with a theory of inevitability. The leaders of the SPD parted company with revolutionary Marxism long ago; once that initial act of treachery had occurred, Social Democratic support for bourgeois policies and politicians followed naturally, together with the predictable selling out of working-class interests. Along this road to reaction, the party quickly turned into a driving force behind the general process of fascistization and played a crucial role in making National Socialism unstoppable. Lukács avoided any speculation about the course that history might have taken if Social Democracy had remained a genuinely revolutionary power—that would have needlessly complicated matters by making it far more difficult for him to rationalize Communist impotence. Fascism, in Lukács' mind, was a "necessary" development, the basic inclination of the bourgeoisie in the current era, as he put it; but fascism emerged triumphant only because Social Democracy blocked unification of the proletariat. What, then, if there had been no Social Democratic class betrayal?

Lukács never suggested anywhere that the original treachery was in any sense historically inevitable, only that events in the development of the party had to happen afterwards just as they did. But if Social Democracy had not committed the original sin of collaboration with the ruling class and its state apparatus many years ago, which damned the party to a road of class corruption and eventual fascistization, would Hitler's brand of fascism have been crushed before it ever gathered its forces? Would capitalism have posed any serious hindrance at all to a united revolutionary proletariat? Once the inevitable transition from capitalism to monopoly capitalism and imperialism was complete, the cyclical economic crises would have beset the state, paralleled by the historical emergence of the revolutionary proletariat. Without the factor of social fascism, which lent fascism proper a good deal of its strength, capitalism would apparently have been no match for the proletariat. This was a line of reasoning not pursued in the party, and Lukács ignored it as well. There is every reason to believe, of course, that if the Stalinists had not been able to blame their own revolutionary impuissance on the SPD, some other "historical" hindrance to proletarian revolution would have been located elsewhere.

But Lukács dealt with the situation as it presented itself in 1933. Here, too, however, a variety of crucial questions went unanswered. Social Democracy had in fact been fascistized, so National Socialism was presumably unavoidable, unless or until the social fascist influence on the workers was shaken off, as Lukács' argument had it. The only variable in the correlation of forces, as Lukács identified them, was apparently the KPD. Social Democracy was showing its true colors, playing out its historical role, and could scarcely be expected to turn over a new leaf of its own accord. The alignment of class forces was thus fixed and could be altered only by the Communists. But the KPD had not been able to break the Social Democratic hold on its rank and file. Though Lukács never said why this was so, from his frame of reference only two possible explanations exist. Either Social Democracy's organizational and ideological strength was utterly impervious to all Communist attempts to "educate" the masses, rendering the entire situation hopeless and fascism unpreventable; or the fault for the stalemate lay

with the Communists and their chronic inability to persuade
the Social Democratic workers of the simple truths about the
two wings of fascism.

The impasse in Lukács' theory was caused by the unavail-
ability of either explanation. The possibility that insurmountable obstacles could ever block the way to providing the workers with an appropriate proletarian class consciousness could
not exist for Lukács, and he was neither inclined nor in a position to remark upon the defects of Comintern policy. Yet no
change in the disadvantageous alignment of forces could ever
be brought about until the Communist party reexamined its
own policies and asked why these policies had failed prior to
1933. Lukács' own theory suggested this conclusion, but he
obviously could not pursue it and ended up eulogizing the very
features of Communist policy that had originally hindered
working-class unity and put an effective stop to joint antifascist resistance. Assuming the rough inevitability of the
SPD's road to social fascism once it had broken with revolutionary Marxism, and accepting also the correctness of the
Communist line, no conclusion can be reached about the rise
of fascism using Lukács' own arguments other than the one
that he rejected: under the circumstances, National Socialism
had been unpreventable. Lukács wrote his book as a "militant
treatise,"[62] a sort of battle strategy for the defeat of fascism.
The political program that can either be inferred from his theory or that he advocated outrightly was, however, identical in
all major respects with Stalin's German policy carried out by
the Comintern, a policy that shared at least some responsibility for the victory of National Socialism.

Even though Lukács' predictions about the future of fascism
make no allowance for any change in the combination of political forces and historical factors behind its rise and eventual triumph, his analysis exudes optimism about its imminent collapse. Lukács gave no indication that he regarded the policy
pursued by the Communist party before 1933 as questionable
and made it clear that this policy would soon yield results. "For
fascist demagogy in dealing with the masses must collapse as
soon as this demagogy is confronted with the revolutionary
united front of the working class, as soon as the active, resolute
revolutionary actions of the proletariat show to the nonprole-

tarian or semiproletarian toilers as well the revolutionary way out of the crisis of the capitalist system" (160). The outcome was a foregone conclusion regardless of "social fascism," said Lukács, which nevertheless continued as the "main social pillar of the bourgeoisie" even after the Nazi victory and would remain so as long as the KPD did not manage to anchor and exploit its influence in and among the masses (189–90).

The bourgeoisie had opted for fascist dictatorship, and Social Democracy could be counted upon to act out its role as social fascism—these factors were constant, leaving only the KPD to reassess the circumstances that made fascism possible. But Lukács apparently felt that a reappraisal of Communist policy was unnecessary and spoke only of the imminent end of National Socialism and the "revolution knocking at the door" (49). The same bourgeois strategy that brought National Socialism into power would cause it to disintegrate from within, virtually spontaneously and evidently without any rethinking of Communist policy. Fascism, Lukács reiterated, had to generate a large mass movement in order to serve the monopoly capitalist system temporarily in a time of acute crisis; the entire theory behind fascism hinged on sovereign contempt for the masses, which it intended to lead into the increasingly cruel bondage of monopoly capitalism. But with the National Socialists running the government, the demagogy that initially enabled them to enlist the masses in this peculiar process of self-enslavement would naturally collide with the daily reality of monopoly capitalism. This contradiction would force the National Socialists to turn their mass movement quickly into an open form of bondage, their social demagogy into a blind instrumentality of monopoly capitalism, and their national demagogy into capitulation to the Versailles system (see 147).

The fascist regime had quickly run out of options; "the fortification of its state apparatus of power [convulses] concurrently its social substructure. . . . It must convulse and undermine it" (237). The stage was set, and not even social fascism could reverse the dynamic of disintegration. Nor, apparently, was the process predicated anymore on the Communists' voluntaristic ability to unite the working class. Such unification, Lukács implied, would happen almost by itself as a consequence of "the necessary flight of the masses" (237) away from the Nazi party and the belated recognition by Social Democratic workers that their own party had led them down the road of betrayal. The process was irreversible: "The 'solution' to the problems of declining capitalism, a solution that fascism in Germany offers, is only a sharpening of its contradictions, an exacerbation of the situation inclining, with the power of a natural force, toward a further maturation of proletarian revolution" (272).

CHAPTER 7

Lukács' Theory of Fascism, Part 2
The Impasse

Lukács' revolutionary optimism was not at all uncommon at the time. Around 1933, it was customary in the Comintern and KPD to think in terms of a crisis of fascism and the imminence of proletarian revolution. The irony is that Lukács was compelled to construct his theory utilizing a limited stock of unchallengeable assumptions and that these approved components effectively eliminated any chance of reassessing the situation as objective new factors came to light. The prescribed optimism about the transitory nature of fascism and the imminent revolution begat a Janus-faced theory that, looking back, provided a ready justification for a disastrous Communist policy by investing the rise of fascism with an air of inevitability, and, looking forward, painted a sanguine picture of fascism's equally inevitable and spontaneous collapse. Whether Lukács had previously subscribed to the fatalistic or "pseudo-revolutionary" theory of allowing the Nazis into power in order to generate more favorable circumstances for a proletarian revolution is a matter of conjecture; it is certainly not unthinkable, however, both because of the inner consistency of the argument and because Lukács traveled in those party circles that had once espoused the notion.[1]

STALIN ON LUXEMBURG AND SPONTANEITY

Be that as it may, the chief influence upon Lukács' theory of fascism turns out to have been the Soviet philosophy debate and the discussions sparked by Stalin's letter to *Proletarskaja revoljutsija.* The criticism of Rosa Luxemburg inspired by Stalin's letter had been preceded throughout the twenties by recurrent protracted debates over the usefulness of her legacy. She had always been taken to task in the Comintern for her celebrated differences with Lenin over such fundamental issues as the leading role of the Communist party and the dictatorship of the proletariat,[2] but when the bolshevization of the Communist parties began in earnest in 1924, a definitive differentiation between bolshevism or Leninism and the complex of ideas associated with Rosa Luxemburg could no longer be put off.[3] By the time the fifth world congress of the Comintern met that same year, "Luxemburgism" had been outlawed in the Comintern as an erroneous political theory incompatible with bolshevism. Without overcoming the mistakes of Luxemburgism, Zinoviev said later, the real bolshevization of the Communist parties was inconceivable.[4] But Rosa Luxemburg was still immensely valuable to the party, which needed the few martyrs it had, and throughout the twenties and even after Stalin's letter to *Proletarskaja revoljutsija,* the official attitude toward her wavered between the rejection of "Luxemburgism" as a set of ideas contrary to the acknowledged principles of Leninism and respect for her person as a revolutionary martyr.[5]

Stalin apparently stayed out of the early disputes. In fact, when he denounced Trotsky's theory of permanent revolution in late 1924 as a "subspecies of menshevism" absolutely inimical to Leninism and the Leninist notion of the dictatorship of the proletariat,[6] he even defended Luxemburg against Karl Radek's claim that the idea of permanent revolution originated in 1905 with Luxemburg and Trotsky. The theory, Stalin said, was the work of Trotsky and Parvus, not Luxemburg.[7] On the other hand, when Stalin passed judgment upon the theory of spontaneity and defended the role of the avant-garde, he did so in terms that sounded like implied criticism of Rosa Luxemburg. The "theory" of spontaneity was the theory of opportunism, the theory of bowing before the spontaneity of the working class, the theory of de facto denial of the guiding role of the avant-garde of the working class, the party of the working class, Stalin charged. The theory of bowing to spontaneity resolutely resisted bestowing upon the spontaneous movement a conscious, planned character; it resisted having the party of the working class take the lead, having the party elevate the masses to the level of consciousness, having the party lead the movement. It was in favor of having the class conscious elements of the movement not hinder those who wished to go their own way; it was in favor of having the party heed only the spontaneous movement and trot along behind it. The theory of spontaneity was, concluded Stalin, the theory of impairing the role of the conscious element of the movement and was the logical basis for *any* kind of opportunism.[8]

Many of these same points resurfaced in 1930 and 1931, both in Stalin's open letter and in the dozens of articles in the Communist press that commented upon it. In the 1931 letter itself, Stalin now assigned responsibility for the theory of permanent revolution not just to Parvus but to Luxemburg after all; they were responsible for having "concocted" [*sochenili*] the "utopian and semi-Menshevist scheme of permanent revolution," permeated throughout with the "Menshevist denial" of proletarian dictatorship as the Bolsheviks understood it. Trotsky merely appropriated the "scheme," forging it into a weapon for use in his battle with Leninism.[9] The real target of Stalin's remarks in his open letter was, of course, not really Luxemburg at all, who had been moldering in her grave since 1918; rather, Stalin was setting his sights on the living Trotsky, and the letter to *Proletarskaja revoljutsija* ushered in a new strategy for dealing with him. Trotsky was no longer to be accorded even the already questionable status of a misguided revolutionary; he was nothing more than a common lackey of the bourgeoisie. (This was the start of the defamation campaign that peaked during the show trials with the charge that Trotsky was in league with the fascists and with Hitler's Gestapo.) "Some Bolsheviks," warned Stalin, "think that Trotsky represents a faction within communism, one, true, that is misguided, one that has committed more than a single foolish deed, one that has even behaved in an anti-Soviet fashion, but a Communist faction nevertheless." These ideas were all entirely wrong and harmful. "In actual fact, Trotskyism has long since ceased being a faction of communism. In actual fact, Trotskyism is the advance detachment of the counterrevolutionary bourgeoisie, which wages the struggle against communism, against Soviet power, against the construction of socialism in the

USSR." That was why liberalism toward Trotskyism, even if it was beaten and masked, was "folly bordering on a crime and on betrayal of the working class."[10]

These themes of spontaneity, the role of the party, dictatorship of the proletariat, and the opportunistic, Menshevist, Social Democratic, and social fascist character of Trotskyism and Luxemburgism were picked up following Stalin's letter and rehashed many times over in the Communist press. Lazar Kaganovich, in an article published in German two months after Stalin's letter, brought Luxemburg's errors on many fundamental issues—the "organizational question" and the question of proletarian revolution, for instance—into even sharper relief than Stalin and explored in greater detail her "close ties" with Trotsky and Trotskyism. The Bolshevik party, Kaganovich explained, had always opposed the theory of spontaneity and "automatism" in the labor movement, fighting tirelessly for improvement in the role of the avant-garde in the revolutionary movement. Too heavy a stress on automatically unfolding economic processes at the expense of consciously formulated revolutionary strategy and tactics was the most characteristic trait of "bourgeois theoreticians" and their "social fascist" lackeys. Trotsky situated himself in the mainstream of these views. What was the essence of "economism" as a mistaken view of revolutionary change? "Concessions to spontaneity, to the automatism of economic development, ignoring the political superstructure and its reverse influence upon economic matters."[11]

Many of these issues had been thoroughly debated in the past, Kaganovich continued, but the nature of the "right deviation" today meant that they had to be dealt with once again because the essence of this deviation was the negation of the revolutionary role of proletarian dictatorship—swearing by spontaneity.[12] These questions had a special urgency for current circumstances in the USSR, and Kaganovich explained the relevance of discussions about Luxemburgism and Trotskyism in the following terms. Coming out openly under the flag of Trotskyism was difficult nowadays, for one could no longer endure oneself to the masses that way and make any capital out of it. Other flags, other slogans, theses, formulations had to be utilized. "This is the issue, Comrades," said Kaganovich, "the new circumstances of the present day: that the Trotskyists, the genuine Trotskyists, the shame-faced, pale-faced, jaundiced, depraved Trotskyists under Trotsky's besmirched counter-revolutionary flag, which has been seized by the worst enemies of proletarian dictatorship, cannot show themselves." That was why the open and camouflaged Trotskyists were reaching for a new flag, for the flag of Luxemburgism, for the flag of Rosa Luxemburg, whom German Social Democrats had executed, in order to misuse her for their Trotskyist purposes.[13]

The German Communists lost no time applying this criticism of Luxemburg to their own history. By fighting its way through to a complete clarification of the role of the party, the KPD had taken the first steps "toward overcoming that Luxemburgian theory of spontaneity and denial of the role of the party which belonged to the most detrimental semi-Menshevist mistakes of the German left."[14] Rosa Luxemburg's various "errors," her incorrect understanding of imperialism and the collapse of capitalism, the role of the party, and so on were cataloged; "the residues of these false views must be uncovered by us completely and must be battled with the utmost resolve."[15] Ernst Thälmann provided a conclusion of sorts to the discussion in his address to a plenary session of the KPD in February 1932. Stalin's letter was an extraordinarily decisive and pioneering political directive.[16] Most important to remember was that Rosa Luxemburg's opinion was false in all questions in which she took a different view than Lenin. Her errors in the theory of capital accumulation, in questions pertaining to the role of the peasantry in revolutionary change, issues involving national minorities, the matter of revolution and proletarian dictatorship, the organizational question, and the problem of the role of the party or, turned around, the spontaneity of the masses—"all of that yields a *system of errors* that prevented *Rosa Luxemburg* from rising up to claim the perfect clarity of a *Lenin*."[17]

The Second International, opportunism, menshevism, social fascism, Trotskyism, Luxemburgism, spontaneity of the masses, on the one hand; Leninism, the leading role of the party, the Comintern, bolshevism, proletarian revolution, and proletarian dictatorship, on the other hand—these were the dichotomies that shaped Communist thinking after 1930, and

Lukács' thoughts on literature and politics in the early thirties reveal him at work patterning his ideas to dovetail with this network of Stalinist dogmas. His differentiation in *Die Links-kurve* between spontaneous writing and literature that con-sciously utilized the principles of dialectical materialism to create realistic art is a measure of his assimilation of the antin-omies consciousness versus spontaneity and their applicabil-ity to art. Similarly, *Wie ist die faschistische Philosophie in Deutschland entstanden?*, which makes a complete mockery of Lukács' later talk about his minimal concessions to Stalinist ideas and his resilience to the ideological tendencies current under Stalin, displays his accommodation to Stalinist political philosophy in the shape that that intellectual practice assumed in the immediate aftermath of Hitler's victory.

When Lukács came back to Moscow in April 1933, he may still have been unsure of the reception that awaited him after the fright of 1931, when his name had been listed along with various other political figures now regarded in the USSR as vir-tual criminals. Like his articles in *Die Linkskurve*, he perhaps thought of his book on fascism as part of an effort to demon-strate his loyalty to Stalin's dialecticians. This suggestion, of course, stresses Lukács' conscious assimilative talents and definitely needs to be taken into account in assessing his atti-tude toward Stalinism. But the entire issue is complicated by the likelihood that Lukács genuinely believed major portions of what he wrote. If this is true, if his adaptation was not com-pletely or substantially cynical, then his position on many im-portant political points in 1933 was indistinguishable from that of the prime articulators of intellectual Stalinism—not just in terms of the words he committed to paper but, more importantly, with respect to his innermost ideas.

One argument in favor of the suggestion that there was a fun-damental unanimity of thought between Lukács and the Sta-linists is the fact that Lukács never categorized his original repudiation of *Geschichte und Klassenbewusstsein* as disin-genuous. His disavowal in 1932 and 1933 of the ideas presented in his own earlier book, in fact, was the sole occasion on which his self-criticism, according to his own account, was sincere and not merely "tactical," and he asked that his study of fascism in 1933 be read as a partial rebuttal of *Geschichte und Klassenbewusstsein*. He criticized his earlier views by singling out supposed similarities between his positions in the midtwenties and Rosa Luxemburg's idea of the spontaneity of the masses. Luxemburg, Lukács wrote in 1933, had assumed an "opportunistic" position in all questions of party organization, largely because she deviated from the "dialectical method" in dealing with issues like theory and practice, masses and class, class and party, and party leadership. That Luxemburg had drawn different, diametrically opposed consequences than the revisionists from her mechanical exaggeration of necessity (theory of spontaneity, the prospects for the mechanical collapse of capitalism discussed in *The Accumulation of Capital*) did not, as Lukács explained it, alter the methodological and ideological essence of the question. "For precisely this lack of insight into the dialectical link between theory and practice led her astray, not only to a direct defense of opportunism in the area of organization (her opinion on the question of the struggle between Bolsheviks and Mensheviks); it also gave rise in her general political theory to a narrowness, an absence of dialectical universality . . . , a rigidity of contrasting issues (her attitude toward Trotsky's 'permanent revolution')" (182–83).

Lukács' remarks about Luxemburg's errors were a perfect reproduction of the standard comments on "Luxemburgism" inspired by Stalin's open letter, and the same was true of Lukács' references (an echo of the philosophy debate) to the indispensable unity of theory and practice in "undistorted" Marxism.[18] Was Lukács merely parroting the hackneyed phrases of the debate or was there more to his treatment of Rosa Luxemburg than the usual disapproval obligatory at the time? Like most of the commentaries published in the German Communist press, Lukács tried to strike a balance between outright rejection of Luxemburg's major ideas on revolutionary tactics and a respect for her accomplishments as a "true" revolutionary, though this appreciation remained rather artificial because the Communists were unable to cite any important tactical proposal of hers compatible with their interpretation of Leninism. Lukács wrote that Luxemburg had revealed herself to be a "genuine" revolutionary insofar as she had thrown her support behind

spontaneous actions of the proletariat vis-à-vis the "arid ratio-
cination" of the party and trade-union bureaucracy. But she had
gone too far in the opposite direction. She had remained generally mired in the ideology of the Second International, as evi-
denced by her support for spontaneous mass movements, support that was not coupled with recognition of the real existing
dialectical relationship between conscious and spontaneous actions, party and class, and so on (see 184).

Lukács' remarks can be taken as an unambiguous plaidoyer
for a Leninist position in "organizational questions," and these
remarks coincide with all the dogmas that emerged on top in
the philosophy debate. Lukács now translated these notions
into a strong emphasis on the importance of dialectical materialism as the proper foundation for defeating fascism. It was imperative, he said, that every Communist examine his own theoretical armament if he was to contribute effectively to the
battle against fascism. In *Geschichte und Klassenbewusstsein*,
for instance, he personally had deviated from dialectical materialism, and he considered it his duty now to explain why he no
longer identified with his earlier work. How could he battle
irrationalism with any hope of success if he was still making
profound concessions to the theory of spontaneity as a result of
the "Luxemburgian vestiges" of his book? How could Lenin's
question "who-whom?" be posed in a dialectically correct fashion and answered properly in concrete instances if the relationship between class and class consciousness was encum-
bered by "idealistic distortions?" "One believes himself to be
fighting honestly, but the enemy is concurrently being supplied—unintentionally—with intellectual weaponry" (56).

EXCURSUS: LUKÁCS' THEORY OF REVOLUTION

What was the point of Lukács' self-criticism? An answer can
perhaps best be found by comparing his 1933 repudiation of
"earlier concessions to the theory of spontaneity" and "Luxemburgian vestiges" with relevant remarks both in *Geschichte
und Klassenbewusstsein* and in his booklet on Lenin, published a year later. In each of these books, Lukács expressed his

views on Luxemburg, spontaneity, and the Leninist conception of the party. Curiously, these particular ideas were not at all at variance with the dogmas of the later philosophy debate or with Lukács' own treatment of Luxemburg in 1933. He spoke out clearly in 1923, for instance, against her "overestimation of spontaneous mass actions";[19] he also expanded his opposition to include, on the one hand, the opportunistic doctrine of "organic" evolution, which taught that the proletariat would acquire power legally at the end of a long, evolutionary path, and, on the other hand, what he called the "revolutionary-'organic'" theory of spontaneous mass conflict. This latter position was based on the assumption that the continual worsening of the economy, the inevitable world war, and the period of revolutionary mass struggles brought about by these developments would, by "sociohistorical necessity," generate spontaneous proletarian mass action.[20]

The theory of relying on the spontaneity of the masses, said Lukács, was misguided because it tacitly assumed that the revolution would be exclusively proletarian and that the masses caught up in spontaneous revolutionary action would not be "contaminated" by participants coming from the intermediate classes. Class consciousness could undeniably be so deeply and instinctively embedded in the proletariat itself that a Communist party needed only to render these natural instincts conscious at the proper moment and channel them in the appropriate direction. The defective thinking in the theory of spontaneity originated, rather, in a total disregard for the problem of the intermediate classes in mass unrest. These nonproletarian elements—the petty bourgeoisie, the peasantry, or oppressed nationalities—lacked the class consciousness of the proletariat; they might further the revolution in particular instances, but they could just as readily switch sides and play a counterrevolutionary role. Under no circumstances, however, were the intermediate classes absolutely fated to develop along the path of proletarian revolution. A Communist party that sat back and left these volatile elements to participate in revolutionary unrest without any guidance could never nudge them in the proper direction or forestall their sudden shift to counterrevolutionary action.

Even if the intermediate classes did not play a decisive role, said Lukács, a revolutionary party such as Luxemburg envisioned it would still be incapable of leading a successful revolution because, assuming that its task lay merely in bringing out latent feelings and drives in the working class and making the subconscious conscious, this view of the proletariat completely overlooked the likelihood of "a terrible *internal ideological crisis*" within the proletariat itself.[21] Lukács' point was that the class consciousness of the proletariat did not develop parallel with the objective economic crisis or uniformly throughout the entire proletariat. Large segments of the working class remained intellectually under the sway of the bourgeoisie so that not even the severest economic turns for the worse would be able to break this influence and shake the proletariat out of its lethargy or false consciousness. The proletariat thus acted in a way that was far less violent and intense than the crisis itself.[22]

These considerations acquired real meaning only when seen from the angle of a "nonfatalistic, non-'economistic' theory." For those who opportunistically postulated an economic process in capitalism leading "inexorably and automatically through a series of crises to socialism," any concern with class consciousness was groundless because proletarian backwardness only signaled that the objective crisis of capitalism had not yet set in with enough severity to spark a spontaneous uprising. Once it had, the proletarian "ideology" could never lag behind the economic crisis. "In such a case," said Lukács, an ideological crisis of the proletariat is ruled out altogether as something fundamentally impossible." An ideological crisis of the proletariat was equally out of the question from a "revolutionary optimistic" standpoint. This outlook, obsessed with the supposed unavoidability of both an economic crisis and the attendant hopelessness of the situation for capitalism, retained the economic fatalism of the opportunists. "In this case as well, the problem dealt with here is not acknowledged to be a problem, except that what was 'impossible' before is now said to be 'not yet' the case."[23]

Any idea that capitalism would collapse as a consequence of impersonal historical and economic laws overlooked a major consideration stressed by Lenin: no situation could be so bad as to block all avenues of escape from it. Regardless of the situation in which capitalism might find itself, a variety of "purely economic solutions" would always be available; it was only a matter of whether these measures could be put into practice, and that depended upon the proletariat—"the action of the proletariat bars the way out of this crisis for capitalism."[24] That this power was handed over to the proletariat at this particular time, explained Lukács, was the consequence of the "naturally ordained" (*naturgesetzlichen*) economic laws of development. These precipitated an economic crisis that blocked the serene further development of capitalism, but even if allowed to develop along capitalist lines, they would never lead by themselves to the simple collapse of capitalism and to a transition to socialism.[25]

The laws of nature or history, then, worked in two directions; they engendered profound economic dislocation, and they gave birth to a proletariat that stood in the way of solutions to the economic crises patterned after past responses because the working class no longer permitted itself to be exploited by the bourgeoisie as an object in those solutions or in economic development in general. "This power of the proletariat is the consequence of objective economic 'regularities'" (*Gesetzmässigkeiten*),[26] but the proletarian transition from an object of economic processes into a subject wholly capable of influencing them was no longer determined by those laws in an automatic, fatalistic way. This was a critical distinction for Lukács: "To the extent, namely, that the proletariat's reactions to the crisis manifest themselves purely in line with the capitalist 'regularities' in the economy, to the extent that they express themselves at best as *spontaneous mass actions*, they basically disclose a structure that frequently resembles the movements of the prerevolutionary period."[27] In the past such movements broke out spontaneously and ended just as spontaneously, as soon as the immediate goals were either achieved or regarded as beyond reach.

All "Menshevist working-class parties" and the unions influenced by them tried to capitalize on this "ideological crisis of the proletariat." Their conscious goal was precisely to hold the pure spontaneity of proletarian actions and uprisings at the level of spontaneity. But:

They can only fulfill their function, however, because of the state of ideological crisis in which the proletariat finds itself; because even in theory an—ideological—natural evolution into a dictatorship and into socialism is an impossibility; because, then, the crisis involves not only the economic undermining of capitalism but the ideological transformation of the proletariat as well, one that has been reared in capitalist society under the influence of the bourgeois way of life. This ideological transformation indeed comes about as a result of the economic crisis that gave rise to the objective possibility for seizing power, but its course of development by no means points to an automatic, "historically lawful" parallelism with the objective crisis. Its resolution can only come about on the basis of free action taken by the proletariat itself.[28]

The destiny of society lay in the hands of the proletariat. All that was new about the current situation was that the blind forces of economic development were pushing society toward the abyss; that the bourgeoisie no longer had the power to lift society over the end point of its economic laws, but that the proletariat now had "*the possibility,*" consciously exploiting existing tendencies, to channel the development in a different direction. "This step certainly issues 'by necessity' from the class situation of the proletariat. However, this necessity itself exhibits the character of a leap."[29] Lukács' conclusion was his plea for a Leninist grasp of the revolutionary dynamic: "If the Menshevist parties are the organizational expression of the ideological crisis of the proletariat, the Communist party, for its part, is the organizational form for the conscious approach to this leap and hence the first *conscious* step toward the realm of freedom."[30]

Lukács stressed many of the same points in his booklet on Lenin. He rejected any suggestion that the class consciousness necessary for a proletarian takeover could evolve on its own. To maintain that a spontaneous revolutionary process of self-enlightenment could occur among the masses, sustained in the party only by theoretically correct agitation and propaganda, was to subscribe to the fallacious notion of an "ideological evolution of the proletariat into its revolutionary vocation."[31] The revolutionary instinct of the workers, said Lukács, could certainly discharge itself in grandiose spontaneous mass actions, but these instincts were insufficient by themselves to preserve permanently "the height of class consciousness achieved through unconscious action."[32] The Communist party, "*the visible embodiment of the proletariat's class consciousness*,"[33] entered in here, and the organization of the party needed to reflect a solution to the problem of how the proletariat could arrive at a definitive conception of its own class consciousness. All who did not reject outrightly the revolutionary function of the party accepted that this did not occur "by itself," either by means of the mechanical effects of the economic forces of capitalist production or through the elemental organic growth of mass spontaneity.[34]

Lenin's concept of organization, wrote Lukács, thus denoted a "*twin break with mechanical fatalism*": with the notion of proletarian class consciousness as a mechanical product of class circumstances and with the idea that revolution itself was but a mechanical consummation of fatalistically unfolding economic forces that, given a sufficient maturity of the objective conditions for revolution, led the proletariat somehow automatically to victory.[35] The party, explained Lukács, had to lay the groundwork for the revolution, acting to accelerate the maturation process of revolutionary tendencies in the proletariat and other repressed groups and preparing the proletariat ideologically, tactically, and organizationally for the kinds of action required in an acute revolutionary situation.[36] Rosa Luxemburg had come close to grasping the dual character of the party as Lenin conceived it, its function in preparing the revolution as "producer *and* product, precondition *and* result of the revolutionary mass movement";[37] but she had overlooked the conscious and active aspect of the party and thus grossly misunderstood all of the organizational principles that flowed from it.

THE DIALECTICS OF SELF-CRITICISM

Lukács' early stand on the question of spontaneity versus consciousness points up the apparent senselessness of his 1933 admission to leanings in the direction of "spontaneity." What makes his confession that *Geschichte und Klassenbewusstsein* disclosed "Luxemburgian vestiges" even more perplexing is that no one had called attention to any such thing. Deborin's objections to *Geschichte und Klassenbewusstsein* published back in 1924, for instance, centered on the book's philosophical dimensions, principally Lukács' reservations about Lenin's theory of reflection and Engels' dialectic of nature.[38] Seven years later, during the philosophy debate, Lukács was listed as a common idealist masquerading as a dialectical materialist; he was not excoriated in any way for his treatment of Luxemburg or Lenin, and in *Die Linkskurve, Internationale Literatur* ("Mein Weg zu Marx"), and his 1934 article "The Importance of 'Materialism and Empirio-Criticism' for the Bolshevization of the Communist Parties," Lukács tended to concentrate mostly on the issue of idealism.[39] If on the issues of the spontaneity of the masses, revolutionary fatalism, or the "organizational question" Lukács was essentially as much in the mainstream of bolshevism in 1923 and 1924 as he was in that of the Stalinist intellectual establishment in 1933, what accounts for his show of repentence?

Lukács' disavowal of *Geschichte und Klassenbewusstsein* contains a number of ironies, the worst being that this instance of self-criticism was the only one where, as he told the story himself, Lukács honestly renounced his past views. Yet this renunciation was precipitated by the very debate in the USSR that soon peaked in the utter debasement of Soviet intellectual life and ushered in the maturest phase of Stalinism. Other ironies abound. In his various rounds of self-criticism during his lifetime, Lukács' position always contained some argument or proposal that provoked a party reaction and induced his act of submission. But in his critical remarks about *Geschichte und Klassenbewusstsein*, Lukács indicted himself in questions of revolutionary theory and tactics for deviations ("the most far-reaching concessions to the theory of spontaneity") that he had not committed and that no one in the party had yet accused him of committing.

Perhaps Lukács saw his criticism of the political theory advanced in *Geschichte und Klassenbewusstsein* as prophylactic. It is thinkable that his self-denigration was motivated in

1933 by latent uneasiness with regard to his standing in the party, a scant two years after the authoritative articles with his name in them had come out in the Soviet press, including *Pravda*. Lukács must have been mindful of the fact that those who spoke for the party could, on a whim, declare virtually any past philosophical or political position to be a deviation, regardless of the true nature of the stand or the context in which it had occurred. In 1933 Lukács was back on Soviet territory; this time he had no opportunity to catch a train to Berlin, and he surely knew it. Maybe he hoped that his *total* break with the philosophical dimensions of *Geschichte und Klassenbewusstsein*, which he may genuinely have disavowed, but also with the book's essentially acceptable or at least defensibly Leninist political side, would help spare him from any sequel to the treatment he had been accorded by those who had spoken in 1931 so contemptuously of "idealists of Lukács' type."

Perhaps the supreme irony of his self-criticism is that Lukács expressed his regrets for having compromised in the past on the question of spontaneity, faulted Luxemburg for her advocacy of such theories, and then constructed a theory of fascism permeated with strong suggestions of the inevitability of spontaneous uprisings spawned by inexorable historical laws that doomed capitalism as fascism to virtually automatic extinction. What might have prompted Lukács to think along such lines? The main influence behind the theory was presumably the straightforward fact that the official Comintern understanding of fascism in 1933 prescribed an identical kind of optimism, one that obliged the party to insist that the masses would presently see through the "glaring contradictions between the promises of the fascists and their practical policy,"[40] desert the party, and join the proletariat. Neither the Comintern nor Lukács could really have arrived at a much different conclusion in 1933. After all, incontrovertible assumptions about capitalism and fascism had been sweeping Communist thought through a prefabricated trough for many years until, in 1933, these axiomatic premises naturally poured into conclusions and prognostications mixing logic with sanguine fantasies that fascism was fated to disintegrate from within. What could Lukács and the rest of the party's ideologues do with their theory of fascism other than spend the rest of the decade anxiously awaiting the coming day when the masses would rise up spontaneously, throw off Hitler's yoke, and, with little in the way of outside help or guidance, carry out a proletarian revolution?

Lukács in Soviet Exile, 1933–1939

Lukács had been in Moscow the first time for several months already when Stalin proclaimed "the all-out offensive of socialism on every front" at the sixteenth party congress in July 1930.[1] Three and a half years later, and less than one after Lukács fled back to Moscow from Berlin, Stalin again addressed a party congress, the seventeenth. Whereas the speakers in 1930 had still been able to celebrate Stalin's genius with at least some moderation, at the so-called Congress of Victors in January 1934 that self-restraint turned into unqualified idolization as one speaker after another apotheosized Stalin in hypertrophied declarations of adoration.[2] As for Stalin's speech, it bestowed an air of reality upon various chimeras of Soviet society. These dominant Stalinist fictions, which entered the Soviet collective consciousness as existential truths, remained intact at least for the remainder of the Stalin years and shaped the official view of domestic and foreign affairs.

THE SEVENTEENTH CONGRESS

The party had much to be proud of, said Stalin. At the fifteenth congress the party had had to prove the correctness of its policy and contend with "certain anti-Leninist groups"; at the sixteenth the remnants of the opposition had to be finished off; but now, Stalin told his audience at the seventeenth to "thunderous applause," there was nothing left to prove and, it seemed, no one else to defeat.[3] The anti-Leninist group of Trotskyists had been defeated and dispersed; the anti-Leninist group of right deviationists had been defeated and dispersed. The policy of industrialization had triumphed, likewise the campaign to liquidate the kulaks as a class and to collectivize Soviet agriculture. To sum it up, socialism in one country had proven feasible after all. "What possible objections can there be to this fact?"[4] These fabulous triumphs were a wondrous contrast to the general decline of the world economy and the rise of Japanese and German imperialism. In the midst of the stormy waves of worldwide economic cataclysms, the Soviet Union stood like a solid rock, holding fast to its course of socialist construction and its resolute policy of safe-guarding peace in the world.[5] When Stalin finished his speech, the almost two thousand delegates to the Congress of Victors rose from their seats and accorded him a tumultuous ovation; by the end of the decade, all but some two dozen of them were dead or dying in forced labor camps.[6]

Economic desolation in the West contrasted with the steady, purposeful strides of industry and agriculture in the USSR. Feverish preparation in the capitalist countries for a new war to redivide the world into spheres of influence compared with systematic, unflinching resistance in the USSR to such a military conflict and with plans for the maintenance of peace. These standardized dichotomies helped forge Lukács' outlook upon his return to Moscow in April 1933. Just months before, the country had been locked in mortal combat "on all fronts" with left oppositionists, right deviationists, left-right (or right-left) blocs, bourgeois specialists, the conspiratorial Industrial party, white guard interventionists, idealists, mechanists, kulaks, Mensheviks, social fascists, Deborinites, Trotskyists, Bukharinites, Luxemburgists, and a host of other mainly fictitious oppositional groupings—literally all figments of Stalin's lurid imagination.

Lukács now stepped off the train in spring 1933 to discover shortly that there was scarcely anyone left in the land to fight. The forces of reaction and imperialism had emerged triumphant in the West, at least temporarily; but socialism had come out on top in the Soviet Union, and the stark contrast between the two worlds of yesterday and tomorrow was attracting "new, passionate supporters" to the side of the Soviet Union with every passing day, some from the toiling masses, others from the ranks of the intelligentsia.[7] The stagnation and decay that reduced untold millions to a state of utter destitution in the

West, along with unbridled fascist reaction and the final, inescapable degeneration of capitalist culture, naturally stood out vividly against the radiant heights that lay before the masses in the Soviet Union. A new world was in the making, a new man being forged. Soviet society stood on the threshold of a new age of culture.[8]

Soviet literature, too, was said to have embarked upon a new era, and the appropriate literary journals overflowed in 1933 with resplendant descriptions and evocations of the "new stage."[9] Fundamental changes had thrown open the door to a new flowering of Soviet literature. The opening editorial in a brand new monthly, *Literaturnyj kritik*, charged that the leadership of RAPP had chosen to ignore the changes wrought during the past three or four years of socialist construction.[10] Lukács' close friend, Elena Usievich, explained that the central committee resolution of 23 April 1932 concerning the "reconstruction" of literary-artistic organizations, the liquidation of RAPP, and the creation of a single Soviet writers' union with a Communist faction within it disclosed the "new situation" created in Soviet literature during the period of socialist construction. Under the influence of decisive successes in the building of socialism, which caused intellectuals to switch to the side of Soviet power, the correlation of forces in literature had changed "in our favor." The overwhelming majority of writers began consciously to subordinate their creative work to the tasks of Soviet power and to the party.[11]

Soviet literature could now boast of impressive successes, all of which had come about as an outgrowth of the class struggle. But the fact that broad segments of the literary intelligentsia had discovered its basic affinities with the goals of socialist construction by no means signaled an end to the class struggle in literature. "The class struggle continues," *Literaturnyj kritik* warned. "It has changed and is in the process of changing its forms. The correlation of forces has shifted. Socialism has consolidated its position, but our tasks have also grown more complicated."[12] Whereas the majority of writers had aligned itself with Soviet power, this new "Soviet orientation" in the work of these recent converts most certainly did not preclude the presence of "tendencies, prejudices, and errors of all kinds" hindering their creative work. These errors dealt the writers setbacks and threatened their new orientation with serious erosion. This circumstance, too, needed to be regarded as a form of the class struggle, albeit "a different kind than the struggle with the class enemy."[13]

Literaturnyj kritik began publishing with articles along the lines of these political-ideological coordinates borrowed from the nascent Stalinist mythology of 1933–34. Under the editorship of one of Stalin's prime exegetes of dialectical materialism, Pavel Judin, the journal looked upon itself as a "militant organ of Marxist-Leninist criticism, an active fighter of bourgeois and petty-bourgeois literary theories, a propagandist of Marxism as the only scientific world view, a propagandist of dialectical materialism—the only scientific philosophy."[14] According to the journal, the major difficulty that Marxist-Leninist critics now had to contend with, in comparison with the situation three years ago, centered around works of art and writers who could no longer be judged so easily "according to the formula 'ours or not ours.'" Large numbers of writers had cast their lot voluntarily with Soviet power; though they desired to be "one of us," their newly found allegiance had failed to appear to a satisfactory extent "in their artistic works."[15] These writers, finally, could only become "one of ours" through the help of the party. However, the creation of a single Soviet writers' union with a Communist faction within it did not connote a relaxation but a strengthening of "party leadership" of the literary movement.[16]

The Communist faction in the union shouldered the major responsibility for keeping watch over literature. This went without saying because the Communist faction was the "preeminent articulator of the party's influence upon literature and the prime leader of the literary movement."[17] Still, rebuking class-damaging tendencies and helping one another in a comradely fashion in aspiring to the common goal of eradicating "class-harmful influences and vestiges" was a task that devolved not just upon the Communist writers but upon every writer who joined the union.[18] This entire enterprise called for great tact and understanding, not threats and injunctions such as those characteristic of the former RAPP leadership. Lenin had spoken often of the necessity of working "side by side, honestly and sincerely" with nonparty members, and "Comrade

Stalin," Usievich pointed out, never tired of emphasizing the same in dealing with Soviet "writer-intellectuals."[19]

For all that, it remained crucial to acknowledge the continuing presence of class enemies in literature and to act and plan accordingly. The triumphant advance of socialism had altered the way in which the class enemy organized his resistance. Comrade Stalin had warned, "with the precision of a genius," that the class enemy no longer showed up with weapon in hand but appeared as a kind and peaceful administrator or bookkeeper in a kolkhoz, mouthing disingenuous phrases about socialism. In much the same fashion, the class enemy was no longer to be found in literature where he had been located two or three years earlier; he was far more clever and dangerous, "carrying out his activity somewhere right along side of us." The "class-harmful theory of formalism," for instance, remained one of the major dangers in literature. "It must not be overlooked that formalism has recently raised its head again and needs to be exposed in theoretically persuasive and concrete terms."[20]

LITERATURNYJ KRITIK

Writers and critics who had emerged from the crucible of the philosophy debate now began taking themselves more and more seriously as "propagandists of dialectical materialism," patterning their criticism after the nascent myths that Stalin definitively raised to the level of dogma at the seventeenth congress. Socialism in one country had won out against all forms of "anti-Leninist" opposition—this was one of two main truisms in the Stalinist dialectic of the thirties, the other being the continuation of the class struggle in ever more intense forms regardless, or better, because of the successes of socialism. Stalin used his speech at the seventeenth congress to help balance these two seemingly mutually exclusive claims, and the conventional wisdom of the thirties soon had it that the class struggle intensified in direct proportion to the country's advance ever closer to the final victory of socialism. Speaking of the various successes of socialist construction and the "victory of the five-year plan," which had completely demoralized anti-Leninist groups and "struck them a blow over the head," Stalin asked rhetorically whether this might herald the end of the struggle and imply that the further offensive of socialism could be dispensed with. No, he answered himself, this was not the case. Was everything as it should be in the party? Would there be no further deviations? No, he said again; the enemies of the party had been scattered, but the remnants of their ideology lived on in the minds of individual party members and cropped up on frequent occasions.[21]

Literaturnyj kritik took an identical stand with respect to Soviet literature, and Lukács found himself in essential agreement with the quintessentially Stalinist positions that the journal defined for itself. He began publishing Russian translations of all his major essays in *Literaturnyj kritik* almost from the very first issue,[22] though in remarks made many years later, he chose to transform his involvement in the journal into the classic example of his ostensible disagreements with Stalinism by ascribing to *Literaturnyj kritik* the attributes of an oppositional publication. But the monthly's "literary theoretical role of opposition,"[23] to use Lukács' own later phrase, was mostly a figment of his imagination—as if Usievich's arch-Stalinist obsession with class enemies lurking everywhere in the guise of writers, her call for "painstaking and profound analysis" of literary works for signs of "class-harmful" activity,[24] and her insistence that party control of literature be intensified were in any way free from the taint of the Stalinist myths that served as the ideological rationale for the terror soon to descend upon the entire country.[25]

There is, accordingly, scarcely a word of truth to Lukács' account of Judin's and Usievich's attacks in 1931 and 1932 upon the "narrow-minded RAPP" and the pair's supposed unselfish interest in a liberal-minded writers' union open to all Soviet writers.[26] Lukács pointed out in 1971 that the original movement to dissolve RAPP and replace it with one writers' union soon split into two wings. "The purely Stalinist wing was content," said Lukács, "to have isolated Averbakh. . . . The journal *Literaturnyj kritik* emerged from the other wing."[27] This rendition is correct as far as it goes, but it is only half of the story and appears designed to cast the most favorable light possible on Lukács' own collaboration with *Literaturnyj kritik.* He could scarcely concede, after all, that the monthly had served as a mouthpiece for an authoritative viewpoint at the same time he claimed to have published anti-Stalinist writings in it. Asked by István Eörsi how much "leeway" the journal had during the years of burgeoning Stalinism, Lukács provided a fraudulent summary of how a prominent journal had managed to survive at the crest of Stalinism, resisting the "Stalinist wing" of Soviet literature and presenting him personally with a forum from which to wage what he called his "partisan warfare against official and semi-official literary theories":[28] "I do not know why, but in any case Stalin regarded the philosophers Mitin and Judin as his own men. Consequently, they played an important role in the central committee, and, in this way, Judin, through Usievich, was able to negotiate concessions for the orientation adhered to by *Literaturnyj kritik.*"[29]

Was Lukács consciously feigning ignorance here of the role played by ordinary Stalinists like Mitin and Judin, charlatans of the worst kind, or had Lukács perhaps been polishing the art of dissimulation over so many decades in expressing his opinions out loud that, by 1971, he had finally forfeited the ability altogether to separate fact from fiction? On the eve of his death at age eighty-five, Lukács was perhaps still engaging in some idiosyncratic version of "the great and splendid expedient of Ketman,"[30] not because he needed any longer to dissemble in order to stay alive but because some form of "Ketman," as Milosz describes it,[31] had become second nature to him. After consciously and subconsciously acting out a role for so many years, Lukács could perhaps no longer "differentiate his true self from the self he simulates" so that, virtually on his death bed, "proper reflexes at the proper moment," proper in the sense of politically prudent, had become "truly automatic,"[32] even at a time when his survival was no longer at stake. Or was Lukács honestly incapable, in spite of his anti-Stalinist talk about the inversion of theory and tactics and his reference to Stalinism in 1962, for instance, as a "paradise for those devoid of talent and those gifted at accommodation," of making elementary connections about the intellectual dynamics of the system under which he had lived for so many years?[33]

Mitin and Judin were certainly influential personalities in

the central committee, to the extent that that institution can even be referred to meaningfully after 1934 as a cohesive body with a voice in policy making.[34] It is also true, as Lukács said, that the Mitin-Judin "faction" feuded often with an even more benighted band of cultural partisans headed by Aleksandr Fadejev. But it is simply preposterous to suggest that Stalinists like Mitin and Judin in any way extracted liberal "concessions" from the central committee to benefit *Literaturnyj kritik*. If Stalin's protégés gained approval for "their" policies in the central committee or, more likely, at much higher levels of the party apparatus, this merely illustrates the privileged status of *Literaturnyj kritik* in the first place in the eyes of Stalin or those closest to him. Lukács himself came to understand the basic principle involved here many years later. He never really troubled to ask himself, he said, whether the origin of or support for a given theory or opinion could be traced all the way back to Stalin. Given the "intellectual centralization" that Stalin created, it was altogether impossible for viewpoints to become the predominant ones without, at the very least, being authorized by Stalin; and for that very reason, Stalin's responsibility for these viewpoints was manifestly evident.[35]

Pavel Judin's programmatic essay on "Lenin and Several Problems of Literary Criticism," which introduced the first issue of *Literaturnyj kritik*, set forth basic theoretical and political principles of criticism that codified the line of the journal right at the start of its existence, and it cannot be argued persuasively that these principles changed substantially over the years. Judin systematized ideas that merged shortly with the prevailing outlook in Soviet literary criticism during the popular front era, and it is important to recognize the essential similarity between Judin's theory and many of Lukács' key theoretical and literary political concepts if one is to assess adequately the basic compatibility of both *Literaturnyj kritik*'s theoretical platform and Lukács' views with the major direction of Stalinist literary policy from 1933 to 1939.

Beginning with the platitude that Marxist-Leninist literary criticism relied upon the teaching of historical materialism regarding basis and superstructure, Judin's comments over twenty full pages of small print amounted to an elaborate historical and philosophical rationalization for the imposition of party controls over literature. Being an expression of ideology and, consequently, belonging to the superstructure, literature was conditioned by the economic relations present in a given society. It was the crudest of oversimplifications, on the other hand, to contend that ideology in general and literature in particular were exclusively and automatically dependent upon the economic basis and had no "relative independence" from it. This latter position was held in one form or another by critics representing or influenced by sociological approaches to literary criticism, and Judin, like Lukács, rejected vulgar sociology out of hand.

The formation of consciousness, he went on to say, was not merely a passive process directly and undistortedly mirroring economic development; rather, social consciousness, as it expressed itself in art, literature, or any other form of ideology, exercised a reverse influence on the economic basis. This was borne out particularly in times of tremendous political and social dislocation, when the pattern of intellectual activity destroyed any illusion that art and ideology stood above the fray and expressed interests somehow independent of the class struggle. During the October revolution, for instance, with the old society fighting for its very life, neutrality in science or art was especially anachronistic. "For or against, with the old world or with the proletarian revolution" was the question that posed itself as science and art began agitating either for or against the revolution. The interrelationship between the basis and the superstructure thus acquired a "special interest" during the time of transition from capitalism to socialism.[36]

Judin's main point was that the key to analyzing works of art lay in the author's world view. Whether he had been "a materialist or idealist as a writer, a conscious materialist or a spontaneous one,"[37] the question of a writer's world view stood at the center of artistic creation for the simple reason that the prevailing outlook of a particular historical era and the writer's own class upbringing and ideological consciousness exerted a powerful affect upon both the content of a work of art as well as the formal techniques "that an artist utilizes to help his ideas and views penetrate the consciousness of the people."[38] Nowadays, however, the "spontaneous materialism" with which past great writers unconsciously burst free of their own ideological class fetters to portray society and historical development accurately was out of place in Soviet literature. A writer needed to study events and acquire a profound knowledge of their rightful place in historical development, as Lenin said, and Judin added that it was impossible to "write truthfully, persuasively, and artistically" if a writer had at his disposal only "confused ideas and disjointed impressions."[39] To combat that danger, for instance, Soviet writers were expected to participate actively in socialist construction.

Judin's comments clearly echo RAPP's earlier demand that all Soviet writers become dialectical materialists, notwithstanding the campaign recently engaged in by none other than Judin and others against RAPP's "narrow-mindedness" on this issue. These affinities were so obvious that Judin could scarcely ignore them, so he made a halfhearted attempt to put some distance between himself and RAPP: "The injunction that a writer master the philosophy of Marxism must not take on the vulgar, warped character that it acquired under Averbakh and others, leading to their insistence that one write in keeping with the method of dialectical materialism ('dialectical materialist creative method')." All that Judin could come up with to demonstrate his differences with RAPP, however, was to stress just like RAPP "that a Soviet and proletarian writer, if he wants to be an artist-thinker, and not simply a chronicler and establisher of facts, must master seriously the philosophy of the proletariat, its world view—dialectical materialism."[40]

The political motivation underlying the "new" Marxist-Leninist criticism is especially conspicuous here. RAPP had called upon writers to study dialectical materialism and practice it in their work by "tearing off the masks" of human behavior, depicting the psychological workings of the dialectic within human beings, and thus revealing "the living man."[41] But RAPP's dialectical materialism had started to develop its own dynamic. This was particularly the case when the organization balked at party attempts to harness its theories for utilization in the various campaigns of socialist construction, attempts undertaken regardless of potential damage to theoretical principles that RAPP felt were valid outside an exclusively utilitarian political context. Judin's call for mastery of the "philosophy of the proletariat," on the other hand, dovetailed with the Stalinist interpretation of dialectical materialism, besides which times had changed: RAPP's bellicose attitude toward non-Communist writers witnessed to the pervasive atmosphere of distrust and suspicion during the First Five-Year Plan and its liquidation of the kulaks, campaigns against bourgeois specialists, misgivings about fellow travelers, and anti-Menshevik hysteria.

After 1932, however, the Stalinists began changing their tone of voice, speaking of impressive socialist successes that had transformed onetime fellow travelers into fledgling followers of the Soviet regime. In contrast to the harsh treatment that RAPP had accorded these intellectuals in years past, the party was now duty bound to assist the initiates along the road to political and literary maturity.[42] In calling attention to both the blemishes and the positive attributes of a specific work, said Judin, Marxist-Leninist literary criticism would lend the writer a much-needed helping hand in working out a scientific world view that was "class conformable" and "ideologically honed."[43] For the time being, during the transitional years from 1932 to the mid-thirties, official policy called for a demonstrative show of tolerance. Behind it, however, lay unequivocal political objectives. In Judin's article these were not very well hidden: "Creative literature is not a personal matter, not merely the private domain of the writer. Creative literature is a weapon to be used in the political education of the masses; it is a powerful device to be employed as a means of influencing the formation of social consciousness and affecting economic affairs."[44]

RESIDUAL INFLUENCES

In Soviet exile, Lukács expanded upon the key ideas that he had pursued in the *Moskauer Rundschau*, related them to different present-day and classical writers, altered or refined occasional minor points, and transposed some concepts to fit the new political atmosphere that Stalin had evoked at the seventeenth congress. But he added no fundamentally new accents to his overall theory, which conflicted with absolutely none of Judin's general tenets, and wrote essays through the remainder of the thirties that were never at variance with establishmentarian literary policy. The picture of these years that emerges from the pages of Lukács' autobiographical writings, on the other hand, is quite different. Lukács contended that his work challenged the cultural establishment. His essays, and articles written by other critics publishing in *Literaturnyj kritik*, attacked Stalinist "naturalist orthodoxy," Lukács said. Engels' letter mentioning Balzac's "triumph of realism" had just been made public, and, in extremely sharp contrast to Stalinism, he and his colleagues held that ideology was no criterion for the aesthetic attributes and makeup of a work of art. Very good literature could be written in spite of a "bad" ideology, as Balzac's royalism proved, and an entirely unobjectionable ideology offered no assurance in and of itself that low-grade literature could be averted.[45]

Lukács' appraisal ignores certain facts and casts a misleading light on others. In no way did Lukács' outlook and the basic editorial policy of *Literaturnyj kritik*, least of all the notion of a "triumph of realism" and all the ideas that went with it, contradict conventional Stalinist policy. Rather, the application of the triumph of realism to past writers was a by-product of the new-found Soviet appreciation of the cultural heritage institutionalized and instrumentalized during the popular front era. But even before the Comintern embarked upon the popular front in 1935, there was no essential difference, for instance, between Judin's initial reference to the "spontaneous materialism" (*materialism stikhejnyj*) of past realist writers and Lukács' understanding of "the natural materialism [*stikhejnyj materialism*, in the Russian translation] of the genuinely great artists (regardless of their often partially or entirely idealistic world view."[46]

The point is that Lukács and *Literaturnyj kritik* did not implicitly or explicitly dispute theoretical positions backed by Stalin or his men. The head editor of the journal, of course, Judin, *was* one of Stalin's men, and that fact ought not to be forgotten. Now Lukács was right to point out that Soviet literary theory split into two camps after 1932, and the editorial line followed by *Literaturnyj kritik* represented one of them. But both of these camps were sanctioned, for a time, by Stalin's cultural overseers. One of the orientations—Lukács called it Stalin's naturalist orthodoxy—adhered stubbornly to a RAPP-like outlook that tended to shun the apparent tolerance toward fellow-traveler writers that emerged in the aftermath of RAPP's dissolution and during the preparatory period leading to formation of the Soviet writers' union. Writers and critics belonging to this camp evidently hoped to keep some of the traditions of the sociological school of literary criticism alive, primarily the categorical linkage between a writer's world view and his "creative method." In the eyes of these critics, a Tolstoy could never have represented imaginatively the interests and viewpoints of any class other than his own, and Soviet writers were expected to become mature dialectical materialists before publishing.

Literaturnyj kritik, whose contributors represented the other camp to which Lukács referred, took a much different attitude toward the classics. These critics argued along the lines of Engels' "triumph of realism" and Lenin's treatment of Tolstoy as a writer who "mirrored the Russian revolution" in spite of his own reactionary class background, and the entire dispute over the question of an absolute identity or possible contradiction between world view and creative method was fought out in a debate in the Soviet press lasting from 1933 to 1936. In these exchanges, the critics who published in *Literaturnyj kritik*, chief among them Mikhail Lifshitz, Lukács' closest friend in Soviet exile, played prominent roles. According to Lifshitz, in fact, the entire campaign against the "vulgar sociologists" was launched with the knowledge and consent of Stalin personally;[47] and, after it had run its predetermined course, the debate ended unceremoniously with *Pravda's* blanket condemnation of the entire school of sociological criticism.[48] The theoretical position that Lukács later characterized as a basic disagreement with Stalinism was consequently little more than one side of Stalin's bifurcated literary line.[49] Lukács' later argument that his theory had pointed to the danger of substandard literature being written in spite of a "correct" world view is also a half-truth in the sense that it obscures other major facets of his attitude toward contemporary writers of various political persuasions. It tends to polish up Lukács' aggressiveness in pursuing the point that good literature could only be written in the last analysis by artists who grasped the dialectic, that is, by writers who were Marxist-Leninists;[50] and it glosses over his habit of challenging the quality of the political commitment made by Soviet or self-professed Communist writers in the West, and usually their doctrinal purity as well, if he took exception to their formal preferences.

Lukács made an absolute fetish over literary forms in Soviet literature. Certain of these he considered "subjective," taken over from the dying culture of the decadent West; and he tied the partiality that some Soviet writers had for such forms, or that Lukács said they had, to their faulty world views. By arguing that art forms were historically objective, coupled in their origin and subsequent evolution to precise social and socially engendered ideological premises,[51] Lukács locked himself into a closed system of logic that compelled him to search compulsively in Soviet intellectual and literary life for "residual influences" of declining Western culture. Modern forms like montage, reportage, or any other "avant-garde" approach to creative writing were in his imagination literary spin-offs of bourgeois decadence; they reflected the inability of those bourgeois writers in the West who practiced them to capture the totality of a fragmented and disjointed capitalist society. Thus, the use of the same methods by Soviet writers to depict a Soviet reality devoid of alienation and social fragmentation was historically anachronistic and inherently antirealistic.

Where were the main impediments to the representation in Soviet literature of the "new man," asked Lukács? "Above all, no doubt, in the remnants of bourgeois consciousness. Our literature did not evolve without being influenced by bourgeois culture and art. The pernicious influence exerted by different currents of this age of decline is manifestly present on different levels of our theory and practice."[52] Ideology was the issue, and Lukács called for a keener awareness of the linkage between questions of form and the improvement of a writer's world view through the eradication, "in the realm of world view,"[53] of residual bourgeois influences. "Our" Soviet literature had not yet embarked upon the path leading to the complete "liquidation" of these residues,[54] he said, adding that at no time in world history was the question of world view of such eminent practical importance as nowadays—here "among us"—in the USSR.[55]

To this general analysis Lukács added his treatment of authorial intention. There were certainly numerous instances where Soviet writers picked up and developed these decadent literary styles with the best of intentions, honestly convinced that they were doing their part in the construction of socialism. "But the best intention and the most honest conviction cannot change the falseness of the method and its unsuitability to express the new; they cannot alter the fact that subjectivism or mechanism are not helpful instruments but impediments for expressing that which is so tremendously new and original and which is occurring daily and hourly in Soviet reality."[56] When a Soviet writer voluntarily shackled himself with such formal restrictions, not even a "Bolshevist temperament" (assuming that he even had one) could help him fight his way free of these self-imposed fetters.[57]

Lukács' rejection of the formal technique and theory practiced by Bertolt Brecht in the West and his indifference toward subjectively praiseworthy intentions differed little from his ambivalence toward much Soviet writing, and his clash with Brecht, Ernst Bloch, and Hanns Eisler over these very issues in 1937 and 1938 during the expressionism debate was entirely consistent with Lukács' determination to have his viewpoint regarded as the authoritative expression of Marxism-Leninism in literature.[58] Assuming that they did not go in for experimental or avant-garde forms, Lukács' feelings toward fellow-traveler writers in the West were far more naturally sympathetic, but his analysis of their shortcomings was equally rigid and patronizing. In his dealings with these writers, Lukács passed through two separate though related phases, and his theories during both periods paralleled Soviet foreign policy. From 1933 to 1935 he dealt with antifascist intellectuals in a manner that conformed to the Comintern's call for proletarian revolution and proletarian dictatorship as the sole means of stopping Hitler and defeating fascism. Then, beginning in 1936, Lukács adjusted his rhetoric and his theories enough to make them compatible with the strategic and tactical modifications of Communist policy that carried the label of the popular front.

DON QUIXOTE, DULCINEA, AND THE GRAND HOTEL "ABGRUND"

Lukács' first detailed assessment of non-Communist intellectuals and their fight against Hitler formed an integral part of his

1933 theory of fascism. If the imperialist evolution of the German bourgeoisie betokened the "pre-history" of National Socialism, the history of philosophy in the age of imperialism foreshadowed National Socialist ideology (42–44).[59] As long as this fact of life escaped those intellectuals who wished to work out their own ideological opposition to the world view of fascism, they would persist in their efforts to fight National Socialism on ideological premises themselves "half or three-quarters" fascist (42–43). So went Lukács' reformulation of his view of pseudo-opposition to fascism as it applied to the intellectuals. The lessons were clear: any writer who succumbed to the illusion that he could battle National Socialism without siding directly with official communism not only sentenced himself to ineffectual resistance but, to all intents and purposes, was fated to become an unwitting ally of the Nazis. The noble intentions that may originally have inspired him were immaterial. "The dilemma: *fascism or bolshevism*," Lukács repeated, "is thus no 'invention' of the Communists. Rather, it is the signature of the epoch in which we live" (39). Every attack on the "revolutionary party of the proletariat" was an unintended act of assistance to fascist reaction. Some of the sincere bourgeois opponents of fascism had learned this lesson quickly, realizing that fascism could not be resisted in isolation and that they had to fight on the side of the revolutionary proletariat. Other intellectuals clung tenaciously to ideological illusions so profoundly anachronistic that these Don Quixotes could not even lay claim to the role of latter-day knights-errant. History stood still for no one, and in the epoch of imperialism and fascist reaction the time was over for illusions about the true nature of society, illusions that were understandable if tragicomical in Cervantes age but entirely out of place today. Lukács tried to be witty in his response:

> Poor Don Quixote, after all, was subjectively much more honestly and fanatically convinced that knight-errantry still existed than the wretched modern-day knights of "democracy." Nonetheless, he reaped only scorn, brought only the lash down upon himself. Today, however, not even his tragicomedy can be imitated anymore. For in his world view the wretched knight was really a knight on horseback, one who

not only made no compromises ideologically (not even an unconscious compromise) with the ascending new world of capitalism, but one who also remained entirely untouched by its ideology. For that reason he was able to raise his lance with unshakable seriousness against windmills and sheep herds. If he had had only the slightest thing in common with the hostile world, he would have become a prosaic idiot or a downright ridiculous impostor, and not the holy fool in Cervantes' immortal depiction. Today, even his tragi-comical way is blocked. The wretched modern-day knights of the "timeless values of democracy" know that the wind-mill is not a giant and, above all, that Dulcinea is an un-kempt peasant maid (47–48).

Fascism or bolshevism—there was no other option today (51). Ideologically this implied that yielding to any form of idealism or irrationalism at the expense of dialectical materi-alism was to take the first step on the road to fascism. "Who-whom" was the question in Lenin's classic formulation; either monopoly capitalism would crush the proletariat and drown all cultural values in the bloody bog of fascism or the working class would shake off the "fascist-monopoly-capitalist" yoke and open the way to a cultural renascence (51).

Whether he realized it in 1933 or not, Lukács conceived of the mass movement that would presently topple Hitler as a spontaneous outbreak of popular Stalinism. The camp of "reso-lute and heroic" opponents to the Hitler regime, a body of op-position that Lukács said was growing daily and witnessing to its heroism in anonymous day-to-day struggles, was incom-parably broader than the exclusively Communist camp or that of "conscious," clear-sighted supporters of dialectical materi-alism (51). As a beginning that was as it should be; but because communism alone, dialectical materialism, provided the requi-site consciousness needed to grasp the social and economic dy-namics of fascism, anyone who "seriously" battled fascism naturally and unavoidably advanced with steady strides toward Marxism-Leninism, whether or not he actually knew it. For the question "who-whom" had to be posed and somehow an-swered by all those who took up the struggle against fascism, though not necessarily in Lenin's precise formulation and not always with the systematic and concrete wealth of understanding inherent in Marxism-Leninism (52).

At this juncture the very idea that any intellectual under any circumstances might reject both Hitler *and* Stalin apparently never entered Lukács' consciousness; it was wholly inconceivable to him. Thus, his pervasive optimism that fascism was foredoomed and bolshevism, in its Stalinist form, preordained by the necessities of the historical process induced him to think in terms of a semi-automatic process, one involving a spontaneous conversion of intellectuals to Stalinism. He did, however, sense the need to dispel beforehand any suggestion that he personally embraced some theory of spontaneity, though his efforts in this regard remained mostly in the realm of rhetoric: "If [the road to a correct fight against fascism] is honestly and resolutely trod, then the worker, as well as the petty bourgeois, the intellectual, and so on will be helped along further by the *experience of their own praxis*. Not spontaneously. Not 'by itself.' Not without the help of Marxism-Leninism, not without coming to terms with it, not without appropriating it to a certain extent" (53).

But Lukács' disclaimer never really translated into a persuasive argument against spontaneity, presumably because historical "automatism" was such an integral part of his theory of fascism. Thus, unlike his view of revolution and class consciousness in *Geschichte und Klassenbewusstsein,* and in spite of his disavowal, he still implied that the necessary awareness of National Socialism and the class consciousness needed to deal with it would essentially congeal spontaneously. True, he claimed that this would occur with the help of Marxism-Leninism and not "by itself." But he left it at that, saying nothing whatever of the leading role of the party. Rather, he appeared to suggest that the masses, including the intellectuals, would come to the Communist party, to Marxism-Leninism, on their own accord because they were led along the right path by lessons learned automatically in their own anti-fascist praxis, assuming, naturally, that they were "resolute," "sincere," and "really" opposed to Hitler.

Later that year Lukács took a broader and more theoretical approach to the role of the intelligentsia in a revolutionary situation. In his unpublished essay "Das Grand Hotel 'Abgrund,'"[60] he argued that intellectuals led a social and political existence conditioned by their class function as purveyors of petty bourgeois ideology, an ideology that was by nature capable of articulating only pseudo-opposition to the monopoly capitalist system. The petty bourgeois intellectuals were buffeted by periodic fluctuations and convulsions in the economic basis equally as much as other members of their intermediate class, which vacillated between the proletariat and the bourgeoisie. The intellectuals thus mirrored the feelings of the lower middle class as it wavered between revolution and counterrevolution and gave ideological expression to this indecision. Once the bourgeoisie began its final decline, this dependence on the economic basis became an acute problem because the producers of ideology spontaneously reflected the process of decay and, whether they wished to or not, played the largest role in maintaining the putrefying forms of exploitation and domination. The more profound the crisis of capitalism and the more crass the barbarism of fascist methods used to sustain monopoly capitalism in power, the greater the dispair of those "ideologues" who recoiled at the thought of becoming sycophants of the fascist system but had not as yet managed to decide in favor of the "salto vitale" to the side of the revolutionary class.[61]

The worsening crisis of capitalism and the growing vitality of the proletarian class struggle, spurred on by the "shining example"[62] of the emerging classless society in the Soviet Union, had brought "the best elements" of the intelligentsia closer to the revolutionary proletariat and transformed them into allies. But Lukács again denied that this was a spontaneous process with a prefigured outcome: between disaffiliation from the bourgeoisie and coalescence with the proletariat there were many turns in the road, many way stations.[63] These served bourgeois designs by keeping numerous intellectuals in a condition of chronic disequilibrium and causing them to stop right at the edge of a precipice, all the while thinking that they were still surging forward with their profound criticism of the existing order. "[The intelligentsia], however, in an objective sense, moves around in a circle, caught up in a condition of chronic despair and on the edge of the precipice."[64] No accident, this circumstance was part of a grand strategy of the bourgeoisie. Because it was no longer unrealistic to think that the intellectuals could be transformed into enthusiastic supporters of bourgeois society, they were manipulated instead into producing a radical-sounding but harmless ideology that appeared to denote fundamental opposition to the bourgeoisie. Though they had come to hold the current society in utter contempt, they were thus held back by their "own" ideology from drawing any "practical conclusions."[65] Not that they had been bribed in any direct sense of the word; "the more clever, unintentional bribery, the transformation of ideological opposition into a component part of the parasitical system as a whole, originates precisely . . . on the basis of the illusion . . . of being able to express vitriolic and radical criticism of the existing order."[66]

For this purpose the Grand Hotel "Abgrund" was erected; from that vantage point, perched at the brink of an abyss, there loomed two possibilities for the intellectuals: a spiritual dead end, a self-renunciation of any meaningful intellectual existence, and consequently the voluntary plunge into the depths of the abyss; or a "salto vitale" into a radiant future.[67] The bourgeoisie, said Lukács, had opened the hotel for business to complicate matters for anyone seriously contemplating a leap in the latter direction. There one lived in the most extravagant intellectual freedom. Everything was permitted, nothing was exempt from criticism. For every kind of radical criticism within the invisible boundaries there were specially furnished rooms: "If one wishes to create a sect for the purpose of a patented ideological solution to all cultural problems, there are suitable meeting rooms at one's disposal. If one is a 'loner,' universally misunderstood and going his way alone, he receives his nicely furnished single room in which, surrounded by all the variants of contemporary culture, he can live 'in the desert' or in the 'monastic cell.'" The Grand Hotel "Abgrund" was set up to meet the needs of all. Every form of intellectual rapture, as well as every form of asceticism and self-flagellation, was not only permitted but actively encouraged. The needs of the lonely and the sociable were equally met, and each individual could be a witness to the activity of every other one; each could have the satisfaction of being the only sane one in a Tower of Babel of general lunacy. "The death dance of world views that takes place each day and each evening in the hotel takes the form for its inhabitants of a pleasant and stimulating jazz band, providing them with relaxation after their strenuous daily course of treatment."[68]

Lukács' wittiness here bears directly upon his Leninist perception of the revolutionary process, and this process unfolded in his mind as he had described it in *Geschichte und Klassenbewusstsein* a decade earlier. The petty bourgeoisie, to which Lukács consigned the intellectuals, responded to the devastating effects of the economic crisis with a spontaneous, confused brand of inarticulate anticapitalism. A reactionary ideology originated along with it, equally spontaneously, but the entire movement was capable at any moment of divesting itself of its reactionary shell and turning revolutionary. These tendencies were accelerated objectively by the deepening crisis of capitalism and subjectively by the "growing influence" of the Communist party. In order to survive, the bourgeoisie had to muster all the means at its disposal to obstruct any process that might disentangle the spontaneous confusion and to keep the movement trapped in the wake of reaction. Grand Hotel or not (whose purpose was to fulfill this objective), Lukács expressed confident optimism about the direction in which the "honest and sincere" intellectuals would eventually leap: "The necessity of a radical break with this ideological arrangement of one's inner life, the necessity of burning this set-up and of the saving salto vitale is growing ever more acute. This necessity is increasingly reaching out to take in the best elements of the German intelligentsia."[69]

REVOLUTIONARY DEMOCRACY

When the Comintern began pursuing the policy of a popular front in 1935, Lukács promptly attributed an extraordinary "historical significance" to it. His earlier anticipation that Western intellectuals were on the verge of a saving "salto vitale" into the camp of the revolutionary proletariat, however, required a certain amount of revision. It now transpired that there was a middle road after all between fascism and bolshevism, and Lukács called it revolutionary democracy. But he changed his underlying concepts very little and retained his customary optimism, which was fed by his infatuation with preestablished lines of historical development. Hitler's victory in Germany represented a milestone in history, he argued, and not just for Germany; for, heartened by popular front "successes" in France and Spain, as well as by the victory of socialism in the USSR, the spirit of revolutionary democracy had come alive as a consequence of Hitler's seizure of power.[70]

Lukács' reading of events in Europe was a recognizable variation on the 1933–34 Soviet refrain that the attainments of socialism wrought during the First Five-Year Plan had encouraged countless non-Communists to declare themselves voluntarily, almost spontaneously, in favor of "Soviet power," of "the party." The pendant to that particular Stalinist myth for Lukács was that formation of a popular front against fascism signaled not just a political event of "global historical" significance but marked ideologically and culturally the commencement of a new era of German literature.[71]

Of course there was an interesting twist to this viewpoint. It implied that the previous analysis had been wrong; the triumphant advance of socialism in the USSR up to 1935 or early 1936 had evidently not been sufficiently impressive in itself to occasion a switch by Western writers to the side of Soviet power, either in the form of an open avowal of Marxism-Leninism and direct loyalty to the local Communist party or a general expression of allegiance to the Soviet Union.[72] But in the West there was now a historical counterpart to socialist successes, namely the "impressive headway" made by the popular front. The only trouble for Lukács, however, was that all these advances, especially those now achieved in the West, had somehow still failed to provide ample encouragement to the intellectuals for their final "salto vitale" from the balcony of the Grand Hotel into the camp of the revolutionary proletariat. Rather, the global historical significance of the popular front had sufficed only to nudge the intellectuals over the brink, where they quickly found a foothold on a ledge that still only overlooked the Communist camp. But these "revolutionary democrats" ought not to be faulted for clinging to the ledge, argued Lukács now; they were "humanistic opponents" of Hitler, a characterization unthinkable for Lukács just months before; and a further process of clarification still lay before them. It was true that they were not yet Marxists, but it would be a "sectarian point of view" to judge them according to their lack of conscious acceptance of basic Marxist or Communist principles.[73] Marxism was not the beginning but the end of the road that they had embarked upon.

Lukács was coordinating his theory with certain tactical inflections in the new Comintern line. The KPD had not managed to attract meaningful numbers of supporters for an antifascist policy that placed proletarian revolution and dictatorship at the top of the party's agenda and slighted any other form of antifascism by insinuating that it was substandard, simply not as legitimate as the Communist brand. Not even the first phase of the popular front, from mid-1935 to mid-1936, had made much of a dent in non-Communist suspicion about the KPD's ulterior motives. In mid-1936, therefore, the Communists began to retreat from a position that had still contained strong overtones of proletarian revolution. The top public priority for the Communists now became a "democratic republic" for Germany once the popular front ousted Hitler and relegated National Socialism to the garbage heap of history.

It should be emphasized that the phrase "revolutionary democracy," Lukács' equivalent of the Comintern's "democratic republic," cropped up in his writing only after that slogan became the centerpiece of the Comintern program. In no way did Lukács anticipate the tactical switch; rather, he reflected it in his writings only after it had been sanctioned. Those who still argued, as he himself had done a scant two years earlier, that the highest law of the age posed the question "fascism or bolshevism" were now nothing but "anarchistic muddle-heads" and "Trotskyist wreckers" in Lukács' mind.[74]

His new line of reasoning was a classic illustration of Lukács' knack, apparently learned from party theoreticians and ideologues, for avoiding anything that smacked of a "discussion of mistakes." Whenever the party abandoned a previous strategy or tactics, it invariably went to great lengths to put the best face possible on a program whose "newness" connoted that the past policy had somehow been faulty. A new general line was usually interpreted accordingly as a necessary and reasoned response to changed historical conditions and not as a belated recognition that previous policies had failed (perhaps with good reason). Lukács developed the same reflex, adjusting his theories on repeated occasions without ever admitting that features of his previous theoretical posture had failed to withstand the test of time.

This should not be construed as a suggestion that the change in 1936 portended deep-seated alterations in the Comintern program. The popular front was an expedient for the Communists, and for Lukács revolutionary democracy was a transitional stage prior to "proletarian democracy," as he referred to the Soviet regime.[75] The year 1936, after all, witnessed the birth of the "Stalin Constitution" amid much fanfare. Stalin himself called it the only thoroughly democratic constitution in the world.[76] Lukács essentially seconded him, praising the differences between proletarian and bourgeois democracy in an article in honor of the draft of the new constitution published just after the first show trial. The existence of a socialist society cast a merciless light upon all the halfheartedness and hypocrisy of democracy in a class society, Lukács said; but the socialist society also assumed the heritage of everything progressive in revolutionary struggles for that democracy and as part of it. "The new constitution," he went on to say, "will become the radiant banner of all freedom-lovers throughout the entire world who enter into the battle against the repression of freedom and the human personality by fascist barbarity."[77] Lukács left little room for doubt that his view of revolutionary democracy, "democracy of a new type" (as he characterized it in a phrase anticipating the euphemism of postwar Eastern Europe), was just a step in the direction of "genuine" democracy such as that practiced in the USSR. "The Bolsheviki have really raised up the traditions of revolutionary democracy in their theory and their practice (in the sense of conserving and lifting these traditions to a higher plateau)."[78] Lukács added that revolutionary democracy would presently transcend the boundaries of a mere defense of democratic rights and liberties against the onslaught of fascism. The struggle of revolutionary democracy by means of a popular front naturally defended democracy in this sense, too, but to safeguard these privileges adequately the struggle had to go beyond these limitations. "[The struggle] must impart to revolutionary democracy a new, higher, more advanced, more general, more democratic, and more social content."[79]

Whether Lukács accommodated his theories to a new party policy by instinct, with cynicism, or after careful analysis leading to genuine conviction, is impossible to tell. Probably his ideas were an amalgam of all these motives, but in the final analysis the private considerations behind Lukács' instrumentalization of official myths to couple his literary theories to Stalin's prime fictions about Soviet society remain a mystery. That Lukács employed these legends, whether he consciously recognized them as such or not, is, on the other hand, hard to dispute. In 1936, for instance, Lukács quoted Stalin's address to the seventeenth congress. Could one maintain, Stalin had asked, that all the residual influences of capitalism had been eradicated in the economy? That could not be stated, he answered himself, and there was even less justification for claiming that the residual influences of capitalism in the consciousness of the people had been overcome. "That cannot be said not just because the consciousness of the people in its development lags behind the economic situation but also because the capitalist world around us still exists, and it is out to animate and maintain the survivals of capitalism in the economy and in the consciousness of the people in the Sovet Union. Against this surrounding world we Bolsheviki must always keep our powder dry."[80]

Stalin's words are a variation of what has been called his "central strategic *motto*, the very heart of Stalinist strategy": classes would disappear "not by means of a lessoning of class conflict but by means of its intensification"; the state would wither away "not through weakening state power but through a maximum strengthening of the state in order to defeat the remnants of the dying class and to organize a defense against capitalist encirclement."[81] In a land in which there were supposedly no real enemies out in the open left to fight and in which, as it transpired on 25 November 1936, socialism had been "essentially achieved,"[82] Stalin's incessant talk about capitalist encirclement and various residual influences within the consciousness of Soviet citizens was his backhanded justification for the coming terror. Whereas Lenin, however explicit he may have been on the use of coercive violence,[83] was fairly clear that terror was used out of weakness, not strength, Stalin contrived the rationale—as the blood purges and terror approached its zenith—that the class struggle sharpened further as the country approached closer to full socialism.[84] On the other hand, Stalin's obsession with remnants and residues of bourgeois consciousness also relied in part on Lenin's remarks that "when the old society dies, the corpse of bourgeois society cannot be nailed down in a coffin and put in the grave. It decomposes in our midst, this corpse rots and contaminates us."[85] The main difference between Lenin and Stalin in this question lay in the latter's estimation of the potential that these "bourgeois residual influences" supposedly had to inflict serious damage on the state and in Stalin's use of the contrived rationale of "capitalist encirclement" to criminalize a "faulty consciousness." Existence was supposed to shape consciousness in a Communist society, but evidently not in Stalin's Russia and not really for Lukács either.

Now Lukács may actually have convinced himself, as he later contended, that his citations from Stalin's speeches were a meaningless decoration to trick the censors and get into print, that he never made any concessions to Stalinist categories of thought. Lukács also never assumed that class consciousness would transform itself into a mature reflection of the new social reality promptly upon the successful execution of a proletarian revolution. On this point he agreed with Lenin's idea about the rotting corpse of a dead society. But it is hard to argue that Lukács' use of Stalin's speech in 1934 served merely decorative purposes. Lukács' approach to Soviet literature was a clearly recognizable variation of the Stalinist myth that the class struggle intensified as the country advanced toward full socialism. Stalin's remarks at the seventeenth congress were significant for Lukács because he claimed the struggle for objectivity in art, which for him was preeminently a question of form, to be part of the battle "against capitalist residues in the consciousness of the people."[86] These issues were by no means exclusively aesthetic ones for Lukács. In 1934 his insistence that the struggle had to be directed against the "ideological encirclement" of socialist construction by rotting monopoly capitalism represented his contribution to the encirclement or siege mentality nurtured and manipulated by Stalin along with his constant appeals for vigilance with regard to agents of the class enemy operating on Soviet soil. "We are dealing . . . with *hostile* ideologies, with different subspecies of menshevism, Trotskyism, and so on," Lukács said, which exploited "the insufficient clarity, this confusion in our praxis, this inadequate steadfastness and resoluteness in our literary theory in order to locate ideological footholds for themselves along this front."[87]

These problems bore directly on the tasks of creative literature, argued Lukács, and could only be resolved on the basis of a correct world view. The role of ideology had to be taken extremely seriously in the literature of the socialist epoch, a literature that mirrored the development of "a *new kind of man.*" More than just the writer's own world view was involved; the ideology of literary heroes was equally crucial, for one of the central questions of "our literature," said Lukács, was to portray adequately the figure of the Bolshevik, which meant above all else that writers acquire the revolutionary theory of communism.[88] Lukács was exploring here the same question that he had first touched upon in his review of Mikhail Sholokov five years before, criticizing the Soviet writer for not placing himself in a position to trace the Cossacks' transitional path from "the elemental," that is from spontaneity, "to consciousness." Lukács found it more opportune in 1936 to take the Stachanovite movement rather than the Cossacks as an example, presumably because Stalin's address to the "first allunion congress of Stachanovites" just a few months earlier had been carried in all the papers.

The Stachanovite movement, Stalin had said, arose to a certain extent "by itself, almost spontaneously, from below," without any pressure whatever from the management of the factories.[89] This popular initiative was a sign of the times; it had broken through to the surface because of a radical improvement in the material well-being of the workers. "Life is better, Comrades, life is gayer."[90] New people, new times, new work norms—this was the logical progression of Stalin's thought.

Lukács took the cue, repeated the substance of Stalin's characterization of the Stachanovite movement, and applied it to a
theory of literature that called for the avoidance of "subjective"
literary forms because, being themselves a reflection of the disequilibrium of capitalist society, they were incapable of representing fluid processes in their totality. Mass movements like
that of the Stachanovites, Lukács explained, witnessed to the
tremendous development of millions of laborers from mere
spontaneity, or unconscious spontaneity alone, to consciousness, and creative literature did its characters and its readers a
grave disservice if it only reflected the last conscious result or
counterposed the final product with the backwardness characteristic of the new man at the start of his transitional process.
"If the new man is not represented in the process of his evolution, then he cannot be adequately represented at all."[91]

But there was another side to character portrayal: the depiction of the class enemy, who was growing more brazen and aggressive with each passing day. Formal problems intruded
themselves here. Lukács had warned that enemy ideologies—
"subspecies" of menshevism, Trotskyism, idealism, subjectivism—lurked behind modern art forms, and the prevalence of
such forms impinged upon the possibilities for an adequate
portrayal of the class enemy. Stalin had often noted that the
further advance of socialism obliged the class enemy, who was
being beaten back further and further, to come up with ever
new and cleverer forms of resistance to the construction of socialism—thus read Lukács' restatement of Stalin's "motto."
The more complicated, well-disguised, and clever the methods
of resistance used by the class enemy, the more important it
was to work out in literature the "intellectual physiognomy of
the class enemy."[92] This would only be possible if Soviet writers rid themselves of the residual influences of a bourgeois consciousness, became schooled Marxist-Leninists, and thus made
proper use of historically correct literary forms. In this and
many other respects, Lukács was in complete agreement with
Stalin, who said three weeks before the first show trial began in
August 1936 that "the inalienable quality of every Bolshevik
under present conditions should be the ability to recognize an
enemy of the Party no matter how well he may be masked."[93]

"TWO AND TWO MAKE FIVE"
OR "SLAVERY IS FREEDOM"

Lukács' preoccupation with the remnants of capitalism in the consciousness of the new Soviet man—which in literature meant tracking down leftover traces of menshevism, Trotskyism, and an assortment of other "isms" in the formal techniques of Soviet writers—reached its climax in the last of his lengthy articles published in Soviet exile. Appearing at the end of the bloodiest wave of terror from 1936 to 1938, "Volkstribun oder Bürokrat?" was steeped in the mentality of the purges. It may have been too early in 1934 for Lukács' loose talk about menshevism and Trotskyism in reference to Soviet writers who employed styles that he rejected to conjure up images of Black Marias stopping in front of Soviet apartment buildings in the early hours of the morning.[94] But by the time he wrote this particular article in late 1938, his warnings about "bureaucracy" in Soviet literature were more or less akin to articulate Stalinist entreaties to be on the lookout for modes of thought and writing contrary to bolshevism.[95]

In "Volkstribun oder Bürokrat?" Lukács availed himself of the same kind of rhetorical legerdemain that he had been resorting to since the early essays published in the *Moskauer Rundschau*. To paraphrase Czeslaw Milosz, Lukács first introduced and defined all the concepts on his terms and proceeded from there to take the contradictions and conclusions suggested by these concepts to be inherent in the real social material that he claimed to be analyzing.[96] But the "social material" in 1938 was that of a terrorized and intimidated populace. In saner times Lukács' kind of theoretical reasoning would have been relatively harmless, but, apparently unperturbed by the implications of his theory in an age of wanton terror, Lukács' callous, scholastic nonchalance about the relationship between his writing and what was happening around him caused him to trip over his own intellectual acrobatics.

Lukács' main point in "Volkstribun oder Bürokrat?" was the same Leninist tension between consciousness and spontaneity (or bolshevism versus Social Democracy) that had provided him with the context for his work at least since *Geschichte*

und Klassenbewusstsein and *Lenin.* In *Was tun?* Lukács explained, Lenin had reviled the opportunistic theory of the
"economists," who chose to attribute a much higher level of
importance to the spontaneity of the workers in their reactions
to economic deprivation and who thus minimized the significance of the "conscious revolutionary." Lenin proved that
"economism" distracted the proletariat from the political
struggle for the collapse of capitalism; in working out the ideological principles of a Marxist party and stigmatizing the bourgeois essence of reformism, Lenin had counterposed two types
of ideologues: the revolutionary tribune and the bureaucrat.
"Bureaucratization"—for Lukács a synonym for trade union-
ism, economism, opportunism, and so on—equaled spontaneity. Spontaneity meant cognitively that the object of interest
and activity was immediate and only immediate. This "theory,"
the ideological apotheosis of bureaucratization, demanded a
confinement to the surface reality of this immediate object and
branded anything going beyond it, which alone distinguished
genuine theory from "theory" in quotation marks, as inauthen-
tic and false.[97]

The true profundity of Lenin's criticism of the theory of
spontaneity, Lukács went on, disclosed itself only during the
age of mature imperialism. For the appeal to spontaneity and
the apotheosis of the immediate surface reality of social phenomena, at the expense of any effort to penetrate the real essence, was a major cultural and ideological aim in the age of
imperialism. "The more firmly the people's cerebral and emotional strivings remain imprisoned in the pitiful abstract dungeon of spontaneity, the greater is the ruling class's security."[98]
This pertained mostly to the labor movement, but also held
true in cultural life because all expressions of spontaneity, even
if they were originally triggered by subjective acts of rebellion
against the system, coalesced objectively with the overall
scheme to maintain the ruling regime in power. The key to es-
caping from the vicious circle of inadvertent assistance to the
very system that incurred the wrath of the workers lay in the
acquisition of a proper consciousness.

The herald of this revolutionary consciousness was the
Leninist popular tribune, and Lenin himself had set an ex-

ample by placing genuine revolutionary spontaneity, a legitimate component of the labor movement as a whole, in proper relation to "conscious awareness" (*Bewusstheit*) so as to grasp legitimate revolutionary spontaneity as really nothing other than "the embryonic form of purposeful consciousness."[99] The role of the popular tribune was to bring this consciousness to life. The champions of a cheap form of spontaneity, on the other hand, confined themselves to ascertaining accomplished facts and brought up the "tail end" of the real movement. Their activity remained barren, a bureaucratic registration ("bureaucratic in the most general and vile sense of the word, as an encumbrance to a vigorous development"), unaffected by whatever enthusiastically "revolutionary" or "proletarian" sounds they might give off.[100]

Herein lay the significance of spontaneity for the ruling class; the extension of spontaneity to bureaucracy enhanced its general effect as a stabilizing, socializing factor in society. Habit (*Gewöhnung*) in capitalism signified stupefaction. Perceiving capitalist spontaneity to be in the natural and normal order of things and reacting to its expressions much as they would to familiar unpredictable natural events like a thundershower or heatwave, the people became "habituated to capitalist inhumanity."[101] Contributing to this general process of socialization and accustoming the masses to the status quo were the writers, who played an important pacifying role by coating daily reality with a tasteful, aesthetic veneer. Intoxication and stupefaction were thus the general spiritual characteristics of the process by which the masses were inured to the horrible inhumanity of declining capitalism, and the class interests of the bourgeoisie demanded that art provide them. Lukács concluded that such sterile intoxication was not just a secondary phenomenon to the dullness of habit; rather, it actually strengthened the worst aspects of habit. In this way the art of decadence flowed into the stream whose waters were supposed to shield the endangered citadels of imperialism from the outrage of the working people—regardless of what individual artists might have intended. "In the spontaneous embryos that produce this kind of art, an honest oppositional intent may well be present on occasion. But being mired in spontaneity and then extolling it theoretically and critically permit no other development than that of a monotonous and barren alternation between intoxication and stupefaction."[102]

From these general "Leninist" premises, Lukács proceeded to draw various inferences bearing upon Soviet reality, for bureaucratism, it transpired, existed in the USSR as well. Adapting his remarks to the main Stalinist myth of the thirties, Lukács said that he who thought the battle to be at a complete end with the extermination of the enemy overlooked the complexity of reality. It was sufficient to recall the criticism of bureaucracy that Stalin and Kaganovich had voiced at the seventeenth congress, and Lukács drew the natural conclusion: "The extermination of bureaucratism is thus part of Stalin's [*das Stalinsche*] program for the liquidation of the economic and ideological survivals of capitalist society."[103]

Of course bureaucratism assumed different shapes in the USSR, Lukács went on; under capitalism it was indispensable as a means of maintaining the establishment in power. In a socialist society, on the other hand, the bureaucratic remnants of capitalism, with their spontaneous side effects, were completely out of place and their pernicious nature was reinforced by the influence of the capitalist encirclement of the Soviet Union combined with the well-planned activity of enemies of socialism. Whether individual bureaucrats were subjectively honest was beside the point; objectively bureaucratism was aid to the enemy because it produced a wall behind which the foe could comfortably hide and readily maneuver and because the bureaucratic handling of problems, even in the absence of evil intent, retarded the economic and cultural progress of socialism. In contrast to the capitalist world, however, which consciously nurtured spontaneity in all its forms, socialism and the further flowering of democracy in the USSR brought a "countermovement" into play against bureaucratism; "the state, the Communist party, and the social organizations wage a conscious struggle for its liquidation."[104]

Lukács might well have appended the Peoples Commissariat for Internal Affairs, the NKVD, to his list of institutions concerned with the "liquidation" of spontaneity, but even without direct mention of the secret police it is difficult to justify giving Lukács any benefit of the doubt about the nature of the threats implied in "Volkstribun oder Bürokrat?" Stalin's entreaties in 1934 in those sections of his speech to the seventeenth congress mentioned by Lukács, when the mass terror was perhaps still only a gleam in Stalin's eye, are worth repeating here. Inveighing against bureaucrats and "office inhabitants" who had developed the knack of paying lip service to party resolutions but ignoring these in practice (his remarks were punctuated by interjections of "quite right" and repeated applause from an audience already living on borrowed time), Stalin emphasized that the struggle to overcome these difficulties required better organization. The party needed purging from such "unreliable, vacillating, degenerate elements."[105] He went on to ask whether the resolutions of administrative organizations would be carried out or disabled by bureaucrats. Would they be correctly enacted or distorted? Was the *apparat* really working in Bolshevist fashion or merely spinning its wheels?[106]

The step from suggestions of bureaucratic torpidity to charges of intentional wrecking and sabotage was plainly a small one. True, Lukács can scarcely be expected to have gleaned the direction of Stalin's impulses from his speech in 1934; but Lukács wrote "Volkstribun oder Bürokrat?" at a time when the psychological and political landscape in the Soviet Union was clear to him, at least according to his later descriptions of his own general political awareness in those years. So unless the myths of Stalinism had in fact completely deadened Lukács to Soviet reality, the real Soviet reality and not the one referred to in the party and government press, he must have had at least some inkling that a theory calling for bureaucratic remnants of capitalism to be hunted down and liquidated, and for "spontaneity" to be stifled by a "class consciousness" imposed by the party, helped exacerbate the already acute atmosphere of mistrust and hysteria that accompanied the purges. Given the practical connotations of such a theory, Lukács' capacity for analyzing the essence of Stalinism many years later without admitting to a trace of moral responsibility for it, even claiming the status of a contributor to a sort of anti-Stalinist counterculture, is remarkable. Stalin's method, Lukács wrote in 1962, aimed at "*an atmosphere of perpetual mutual mistrust*, at vigilance exercised with respect to every citizen; it is the feeling of a permanent siege condition."[107]

By 1938 the imperatives of survival had evidently contributed to the formation of a certain finesse in Lukács at foreseeing the potential usage of his theories to discredit him politically. He thus became adept at finding the rhetorical means to incapacitate possible criticism before it was voiced. If capitalism automatically gave rise to "spontaneity" for the purpose of retaining power and, by means of the encirclement of the USSR, sponsored similar tendencies within Soviet frontiers, and if socialism engendered a reflex countermovement against bureaucratism, then perhaps this natural response was itself a spontaneous phenomenon. Perhaps all these expressions of "automatism" guaranteed that the further development of socialism could be left to the laws of history. Here the Stalinist dictum that the class struggle intensified as socialism reached higher plateaus of development came into play, and Lukács fitted it seamlessly into "Volkstribun oder Bürokrat?" in the form of another reference to Stalin's keynote address at the seventeenth congress.

In a concretization of Lenin's doctrine of spontaneity and consciousness that was "as original as it is profound," said Lukács, Stalin had applied that doctrine to the question of the withering away of the state and demonstrated that any attempt to view this as a "spontaneous process" was to display lack of concern, a do-nothing attitude, and disarmament in the face of the enemy. The supporters of such a "socialistically" rejuvenated theory of spontaneity felt, Lukács quoted Stalin, "'that one could lay down one's arms and in good conscience go to sleep in expectation of the coming classless society.' Stalin showed 'that the classless society cannot come about, as it were, of its own accord. It has to be fought for and built by the efforts of all working people.'"[108] Explaining how, Lukács also quoted Stalin's key passage: "'By strengthening the organs of the dictatorship of the proletariat, broadening the class struggle, abolishing the classes, liquidating the remnants of the capitalist classes, and in battles with external and internal enemies.'"[109]

Lukács now applied these lessons to Soviet literature. In belles-lettres, too, the residual influences of capitalism could not be overlooked, and the 1936 campaign against formalism and naturalism was a case in point; the fact that these styles insinuated themselves into Soviet literature bore out claims that their "social roots" were identical to those said by Lenin and Stalin to have caused bureaucratism. "These literary styles grew out of the soil of capitalist decadence,"[110] and the naturalists and formalists of Soviet literature had taken them over from Western literature. The more adeptly they were used, the more automatically bureaucratized became the attitude of their practitioners toward questions of form, and only writers with profoundly bureaucratized, inwardly indifferent attitudes toward the form and content of the new life in the USSR could possibly desire to represent the birth of a new socialist man with the artistic methods of decadence.[111] Of course great strides had been made in Soviet literature, and generally "the development of socialism caused this type of 'literature' to disappear."[112] But those artists who had not inwardly overcome the remnants of decadence had quickly come up with new forms of antirealism, for instance, a kind of formal, empty, bureaucratic optimism. For bureaucratic optimism there existed "only results that, without exception, represent effortless victories won without any struggle. The resistance of the external enemy, the inner resistance in the people themselves, resistance that hampers the birth of the socialist man and, in individual cases, completely thwarts it, does not exist for [these optimists]."[113]

Lukács' conclusion: the Leninist contrast between the popular tribune and the bureaucrat retained its pertinence for contemporary socialist literature because capitalist encirclement and the residual influences of capitalism allowed a bureaucratizing influence on Soviet literature to persist. Six years of theoretical activity under the conditions of Stalinism had culminated for Lukács in entreaties for the cleansing of Soviet literature from "survivals of capitalism," a plaidoyer that invited political police tactics in dealing with literature; and Lukács issued his appeals with the assurance that he had every right to make them. Though he declined to put his conviction into words, Lukács surely regarded himself as a popular tribune following in the footsteps of Lenin: "As a tribune of the revolution, Lenin took up the battle against spontaneity. He succeeded in transcending immediacy[114] to acquire a clear consciousness with respect to the movement as a totality . . . on the strength of that adequate understanding which only the materialist dialectic, Marxism, makes possible."[115]

In executing his self-assignment as a popular tribune, Lukács made preposterous demands upon Soviet writers. Or had the phantasmagoria of Stalinism actually become true life for Lukács? On one side stood the triumph of socialism on 25 November 1936, the most democratic constitution in the world, and Stachanovite workers; but on the other stood capitalist encirclement, residual influences of bourgeois consciousness, bureaucratism, spontaneity, and enemies of the people; it was thus vitally necessary to liquidate all "remnants of the Bukharinite-Trotskyist spies, wreckers, and traitors,"[116] these "monsters," "scum of humanity," "wretches," and "lackeys of fascism"[117] in order to clear the way for the new homo sovieticus—did Lukács mistake this fictionalization of Soviet ideology for the actual state of affairs? "All happenings are in the mind. Whatever happens in all minds, truly happens," Orwell wrote several years later; perhaps, too, cerebrally motivated zeal was not enough in Lukács' case and his orthodoxy had eventually been absorbed into unconsciousness.[118] Perhaps in Soviet exile Lukács indeed lost the ability to distinguish Soviet fact from Stalinist fiction. If so, it may have made little difference to him at the time; for Lukács, to quote Orwell again, reality may have been "inside the skull,"[119] in which case true reality lost its meaning for Lukács because his reality originated in an imagination filled with the spectral images of Stalinism. Yet the literary portrayal of Soviet life evidently struck Lukács' aesthetic senses nonetheless as superficial and psychologically oversimplified, and he argued for a replacement of "bureaucratic optimism" with a different brand: "The unflinching contemplation of external and internal threats, the unflinching exposure of obstacles and impediments, the full understanding of dialectical contradictions that, by nonsynchronous [*ungleichmässig*] routes, bring about the final liberation of mankind, that is, the optimism of the tribune of the socialist revolution."[120]

Prima facie this sounds, at least in part, like an appeal for protest, a cry for social and political criticism. But Lukács was either utterly cynical or entirely blind to the fact that the literary representation of the "obstacles to socialism" could lead in only two possible directions: either to a writer's suicidal true-life reflection of Soviet reality in a typescript that would never have passed the first editorial reading in a Soviet press anyway, or to a depiction of divers "internal and external threats" and sundry "dialectical contradictions" along the lines of Stalin's motto about the intensified state of class warfare as socialism expanded and prospered. If Lukács was not being cynical in demanding the impossible from Soviet writers and was not, with equal cynicism, calling for the fictionalization in literature of what he knew to be a fictionalized reality already, the only remaining explanation for his arguments is the suggestion that, by 1938 at the latest, the Stalinist mystique, with all its self-certifying dogmas, had come to be identical for Lukács with what he supposed to be the true reality of Soviet life. Perhaps Lukács had genuinely "lost the power of grasping that the world," Stalin's world, "could be other than it is."[121] If so, then Lukács was playing out the same tragedy that he reserved for unwitting apologists of capitalism and fascism in the West: providing a polished veneer for an underlying inhuman reality and pacifying his readers—"habituating" them—into acceptance of the regime and its policies as an expression of lawful historical regularities. Like ideology and political theory, Soviet literature had descended to the level of an adjunct to Stalin's exercise of political power, and Lukács helped to supply the theoretical rationale for this political degradation of art.

A quarter of a century later, he came up with this seemingly guileless description of the plight of literature in Stalin's time: all the branches of science and every kind of writing was to serve exclusively the needs of political agitation decreed from above, by Stalin. Any independent perception and treatment of reality in literature became increasingly discredited, for "party-minded" literature was not supposed to reflect creatively objective reality but to illustrate in literary form the resolutions of the party.[122] As true as this is, how Lukács' crusade against "spontaneity" and all that he had been subsuming for years under that rubric provided the theoretical underpinnings for a different, non-Stalinist brand of literature, an anti-Stalinist counterculture, was a secret that Lukács took with him to the grave.[123]

The Dialectic of Reality

When German troops approached the outskirts of Moscow in late 1941, the writers' union evacuated Soviet and exiled German writers from the capital. Lukács traveled first to Kazan and then to Tashkent, where he began work on a new study of National Socialist ideology.[1] Eight years had elapsed since his last book on German fascism, and the dialectic of reality in Germany had not unfolded quite as Lukács had predicted in 1933. The inherently disintegrative tendencies of fascism had not precipitated severe economic dislocation, nor had the "glaring contradiction between the promises of the fascists and their practical policy" (Pieck) opened the eyes of the masses to the trick played on them. There had been no economic collapse, no spontaneous outbreak of popular unrest, no proletarian revolution, no Soviet Germany modeled after the system in the USSR. Contrary to Lukács' expectations, National Socialism had lost none of its vitality, and the masses still backed Hitler, it seemed, to the hilt. The opening campaign of the war in Russia had especially shocked German Communists living in Soviet exile with graphic evidence of the inadequacies of their own theory. True, the party had always insisted that Hitler meant war, and, once they had recovered from the initial surprise of the invasion, the Communists fitted it easily into their schema as the Great Patriotic War of the Fatherland. What the theory simply did not allow for was the spectacle of the soldier-sons of the German working class firing on the Workers' and Peasants' Red Army.[2]

These considerations obliged Lukács to take a second look at his own theory, and the modifications that he introduced disclose several aftereffects of popular front thinking. That policy, originally sanctioned by Stalin and carried out by the Comintern, had been put to rest by 1939 at the latest. The Communists, however, never really detached themselves officially from the acknowledged aims and objectives of a popular front and blamed its collapse on a combination of Social Democratic obstinacy, anti-Communist hysteria, and Western duplicity in ignoring the Soviet interest in collective security and trying to strike a separate bargain with Hitler. But many of the popularized ideals of the policy remained valid for the Communists anyhow, even (though more dormantly so) during the years of the Hitler-Stalin pact. They then resurfaced, slightly altered, with the outbreak of war and formation of the alliance. But history had taught the Communists certain lessons. It was generally recognized that the pursuit of ideological-programmatic aims like proletarian revolution and dictatorship, that is, goals patterned after the tactics of the twenties and early thirties, would only isolate the Communists from the mainstream of antifascism. "Democracy," first substituted for proletarian dictatorship during the popular front era, was now the height of the Communists' public ambition, and they remained its indefatigable advocates throughout the war.

THE LAND OF POETS AND THINKERS

Lukács had evidently been sure by the later thirties that the popular front was an appropriate political strategy congruent with the logic of history, and he never seems to have taken it for a mere political expedient. His 1942 study of National Socialism, with the ungainly title *Wie ist Deutschland zum Zentrum der reaktionären Ideologie geworden?*,[3] bears out the contention that the basic propositions of the popular front, along with the shock of war, had caused Lukács to rethink the debacle of 1933. There are certainly no direct indications in the manuscript that he now looked upon his previous ultimatum "fascism or bolshevism" as a grievous mistake; but the book reveals that Lukács had modified his views, and his silence in 1942 about his earlier obdurate opinions and erroneous predictions might be just another case of his refusal to acknowledge his own (and the party's) past illusions once they had finally burst. Besides, any admission of theoretical errors in his understanding of fascism in 1933 would have implied at least an abstract acceptance of personal accountability for the consequences of those errors, and Lukács habitually shirked the responsibility for his theories when the dialectic of reality failed to confirm his assumptions about the necessities of the historical process.

Lukács' adjustments in 1942 still left the vital conceptions of his earlier theory of fascism intact: the spontaneous bitterness of the masses arising out of the personal deprivation that they had experienced because of the economic crisis begat a form of inchoate anticapitalism and made them receptive to the social demagogy of the fascists. Lukács' conclusion: "The masses . . . sensed so profoundly the lack of solutions and prospects for the future inherent in their situation that they reached out to grasp at any straw offering them the slightest hope of immediate salvation."[4] The "mythos" of fascism promptly exploited their hopelessness in order to trick them into supporting the annihilation of all revolutionary organizations and institutions. It is easy to spot Lukács' old theory of gullibility in these general elaborations, but the simple explanation that the naive masses were frantically grasping at straws in 1933 left as many questions unanswered in 1942 as it had when Lukács first aired the idea eight years earlier. In 1933, after all, the masses had a choice. Why, then, had it proven impossible to disabuse them of the notion that Hitler meant salvation and to educate them to the nature of a brazen form of deception whose murderous objectives could be summed up in the Communist press or in Lukács' writings in a few choice sentences? The "instinct which makes man revolt against a reasonable explanation of all phenomena" was indeed mysterious to Lukács,[5] so he discarded the problem of why the masses overlooked the Communist party when they truly longed for an anticapitalist revolution without indicating that the question even existed.

It is true that Lukács' selective reasoning can be treated to a limited extent as implicit criticism of earlier political tactics, and it is senseless to look for or expect an admission by Lukács in 1942 that he had shared the party's illusions in the early thirties. But his later habit of glossing over his personal support of past ill-starred policies and defending himself by taking the offensive is a different matter altogether. His liberal views on political tactics could be traced from the "democratic dictatorship" of the Blum theses to the antisectarian concept of "revolutionary democracy" in the popular front, he said; moreover, he had always opposed Stalin's theory of social fascism.[6] But Lukács' judgments from 1931 to 1935, his entire political and literary theoretical outlook and attitude in these specific years, belies this particular legend and casts an exceptionally harsh light on his retrospective criticism of policies that he had once supported politically and legitimized theoretically. In 1946, to take just one example, Lukács was a vocal advocate of "democracy" as the only way of eradicating fascism, and he issued passionate warnings against erecting barriers between "Eastern and Western democracy," between bourgeois culture and socialism. But he never indicated that he personally had once participated in the erection of such "barriers" or analyzed the reasons why. These false dilemmas from the prewar years now needed to be done away with, he concluded. "The false dilemma of fascism or bolshevism contributed immensely to the ideological weakening of the progressive forces prior to the war."[7]

Though Lukács' sociohistorical analysis of fascism may have remained basically the same in 1942, he now had to address a complex of key questions somewhat differently. Foremost among them was the issue of mass German collaboration in the crimes of fascism. Lukács now came out strongly against the "mechanically crude distinction" that had been made for years between fascism and the German people. Any outlook that regarded the Germans as having fallen under the sway of a small, tyrannical clique was mistaken; the land of poets and thinkers had degenerated into a nation caught up in organized and systematic barbarity (21). Continuing differentiations between the fascists and the Germans led straight to an erroneous perception of fascism, "as if the adventurer Hitler had succeeded by some sort of trickery in impelling himself into power and then retaining his hold on power by despotic means" (22–23).

This erroneous perception, of course, was the basic argument that Lukács and the party had adhered to for many years, but certain realities and various dogmas that conflicted with them compelled Lukács in 1942 to harmonize two essentially irreconcilable points of view. Ten years of National Socialism and

German troops just outside Moscow brought home to him the fact that his treatment of the Germans in 1933 and his forecast for the immediate future had treated the people too benevolently. Nevertheless, Lukács still had to be mindful not to regard the Germans collectively as being altogether indistinguishable from the fascists because this opposite extreme violated his own convictions and, perhaps equally important, contradicted a prime component of Stalin's German propaganda. In his army decrees of 23 February and 6 November 1942,[8] Stalin had warned about the dangers of permitting the battle against Hitlerism to degenerate into a struggle against the German people as a whole, said Lukács. Should that happen, an incorrect, mechanically crude distinction between Hitler and all currents present in the German people would then be replaced by an even more mistaken identification of fascism and the Germans.[9]

BEFORE THE COURT OF HISTORY

There was thus comparatively little leeway available to Lukács to explain the grass-roots support of National Socialism. He had to locate explanations situated somewhere between the polar extremes of collective guilt and mass coercion, but he was plagued continually by the inescapable logic of his arguments, for these all tended to carry him alternatively in the direction of one vexing extreme or the other. Lukács' starting point was his view of Hitler's subjugation of the Germans as a "factor of their historical destiny" (24–25). The problem with this approach, apart from Lukács' queer use of the fascistized term *destiny* (*Schicksal*), was its inherent allusion to the inexorable workings of historical laws. It implied that the German people had finally ended up in the place that history had reserved for them—on a garbage heap of brutal reaction and bloody fascism. But Lukács did not believe this himself, even though he was seemingly mesmerized by the development of reactionary trends in German intellectual history, and this particular interpretation conflicted with Stalin's distinctions between the German people and Hitler. If history had somehow decided beforehand that the Germans as a nation were to play the role of global reactionaries and fascists, what was left of Stalin's periodic reminders that the Soviet Union waged war against "the fascists," not the German people, and that the Hitlers came and went, whereas the German people and the German nation remained?[10]

Lukács tried to settle on some middle ground. He pursued a number of general points about the German road to fascism with an eye to freeing his theory of the implication that a binding, inflexible logic was in force while he concurrently and often contradictively analyzed National Socialism as a natural outcome of many quintessentially German philosophical and political trends. Lukács saw the contradiction and tried to extricate himself from the impasse by denying that he believed in historical necessity with respect to fascism. To perceive a certain phase of national development as a facet of a people's historical destiny by no means signaled recognition of a fatalistic necessity, he pointed out. "For, above all, there are junctions in the history of every nation, historical crossroads at which the destiny of the coming years, sometimes even decades, is settled upon by way of the struggle of class forces, by way of the back-and-forth grappling between tendencies and countertendencies within the people" (23–24).

Lukács' explanation makes some sense from a Marxist perspective, but it raised the familiar question that Lukács steadfastly refused to address: was 1933 such a historical crossroads or the logical culmination of several decades of essentially prearranged development? At what point, in other words, were the Communists no longer historically capable of altering a set course of events, excused by history, so to speak, from any responsibility for a series of social and political occurrences whose outcome was a foregone conclusion anyway and compelled to await the next opportunity when history would arrive at a "juncture"? In 1933 Lukács had spoken unambiguously of a fork in the road, which he called "fascism or bolshevism"; that being the case, why had the masses selected fascism? Lukács suggested a variety of reasons to explain their choice, but all of his explanations are single-faceted. He accounted for the attractiveness of fascism to the masses as a consequence of decades of an ideological and political culturalization process that

climaxed under the favorable conditions of the specific historical situation existing around 1933. Lukács wrote, then, as if
the people were really powerless in 1933 to do other than embrace fascism because of a combination of irresistible demagogy and the various intractabilities of the economic crisis. But
the implications of his theory placed Lukács right back in the
mainstream of arguments pointing toward inescapable necessity and undermining his idea of historical crossroads. The triumph of reactionary barbarity in Germany was by no means a
historical coincidence, Lukács went on to argue; it was no mere
misfortune that befell the German people from out of the blue;
rather, fascism was the outgrowth of an important trend of German political and ideological development (35).

At this point Lukács seems to have maneuvered himself into
a blind alley, which may explain why he concentrated most of
his attention in 1942 on developments after the Nazi accession
to power and not to any exploration of the crossroads of 1933.
His basic theory for the years after 1933 reads as follows: "Once
a decision has been settled upon at such a turning point (and
such a decision is never coincidental), then there follows the
necessary consummation of certain tendencies that must remain predominant for a shorter or longer period of time. The
struggle between tendencies and countertendencies then plays
itself out, though by now under more or less radically changed
conditions, and it is entirely possible that years can pass before
a new turn again becomes possible on the basis of objective
circumstances" (24–25). The danger now, he warned, was that
historical development might again place Germany in a situation offering objectively advantageous conditions for a democratic renewal and catch "the subjective factor" off guard.
"Being prepared is of the utmost urgency; this also goes for
politics and cultural politics" (37).

Now this particular explanation may actually be Lukács'
cautious way of smuggling a note of criticism about former policy into his manuscript. His reference to the "subjective factor"
that might (again?) fail to prepare itself adequately in advance
to deal with a historical turning point may be an insinuation
that the Communist party had been ill-prepared the last time
around. However that may be, this conceivable criticism fails
to affect the substance of Lukács' version of why the masses

were so easily taken in by National Socialist demagogy, and, pursuing his theory, Lukács again ensnared himself in contradictions. Working within the circular arguments of interrelated dogmas, Lukács somehow had to modify his theory of 1933 to account for Hitler's mass backing. For however little the party's view of National Socialism had changed otherwise, by 1942 at least some allowance had to be made for the complicity of the masses. Lukács began by arguing that fascism differed from earlier forms of terror and reaction. Whereas "white terror" after past unsuccessful revolutions was chiefly the preserve of the military and the police, assisted by certain strata of the lumpenproletariat and lumpenbourgeoisie, Hitler's "pseudo-revolutionary mass hypnosis" set itself the goal of incriminating millions of Germans in fascist barbarity. "To the shame of the German people, it must be said that the national and social demagogy of fascism achieved its ends to a far-reaching extent" (179).

The incrimination of the German people and their collusion in fascist barbarity was the new general dimension to Lukács' theory of fascism, but he still had to explain the process by which this collusion first came about. The trouble was, his efforts to bring his thinking into greater conformity with reality simply raised more questions than they answered. What historical right did Lukács have to blame the German people for Hitler, considering that they had yielded to the accumulated pressure of reactionary ideological and political trends with the momentum of decades behind them and especially if Lukács might indeed have acknowledged, however privately, the failings of Communist policy in the early thirties? If the KPD had not played its proper subjective role as the avant-garde of the proletariat and the organized form, the "visible embodiment," of proletarian class consciousness, then popular resistance to Hitler could have been spontaneous at best. Yet as Lukács interpreted the revolutionary process, spontaneous rebellions always partook of "bureaucratism" and played straight into the hands of the ruling class. According to Lukács' own central ideas, this kind of a development lay in the natural order of things, making it hard to figure out how he could use precisely this development, or lack of development, to justify in his own mind the condemnation of an entire nation.

The difficulty that Lukács encountered in his efforts to bring his theory into sharper focus with respect to the question of mass complicity sprang to a large degree from his apparent inability to grasp the human element in fascism's rise to power. He thus shifted back and forth between an account that attributed Hitler's mass following to normal human frailty and his much older view of economic and historical determinism, without ever managing to blend the two convincingly or avoid the impression that his oscillation was caused by his own confusion.[11] An illustration of the former approach was his comment that fascism ensured itself of popular support by awakening the worst instincts of petty envy, abject backbiting, latent sadistic impulses, and contemptible careerism. At the same time, fascism played on the honest but confused national and social revolutionary longings of the masses, whose misguided representatives, hypnotized by Hitler, committed the most abhorrent crimes in the belief that they were bringing about the long-cherished national renewal (179–80). In this manner Lukács counterpoised the two extremes of collective guilt and what might be called a historical accountability for fascism made less severe because of the masses' diminished capacity to assume responsibility for their own actions. But from this two-sided human explanation, which is not unreasonable, Lukács seemed to conclude after all that external coercion and repression, rather than voluntary or semivoluntary collusion, had finally tipped the scales. Fascism had fastened an iron ring around the German people; those Germans not actively involved in fascist criminality were pressured and terrorized into at least some form of personal involvement to avoid a life made unbearable in an atmosphere distinguished by unending fear of denunciation and inhuman torment.[12]

But Lukács' summation of conditions in Germany ten years after Hitler took over power then switched right back to the basic charge of complicity: "This moral corruption, which has taken over the broadest strata of the people, . . . is the specific nature of German fascism. This nature sets it apart not just quantitatively but also qualitatively from all earlier forms of white terror" (181). Even so, neither the version stressing the preponderant factor of coercive violence and terror nor the deterministic approach, explanations that restated the two polar extremes of identifying the people with fascism or separating them from it, seemed to clear up the confusion in Lukács' mind. Confronted with the element of mystery in human behavior, which eluded dialectical explanations, Lukács mixed his theories. The objectively necessary contradictions of fascism, deriving from the unbridgeable gap between demagogic proclamations of national and social renewal and the actualities of reactionary imperialist politics, could only be glossed over temporarily by keeping the masses in a state of thoughtless delirium and hypnosis (183). Still insufficient by themselves, these factors were then rounded out by the key component: "It is the Führer mythos, culminating in the redemptive personality of the Führer, that created such a general atmosphere in which this kind of credo quia absurdum was first made possible" (185).

Perhaps because his other explanations left him dissatisfied, Lukács now gave in to a certain urge to move toward a theory of fascism that hinged to a significant degree on the Führer principle. In so doing he made a complete about-face. In 1933 he had written that the pre-1933 type of Hitler would soon give way to a different type, one who would jettison the national and social rhetoric and hand over state power to monopoly capitalism. Whether this transition would involve a "personnel change" or whether Hitler himself would remain in service as a plastic wall sculpture holding a loud speaker was a question of the "twenty-fifth magnitude" (148). In 1942, at least in one passage, Lukács argued similarly. The accomplishments of fascist propaganda were unrelated to Hitler's "genius"; had Hitler not been around to do the job, some other "genius" of reaction would have stepped forward and offered his services (148). The difficulty with this archetypical Marxist-Leninist estimation of Hitler is that it fails to square with Lukács' assessment of the Führer figure elsewhere in the book. From American advertising Hitler had learned that mass suggestion was the secret and that a Wagnerian *Gesamtkunstwerk* had to come into play: "Not only the internal components of propaganda have to aim at suggestion and hypnosis, rather, all the atmospheric external attributes, everything auditory and visual, have to be arranged in order to place the listeners in a will-less trance in which they believe everything that they are told" (172).

This is little more than a reformulation of Lukács' old theory of gullibility, which by 1942 came across as a state of diminished capacity. The essence of fascism was to incriminate as many people as possible in Nazi atrocities, Lukács continued, and to draw them into the process of barbarization through the use of propaganda, coercion, terror, fear of denunciation, and so on. "What is peculiar to these outrageous crimes is that they are committed by people whose sense of morality and ethics has been confused by the influence exerted for many years by fascist ideology and practice, by people who are altogether unable to find their way in this chaos and who give themselves over, without resistance, to the bloody ecstasy of war propaganda" (200). This analysis is certainly not inaccurate, nor is it unconvincing from a Leninist frame of reference; a key principle of Leninism held that the intelligentsia introduced class consciousness to the masses from the outside, and—in support of his theory of the popular tribune in his 1939 essay—Lukács had quoted Lenin's remarks to the effect that a revolutionary consciousness was inculcated in the workers outside the boundaries of the economic struggle between laborers and owners. The formation or consolidation of class consciousness on the basis of the economic process itself was excluded as a possibility, Lenin said, and Lukács elaborated: "The embryo of spontaneity yields fruit . . . only through conscious work. . . . The tribune awakens this conscious awareness."[13] From this angle Lukács' reference to the years of fascist influence on the masses makes perfect sense; after 1933 there were, after all, few countervailing forces and no "popular tribunes" left in Germany. Though Lukács made no mention in his 1942 manuscript of Lenin's understanding of the origin of class consciousness, it certainly helps explain Lukács' thinking. It provides no answer, on the other hand, to the old question of what had gone wrong in the years leading up to 1933, when there should have been limitless opportunities to inculcate a proletarian class consciousness.

Delirium, incapacitation, hypnosis, mass suggestion, Führer mythos and Führer principle—at least some of these descriptions verge on the numinous or the metaphysical, and none was exactly the stock in trade of a Marxist-Leninist. But Lukács appears to have been stymied by the imponderables of human behavior. Dialectical materialism had taught him certain lessons about the world and society, but by 1942 the dialectic of reality called those lessons into question. In 1933 Lukács had predicted confidently that the fascist "solution" to problems besetting declining capitalism was actually only an exacerbation of the contradictions and an intensification inevitably leading to proletarian revolution. "The sharpening of contradictions in daily reality engenders by necessity a mountingly acute contradiction in philosophy as well," he had written in closing, adding that efforts to patch up these gaps could not retard the process: "here the empty balloon of monopoly capitalist philosophy bursts by the force of its contradictions" (272).

But for reasons that Lukács had difficulty explaining, the balloon had not burst after 1933; the logic of history had proven far more complex and elusive than Lukács had thought, and in 1942 he was obliged to seek refuge in a theory of fascism that hinged significantly upon a very non-Marxian principle of individual leadership. Ironically, his reversion to a theory in which the personality of a single human being, a savior, played an indispensable role paralleled the hypertrophy of the cult of Stalin's personality in the Soviet Union. If the leadership principle was difficult to reconcile with a Marxist analysis of monopoly capitalism in its declining era, the glorification of Stalin should have been equally incompatible with an understanding of the historical dynamic involved in the triumph of the revolution and the construction of socialism.[14] But at the eighteenth party congress in 1939, the building of a socialist society was eulogized as "the great Stalinist cause" and Stalin himself was pronounced the "genius-architect of Communism."[15] Celebrating Stalin's sixtieth birthday, Lazar Kaganovich noted that Lenin had been a great driver of the locomotive of history and that "such a great driver today is our Stalin." His great service had been to open the throttle of the locomotive still wider and keep it on the socialist tracks.[16] Today the Soviet people said to their great locomotive driver: "You have not only kept the locomotive of history on the tracks, you have increased the speed in spite of all the obstacles created by our treacherous enemies; you have brought the great train of the revolution to Socialism

Station."[17] To help explain the age in which he lived, Lukács, who believed to the day he died that "things would have been impossible without Stalin"[18] and who thus recognized the validity of a kind of Führer principle in the Soviet Union as well as in Germany, had reverted to a dichotomization and personification of the historical process.

THE STORMING OF THE BASTILLE

In assessing the measure of German national responsibility for Hitler, Lukács oscillated between the extremes of a broad partnership in crime and a form of national accountability tempered by historically extenuating circumstances; and his inability to theorize and speculate free of the fetters of constrictive dogmas that nudged him first in one direction and then in the other caused his hesitation in reflecting upon the future of the German people. The actual dimensions of popular German "countertendencies" to the fascist contamination of the masses were impossible to ascertain, he said, though this was precisely the critical question. For in the absence of antifascist impulses at a grass-roots level, the military defeats suffered by Germany would not give birth to a popular ground swell capable, either partly or entirely on the basis of its own vitality, of dislodging the Hitler regime. The task of removing the Nazi system and democratizing the nation afterwards would thus devolve exclusively upon the allies (201).[19]

Lukács then tried to enhance his speculation about the future with more concrete details leading to an eventual prognosis, but he succeeded only in raising vital questions that he was unable or unwilling to answer. For instance, given his overall evaluation of the "moral corruption" of the German people, which was understood as a mental state induced by a combination of both active and passive collusion in Nazi criminality, why think that the masses would ever rise up against Hitler? Lukács had reckoned with just such quasi-spontaneous uprisings ten years earlier, but he had been badly mistaken; and in 1942 he still stuck to a theory that relied significantly on spontaneity. Lukács' theoretical options were strictly delimited by an assortment of dogmas; he had to speak of German opposition to Hitler or come into conflict with Stalin's differentiation between the fascists and the people. But by providing for the possibility of rebellion, he had to establish some motivation for it, and his resulting explanations remained inarticulate. In Lukács' mind the internal contradictions of fascism were no longer the trigger to an uprising at all; rather, military defeats were somehow supposed to make the dormant moral sensitivity of the masses come alive. Of course, Lukács was compelled to argue approximately along these lines because any suggestion that the moral integrity of an entire nation could be obliterated entirely was out of the question for him or any Marxist. The presence of a class consciousness of some sort had to be asserted—too much was at stake ideologically to concede that the Nazis had eradicated it altogether.

Lukács' notion of the rejuvenation of class consciousness, however, rested on simple wishful thinking. "It is the defeats of the fascist armies in the war against the Soviet Union that have finally begun to pick apart this [fascist] mythos and cause an awakening among ever growing segments of the masses," Lukács said, but his optimism sprang from a fiction: "Letters from the front and from the homeland and the statements of POWs show clearly how this process of differentiation, however slowly and contradictively, is going forward among ever growing segments of the masses" (183). Lukács appears to have believed that this process was actually occurring;[20] most of the other German exiles apparently did also, though Lukács admitted to a measure of uncertainty. Just how many blows the Hitler regime would still endure before definite strata of German society began to resist the regime and shake off the fascist yoke no one could tell for sure (201).

For Lukács, this revolt, when and if it came, would evidently not reflect mere popular discontent with a losing war; rather, Lukács expected the military defeats somehow to instill new life into deadened feelings of class consciousness. But Lukács was apparently not unmindful of his mistakes in 1933 and refused to give in completely to an overly easy optimism. He came out instead on both sides of the issue. Just as he had wavered in his assessment of the German people, he now vacillated between certainty that a popular uprising was only a matter of time and general pessimism about its prospects for

ever occurring. German history, he said, offered few assurances
that Germany would be able to liberate itself from fascism on
the strength of its own efforts (201). Social progress, after all,
had usually occurred in Germany's past only as the consequence of lost wars. Napoleon's defeat of the Prussian army at
Jena and the end of the monarchy in World War I were just two
examples of Mehring's sardonic reference to the way the Germans stormed the Bastille. Having expressed his pessimism,
however, Lukács quickly reverted to a more optimistic analysis. A third such military catastrophy was brewing, and the Germans were developing a growing awareness that the defeat was
unavoidable. Everything depended now, he wrote, on whether
the "growing dissatisfaction" with Hitlerism and the "growing
outrage" in Germany at fascist barbarity would crest in a
"genuine" inward storming of the Bastille.[21] In any event, the
third storming of the Bastille, by which Lukács understood the
military collapse of the Hitler regime with or without the help
of the masses, was unavoidable. Germany could not continue
to resist the combined might of all "freedom loving peoples"
and the military alliance of the most powerful nations in the
world (202–3).

DEMOCRACY

Lukács' inability to settle on the exact nature of German mass
complicity in fascist crimes carried over to his prognosis of the
future German state. Hitler's demise would presumably mean a
democratic regime, though the extent of this democracy and its
specific attributes would hinge on the circumstances and forces,
internal and external, that brought the transformation about
(205–6). For the future, one of the most urgent tasks was to
begin laying a solid ideological foundation for a large-scale
democratic reclamation of the German mentality "on the basis
of its own internal strength" (206). This restoration process presupposed a general awareness that the predominant ideological
currents of the last several decades were dangerous and misguided. Whether the Germans would arrive at this recognition,
even after Hitler's defeat, was impossible to say for sure. Much
depended upon the level of participation "by inner German

forces" in the "third storming of the Bastille." The greater the German involvement in that process, however, the more favorable for the formation of a German democratic world view. "But even in the most advantageous case," Lukács warned, "under no circumstance can such a turnabout happen by itself and *under no circumstances entirely spontaneously*" (210).

How did the Communists figure in Lukács' vision of the future? His reference to the limitations of spontaneity indicates, not surprisingly, that he reserved a pivotal role for them in the process of democratization; his description of party involvement, though, is extremely vague. Perhaps this was deliberately so. Stalin's postwar policy throughout Eastern Europe originally downplayed programs of an orthodox Marxist-Leninist nature in the hope of installing the Communists in the forefront of a broad popular movement for antifascism and "democracy." Marxist-Leninists, said Lukács, citing Dimitrov's address to the seventh world congress in 1935, were responsible for convincing the German people that democracy ought to be a vital national concern. Lukács added that if they wished to play an influential part in a popular democratic crusade, the Communists needed to persuade the masses and the intelligentsia that the doctrine of Marx and Engels was inextricably intertwined with the struggle for the democratic liberation of Germany. The people had to be brought to an appreciation of Marx and Engels as outstanding figures of "*German history*" and the development of "*German* democratism," regardless of the internationalism of their ideas (217).

Lenin's name and Stalin's too were conspicuously absent from Lukács' remarks; nor did he make any mention of the Soviet Union. Pursuing this unabashedly nationalist line of argument, Lukács was already anticipating postwar Stalinist policy in Eastern Europe. Again acting out his role as a self-appointed popular tribune, he was promoting a new policy "for the masses" and equipping it with the necessary theoretical adjunct. But Lukács was also on the verge of making the same kind of blunder that he had committed repeatedly in earlier years. Just as in 1930 and 1931, he again appears to have taken the official theoretical facade hiding political expedience for the articulation of historically necessary modifications of party policy. Lukács once more misjudged the dynamics of Stalinism.

He misinterpreted Stalin's determination to ensure Soviet influence in Eastern Europe as the substance of historical necessity. From 1945 to 1948 in Hungary, Lukács acted as a tribune
for people's democracy, apparently not realizing that the modalities of Stalin's democracy were not what the party claimed they
were. In 1948, then, with the onset of the cold war and with
political power in the Eastern European people's democracies
more or less in the hands of local Communists, Georgi
Dimitrov pronounced these "democracies of a new type" to be
basically identical with proletarian dictatorship after all.[22]

   This turn of events actually seems to have taken Lukács by
surprise, and before long he and the party reenacted the familiar ritual. The Hungarian Stalinists Josef Révai, László Rudas,
and Márton Horváth accused Lukács of a "right deviation"—he
had, they said, downplayed the role of the dictatorship of the
proletariat in people's democracy.[23] Lukács hastily backed down
and renounced his "faulty" views. His 1971 version of these
events, by the way, is about as accurate as many of the other
tales that fill the pages of his autobiography. His account of the
"Rudas debate" (the attacks on Lukács in 1949 began with the
criticism by Rudas) reads as follows. Since the Blum theses,
Lukács contended, he had adhered to an uninterrupted line to
which he was never untrue. Initially, Mátyás Rákosi and his
people accepted this in the sense that they tolerated it; and no
one needed to think, Lukács went on, that his ideology was
ever understood by anyone as official ideology. At the end of his
article, Révai had also mentioned the Blum theses as the original cause of Lukács' mistakes. "And this entire debate proves
that the dictatorship that broke out in the fifties had been a
dictatorship from the beginning"; it was not true that it had
been preceded by a period of democracy.[24]

   Of course the dictatorship that "broke out" in the early
fifties had been a dictatorship all along, if only a latent one for
the first three or four years, that is, one that increased its dos-
age of coercion gradually to make the erosion of political pluralism and popular self-determination appear less evident. But
why had Lukács entertained any illusions about the ulterior
motives of common Stalinists in the first place? Why did he
take Rákosi or Ulbricht seriously when they spoke so passionately of democracy? Lukács actually believed in the intrinsic

worth of people's democracy as a theoretically correct policy; in this respect he was not untrue to his understanding of a democratic dictatorship in 1928 and revolutionary democracy in the thirties. At the time he by no means regarded the Eastern European democracies as political shams calculated to provide the Communists with an initial foothold on power, and he quickly helped ground the political concept in theory in his immediate postwar writings. In his view, he said in his autobiography, and this view went back to the Blum theses, people's democracy was a form of socialism that grew out of democracy. According to the other standpoint, he added, people's democracy was a dictatorship from the very beginning; from the outset, people's democracy was intrinsically the same form of Stalinism into which it evolved after the Tito affair (188).[25]

But in 1946 and 1947 an abstract theoretical principle again appeared to mesmerize Lukács to such an extent that he overlooked the inherent potentiality for cynical abuse of the idea. Lukács' own intentions may have been ingenuous in 1945; as usual, that is extremely difficult to establish. But only three years earlier he had written that "in historical matters what counts is the objective result of an accomplished act, not the intention behind it."[26] Measuring Lukács against his own standards, it is hard to absolve him of some responsibility for having helped give the democratic masquerade from 1945 to 1948 an articulate theoretical rationale and ideological respectability. In 1946, for instance, he described the new type of democracy as the result of a countermovement called to life by fascism, a countermovement that marked the beginning of a reestablished alliance between socialism and democracy. "The battle of the nations against the fascist 'new order' sparks— admittedly on various scales in various countries—such popular countermovements, out of which crystalize the democratic forms of life for a new Europe."[27] It was vital that the new democracy become a beacon light comparable to 1793 or 1917, he said and explained his concept of democracy: "Europe is fighting for its new physiognomy. Today the struggle is waged formally between the different types of democracy over the question of whether democracy is to be purely a political-judicial form of state or a real way of life for the people." Behind the question hid matters of power: whether the democratic way of life would continue to represent the anonymous rule of the "two hundred families" or whether it could be developed further into a genuine form of government for the working people.[28]

Lukács' notion of the "further development" of democracy is not that much different in principle from what Stalin and his spokesmen had in mind from 1945 to 1948, and many of Lukács' general formulations and descriptions of the modalities of democracy in its only "genuine" form were basically interchangeable with the definitions filling the pages of the Communist-controlled or party press of Eastern Europe at the time. Most of these naturally made use of frequent references to Soviet democracy and, especially in 1946, extolled the ten-year-old Stalin Constitution as "the only truly democratic constitution in the world."[29] Nor were these interpretations of Soviet democracy at all new to Lukács; the nineteen years that had elapsed since "proletarian democracy lifted up its head triumphantly in summoning the proletarian dictatorship to power," he had written in 1936, brought "proletarian democracy to full maturity." The Stalin Constitution anchored the results of the victories of socialism achieved thus far.[30]

Yet Lukács later spoke as if democracy in Hungary and Eastern Europe had somehow been betrayed in the late forties, even though in 1946 he had pointed to 1917 as a model for the new democracy. Asked in 1971 if he felt that the popular democratic road to socialism could have been continued if the international situation had not deteriorated, Lukács answered in the affirmative. But such an outcome would only have been possible, he added, if there had been no Stalinism in the Soviet Union.[31] This, however, is the crux of the whole issue. If Lukács at the time had understood Stalin as a political personality and the dynamics of the political and ideological system that operated under him, why was he taken off guard when people's democracy turned out to be a hoax in late 1948? Or had he honestly felt in 1946 and 1947 that Stalinism was capable of fostering genuinely democratic impulses? He had certainly felt that way during the thirties, and there is no compelling reason to believe that his celebration of Soviet democracy and the Stalin Constitution in the thirties was merely part of some "theoretical masquerade." However that may be, his credulity in the immediate postwar years was certainly no graver a misjudgment than the trustfulness that he had exhibited both prior to 1933 and afterwards in Soviet exile, where he produced many writings useful as a theoretical rationale for establishmentarian political and literary political tactics. All these factors lend credence to the contention that Lukács was actually as unaware of Stalin's ulterior motives or basic impulses in Eastern Europe in 1945 as he had been, for instance, in the course of the philosophy debate a decade and a half earlier.[32]

As long as a specific political policy remained in force corresponding with the theoretical adjunct that Lukács was supplying, he was by no means merely "tolerated" in the party but welcomed. Dexterous, accommodating intellectuals, especially the rare quick-witted kind, were a functional requisite in the Communist party, for they were charged with the important responsibility of supplying the ideological fictions that backed up political actions and fait accomplis; and if these intellectuals were perhaps not already wholly corrupted and actually believed some or all of their own fictions, so much the better. That, after all, was probably the ultimate instinctive goal of the party's form of ideological terror—rendering orthodoxy unconscious, to borrow Orwell's phrase.[33] In any event, when the tactics either changed suddenly or were carried through to a conclusion that Lukács had failed to foresee, leaving him too little time to adapt, he was left dangerously exposed and subject to attacks by Stalinist functionaries often motivated simply by the special animus that they had entertained toward him for years anyway. These functionaries were usually would-be intellectuals themselves, and they may well have resented Lukács especially because he was so gifted at what he did. When he was in harmony with the party, after all, he proved a hard act to follow for many of the party's intellectual charlatans.

Summing up the events of 1949 more than two decades later, Lukács came up with a description of his involvement in them that managed to brush aside any serious soul-searching related to his own accountability for the political circumstances to which he and many others had then fallen victim: "The Moor has done his job, the Moor may go; Lukács, consequently, isn't needed any more."[34]

. . . .

CHAPTER 10

Conclusion

Lukács made a cult of history, and it anesthetized his mind. It numbed his sense of reality and eventually addicted him to the illusion that his own view of the dialectic and the dialectic of reality corresponded with each other. Lukács never entertained the slightest doubt about this original principle, and he remained a dogmatist all his life, resolving existential and empirical antinomies by all the casuistry at his disposal—even when history deluded him. On one of those occasions, his belated recognition that the Germans as a people had not behaved according to history's universal imperatives by carrying out a proletarian revolution after 1933 may have dampened his historical optimism temporarily. But Lukács quickly recovered his general confidence in the logic and predictability of history. As a Marxist, of course, he believed that there was meaning to history and that history was evolving toward justice on earth, which would ultimately emerge from the crucible of an apocalyptic collision between the forces of good (socialism) and evil (capitalism, fascism). This indwelling conviction had long since become instinctive to Lukács by the thirties. Socioeconomic processes unfolded in accordance with eternal historical laws, and the classes of human society were inexorably swept along by them. These immutable forces of history could, however, be identified and defined. Following the lead of the proletariat, mankind could then adapt itself to the laws of evolutionary and revolutionary development and thus—merging freedom and necessity, subject and object, theory and practice—participate in the historical process.

"*The absolute dominion of the whole, its unity over and above the abstract isolation of its parts: this is the essence of the dialectical method*," Lukács wrote in 1919, this was "orthodox Marxism";[1] and if empirical facts appeared to contradict the whole, he quoted Fichte, "so much the worse for facts."[2]

These remarks, written not long after his conversion to Marxism, bear witness to one of Lukács' earliest steps in the direction of a final "enslavement through consciousness."[3] The opportunity to ignore consistently the empirical reality of Russia, however, did not present itself until 1930. By the time Lukács arrived in Moscow, the first wave of forced collectivization and dekulakization had receded, at least marginally, and Stalin had delivered his famous speech, "Dizzy with Success." In it he blamed the "excesses" of his own policy on overzealous subalterns who were supposedly in too great a hurry to build socialism. Stalin's first show trial, the Shakhty trial of 1928, was already history, and he was busy planning the next. In 1930, just in time to help justify more repression in the countryside, the clandestine "Toiling Peasant party" was dug up, its members supposedly having been recruited from among former kulaks and social revolutionaries. Late that year the technical specialists belonging to a nonexistent Industrial party went on trial, charged with wrecking, subversion, espionage, and sabotage, and with organizing foreign intervention and the armed overthrow of Soviet power. Before Lukács left Moscow for Berlin, the members of yet another fictional body, the "union bureau" of the Menshevik party, were hauled into the courtroom for a fourth production.[4] By then collectivization had already led the country to the brink of catastrophy; millions of peasants had been uprooted and deported to desolate arctic regions of Siberia, where many of them soon perished of hunger and exposure, and a planned famine in the Ukraine presently turned the entire region into one vast concentration camp that eventually claimed upwards of six million lives.

After eighteen months of experiencing Soviet reality, Lukács moved to Berlin, where he arrived brimming with enthusiasm for the earlier than anticipated realization of the First Five-Year Plan. The internal and external situation in the Soviet Union had been fundamentally transformed, he said; in the West the capitalist system had been buffeted by a crisis of unsurpassed severity, and its coming collapse was manifestly evident. In stark contrast to this political-economic conjuncture, however, stood the construction of socialism in the USSR; in city and countryside, the First Five-Year Plan was being fulfilled in four, no, in three years.[5] The correlate in Lukács' mind read: *"The*

undeniable advance of socialist construction, which fills the
working class masses throughout the entire world with enthu-
siasm, has to be leaving a visible imprint on the minds of
thinking intellectuals."[6]

Just a few years later, in 1933 and 1934, Lukács was convinced that intellectuals who participated "seriously" in the
antifascist struggle would be led virtually automatically on-
ward and upward along the path leading to Marxism-Leninism.
He argued along the same lines in 1936, first in the essay
"Erzählen und Beschreiben," then, with minor modifications
occasioned by the popular front, in *Der historische Roman*:
revolutionary democrats who had embraced the popular front
and the cause of revolutionary democracy had not, it was true,
become conscious Marxists, and to expect this of them was the
worst kind of sectarianism. It was imperative, rather, to see
that Marxism was the end of the road that they had embarked
upon, not its beginning. But the process had set itself in motion, built up its own internal momentum, and intellectuals
consistently loyal to the spirit of revolutionary democracy (as
Lukács defined it) were bound to be swept along by the high
tide of socialism. Marxism for them was merely a matter of
time.

Lukács' automatism had a direct analogy for him in the Soviet Union. Extolling the 1936 Stalin Constitution and "the
problem of the personality," Lukács pointed out that no obstacles blocked the path of future personal development, maturation, and self-expression for anyone who was at one with society, that is, for the true personality. As for the malignant
residual influences of capitalism, the iron severity of the dictatorship of the proletariat would see to these bourgeois survivals, whereas "those who are stumbling and vacillating will
be reeducated by proletarian democracy, to proletarian democracy, by means of their own praxis and their own experience."[7]
By 1936 at the very latest, Lukács' social and political automatism, his mesmerization by his own logicality, had effectively thrown open the doors to a theoretical rationalization of
mass murder, whether he fathomed the implications of his own
theory or not. For if their own experience as members of Soviet
society did not automatically, spontaneously, convert or "reeducate" certain strata of Soviet citizenry to proletarian de-

mocracy, the source of the breakdown must presumably lay in human subjectivity, for the last place that Lukács would ever have looked for a blockage in the historical process was in his original dialectic, in this case in the dialectic of "proletarian democracy" itself. Instead, pursuing his own logic to its natural conclusion, Lukács would have been compelled to argue that the reasons for any materialization of political and social recidivism lay with the residual influences of capitalism polluting the citizens' minds to begin with. The iron severity of proletarian dicatorship was there to deal precisely with that kind of contamination.

Ten years later, in 1946, the political circumstances in liberated Europe had changed radically, but not the dynamics of the historical process as Lukács was accustomed to viewing them. Characterizing the coming democracy and the new citizen, the *citoyen*, much as he had earlier imagined the new Soviet man, Lukács posed rhetorically the question that he thought might naturally occur in response to his theory of social development under the conditions of the people's democracy. Would the new man, in this case the reborn *citoyen*, come into being to erect the new democracy or would the institutions of the new democracy reeducate the people to citizenship (*Citoyentum*)? In reality, he answered, this question posed a false dilemma, because "by struggling for the new democracy, in the process of building it, the spirit of citizenship awakens within the people; by re-forming themselves ideologically, they stimulate the struggle to erect new institutions of democracy."[8]

Orwell's Lukácsian dilemma with respect to the masses appears to have been less of an issue in Lukács' own later thinking: "Until they have become conscious they will never rebel, and until after they have rebelled they cannot become conscious."[9] For Lukács, the way out of this vicious circle had always been found in the unity of theory and practice, the essential identity of historical subject and object as the proletariat progressed by way of conscious acts toward awareness of its historical role and toward the realm of freedom. Consciousness— class consciousness—came in the very act of revolting against and surmounting the old order. In *Geschichte und Klassenbewusstsein* the passage from the realm of necessity to the realm of freedom was to take the form of a "leap" in its final stages. In 1946 the dialectical process, it seems, had evolved into one of almost sheer automatism. Building the new democracy and "re-forming" themselves ideologically, the masses, the new *citoyen*, automatically impelled society forward toward the establishment of democratic institutions.

But what if Lukács' "citizenry" declined to act as it was supposed to? What if the dialectic again broke down? What if the masses turned their backs on history and refused to cooperate with this natural process of "democratization" because, for reasons unfathomable to Lukács, they mistrusted it? Curiously, in this context Lukács makes no note of the Communist party. But the locomotive of history stopped for no man, and, it seems, refractory *citoyen* would have to pay for their recidivism. Because the new democratic order did not yet exist, the potential power of the state was presumably to devolve in the interim upon the Communist party, which surely did exist and represented the state in its incipient form; and the party would be called upon to deal with all the residual influences of historically superseded outlooks and prejudices within the people with respect to what was ostensibly their own democracy. After all, according to the authoritative Dimitrov, this democracy turned out to be just another form of the dictatorship of the proletariat by late 1948, and such a dictatorship was accustomed to dealing with "residual influences" with merciless severity, as Lukács had put it in 1936. Thus, if history failed to bring the citizenry smoothly into line by itself, then the party would step in to carry out the will of history with coercive violence. Or were the imperatives of history and the exercise of terror to enforce them one and the same for Lukács, a unity of theory and practice?

This unity had existed for Lukács in the thirties, though he never put it quite so bluntly. In fact, terror was not supposed to exist, so for Lukács there could be nothing of the sort in the USSR. Bernard Shaw, Lukács said in 1931, had been to the Soviet Union, saw the future, and it worked. "As a venerable critic of democracy, he understood that proletarian dictatorship produces an entirely different responsibility on the part of those who work for it than democracy; that the workers' attitude toward the exertion of their energies, toward sacrifice with respect to momentary interests, is entirely different than in capitalism; that 'forced labor,' 'GPU terror' are stupid and undignified lies, etc."[10] Stalinism was still in its infancy in 1931 (though it was maturing rapidly), and the direction of the Soviet regime under Stalin's guidance was not yet plainly evident. Collectivization, executions, punitive expeditions, forced requisitions and the resultant artificially induced famine in the countryside, mass deportation—these concomitants of proletarian democracy were all concealed from the eyes of outsiders, and many of those who were in a position to know about them chose not to. Lukács saw instead only the brilliant success of the First Five-Year Plan—fulfilled in three—described so vividly by the Soviet press. But, it might be argued, he could not conceivably have known the full truth at the time. Even a quarter of a century later, after the twentieth party congress, Bertolt Brecht, for one, was still arguing that a lack of facts made it too early to undertake a historical assessment of Stalin.[11] If the validity of this argument is accepted for Lukács back in 1931, when there was still some justification for it, then it would be premature to expect to find in Lukács a linking-together of Orwell's "knowledge with ignorance" or "cynicism with fanaticism"; rather, Lukács' reasoning in 1931 would have been infused with a conventional blend of common fanaticism and simple ignorance.

But this only applies to 1931. Even Eörsi, who knew Lukács well, was baffled by his behavior in the immediate postwar years. Why, Eörsi asked himself, did Lukács act as if he knew nothing about the chains that fettered the physical and spiritual existence of the Soviet people upon his return to Hungary from the USSR? Why did he pretend to know nothing of the atmosphere of universal anxiety that hung over Soviet society and to be ignorant of labor camps that functioned smoothly as death camps? Eörsi answered the question by quoting a remark made by Lukács two years before he died, words to the effect that even the worst socialism was still a vast improvement over the best capitalism.[12] Lukács' comment is a partial answer to Eörsi's original question, but it cannot be accepted as a complete explanation because to do so assumes that a comment made in 1969 can be immediately used to gauge Lukács' behavior prior to Stalin's death. To cite Lukács' preference for "the worst socialism" over "the best capitalism" as an explanation for his actions right after the war ignores the full extent of Lukács' infection by the political pathology of Stalinism, which certainly lingered on from the time of his return to Hungary in 1945 at least until Stalin's death in 1953. It is a view that presumes the presence of a pristine rationality guiding Lukács' actions and outlook. There can be no doubt whatever that such a rationality existed and that this distended cerebralism was, in fact, the overriding determinant in Lukács behavior. But to focus exclusively on such psychotic logicality overlooks *simple fear* as a motivating factor and fails to consider that Lukács' hyperrationalism might well have been at least a partial reflection of fear, perhaps in a perverse sense even his private salvation from it.

Lukács, after all, had just lived through thirteen years in a society lastingly scarred by years of the bloodiest unrelenting terror. If one assumes that the quotidian reality of life in Stalin's Russia demoralized Lukács just as it demoralized countless other Soviet citizens, then there is no reason to think that his anxiety simply evaporated the moment he crossed the Soviet border and set foot on Hungarian soil and that it left no trace at all upon him.[13] If his differences with party Stalinists in 1949 over the question of democracy are viewed to a significant degree as a misunderstanding caused by the fact that Lukács originally took the official policy of the people's democracy at face value, and if his prompt self-criticism is interpreted as at least a partial expression of lingering fear, then Lukács did not manage to overcome at least some of the aftereffects of the spiritual contamination caused by thirteen years of unmediated Stalinism until well after Stalin's death. After 1956, then, Lukács never practiced self-criticism or kowtowed to Hungarian sub-Stalins again.[14]

What kinds of arguments concerning Soviet society did the combination of hypertrophied rationality and corrupting fear produce from Lukács when he returned to Hungary? Arriving in Berlin from Moscow in 1931, Lukács was probably generally ignorant. But ignorance was no longer an excuse in 1945. Lukács' claims in his post-Stalin writings to have been a prime Hungarian advocate in the late forties and early fifties of a non-Stalinist democracy, a people's democracy, ought to be examined alongside his impassioned defense of the Soviet Union in the last years of Stalin's life.

While Lukács was writing his final chapter to *Die Zerstörung der Vernunft*, treating the subject of irrationalism in the postwar era, men like David Rousset and Viktor Kravchenko were making headlines around the world with their shocking disclosures about the existence of a network of concentration camps in the Soviet Union. These startling revelations, the realization that Rousset's *univers concentrationnaire* applied to Russia as well as to Germany, took the world largely by surprise. In 1950, for instance, Rousset, a member of the International Commission against the Concentration Camp Regime, sued the Communist newspaper *Les Lettres françaises* for libel for alleging that Rousset misrepresented a quotation from the Soviet penal code. In the course of the trial, at which the former Soviet prison-camp inmate Alexander Weissberg testified, numerous facts concerning the system of forced labor camps in the USSR came out, facts that many in the West still refused to believe. Sartre, for instance, argued steadfastly that such evidence should be ignored, even if true, because it might otherwise cause the French proletariat to despair.[15] In this atmosphere Kravchenko's *I Chose Freedom* came out in print. The author was immediately subjected to a vicious, unrelenting smear campaign in the Communist press, the favorite slander being that Kravchenko's book, which contained detailed, first-hand information about the camps, had been faked by the American secret service. Kravchenko sued *Les Lettres françaises* for libel and won the case.[16]

In trying to refute the revelations of a Rousset, a Kravchenko, or the "demagogic absurdities" of Albert Camus in his dispute with Sartre over Soviet concentration camps,[17] Lukács likewise tied the appearance of publications containing documentary evidence about Soviet concentration camps to a concerted effort by the legatees of Goebbels and Rosenberg to defame the USSR. This flood of publications and the outlooks of "renegades" were a prime illustration for Lukács of the revised tactics of the bourgeoisie in comparison with their former modus operandi, the indirect apologia. The major ideological goal of "capitalist science" in the postwar era, Lukács said, was to articulate convincing arguments that would retard the steadily growing worldwide attraction of the socialist alternative.[18] "The successful resistance of the Soviet army against the most powerful land force in the world, its overpowering victory over Hitler, the monumental peaceful construction projects of the postwar years, the ability likewise to produce atomic bombs, and so on and so forth reveal indisputably to the entire world the high economic and technical standard of the socialist economy and its trend of development, which points continually upwards."[19]

It is a simple matter, of course, to spot Lukács' older argument that the magnetic pull of socialism was drawing ever larger numbers of the Western proletariat and intelligentsia into an orbit of enthusiastic support of the Soviet system. Whereas in years past the global bourgeoisie had argued demagogically in terms of the imminent collapse of that system, different means had to be employed in the present age to belittle and besmirch the reality of dazzling Soviet successes. Examining these means exposed the continually plummeting ideological level of anti-Soviet propaganda.[20] Echoing his 1931 dismissal of "stupid and undignified lies" about Soviet secret police terror and forced labor in Russia, Lukács noted: "Attempts to mount a new offensive can only be made through obvious calumnies, through the false testimony of paid police agents."[21]

The disclosures of Kravchenko's book, facts about the Soviet system of camps that Lukács knew well to be true (assuming that he took the time to read Kravchenko's book), had thus triggered one of his old reflexes. The "Kravchenko principle" of arguing against the Soviet system with hypocritical cynicism about supposed freedom and democracy in the West was an ideological offensive; what had been defensible in Hitler's time only through a defensive form of indirection was now possible by means of an ideology sustaining a *direct* apologia of monopoly capitalism.[22] Added to that, said Lukács, was the fact that this propaganda not only worked with crass lies (the "Kravchenko method") but also depicted diverse crimes committed by imperialism as nonexistent—bacteriological warfare in Korea, mishandling of Korean and Chinese POWs, and so on.[23] At this point the "renegades" leaped into the breach in the battle against communism, though their activity by no means marked an unprecedented phenomenon. The international propaganda and provocational activity of Trotsky during the two world wars was a similar occurrence; then, too, there had been the assorted Eastmans, Doriots, and so on. "But today it is not merely the ordinary police agents of Kravchenko's ilk, etc., who are placed in the forefront of world publicity, but precisely the most esteemed writers like Dos Passos, Silone, Koestler, Malraux; and prominent politicians like Ernst Reuter, publicists like Burnham, and many others are renegades of Communism."[24] The "authenticity" of their revelations about communism was particularly valuable ammunition in an age when anti-Communist propaganda had descended to the level of a Kravchenko. Every lie and slander was welcome in this kind of smear campaign.[25]

Lukács was just as bent upon refusing to acknowledge the existence of slave labor camps in the USSR in 1952 as he had been twenty years before, when his fanaticism may still have been partially infused with unadulterated ignorance. The ideological inferences that Lukács drew in 1952 also had a familiar ring and highlight the internal consistency of certain key ideas since the early thirties. Whereas the Grand Hotel "Abgrund," Lukács' clever symbol for the indirect or critical apologia of monopoly capitalism, stood for bourgeois strategy in the early thirties, individualism and nonconformism had replaced inferential advocacy of the existing establishment two decades later.

Nonconformism in the West was an objective lie, Lukács explained, one that inevitably sprang from the soil of monopoly capitalism; subjectively it was often a sign of self-deception and self-delusion. But such was the general character of the "free world" today, and thus it had been under Hitler. The only difference was that this lie had been hidden from some by the colorful veil of myths, whereas others had regarded Hitler's demagogy and tyranny as the only obstacle to the arrival of a blessed age of nonconformist individualism. But the veil had been lifted, the frenzy was past, and it was clear to everyone, said Lukács (in an adaptation of Stalin's favorite phrase "the whole world knows"), that the impulse toward an apologia of the capitalist system in its present aggressive, warlike form was the precondition for a toleration of nonconformism. Hard as it was to imagine, the ideology of the cold war had actually experienced a drop in level compared with the Hitler era—just contrast Hans Grimm with Arthur Koestler, Lukács said.[26] Whereas Hitler had been able to pull together everything reactionary over a hundred-and-fifty-year span of irrationalist development, leading irrationalism out of the salons and onto the streets, the socially conditioned impulse toward the direct apologia precluded even this possibility today.[27]

Rather than enhancing the sophistication of his general arguments, the end of Lukács' years of exile brought only a theoretical tawdriness here that registered in his reworking of the most sordid vulgarities of the cold war. Lukács pointed his finger accusingly at the shameful drop in the standard of "mainstream bourgeois ideological thinking," but it was really Lukács' own habit of thought that had been even more profoundly vulgarized. The addled logic of the political pamphlet that he appended to *Die Zerstörung der Vernunft* as an afterword outstrips in many respects Lukács' lowest-grade writings of the thirties and really crowns the logical absurdities of the entire volume with a piece of utter nonsense. This, perhaps, was the price to be paid for the spiritual demoralization caused by thirteen years of Stalinism, and now the dialectic of reality was again treating Lukács with contempt, jeering at him, as it were, for his arrogant presumption that history had selected him alone for initiation into its dialectical arcana. Lukács was compelled to believe that the Soviet Union's real achievements matched Stalin's most extravagant claims about them. But this reality was largely a figment of Lukács' own imagination. There were not supposed to be concentration camps in Russia, so for Lukács these labor camps had no objective existence. Similarly, his dialectic told him that the toiling masses and the intelligentsia in the West ought to be flocking to the side of Soviet power; that Lukács had been reiterating this claim for at least two decades and that it had never happened as the dialectic supposedly foreordained it, did not defer him from his analysis in 1952. For this reality, too, was located only inside Lukács' head.

This, however, was the only reality that mattered to him. Because the empirical facts of Soviet concentration camps interfered with his cerebralism, the hyperrationalism with which Lukács defined the whole, so much the worse for these "facts"; and persons who revealed the existence of something that could not and therefore did not exist in his mind were consequently irrational—apologists of main-line monopoly capitalism, architects of the coming war, heirs to Goebbels. Reality was not unfolding as Lukács expected, the intellectuals were not stampeding to the side of Soviet power, so brazen lies about some fantastic and phantasmal *univers concentrationnaire* that stretched across the vast reaches of the Soviet Union, lies confusing the natural inclination of the masses to align themselves with the USSR in an act of quasi-spontaneous allegiance, had to be ultimately responsible, much as the combination of fascist and social fascist demagogy had befuddled the people in their infinite gullibility two decades before.

Was Lukács consciously aware at the time that he was lying? If one applies to him some of the traits that make up Milosz' Gamma, the Slave of History, Lukács knew that "not one word" he pronounced about the camps was his own. "I am a liar, he thinks, and makes historical determinism responsible for his lies."[28] If Lukács' inner motivation was sheer madness, frighteningly syllogistic, then its overriding attribute was precisely the method behind it; the method *was* the madness, a Procrustean intellectualism that itself defies rational analysis by the historian. This political pathology transformed Lukács into a victim and an executioner: he executed the same doctrine that victimized him. Lukács demanded that history permit him to play the role of prophet and soothsayer, that it reveal to him the mysteries of its immutable and, to most ordinary mortals, inscrutable laws. When it cheated him out of his rightful role as a popular tribune by confronting him with developments whose predictable regularity stubbornly withstood his best efforts to penetrate them, Lukács revolted by inventing a reality of his own that conformed to *his* dialectic, a visionary dialectic itself deduced not from a rational observation of empirical reality, but rather one to which Lukács had already affixed his preconceived schema. What failed to mesh smoothly was then snipped away, forfeiting any right to an objective existence. To paraphrase Orwell, Lukács carefully cultivated the power of not grasping analogies, not perceiving logical errors, not understanding simple arguments if they were inimical to his dialectic, and shying away from any train of thought that contained within it the seeds of heresy—a deviation.[29]

Orwell, in fact, may come as close as one can to articulating the essence of Lukács' syllogisms: "*Doublethink* means the power of holding two contradictory beliefs in one's mind simultaneously, and accepting both of them. The Party intellectual knows in which direction his memories must be altered; he therefore knows that he is playing tricks with reality; but by the exercise of *doublethink* he also satisfies himself that reality is not violated. The process has to be conscious, or it would not be carried out with sufficient precision, but it also has to be unconscious, or it would bring with it a feeling of falsity and hence of guilt."[30] Thus, following Orwell, Lukács knew and he did not know; he was conscious of complete truthfulness while telling carefully constructed lies, he held at the same time two opinions that canceled each other out; he knew they were contradictory but believed in both of them. He consciously induced unconsciousness, and then, once again, became unconscious of the act of hypnosis that he had just performed upon himself.[31] These thoughts provide at least some clues to Lukács' mental processes prior to Stalin's death.

Later, after Stalin had been entombed and the expression of an opinion was less likely to demand the ultimate sacrifice, Lukács not only acknowledged the existence of Soviet slave labor camps and unbridled terror (without admitting that he had ever denied it), he outdid himself in aperçus regarding the quintessence of Stalinism. Lukács, whose orthodoxy had years ago slipped into unconsciousness, apparently broke the hypnotic spell that Stalinism had cast upon him and stood up for his convictions after 1956 in dangerous situations that demanded a good deal of personal courage. Imre Nagy's fate, after all, could just as easily have been Lukács'. But he held to his anti-Stalinist convictions without conceding that he had ever been spellbound by Stalinism in the first place; and once he had awakened from his reverie, he began systematically constructing the sophisticated myth of his own political infallibility and primordial anti-Stalinism—he had "always" supported this and "always" opposed that. Lukács' later disingenuousness in these matters was just as much a self-serving pathology as the one that had led to his captivation by a cannibalistic dogma in the first place.

Following the Soviet invasion of Czechoslovakia, the eighty-three-year-old Lukács muttered once in Eörsi's presence that the whole experiment begun in 1917 had presumably failed. The entire undertaking would have to be started up again elsewhere.[32] Eörsi never heard Lukács repeat words to that effect again. Instead, one year later, he made his comment about the worst socialism being superior to the best capitalism and repeated his opinion again the year he died.[33]

If indeed he had much of a conscience in such matters (a question that by no means needs to be taken polemically), Lukács may have assuaged it by convincing himself of the truth of his remark, which contains a not very subtle rationale for his own moral complicity in some of the most horrific crimes ever committed. As early as 1920, Lukács had already dealt with the ethical concerns raised by personal involvement in a process that demanded acts of wanton violence or, at the very least, acquiescence in and approval of the execution of such violent deeds by the prime instrumentality of history—the Communist party. It was merely a question of a secularized form of religious faith in history. This religious faith, Lukács had written in *Geschichte und Klassenbewusstsein*, was nothing more here than the "methodological certainty that the historical process continues on its way to the end *in and through our deeds*, untroubled by all momentary defeats and reversals."[34] Lukács, then, had always been willing to bloody his hands, if only symbolically; to apply one of Brecht's phrases to Lukács, he was not one who squeamishly wished to slaughter the calf—sacrifice it might be a better term in Lukács' case—without seeing the blood.[35]

But behind all this sophistical self-exculpation lay a shocking sort of egocentricity and an utter insensitivity to human life and human suffering. After all, Lukács' preference for Stalinist Russia (though he had been quick enough to leave when he had the chance in 1931) was not a private decision in favor of the "worst form of socialism" that affected him and no one else. Freedom of choice was denied to millions of others, and, unable to act upon their preference, millions were sacrificed on Lukács' altar of history. For them the best capitalism would have guaranteed them life, and even the worst possible form of it would not always have meant a completely unbearable, unlivable existence. Yet even if it had, who gave Lukács the right to demand from these millions of men and women the ultimate sacrifice for his faith in a future, chimerical utopia? History, he would no doubt have replied, but this could scarcely have comforted most of Stalin's ordinary victims, for neither they nor their children, who either died unborn or perished along with their parents, would live to see that radiant future, or even a comforting distant glimmer of it.

As for Lukács, his secularized god was more than just an impersonal motive force in the world, and he did not see himself as merely another human being buffeted this way and that by the turbulence of history. Stalin and Soviet socialism gave Lukács a sense of purpose that he could not have acquired anywhere else. Marxism-Leninism in its Stalinist form bestowed meaning upon his life; it rid him of an agonizing sense of personal alienation and lifted his work to the dignity of perfect truth. In his mind Marxism-Leninism lent historical legitimacy to his political, philosophical, and aesthetic thought and to the practical manifestations rationalized by it, thus assuring his ideas an immortality that rescued the labor of a lifetime from the usual corruptibility of the intellectual accomplishments attained even by the great philosophers and thinkers who preceded him.

The unity of theory and practice was a binding principle for Lukács, a more serious, even ominous proposition than he could perhaps ever admit to himself. For throughout much of his life his writing and personal commitment to his ideas were inseparable from his attachment to Stalin's theoretical dialectic, which, in turn, was an indissoluble part of Stalin's practical reality. However, Lukács was aware enough of Stalin's crimes after 1953 to realize that he must sever his work retrospectively from Stalinism if his writings were to retain any lasting significance in the eyes of posterity. That Lukács had made a pact with history to establish heaven on earth was a gamble for which he never felt the slightest constraint to apologize; but that he had likewise staked his own soul on the party, Stalin's party, was evidently too grievous an error to be classified as a momentary personal lapse or reversal, and he turned himself into an anti-Stalinist late in life, acting on his principles after 1956 with a brand of civil courage perhaps inspired by a bad conscious about his past.

But even then, orthodoxy, borrowing Milosz' phrase, could not release its pressure on Lukács' mind, not even after Stalin's death, or it would have ceased to be orthodoxy;[36] and as Lukács must have realized, without theoretical orthodoxy his complete system of ideas, going back several decades, would have lost its entire internal cohesiveness and validity. His work would have been subject to the normal corruptibility that comes with time, relativizing or decomposing most human accomplishments, and, in Lukács' case, threatening to pass sentence on his own life and work with a historical verdict of meaninglessness not at all unlike the one that he had pronounced upon a fascistic Nietzsche. But that kind of accountability, normal human frailty, passing relevance at best or historical nothingness at the worst, the perishability of all he had lived and strived for—Lukács recoiled inwardly at the very thought that his work may have amounted to nothing more. He craved a universal, timeless validity, addicted himself to the illusion that he was achieving it, and paid the full price for his earthly fantasy. He stretched out his hand to seize a transcendent immortality and perhaps even died convinced that it was in his clutch, but he managed to secure scarcely more for himself than a fleeting sort of fame that bears little resemblance to his original vision.

Brecht

CHAPTER II

The Victim

*To begin with, about all one can say is that the bolsheviks
simply did not know how to develop a literature. . . . the
assumption of power by the proletariat took literature by
surprise.* —Brecht, *Arbeitsjournal*

By the late thirties Bertolt Brecht had grown bitterly disillu-
sioned with Soviet cultural policy. The "theoretical line" in the
USSR thwarted all that he had worked for over the last two
decades, he told Benjamin in 1938.[1] In his journal he added that
Soviet literature and art struck him as "shitty."[2] Five years later
his disenchantment, in this instance with Soviet literary criticism, hit a new low. When studies were undertaken at all, they
were tantamount in character to a trial. The tone was appal-
lingly unproductive, venomous, personal, and concurrently authoritative and servile—obviously no atmosphere in which a
"vibrant, militant, exuberant literature" could thrive.[3] Something had gone wrong along the way, and Brecht seemed aware
of the fact that more than the passing prevalence of an especially constrictive line advocated by one group of hidebound
functionaries was involved. He attributed Lukács' overriding
authority as a literary critic, for instance, precisely to his geo-
graphic locality in Moscow and the political-ideological backing that it lent his arguments.[4] Yet Brecht was peculiarly reti-
cent about taking the problems he spotted in Soviet literature
back to their original source. The plain fact that Soviet literature was plagued by the effects of Stalin's literary policies in
force over the last decade or so escaped Brecht. He somehow
missed the various link between Stalin's political policies and
the literary and cultural modalities spawned by them, so that
the damage naturally done to Soviet art in Stalin's time took
Brecht largely by surprise. Although the situation in the Soviet

Union had been building to a climax since the early thirties, Brecht ignored the many conspicuous warning signs and was caught off guard by the impact of Stalinism upon Soviet art and by the corresponding consequences for the reception of his own work in the USSR.

BRECHT AND THE STALINISTS

Brecht's prospects in the Soviet Union, however, had not always been as bleak as they became in the late thirties. He had several close friends living in the USSR, and they stood up for him and his work with periodic success. The result was an odd state of affairs. The German and Russian Stalinists thrived on confrontations with Brecht because in their eyes his modernistic theory of epic theater mirrored the "decadence" that infused bourgeois art in general and clashed with all their freshly hallowed principles of socialist realism. How, under such circumstances, did Brecht manage to get any of his writings into print at all in the USSR? What accounts for the various favorable reviews and articles that appeared on occasion in the Soviet press? Brecht's modest successes were a by-product of conflicting official policies whose shifting configuration in the thirties and early forties allowed the natural affinities between him and the Soviet avant-garde to yield sporadic results. Specifically, his fortunes in the USSR were tied directly to the friction generated by two political dynamics contending with each other throughout much of the thirties: the popular front, which acted as a tranquilizer upon the Stalinists in their dealings with Western writers; and the vassalization of Soviet cultural life under Stalin that eclipsed brilliant theatrical experimentation and literary innovation in Soviet art and blotted out much of Brecht's work in the process. The dynamics of the two policies were never very evenly matched, and the eventual outcome was probably inevitable. But the contest waxed and waned enough for Brecht to slip into recurrent breaches in the Stalinist line with a handful of his plays, a sampling of his poetry, an occasional essay, a few "Lehrstücke," and the *Dreigroschenroman*.

The antagonism toward Brecht in the pre-Hitler years, caused chiefly by RAPP's domination of the BPRS and by Lukács' determination to assert himself in literary-theoretical matters during his year and a half in Berlin, relaxed somewhat after Hitler's accession to power. Then, to a modest extent, even Brecht became an object of the Stalinists' affections. During the lull before the formulation of more exact and prescriptive definitions of socialist realism and as a Communist-backed united front of writers gradually took shape, Brecht's name was apparently placed fairly high on the list of writers whose backing of a united front the party's cultural politicians considered imperative. As things transpired, however, Brecht happened to broach the subject of organizing writers for resistance to fascism with Communist literary functionaries first. He evidently thought of convening a writers' conference, for instance, well before it occurred to Johannes R. Becher. As early as June 1933 he proposed the organization of "an authorized conference for a number of colleagues . . . , at which the goals and methods of our future work will be laid down once and for all."[5]

Even though Brecht may have envisaged a different kind of meeting than the one that took place two years later in Paris, his proposal might have been part of the original stimulus behind the Communists' plans for a "world conference of all antifascist writers" that Becher first outlined in a letter to Moscow in October 1933.[6] But regardless of possible tactical differences concerning the management of the conference, both Brecht and Becher shared one mutual concern. The intellectuals attending the meeting needed to be steered into acceptance of a view of fascism that called for the proper proportion of opposition to Germany *and* support of the Soviet Union and international communism. Now was the time to begin, Brecht told Becher in June. The left-wing bourgeois writers currently had no set platform or viewpoint for the struggle against fascism, and "they aren't given one when their names are borrowed now and then for this or that cause. Precisely the circumstance, too, that they now sense their lack of orientation and defenselessness to some extent would give us a real chance with them, though the time to act may very well be limited." If ever, then they could be won over for real political schooling right now, said Brecht.[7]

The main difference between the conceptions held by Brecht and Becher was that Brecht made no secret of what he understood by cooperation with non-Communist intellectuals; he called it political "schooling." The party's writers and cultural functionaries, on the other hand, Becher among them, took a different approach: they were somewhat disingenuous about their ulterior motives. As the Communist plans for a writers' congress gradually took shape in 1934, Becher now approached Brecht, who apparently still had little patience with what he regarded as an unduly tactical strategy. "I shudder just a bit at the thought of get-togethers for the purpose of being among each other," he informed Becher; "one counts the heads of one's loved ones and assures oneself that everybody thinks alike, etc."[8] When the congress finally met in June 1935 in Paris, Brecht's speech reflected his uneasiness at the thought that the Communists might go out of their way to slough over the essence of fascism in their haste to achieve a superficial unity. So Brecht made his point emphatically: "Comrades, let's speak about the status of ownership. That is what I wanted to say in opposition to the spread of barbarity in order that it be said here or so that I was among those saying it."[9] In spite of Brecht's plainspokenness at a congress planned by the Communists to gloss over touchy ideologized issues like "the status of ownership," there is no evidence to suggest that his speech annoyed anyone in an official position in the party. The Communists, in fact, continued to attach importance to his involvement in the united front.[10]

How significant a factor was the literary united front in forestalling a reoccurrence of attacks upon Brecht such as those published in *Die Linkskurve* by Lukács and others in 1931 and 1932? The full extent of the role played by the new literary-political policy cannot be measured entirely; but combined with the respite in Soviet literary politics between the dissolution of RAPP and the real onset of literary Stalinism in 1936, it created an atmosphere in the Soviet Union more congenial to Brecht's work than would exist again for years to come. Responsibility for Brecht's good fortune from 1933 to 1936 rests with a close-knit group of friends and supporters in Moscow: Sergej Tretjakov, Bernhard Reich, Asja Lazis, Mikhail Koltsov, and Margarete Steffin, who proved to be Brecht's greatest asset. Her first trip to the Soviet Union had coincided with Brecht's, and, with the assistance of the KPD,[11] he helped arrange a stay of several weeks for her in a Crimean sanatorium—Steffin was tubercular—during his and Dudov's visit to Moscow to attend the premiere of the film *Kuhle Wampe* in May 1932.[12] Just over two years passed before Steffin returned to the Soviet Union,[13] staying this time for several months in Leningrad, Moscow, and Georgia[14] before returning to the West, apparently together with Brecht after his visit to Moscow in March, April, and May 1935.

Der Dreigroschenroman (in German and Russian) and *Die Rundköpfe und die Spitzköpfe* may not have been published in the Soviet Union had Steffin not been on the spot. Shortly after her arrival in Moscow in mid-September 1934,[15] Brecht wrote her that *Der Dreigroschenroman* ought to be the easiest to sell. "You should be able simply to walk right into the State Publishing House [Goslitizdat], where they speak German. They ought to pay more for a manuscript, but it would be good to have some of the page proofs to show them that it is being printed. That's what Wieland Herzfelde says, who is here at the moment. A Russian signature ought to bring at least 350 rubles, but let them make their own offer."[16] A month later Brecht sent Steffin the latest information. The novel was supposed to be out that very day in Amsterdam, though he still did not have a single copy and would send Steffin the first. "What are things like in Moscow?" he asked her. "Tell me more about the atmosphere there! . . . Who else did you speak with?" It would be good, he added, if Goslitizdat would publish some of his work.[17]

By December Steffin had a signed contract for the *Dreigroschenroman;*[18] whether this applied just to the German edition to be brought out by the Verlagsgenossenschaft ausländischer Arbeiter (VEGAAR) or also to Goslitizdat's Russian version is unclear, but the two editions were originally supposed to appear simultaneously.[19] The translation itself was evidently also arranged for the late fall or early winter 1934; it was to be prepared by Valentin O. Stenich, whom Steffin first met in the offices of VEGAAR. Stenich had rewritten the libretto for Meyerhold's Leningrad production of Tschaikovsky's *Picque Dame* and had also made a name for himself with excellent translations of Dos Passos, Joyce, Faulkner, Kipling, Malraux, and others.[20] He died in 1939 at the age of forty-one, presumably a victim of the purges.

Prospects for Brecht's work seemed promising elsewhere. Nikolaj Okhlopkov, a former actor and student of Meyerhold and since 1930 director of the Realistic Theater, decided that he wanted to stage *Die heilige Johanna der Schlachthöfe.* Whether Brecht was first introduced to Okhlopkov in 1932 or not until 1935 is uncertain, but a production of the play was already being talked about in mid-1933. In July Brecht told Tretjakov that—"now as before"—he would like to come and work in Russia in the fall, inquiring specifically, "How are things coming with 'Heilige Johanna'? Have you ever heard anything, by the way, about the actress Carola Neher, who left Germany over a half a year ago and is supposed to be in Russia? I heard that she traveled first to Odessa. She learned Russian and had also entered the German [Communist] party. Perhaps you could inquire after her among the Germans (maybe you could ask Piscator)? She would be a marvelous Johanna."[21] After Tairov's staging of *Die Dreigroschenoper* in 1930 for his Chamber Theater (Kamernij teatr), *Die heilige Johanna* would have been just the second of Brecht's plays to be performed on a Soviet stage. As things turned out, however, this production never materialized. Rehearsals were scheduled to begin in September, Tretjakov informed Brecht in July, though he had evidently not yet finished his translation of the play.[22] Tretjakov told Brecht that he would be talking soon with Okhlopkov, Neher, and Erwin Piscator—"in order to discuss the theater questions and especially the Johanna perspective."[23] A production never resulted, but, in spite of what Reich implies, there appears to be no reason to assume that political pressures were brought to bear this early upon Okhlopkov and blocked his plans.[24] It was still only 1935.

Nor should hasty conclusions be drawn from the situation in which Tretjakov now found himself. He certainly sensed that problems were in store for his type of factual, publicistic writing. He had spoken at the first all-union congress of Soviet writers in August 1934 (Brecht, by the way, had earlier been extended an invitation),[25] and he was definitely troubled by the atmosphere there. "At the moment we are at a cross roads," he wrote Brecht; "one-sided intellectualism (technicism) is being sharply attacked by the emotional principle. Emotional complexity is demanded." There were a series of principally new circumstances that needed to be discussed and studied, he said, adding that he would particularly like to do that with Brecht.[26]

Tretjakov's nervousness about the future does not mean, though, that he in any way sensed the severity of what was coming for Soviet literature; neither he nor Brecht nor very many others ever dreamed in 1933 or 1934 that Soviet art under Stalin was about to become so utterly vassalized. In fact, Tretjakov's involvement in past vituperative literary theoretical polemics that culminated neither in political delicts nor, worse, in bloodshed may have lulled him into a false sense of security, even though he knew well that there was strong opposition in the USSR to any kind of writing that smacked of the avant-garde or experimental. But if there ever had been any sort of favorable atmosphere for Tretjakov's kind of work since the late twenties, it was rapidly worsening. A hint of cynicism comes out in a letter that Tretjakov wrote Brecht about the upcoming writers' congress in Paris, which Tretjakov did not attend: "You are an old comedian if you are surprised that I do not have 3 weeks for the congress. That is certainly not private business of mine."[27] But the temptation to look for auguries of Tretjakov's arrest either in the difficulties he was now experiencing or even later in 1936 and the first half of 1937 should still be resisted, in spite of the note of cynicism. Like most of the other six hundred Soviet men of letters victimized by the purges, Tretjakov was arrested—as a Japanese spy—with no prior warning; he was never denounced for his views on literature anywhere in the Soviet press just prior to his disappearance, nor are there indications that he feared for his life more than any other Soviet writer beginning in mid-1936.[28]

Still, Tretjakov and Brecht knew that they had to cope with a brand of Soviet criticism and with Soviet-influenced literary critics outside the USSR antagonistic to their views on literature. When Alfred Kantorowicz reviewed the Amsterdam edition of *Der Dreigroschenroman* in Willi Münzenberg's Parisian journal *Unsere Zeit*, for instance, Brecht, having been informed that Kantorowicz was Becher's "secretary,"[29] promptly complained to Becher that that fact invested the article with the quality of an official or authoritative pronouncement. "Brecht is not interested in *edifying* but in *educating*," Kantorowicz had written; "his writings are not amusement but *educational aids.* He wants to stimulate thought. He does not have his readers or his spectators identify with the characters, he places them *opposite* the characters as observors." Those who had been inclined to regard Brecht as a cynic would now have to realize that he was a moralist, albeit one "with revolutionary consequences."[30]

The patronizing tone in Kantorowicz' compliments irritated Brecht, who wrote Becher that the "slimy friendliness" dressing it all up was of no interest whatever given the central point of criticism—"the novel is supposedly not realistic and it is idealistic."[31] Now Brecht may have erred in thinking that Becher, who was not privately ill-disposed toward Brecht, had any personal involvement in the publication of the article.[32] But Brecht in any case felt provoked and offered the following defense. In criticism like Kantorowicz', it was assumed that all nonrealistic novels were consequently idealistic. This could perhaps be taken as a point for discussion if not for the fact that only those novels lacking creative imagination were assigned the quality of being realistic. He thought, said Brecht, that a work was only idealistic when consciousness was suggested as the determining factor for the respective reality of social institutions. Because he depicted the determining influence of economic circumstances and class allegiance upon the consciousness of the characters, he felt that he had been writing a materialistic novel. "Because I depicted reality so that cause and effect can be clearly seen and one can intervene (there being no point in interpreting the world as opposed to the need to change it), I thought I had written a novel for realists, not just a novel in which reality comes up. Well, I stand corrected. I just wish it would occur in a less superficial and arrogant RAPP-like manner."[33]

Becher said that he concurred. He promised to publish a piece of countercriticism that would take issue with Kantorowicz in the near future,[34] except that the matter hardly ended there. Otto Biha (writing under the name Peter Merin) had either decided on his own to write an article about Brecht, one that objected to gratuitous criticism, or he was now asked to submit one. For some reason or other, Kantorowicz also offered to send an article, a new one presumably, to Willi Bredel, who was then working in the editorial offices of *Internationale Literatur* in

Moscow. Bredel answered Kantorowicz' inquiry: "I just heard from Peter that he has an article on Brecht finished, a long one. I am writing him now that he should send it to us. If he does, please don't get upset that I asked him for the piece: it has been such a long time since we published anything by Peter." If Merin did not send the Brecht article, then Bredel would ask Kantorowicz for one.[35]

Merin's article came out later in the year. Meanwhile, *Unsere Zeit* published not one but two short pieces about Brecht's *Der Dreigroschenroman*. Bodo Uhse wrote the first, a favorable review, and a certain Paul Haland published the second. Why Brecht, the brunt of vitriolic attacks in Germany, should be subjected to criticism "from within the camp of friends" perplexed Uhse; *Der Dreigroschenroman*, after all, had a place next to the great classical prose achievements of German literature, and Brecht's use of the language was on a par with Luther's, Kleist's, and Büchner's. "It is not a question of whether Brecht's didactic utterances are correct down to the last dotted 'i'; they are not correct, and not only the dotted 'i' is false." But the real question was, "whom does the book help and whom does it harm? . . ."[36]

Uhse shied away from underscoring theoretical differences that only obscured the overriding political significance of Brecht's work. But Haland had the last word, certainly not by coincidence, and his opening remarks smacked of the same sort of "slimy friendliness" that had disgusted Brecht in Kantorowicz' article. No one denied that Brecht was a talented playwright. His theory was debatable, his poetic talent and the stage effectiveness of his dramas were not. "Bert Brecht is one of us and belongs to the future of the proletarian revolution."[37] Haland then turned on Brecht. He had changed, "in a way that we approve of," but Brecht's transformation was regrettably less apparent in the *Dreigroschenroman*. The novel confronted the praxis of the bourgeoisie with bourgeois ideology spread by individual members of the ruling class. That confrontation developed into merciless criticism. "Except, such criticism only proves that this world is the worst of all worlds. The proletariat as the designated spokesmen of the historical criticism of the bourgeois social order is not present in Brecht's novel."[38] Only one brand of anticapitalism deserved to be taken seriously, the socialist anticapitalism of the proletariat. All other kinds of criticism ran the danger of being misused and were often "misuse" themselves. Not that he (or "we," as Haland put it) was out to assign topics to writers, but the lessons that Brecht imparted were not clear enough.[39] Haland concluded by saying that the writers who aligned themselves with "us" would be expected to choose their topics in close connection with "pressing reality" and with the demands that arise out of it.[40]

The more contentious Stalinist wing of the party's literary critics had spoken out publicly against Brecht for the first time since the debates in *Die Linkskurve*.[41] All the same, publication of *Der Dreigroschenroman* was proceeding without a hitch in the Soviet Union, and it appeared likely at the time that *Die Rundköpfe und die Spitzköpfe* would be both staged and published in book form. Brecht wrote to Steffin, who was back in Moscow, to ask that she sing his praises "in Mecca."[42] By then the date of his own departure for Moscow was nearing. In early March he told Steffin that he expected his visa within a week or so, and he would depart immediately upon receiving it.[43] "What is the name of the organization that issued the invitation," he asked, "Morp or Mort? I can't figure any of this out."[44] He also wondered whether his *Versuche* were going to be published and whether he would be received in the Soviet writers' union.[45] He apparently arrived in Moscow to find that a tentative agreement to produce *Die Rundköpfe und die Spitzköpfe* in both Moscow and Leningrad had been reached, even though the play had yet to be translated into Russian.[46]

MOSCOW 1935

Brecht was treated as a celebrity. Gustav von Wangenheim, Brecht said in a letter to his wife, had behaved "piggishly and in an unforgettable way," but there was nothing unusual about that because his relations with Brecht had been strained for a long time.[47] Otherwise, a reception was arranged in Brecht's honor and attended by representatives of the German cultural and political elite in Moscow at the time, including, among others, Wilhelm Pieck, Arthur Pieck, Fritz Heckert, Margarethe Lode, Erwin Piscator, Becher, Reich, Lazis, and Friedrich Wolf.[48]

Béla Kun and Valdemar Knorin (both of whom disappeared within a few years)[49] were there from the Comintern; Sergej Tretjakov and Semjon Kirsanov represented the Soviet writers.

At least some of the talk during Brecht's visit revolved around Piscator's dream of a resident German theater in the USSR. The plans were never realized, and at the time Brecht had little hope that they ever would be. He wrote Helene Weigel that things were rather foul as far as a German Theater was concerned. "There are few actors, only poor ones apart from Neher, but she is not especially appreciated."[50] He also tried to land an acting role of some sort in the USSR for Weigel, but came up with nothing, a minor part in a film about Georgi Dimitrov being rejected because Wangenheim was the scriptwriter.[51] Opportunities were simply not available, not even for Neher, though plans continued to be made for a German theater. Tentative talks were also underway for a theater in Engels, the capital of the Volga German republic, but nothing ever came of this project either, which Brecht dismissed as "scarcely a third-class affair."[52] But Brecht apparently regarded these matters as minor irritants and left Moscow with no reason to complain about the way he had been treated. He wrote Koltsov, who had asked Brecht to attend the upcoming writers' congress in Paris, that his trip to the USSR had been extremely refreshing in every respect; he noticed it in his work. "I spent several days in Leningrad, where I was likewise welcomed with unusual friendliness. The trip home, too—everything went well."[53]

Upon his return to Skovsbostrand, Brecht began pressing Tretjakov for information about Okhlopkov's plan to produce *Die Rundköpfe und die Spitzköpfe*. Okhlopkov was not moving ahead very quickly, perhaps because he was preoccupied with his search for a new building to house his company, and Tretjakov had trouble locating him to discuss his intentions.[54] July was half over, and Okhlopkov was still out of town; "that's why the Rundköpfe can't get moving," wrote Tretjakov,[55] who then also left town, postponing any discussions between him and Okhlopkov until mid-September, when he finally wrote Brecht: "Okhlopkov has come back. He signed a contract with Stenich for the translation of Tschuchen [*Die Rundköpfe*] and asked me if I'd like to edit it after translation. O.k."[56]

At about that time, two articles dealing with Brecht's work

appeared in Soviet periodicals. Peter Merin's in July was the first, and a Russian, A. Brustov, published the second in September. Both critics were at some pains to treat Brecht equitably, the result being a fair amount of praise tempered by their reticence to endorse his theory. Merin divided Brecht's writing into two phases, classifying works written prior to 1930 as his "poetics of negation." About the first category Merin explained that the forces acting according to class were hazy in this period of Brecht's work. "All the elements of negation are drawn in. But the opposite poles are lacking. The other side and its power is absent."[57] Merin then turned to the later works, *Die Mutter*, *Die heilige Johanna der Schlachthöfe*, *Die Rundköpfe und die Spitzköpfe*, and the *Versuche*. These showed a transition "from the creative period of social criticism, of the negation of things as they exist, to a work of affirmation of the coming order."[58] *Der Dreigroschenroman*, however, came in for criticism that almost echoed Haland's. Why had Brecht neglected the type of capitalism characteristic of the present day? Where was the working class? Brecht had certainly not ignored modern capitalism altogether, nor was he oblivious to the presence of its "future conquerer," the working class. But he had opted to focus upon a sick, putrefying, and expiring order without bringing in those who would administer the penalty of death. Still, Merin chose to emphasize the positive. The underlying idea of the book, along with the most important portion of Brecht's work, remained a pamphlet-like exposure of the bourgeois world in its superstructure. "There thus originates a large-scale contemporary satire of capitalist ethics, of fascist ideology."[59]

Brecht's theory was a different matter. Although Merin tried to be conciliatory, his comments had a slight air of condescension about them. Sooner or later Brecht was bound to abandon his experimentation and adopt a reasonable attitude; it was imperative that he do so, moreover, because all artistic creation mired in formal experimentation ended in art that distorted reality. "Brecht's development especially proves how important it is to pay attention to those contemporary talents who are searching in the maze of formal matters with an eye to drawing their abilities into the service of progress." It could be that Brecht's artistic theory was incapable of achieving the desired result, Merin said; still, it was hard to fathom why anyone would reject summarily such a fruitful artistic praxis, which transcended the theory anyway.[60] The revolutionary and artistic significance of Brecht's work, after all, was unchallengeable, and poets ought to be recognized not by their theories but by their actual writing.[61]

Brustov pursued a related line of argument. Brecht's early works failed to depict the proletariat—"the only force capable of leading the world out of the blind alley." He saw the world falling apart, but regarded its condition as immutable and enduring.[62] Be that as it may, Brecht was still the most significant playwright and poet of postwar Germany; no German writer since Heine had hit upon such a brilliant combination of anecdotes, irony, satire, and content. "There is nothing in contemporary German literature to compare with the stridency of [Brecht's] criticism, his sarcasm, and his aggressiveness."[63] Brustov then went on to raise the question of Brecht's theory in a section entitled "Catharsis or Cigar." The theory fell apart under close scrutiny, he argued, but to all intents and purposes Brecht went beyond it in his writing. "Brecht poses a question that rules out a third alternative: catharsis or cigar? He chooses (or thinks he chooses) the latter. But as surely as the viewer of Brecht's plays falls into a state of catharsis, he just as certainly forgets about his cigar and lets it burn a hole in his pants!" This pointed toward catharsis plus a "smoking observer."[64]

Brustov punctuated his praise of *Der Dreigroschenroman* with familiar objections. However dazzling the satirical form used to cloak Brecht's criticism of bourgeois society, the proletariat, the class charged historically with executing the death sentence imposed upon this society, was inexcusably absent. Brecht had, after all, witnessed the proletariat at the height of its strength and vitality; moreover, he believed in the proletariat as the eventual victor, the builder of socialism. Yet "no trace of this knowledge" showed up in the novel. If Brecht had overcome this deficiency, *Der Dreigroschenroman* would have become the "epochal book of our era" that Brecht intended it to be. Instead, the idea remained only imperfectly realized, outstanding within certain bounds, but a torso nonetheless. Brustov was confident, though, that Brecht would fill in the gaps; his "exceptional talent," his "genius," virtually guaranteed it. "The struggle for liberation of the German proletariat from fascist dictatorship, the fight for the Soviet power of German workers and peasants, has acquired a resounding voice.[65] He will continue to supply the antifascist united front with an even greater number of powerful works."[66]

DAS WORT

In late 1935 or early 1936 Steffin returned again to Moscow, and many of the projects begun the year before were wrapped up. In February Steffin wrote Brecht that *Die Horatier und die Kuratier* was in print and scheduled to appear in two weeks.[67] *Der Dreigroschenroman* was about to go on sale in German,[68] Steffin wrote, and Stenich would be bringing her the manuscript of the Russian translation tomorrow. The publisher had it a few days later, and Steffin wrote to say that it would be out "soon."[69] Prospects for a licensed VEGAAR edition of Herzfelde's planned four volumes of Brecht's plays (to be published by the Malik Verlag) and for a poetry volume also appeared promising.[70] Although trouble for literature and art was now brewing in general terms in the USSR (in her letter to Brecht Steffin mentioned the "formalism discussion" that was filling the pages of the Soviet daily press), Okhlopkov was still interested in staging *Die Rundköpfe und die Spitzköpfe* both in Moscow and in Leningrad's Music Hall. Moreover, Lenfilm had suggested that Brecht write the script for a film version of *Schweik*,[71] and Goslitizdat hoped to publish *Die Rundköpfe und die Spitzköpfe*. Brecht proposed that two more plays be included in the volume, but Steffin told him on 5 March that *Die Rundköpfe und die Spitzkopfe* would be coming out alone. She provided no further details. Steffin also reported that Semjon Kirsanov had agreed to translate the play and was advanced five thousand rubles. After he failed to deliver a single line, Stenich was approached instead, and Kirsanov agreed to work off his advance by doing twelve songs for the play. As far as Brecht's royalties were concerned, both Steffin and Stenich thought that Okhlopkov should assume responsibility because he was staging the play.

Brecht, by the way, was anxious to visit Moscow himself at

the time, but Steffin told him somewhat cryptically that, according to Stenich's "privately" expressed opinion, there was no point in it.[72] Still, by the end of 1936 Brecht had few grounds for dissatisfaction. *Die Rundköpfe und die Spitzköpfe* appeared that year in translation,[73] and Tretjakov's book of portraits (including one of Brecht), *Ljudi odnogo kostra*, also came off the press.[74] Okhlopkov's plan to put on *Die Rundköpfe und die Spitzköpfe*, on the other hand, fell through. Although the authorities shut his theater down just one year later, there is no hard evidence that a worsening political and artistic climate caused Okhlopkov to abandon his plan to stage Brecht's play. Nor, however, can the possibility be ruled out altogether.

In view of the prevalent hostility toward Brecht in the German section of the Soviet writers' union, particularly among those who headed the section, it is difficult to understand why he was asked to edit the new monthly *Das Wort*, which was originally planned as the official organ of the German section. The reason is that those men who disliked Brecht the most were least involved in the early stages of the journal's planning. Key roles were played instead by Mikhail Koltsov and his companion Maria Osten. Brecht had probably met Koltsov for the first time in 1932, and Koltsov, in fact, had a hand in the showing of *Kuhle Wampe*.[75] Their relations grew more cordial in 1934 and 1935, probably because of Koltsov's position as head of the foreign commission within the writers' union, and the selection of Sergej Tretjakov to be Koltsov's deputy points to still further associations between the three men.[76]

These connections appear perfectly understandable considering the literary theoretical affinities. Koltsov was a journalist with a solid reputation as an *ocherkist* long before he wrote his *Spanish Diary*. His opinion of socialist realism as it acquired its "theoretical" contours in the course of 1936 is unknown, but it seems unlikely that he would have disdained Tretjakov's kind of artistic publicism—"bio-interviews," literature of fact, and the like—because his own work fit into the same general category. Given these circumstances, it is likely that Koltsov was directly responsible for placing Brecht on the editorial board of *Das Wort* alongside the fellow traveler Lion Feuchtwanger and the Communist Willi Bredel; and, most importantly, the Jourgaz publishing operation that Koltsov headed was in charge financially and technically of bringing out *Das Wort*. In addition, Maria Osten, who had become friendly with Steffin, worked together with Wieland Herzfelde in early 1936 to get the journal off the ground.[77] By 1 April Osten had received Brecht's agreement to serve as an editor,[78] and she continued to correspond with him and Feuchtwanger from Moscow until Bredel arrived from Paris in May to take over the daily chores of running *Das Wort*. Osten then left for the West,[79] where she continued to work for the journal. By 24 June she was with Brecht, evidently in Paris,[80] and met also with Walter Benjamin to arrange for his collaboration with the journal. She stayed with Brecht for a few weeks before joining Koltsov in Spain.

Brecht's initial editorial involvement in *Das Wort* was problematical. He was extremely unhappy with the journal at first and asked Piscator in October 1936, for instance, to write something for the journal to improve it a little. "It makes you sick to your stomach."[81] But Brecht was scarcely a model editor in his efforts to raise the quality of the journal. His verdict in the early months regarding the publication of various manuscripts evidently fell into one of two categories, acceptance or curt rejection, and he supplied little in the way of reasons for either. Bredel wrote Herzfelde in December 1936, for example: "The objections that B.B. has against Winder's 'Tochter des Bombenkönig' are unfamiliar to me; he demanded categorically that it not be published. Maybe the two 'know' each other." Herzfelde, for his part, considered it unpardonable to reject a manuscript because the editor disliked the author. He told Bredel to demand a concrete explanation.[82] Although this may be a characteristic example of Brecht's posture at the beginning, by early 1937 Bredel's unhappiness with his coeditor had vanished. He wrote Osten in March that what stopped the journal from achieving real quality was only the regrettable but unavoidable circumstance that the editors lived in three different cities.[83]

But just when Brecht's interest in the journal picked up and some of the early difficulties in running it had been ironed out, Brecht's enemies started causing trouble. His first brush with the German Stalinists came in the form of a quarrel with Julius Hay.[84] Bernhard Reich had published an article in the January

1937 number of *Das Wort* that included too much praise of Brecht's *Die Rundköpfe und die Spitzköpfe* and too little of Hay's *Der Damm an der Theiss* and *Haben* to suit Hay. In contrast to the brand of criticism regularly practiced by Hay himself,[85] Reich's critical remarks had no denunciatory undertone; he voiced his opinion politely and unabrasively, explaining that Hay tended to go in for widely diverse topics that reflected an element of political circumspection caused by his uncertainty in the question of artistic tactics during the period of the popular front. As a result, Hay "camouflaged" his work. Reich's version of Hay's thinking ran like this: "Out of consideration for the natural allies of the proletariat, who are captivated by various illusions and traditions, one ought to 'camouflage' one's terminology and subject matter. One ought to locate neutral, peripheral topics, so to speak, not take immediate, revolutionary material as one's point of departure, and weaken the presentation, show an interest in 'human matters.'" In his opinion such thinking missed the point altogether. "What is urgently needed is a genuine art for the masses,"[86] said Reich.

When Hay read the article, he lost his temper and fired off a letter to Brecht demanding that an article he enclosed be published. The essay—Brecht described it in a letter to Piscator as "a nice, dirty little article . . . with clumsy attacks upon Reich, me, and, camouflaged, upon you"[87]—prompted Brecht to write letters to Reich, Hay, and Becher. Brecht told Reich that he had just received copies of the Russian version of *Die Rundköpfe und die Spitzköpfe,* and he hoped that "the Russian comrades" would read it with more understanding than "our stack of Hay" had shown. "It will interest you to know," he went on, "that Hay (who is no more alone with his opinion than any philistine with any opinion) raises chiefly 2 crafty objections: *First*, the play is water on the mill of the fascists inasmuch as it takes up the fascist claim that racial characteristics of arians are clearly distinguishable from those of Jews (anatomically, too). . . . *Second*, I did not depict fascism because fascism can not exist in an agrarian country." Brecht realized immediately that Hay had not acted on his own, and he feared that Reich may have incurred the wrath of persons in Moscow capable of making things difficult for him. In Brecht's view, people who, with things as they were now, were determined to discuss nothing but questions of form and to that end jumped at opportunities to pick fights were a "very unpleasant sort of formalist."[88]

Brecht told Hay that it had never entered his mind to kill criticism of his own work and theory; if Hay could come up with an informative essay minus the invective, however much it took issue with Brecht, *Das Wort* would publish it. But Brecht would not stand for polemics that were bound to precipitate a divisive debate. "I would advise you," he told Hay, "against publishing this particular article; it does not serve our common cause, and you would do better not to make an issue of it."[89] In the third of his letters, Brecht explained his position to Becher. Because Hay had really meant to attack him, said Brecht, he could not have avoided answering Hay if the article had been published; "and I was far more afraid of the impact of my counterattack than I was of the attack." Those people like Hay had simply forgotten all practical matters connected with the real fight on account of their formalistic interests, Brecht went on. "You can imagine that it was not entirely easy for me simply to play the editor here, mumbling all sorts of phrases like 'you may have missed the right tone a bit' and 'we can't be fighting among ourselves in front of everybody,' by simply not publishing the little piece and answering his letter, instead of using such a marvelous opportunity to speak my mind in *writing* and to bury the subject." A public debate on literary forms was in no one's interest, and Brecht asked Becher to explain his standpoint to "the comrades" in Moscow. "In a word, we can do without Hay fever."[90]

After this particular skirmish (directly or indirectly, Georg Lukács had his hand in it),[91] Hay bore a grudge against Brecht, making at least some of the coming events probably unavoidable. As an editor of *Das Wort*, however, Brecht enjoyed a measure of protection from the men around Lukács who were anxious to even the score with him. But when Willi Bredel left for Spain in early 1937, his position as Moscow editor of the journal was taken de facto if not de jure by a pair of Lukács' acolytes, Fritz Erpenbeck and Alfred Kurella, and the situation from then on deteriorated rapidly. A mark of the changed circumstances in the Moscow office of *Das Wort* was the treatment accorded Walter Benjamin, whose difficulties in dealing with the journal mounted. Bredel had told Benjamin in late March 1937 that he wished to wait for the time being with the publication of Benjamin's "Das Kunstwerk im Zeitalter seiner Reproduzierbarkeit" because it was too lengthy.[92] With Bredel out of Moscow, though, the new acting editor reached a quick decision. The article was being returned to him at Bredel's request, Erpenbeck wrote Benjamin, adding: "Apart from the fact that it is too lengthy for our journal, we just received an essay a short time ago that deals to a large extent with the same problem."[93] More rejections followed. Benjamin's review of *Der Dreigroschenroman* was returned to him "because it is inappropriate for us to publish your piece in our journal so long after Brecht's book came out. Unfortunately, I cannot tell you myself why this manuscript lay around so long here."[94] When Benjamin inquired about the fate of his second "Pariser Brief" ("Fotografie und Malerei"), which the editorial board had actually commissioned and whose acceptance Bredel had expressly confirmed ten weeks earlier,[95] Erpenbeck replied that a decision had to await Bredel's return from Spain,[96] probably knowing full well that Bredel would not be back in Moscow soon. The article never appeared. In late 1937 Brecht prodded Erpenbeck into commissioning Benjamin to review the first two volumes of Brecht's plays published in the Malik edition,[97] but this review never found its way into the pages of *Das Wort* either.

Then, after a hiatus of two years or so, the attacks upon Brecht started up again. The first, and one of the harshest, appeared in *Literaturnyj kritik*. Written by Lukács' friend V. Aleksandrov, the criticism of Brecht's *Die Mutter* had the unmistakable ring of Lukács to it. Comparing Brecht's adaptation with Gorky's original novel, Aleksandrov bandied about words like "mathematical formulas" to describe the dialogue. Certain kinds of "logic" or a textbook on geometry could be adapted like this for the stage, but not Gorky's novel. Such arithmetic was occasionally "quite witty," but arithmetic it remained, "as if the play were supposed to strike the spectator as a logical equation."[98] Ilja Ehrenburg had once employed such geometry to create his Nikolaj Kurbov, an approach to writing characteristic of someone who "overate and poisoned himself with the foul emotionalism of decadent bourgeois art and who has no desire to look for a different form of healthy emotionalism." Brecht might have the best of intentions, said Aleksandrov; he might despise the bourgeoisie. But this intentional flaunting of didacticism should be regarded "above all else as a *formal*, innovative technique." No wonder Brecht's didactics were directly linked to formalistic art, Aleksandrov went on; "they spring not from the new relations that exist between human beings but from the quest for newness [*novizma*]. Brecht failed to grasp and embrace Gorky's humanism and realism, and yet precisely such humanism and realism must be learned. For they are the true instruments required in the struggle against, among other things, the bourgeois decadence that Brecht opposes even as he bases himself upon the 'achievements' of this selfsame decadence. Decadence, however, is not an achievement at all but a sickness, one that must be overcome forthwith."[99]

The expressionism debate began in *Das Wort* three months later, one of the prime purposes of which was to hector Brecht into an open defense of his ideas on theater. Although he refused to let himself be provoked at first, Lukács' article "Es geht um den Realismus" finally goaded Brecht into writing.[100] He had seen the article in manuscript form and immediately insisted to Erpenbeck that it not be included, as scheduled, in the next issues of the journal.[101] But Brecht's protestations were ignored, and Lukács' article appeared in *Das Wort*. In a communication written a few weeks later, Brecht then promised Alfred Kurella that he would be sending his own essay "Volkstümlichkeit und Realismus" to Moscow for publication in *Das Wort*,[102] but Brecht's indirect response to Lukács never appeared in the journal, nor did another essay that had clearly been earmarked for publication in *Das Wort*, "Weite und Vielfalt der realistischen Schreibweise." Whether Brecht ever actually sent the articles is not entirely certain; he may have suspected that they would merely serve Lukács as a negative illustration of certain points Lukács would then make in a final, canonical statement. Though Brecht warned Bredel in summer 1938 that his patience with this kind of behavior was wearing thin,[103] he continued on as editor until the journal folded in March 1939 following Koltsov's arrest four months earlier.

"DISTORTED REALITY"

Several months later, Brecht's fortunes in the Soviet Union took a modest turn upwards when Lukács' influence among Soviet literary critics began to wane as a consequence of the gradual change in Soviet literary policy caused in part by the end of the popular front era.[104] In early 1939 some of Brecht's friends ventured to criticize Lukács' disciple Hay, though still very tentatively. They appear to have gone about it by using the same type of tactics employed in the past by the Lukács circle. They published an essay by Hay in a periodical that they controlled or strongly influenced, *Teatr*, and followed it up with articles of their own. These were written by Timofej Rokotov (chief editor of *International Literature*) and Bernhard Reich.

Hay's essay, "The Road to Realism," which appears to have been a version of the article whose publication Brecht forestalled in 1937, began with criticism of "political" theater in Weimar Germany. The salient points: this "topical" (*zlobodnevnyj*) theater had restricted the number of available themes, confined the front of the revolutionary struggle by underrating the broad humanistic appeal of communism, and "ignored" the classical heritage. Certain revolutionary writers and artists had set out to create art for the broad proletarian masses; "instead, they failed to take advantage of all the possibilities available to them and persisted in following a sectarian path in their work."[105] It would be "unjust," however, to forget about certain "very positive developments" that paralleled this general incorrect trend in art, said Hay; some writers were disinclined to circumscribe the sphere of their activity, and these artists (Hay counted himself among them) went about the task of exploring different possibilities vigorously and with great resourcefulness. They discovered a sort of Aesopian language, a form of "camouflage," and came up with "interesting and valuable results." A prime example of these writers was Gustav von Wangenheim, whose plays were performed time and again even after Hitler's accession to power and up to the burning of the Reichstag. They managed to attract far greater numbers of spectators than plays with a "distinct political tendency," Hay contended. After February 1933 the new situation demanded new techniques, and Wangenheim broke free of the now outdated approaches. Bertolt Brecht, on the other hand, "who displays an uncommon degree of talent," persisted in working in the wrong direction and tried to turn "a passing, transitory phenomenon into a principle." Life had shown this to be a hopeless undertaking; *Die Rundköpfe und die Spitzköpfe*, for instance, failed to attain its political purpose, the exposure of fascism's racist demagogy. But in recent years Brecht, whose "talent not even his own false theory can stifle," moved forward on the road to realism. *Die Gewehre der Frau Carrar*, for example, or *Der Spitzel* and *Die Rechtsfindung* served as proof that Brecht had "successfully liberated himself from the formalistic 'epic doctrine'" and that he was well on the way to writing realistic plays.[106]

Rokotov's and Reich's articles followed in the same issue of *Teatr*. Neither piece was at all polemical, neither mentioned Hay by name nor took specific issue with his remarks, and the recent works by Brecht that came in for praise were the same ones mentioned by Hay.[107] Perhaps no more could be risked at the time, but within a year Lukács' standing in official Soviet literary circles had eroded almost entirely, and his critics ventured out into the open. The swift deterioration of Lukács' authority was accompanied by certain cautious overtures to Brecht. Rokotov wrote him in August 1939: "As you may know, our mutual friend Martin Andersen Nexö is currently visiting here in Moscow. A short time ago, I had a long conversation with him about literary matters, in the course of which Martin Andersen Nexö, among other things, expressed his surprise that you have no ties with our editorial staff at all." Nexö had told Rokotov that this was an oversight on Rokotov's part and asked him to write Brecht. He was all the happier to fulfill Nexö's request because the editorial staff of *International Literature* followed Brecht's work attentively and had read his one-act plays about the Third Reich published in the French *Commune* with real interest. "These plays enthralled us to such an extent," Rokotov went on, "that I turned specifically to the secretary of the Parisian league of German writers with the request that he send us the manuscripts of these plays in the original." Rokotov intended to publish a collection of anti-fascist plays in the very near future, and Brecht's plays would be a real addition to this volume, of which Rokotov was the editor.[108]

Rokotov added that the entire editorial board, himself naturally included, would be pleased if permanent and cordial ties could be established between the journal and Brecht, perhaps trying to impress upon Brecht that the editions of *International Literature* published in languages other than German were not in the hands of the same persons who ran the German version. "You probably know that our French and English editions are completely different from the German edition of the 'IL,'" Rokotov remarked. "In case these should be of interest, it would be my pleasure to send them to you. . . . Our Russian press has not published anything about your present work for quite some time. We would be happy to have a letter from you that we could publish in the 'IL' in order to acquaint our readers with your creative plans." Rokotov thought that one or two of Brecht's one-act plays could also be printed in the Russian edition of *International Literature*, in addition to the collection.[109]

The timing of Rokotov's letter was not especially good. Hitler and Stalin reached their agreement a week later, and no antifascist book by Brecht or anyone else saw the light of day for the next two years. But even though the various editions of Brecht's *Furcht und Elend des Dritten Reiches* published in the Soviet Union had to await the outbreak of war,[110] the pact did not prevent some stridently polemical articles directed at Hay and Lukács from appearing in print. In early 1940 N. Kozjura published a blistering denunciation of Hay's *Haben*, which had just appeared in Russian. The play was supposed to illustrate Marx' notion of the dehumanization caused by the ownership of private property. The artistic realization of this profound idea, however, had "regrettably" been undertaken in a vulgar sociological fashion. The attempt to portray the intractabilities of an economic social system and the individual human beings caught up in its cogs was carried "to the point of absurdity" in Hay's play, resulting in a caricature. At the heart of it all was the "venerable history" of Hay's literary techniques, Kozjura said, and she went on to use the same epithets against Hay that he and others in Lukács' circle were so fond of employing. These techniques sprang "purely and simply from the arsenal of decadent dramaturgy." The play was devoid of human beings; there was no evolution in their mental processes, no interiorized or individualized tragedy that made the crimes later committed by them plausible to the reader. "The distorted, hysterical, unnatural caricatures are an offense to an elementary sense of artistic good taste." That a Soviet publisher had brought out this book, "archaic in its errors, tasteless, and boring,"[111] was unpardonable.

Then Reich vented some of the pent-up frustrations of recent years. In June 1940 he accused Lukács of attempting to "revise and distort Marxist-Leninist views on art."[112] Several months later he leveled a devastating attack entitled "Distorted Reality" upon the leading figures of the German section of the Soviet writers' union, beginning with Becher, proceeding to Hay, and finishing up with Lukács. Becher had recently reviewed for the *Literaturnaja gazeta* Hay's play *Der Putenhirt*, which *Internationale Literatur* had published. His review, as Reich must have spotted immediately, was meant as much as a refutation of Brecht's work than as an appreciation of Hay's. Underlying it all was Lukács' general notion of decadence. "Particularly in the leftist-oriented literature of the West there were countless supporters of 'epic' dramas, or a revue-like documentary drama, which under a revolutionary facade accommodated itself in this manner to the disintegrative tendencies of capitalism," said Becher. Hay, on the other hand, had resisted attempts to "enrich," that is, to "dissolve" the drama lyrically, epically, novelistically, or with methods of reportage. The need for the "creative representation of human beings," the "lure of originality," "arbitrary, loosely stringed-together sequence of scenes," "'up-to-date,' long-winded, boring didacticism"—the various pejoratives were addressed to Brecht, and the diction was Lukács'. Becher concluded with words that likewise parroted Lukács: "Capitalism must be battled not just in word but also in deed. But in the realm of art, deed is creative representation. Only a profound, all-embracing representation of human beings is effective against the barbaric dehumanization engendered by contemporary capitalism on all of its battlefields, and it is artistic perfection that upholds us in our belief in human perfectability and in a different, better world. Literary 'shadow games' of whatever sort necessarily fail vis-à-vis the barbaric brutality of imperialism."[113]

Reich used Becher's compliments of Hay to rail against his, Reich's, and Brecht's longtime detractors. Hay's "demagogic" distinction in *Der Putenhirt* between the various social strata that existed in a capitalist system made him guilty of grievous errors. Becher, who understood the nature of these mistakes, had nonetheless expressed his "solidarity" with Hay.[114] Reich's line of reasoning then dipped to the same low level as his opponent's and took on the identical kind of denunciatory tone typically employed by Lukács and his followers. Hay neglected to portray the intensity of the class struggle, and the "idealistic" impression that the play left in the reader's mind was inexcusable given the current state of world affairs. How was it, in fact, that Hay, a political émigré who had found a "second homeland" in the Soviet Union, lost his ability to empathize with daily life abroad?

Reich then brought up various plays that Hay had written previously, including his trashy account of spies in the USSR, class vigilance, and the ever-alert eye of the Soviet secret police, *Tanjka macht die Augen auf*. This play demonstrated Hay's inability to deal with such matters on a serious level. "He has not yet found his bearings in Soviet reality," was the way Reich put it.[115] Then he came to Lukács: "We can scarcely go wrong by ascribing Hay's efforts to picture contemporary reality in an indirect, weakened form, and his predilection for depicting life that produces only a faint and indistinct echo of the sound of revolutionary struggles, to the influence of Lukács' 'theory.'" Whereas Hay, in *Haben*, had still managed to hold his own against this "baleful" influence, he had capitulated to it in *Der Putenhirt*, sending "Lukács and his sidekicks" into raptures in their praise of an obviously unsuccessful play. Becher had spoken of the "programmatic" quality of *Putenhirt*. "In a certain sense, this is correct," said Reich; "but what kind of a program leads inevitably to a politically pernicious falsification of contemporary life? This program ignores the ideological content of sharp conflicts that characterize the reality of today's world. Lukács and his sidekicks extol *Der Putenhirt*, in which they see, justifiably so, the creative realization of their aesthetic theories."[116]

Thus ended this latest episode in Brecht's running battle with proxy German Stalinists. War broke out several months later, and the various issues that he and his detractors had debated throughout the thirties and early forties were not rehashed again until after Brecht's return to the Soviet zone of occupation.

BOLSHEVISM AND THE ENEMIES
OF LITERARY PRODUCTION

The Soviet Union was like a puzzle to Brecht. He managed to put some parts of it together perfectly, but he proved less adroit when he wedged other pieces into places where they did not belong. He then mistook the emerging image for an unvarnished and authentic representation of Soviet reality, whereas the picture was actually badly disjointed. As a result, he completely misinterpreted some basic facts about the way things were done in the Soviet Union under Stalin. Brecht knew, for instance, that the major source of his personal difficulties lay with men like Lukács, Gábor, Kurella, Erpenbeck, and Hay. "With these people," said Benjamin to Brecht on one occasion, "you just can't make much of a showing" (*ist eben kein Staat zu machen*—cannot "make a state"). To which Brecht replied sarcastically, "Or *just* a state, but no commonwealth. They are enemies of production, that's all. Production makes them uneasy. It cannot be trusted. It represents what is unpredictable. One never knows what will come out of it. And they themselves do not want to produce. They want to play the role of the apparachik and have control over others. Each of their criticisms contains a threat."[117]

This particular characterization is essentially sound. But the reasoning behind it is faulty all the same, and because Brecht was unable to spot the underlying flaw, he was singularly inept when it came to bringing the larger picture of Stalin's Russia into focus. Brecht evidently believed that *apparatchiki* of the kind he had just described, with their insatiable urge to prescribe and mandate, perhaps had functions of some kind to fulfill in the state and party apparatus, but they should be kept at arm's length from literature. Brecht apparently had no idea that precisely this species of party bureaucrat was responsible for what he imagined were great revolutionary changes in the country and that such men would be loath to keep their hands off literature. A prominent part of the puzzle was missing, but Brecht, it seems, failed to realize that the piece was even lost. "It does not even have to be claimed that [the methods of the bolsheviks] failed in this area," he said of Soviet literary politics; "perhaps it suffices to say that the methods that they applied in this area failed."[118]

Brecht draws a fine line between "Bolshevist methods" in general (these he commended) and the methods that the very same Bolsheviks applied to literature. These, Brecht apparently believed, were in some way not consistent with bolshevism. The faceless bureaucrats who managed the affairs of government in the thirties had a natural urge to oversee Soviet literature and every other form of intellectual endeavor. In so doing they resorted to the same methods that they employed to bolshevize the Soviet Communist party, dekulakize the kulaks, and liquidate real and fictional opponents of the system. What compelling reasons were there for Brecht to count upon the same functionaries to exclude literary life from their regulation and regimentation of Soviet society?

The Apologist

But people will not say: the times were dark
Rather: why were their poets silent?
—Brecht, "In finsteren Zeiten"

Is it best then to keep silent?
—Brecht, "Ist das Volk unfehlbar?"

In 1943 Brecht commented upon "the most frightful instruments of oppression and the most frightful police force which the world has ever known." Denouncing Hitler for having "ravaged his own country" before ravaging others, he expressed his outrage that "whole armies" of citizens had been locked up in concentration camps and that the number of prisoners in Nazi Germany added up in 1939 to the staggering sum of 200,000.[1] By way of comparison, figures reputedly compiled in 1956 for a secret politburo investigation of Stalin's crimes place the prison and camp population in the USSR in 1938 at 16 million. Before 1935, 22 million persons perished in the collectivization of agriculture through famine and terror, and some 18,840,000 persons, fully one quarter of the adult population of the Soviet Union, are said to have "passed through the Lubjanka and other affiliated institutions" from 1935 to 1940. Around 7 million of these were executed in prison, the overwhelming majority of the rest died in camps. After 1940 and until Stalin's death in 1953, in the vicinity of 9 million more died in other assorted campaigns of violence and repression.[2]

DOUBT, DICTATORSHIP, AND HISTORICAL USEFULNESS

What accounts for Brecht's silence with respect to these "dark times"? He explained away the atrocities by contriving every imaginable extenuating circumstance. He began by toying with the concept of freedom. The urge to be free meant different things at different times, always depending upon the social class in pursuit of liberty. The bourgeoisie curtailed freedom of speech by manipulating the technical means by which opinions could be turned into factors in the struggle for power. In the USSR, by contrast, information was disseminated differently. "It is no coincidence that the speakers at the Soviet congress consulting about the Stalin Constitution repeatedly acknowledge the claim of the proletarian class to all printing presses, paper reserves, meeting rooms, and radio stations."[3] But the incongruity of Brecht's evaluation of conditions in the USSR is that he set his normal suspicion aside and took ordinary Stalinist rhetoric in 1936 at face value. In so doing, he ignored his own advice to Tretjakov just a few years before to the effect that Marxists were not interested in what statesmen said about their policies but in what they did.[4]

The "proletarian Soviets" had their own way of "organizing" opinions,[5] Brecht argued. It was a unique approach to molding and influencing public opinion that had nothing in common with the crass propaganda or demagogy of the bourgeoisie. This was understandably so, for without clear methods of enlightenment, persuasion, and conversion it was ridiculous to think "that the gigantic work of collectively constructing industry (without private initiative), the collectivization and mechanization of the agriculture over one sixth of the earth, the achievement of two five-year plans . . . could have been decreed dictatorially and to the exclusion of any criticism by a few people sitting in armchairs."[6] It never crossed Brecht's mind that the feat of collectivization and industrialization might indeed have been carried out because a few men at the top set the entire process in motion. He deduced instead that the revolutionary transformation of town and countryside had to have enjoyed the wholehearted, if occasionally critical, support of the people. Brecht knew, on the other hand, that a measure of repression had been involved; the criticism of some peasants had not been "constructive" and was thus dealt with accordingly. In Brecht's mind, though, such violence fit into the category of historical necessity because "without the repression of those peasant masses who balk at supporting the construction of a powerful industry in Russia, a condition cannot be brought about, that is created, in which dictatorships are superfluous."[7]

Brecht apparently had little difficulty blotting images of a bloody civil war waged against the rural population of the country out of his mind; he utilized the word "repression" seemingly without conjuring up visions of mass deportation by cattle car, brutal cold, starvation, and murder. Some 22 million persons presumably perished in the campaigns of forced collectivization, and Brecht contented himself with cerebral rationalizations. The Bolsheviks had to turn agriculture itself into an industry, he said, and that was "violent business."[8] Brecht was perfectly willing to regard the end as a justification of the means. Certainly he may have been ignorant of the full dimensions of the horror, but he could easily have taken Stalin at his word in the essays collected in *Problems of Leninism* and republished in hundreds of thousands of copies as classic expositions of Marxism-Leninism. These writings were read and studied by all Communists in the thirties, and it is unlikely that Brecht was unaware of them. In one particular speech, Stalin had upbraided the Zinovievist-Trotskyist "opposition" for advocating a policy of harmlessly "scratching the kulaks." Real bolshevism, contended Stalin, meant something else altogether: "To attack the kulaks means to smash the kulaks, to liquidate them as a class. Without these aims, attack is a mere declamation, mere scratching, empty noise, anything but a real Bolshevist attack. To attack the kulaks means to make proper preparations and then deliver the blow, a blow from which they could not recover." Would Brecht perhaps have wondered what Stalin meant by liquidate? Just how permissible was the harsh measure of "dekulakization," expropriation and deportation of the kulaks, Stalin had asked himself? "A ridiculous question," he answered; "don't lament the loss of the hair of one who has been beheaded."[9]

What is striking about Brecht's assessment of Stalin and the Soviet Union is the methodical zealousness with which he suspended his usual skepticism. Various forms of disbelief were normally basic requisites to Brecht's approach to the apparent reality of the world around him and the claims made about that reality, but not in the case of the Soviet Union. He assailed a skeptic like André Gide, who had written two books critical of the USSR, for his lack of perspective and one-sided skepticism; it was not broadly enough applied—"not directed at all sides." [10] But was Brecht's more so? True, he later began questioning certain developments in the Soviet Union that troubled him. Very skeptical answers resulted whenever he brought up Russian matters in Brecht's presence, wrote Benjamin in 1938. [11] As it was, though, Brecht's skepticism invariably touched only upon "details." He thought that he had no obligation to concern himself with inconsequential matters such as the "horrible things" connected with the show trials, according to Sternberg. What he was concerned with was the "overall line." [12] Brecht's cardinal failing, the dominant flaw in his "dialectic," was his predilection for viewing unpleasant "details" as isolated occurrences or transitory, atypical phenomena, rather than looking at the broad pattern of behavior that produced them.

Brecht used the issue of collectivization to make the point that governmental policy in the USSR was not exempt from criticism, though it was couched in sui generis terms. "It is true that the general line of the party is not criticized in newspaper articles and not set down or turned around by groups chatting by the fireside. No book is published against it." But "life itself" criticized the general line. When the collectivization of agriculture had endangered the entire country a few years earlier by its "overly hasty tempo," no article against it had come out in the press. "But was the tempo maintained?" It was not, and it must therefore be assumed that criticism had indeed been voiced. "Could perhaps that which had resulted in a reduced tempo be called criticism? It would be an unaccustomed kind of criticism, a new species, but what is wrong with that?" [13]

Brecht may have been helped along in this indirect plaidoyer for restriction of a free press by Stalin's article "Dizzy with Success," in which Stalin blamed his subalterns for overdoing things in the collectivization campaign. Brecht's logic in the above passage was certainly redolent of Stalin's, and he added by way of explanation: "In driving a car, sitting at the wheel, I criticize the direction of my automobile by steering." [14] But there is a certain amount of involuntary irony to Brecht's metaphor. Applied to Stalin's behavior, the following scene would have to be pictured: at the wheel of a car careening wildly down the road, Stalin, after first running over the "left" opposition, swerves to the right. He then veers back to the left after hitting the right wingers, and finally, because he was going too fast, loses control of the car altogether and almost runs it off the left side of the road, killing several million peasants who failed to get out of the way quickly enough. After hitting a few too many and inciting the anger of the rest, he slams on the brakes, jumps out, and, gesticulating wildly about irresponsibility, accuses his party comrades who forced him to give the car too much gas of being intoxicated by success and making "reckless attempts to settle all the problems of Socialist construction 'in a trice.'" [15]

In the thirties Brecht never quite fathomed the role that brute force played under Stalin. He believed that dictatorships of all kinds evolved as part of a natural historical process. They were necessary tools of any kind of repression, Brecht wrote. "If the struggles of the repressing class with the repressed classes are severe, then they even lead as a rule to the dictatorship of individual persons within the repressing class." This was because the class responsible for the repression needed strict discipline and, in view of a powerful enemy, was not able to allow its own heterogenous interests to express themselves strongly." [16]

According to the Bolsheviks, however, there was a critical difference in their case. For them, wrote Brecht, the decision to reject or enforce a dictatorship in the only form that had appeared thus far, one culminating in a single person, was based on the consideration of whether such a dictatorship "retarded" or "facilitated" the forces of production. [17] Brecht sided with this reasoning, and his capacity to inquire critically into major features of Soviet policy and the real substance of Stalin's rule suffered from serious erosion because of it. Brecht put his faith in the historical exigencies that placed one man at the top of a power pyramid, but he overlooked the process by which the base then thinned out quickly. He apparently failed to realize that as the men around Stalin who used to have some say in the government fell by the wayside, the number of persons able to influence policy shriveled essentially to one. Where was the Bolshevik whom Brecht evidently expected to scratch at Stalin's office door, inform him of the politburo decision that he was now hampering the forces of production, and request that he now relinquish his duties? By late 1936, 1937, and 1938, after all, "Bolsheviks" (especially those in the central committee and politburo) were a vanishing breed.[18]

Not that Brecht had no reservations about Stalin at all; he was ill at ease, for instance, with the praise lavished upon him[19] and wrote in *Me-ti*: "Ni-ens [Stalin's] reputation has suffered on account of disreputable praise. There is so much incense that the picture becomes impossible to see, leading to the comment: Something is being hidden here."[20] Praise like this smacked of bribery. Of course something was wrong, but the correct inferences again seemed to slip away from Brecht, who sought refuge in his skewed dialectic. The adulation of Stalin served a useful purpose and furthered the historical cause. It was true that praise had to be procured wherever possible if it was needed. "To make them praise a good cause, bad people have to be bribed. And there was need of much praise in those times, for the way was dark, and the one leading the way had no proof."[21] What mattered to Brecht was not the superhuman image of an earthly divinity, of demiurgic greatness; it was a question, rather, of Stalin's "usefulness." He described this particular distinction in one of his poems[22] and wrote similar passages into *Me-ti* ("Me-ti suggested that Ni-en [Stalin] not be called the Greatest all the time, but rather the Useful One"[23]). This kind of reasoning caused Brecht to lose his way again in another of the dialectical word games that so often tainted his thinking. The time was not right to employ "usefulness" as a term of praise, for: "The useful ones had been without any fame for too long; thus, the comment that one was useful now no longer brought anyone the trust that he was capable of leading. Before, the leaders had always been recognized by their capacity to be useful to themselves." Me-ti soon saw the unfitness of his suggestion and said himself that what he actually wanted was for the useful ones to be acknowledged as great. But precisely that was now occurring with Ni-en, Stalin. "The pack of repressors who used to control power always tried to prove to the repressed that the greatest of repressors was actually very useful. Now the Useful One is being called great."[24]

Brecht backed himself into an approval of the personality cult, shunting all substantive criticism of Stalin off to the side to make way for an historically adequate appreciation of his "enormous services."[25] In fact, many of Brecht's arguments in the thirties have the sound of the sophistry that filled the pages of Stalin's newspapers and the Communist press abroad: because criticism of Stalin undercut the struggle against fascism and paved the way for war against the USSR, all genuine antifascists were duty bound to defend occasionally unpleasant but necessary developments in Russia. Brecht wrote, "the struggle against the Soviet Union is waged by many intellectuals according to the slogan *For Freedom!*" Fingers were pointed accusingly at the overwhelming absence of freedom in which the individual as well as the masses of workers and peasants were supposedly living in the Soviet Union. "The subjugation supposedly emanates from a number of powerful and violent people, at the head of whom stands a single man, Josef Stalin." Not only fascists, bourgeois democrats, and Social Democrats, but Marxist theoreticians too shared this attitude. The Marxist thinkers would naturally challenge any suggestion that they opposed the Soviet Union itself, even when fascists and democrats of one form or another regarded them as allies. They would say they are only against the "'condition in which the Soviet Union currently finds itself,'" against a number of powerful and violent people there, against a single man, Josef Stalin.[26]

Thinking along these lines was reckless and irresponsible in Brecht's opinion. For if the USSR became embroiled in a war, the "Marxist theoreticians" would find their stance untenable. By discriminating between the Soviet Union and Stalin, they disarmed themselves of the capability to defend the country unless the Soviet Union parted company with Stalin; a Soviet victory in war would be undesirable if it came under Stalin's leadership, if it were Stalin's victory. Therefore, the Marxists found themselves hard-pressed to escape the charge that their argument "only against Stalin" smoothed the way for a military buildup against the USSR.[27] As so often happened with Brecht's reasoning in such matters, as long as his basic premise went unchallenged, the rest of the argument followed with an almost compulsive logic. But it was quintessentially Stalinist for Brecht to subscribe to an equation that, with only slight modification, made it impossible to combine antifascism with criticism of Stalin or the USSR and that considered such criticism as an indirect form of assistance to Hitler's Germany.

The biggest lie linked fascism and the threat of war with Trotsky and the show trials. Brecht was unmindful of the fact that Soviet politicians, Stalin especially, had been obsessed with the threat of an imminent "imperialist" war against the USSR or foreign intervention ever since the revolution.[28] Brecht failed to realize, particularly after Stalin began tightening the noose around the country's neck after 1927–28, that this war hysteria was meant mostly for domestic consumption and believed least of all by someone like Stalin. Talk of foreign enemies and their stooges inside the Soviet borders—all the underground peasant, bourgeois-specialist, and Menshevik parties—created a siege mentality that made it easier for internal critics of the regime to be stigmatized as traitors by pointing to the need to rally around the *vozhd*, the leader, in times of crisis. And for the Stalinists crises never ceased existing. After the mid-thirties, of course, the threat of war was very real, but Stalin still exploited it as a screen to veil his blows at former and purely imaginary oppositionists within the party.

The show trials were a prophylaxis, a preventive defense of the homeland, the *rodina*, against fascism and Trotskyism, the Stalinists said. Brecht swallowed the lie, even if he quibbled over occasional details and chose not to come out publicly in favor of the courtroom spectacles. His private utterances about the trials, which in terms of his specific points were virtually interchangeable with passages in Vyshinskij's speeches, fall into place within this general scheme of things. The trials helped prepare the country for the war soon to be waged against it, said Brecht,[29] becoming so enmeshed in the snarled logic used by the Stalinists to account for the trials that he overlooked the simple truth: under Stalin's direction the NKVD had embarked upon a campaign of wanton terror. Brecht talked of the Soviet Union as a one-man dictatorship, but then somehow missed the point of it all. Perhaps his gaze was fixed too intently upon Germany. Hitler was a dictator, yet Brecht thought that he knew who pulled his strings; he was a marionette of big business, nothing more. Brecht might have felt that in a similar fashion Stalin, too, was answerable to others in the party hierarchy or state apparatus who collectively wielded real power in the country. In any event, Brecht never seems to have realized that Stalin called all the shots, set all the policies, predicated most of his actions on the requirements of preserving his own power, and had Bolsheviks young and old led to slaughter as the mood struck him. Brecht's notion of dictatorships "that tore out their own roots"[30] somehow failed to allow for the possibility of a dictator who had amassed as much unchallenged personal power as Stalin.

If Brecht had adequately assessed Stalin's real character at the time, he might have grown suspicious about the trials and the confessions. As it was, he seized upon the same dialectic that had led him astray on other occasions. The lack of evidence at the trials was apparently little more than a beauty mark. Brecht wrote: "Me-ti reproached Ni-en because he demanded too much trust from the people in his trials against his enemies in the league. He said: if one demands of me that I believe something believable (without the proof), that is as if one demands of me that I believe something unbelievable. I will not do it. Ni-en may have benefited the people by the removal of his enemies in the league, but he failed to prove it. By a trial without proof he harmed the people."[31] Stalin's "mistake" lay in the failure to produce evidence, then, but Brecht apparently never questioned the rough truth of the accusations[32] and chastized Stalin only for committing an error in judgment. He ought to have taught the people to "demand" evidence, "especially from him, the one so generally useful."[33] Could Brecht really picture Stalin insisting that the people demand proof from him when the general rule in the secret police was, "Give us the man and we'll make the case?" That Brecht apparently could is a mark of his grasp of Soviet reality in these years. But proof or not, nothing that had thus far transpired in Stalin's Russia could possibly serve in Brecht's opinion as justification for an antifascist to *question* the USSR. Why? Because such an attitude against the Soviet Union would necessarily develop "entirely automatically and in the shortest span of time" into an attitude against the Russian proletariat, currently threatened by world fascism and war, and against the socialism then in the process of being built.[34]

Brecht's thinking in the matter of the trials likewise disclosed serious flaws when he took up the question of the political objectives of the "conspirators." Their goals were based on "defeatism," their major miscalculation having been the conviction that no possibility existed for the construction of socialism in one country and that fascism would prove to be durable in other lands. For that reason, argued Brecht, the defendants secretly conspired to *restore* capitalism in the USSR. Such logic was one of the chief arguments of Stalin's prosecutor Vyshinskij. But Brecht still had to account for the confessions, whose believability, he said, hinged only on the articulation and understanding of a political program that culminated naturally in the defendants' "remorse" once they realized the depth of their own depravity.

Brecht's (and again, Vyshinskij's) dialectic: the men now in the dock had come to believe that an unbridgeable chasm yawned between the Soviet regime and the masses and between workers and peasants, a gap that was placing worker control of the means of production and of the army in jeopardy. The defendants were therefore understandably anxious to make the concessions necessary to strike a deal with foreign powers as a means of saving what they could in the USSR and staving off a total national collapse. Their cooperation with "capitalist [read: fascist] general staffs"—"certain negotiations with fascist diplomats"—may well have been mere contact with individual persons in the pay of these foreign powers.[35] But this fine point was immaterial, for they found themselves surrounded by "all the rabble that is interested in such defeatist conceptions."[36] Brecht concluded that the accusations needed to be made "conceivable." If the politicians charged in the trials had slumped to the level of common criminals, then this type of career needed to be explained to western Europe as a political one, that is, as a brand of politics leading to common crimes. Behind the actions of the accused there was a thinkable political conception that needed to be rendered visible, and such a conception was defeatist through and through. "It is, figuratively speaking, suicide out of fear of dying." But it was instructive to trace how it may have arisen in the minds of such people. "The tremendous natural difficulties of constructing the socialist economy along with the rapid and profound deterioration of the situation in which the proletariat was thrown in several large European states created panic."[37]

This panic impelled the accused along a path of compromise not unlike Lenin's partial restoration of capitalism during the

New Economic Policy (1924–28). Of course NEP had been correct and called for within the context of the times, said Brecht, but nowadays any such program was anachronistic, counterrevolutionary, criminal.[38] As for the confessions in particular, Brecht solved the riddle easily. In the few years that had passed since this conception originated, its anachronistic nature had become evident even to those responsible for it. They were no longer able even to maintain their own previous opinions and came to regard them as criminal weakness, as unpardonable betrayal. The false political conception led them into a deep isolation and far into the realm of common criminality. "All the vermin inside and outside the country, everything associated with parasitism, professional crime, and informing [*Spitzeltum*] nestled in among them," and with all this rabble they shared the same goals.[39] He was convinced of the truth of this explanation, said Brecht.

VIRTUES AND VICES

Socialism looked upon its own distorted mirror image in fascism, with none of its virtues and all of its vices, reads Brecht's journal entry for 19 July 1943.[40] This juxtaposition of virtues and vices in Soviet Russia occurs frequently in Brecht's writing, especially in *Me-ti*, always with the implication that the residual vices plaguing the system were outweighed by its historically guaranteed virtues and would eventually be overridden by them.[41] The developments that Brecht placed in the category of virtues are clear without further elaboration; what, on the other hand, was he prepared to subsume under the other rubric? Violence and terror? Did he understand what was happening or did the same fixation that caused his myopia with regard to the trials cloud his vision here, too? Brecht's dialectical approach to the problem of collectivization funneled his thinking in a direction that to all intents and purposes ended with him condoning the repression of any "rich" peasant— "kulak" was the derogatory term—who owned more than a few small animals. Whether Brecht was actually aware of the full dimensions of "dekulakization" is beside the point. For as long as he accepted the necessity of "repressing" a dozen peas-

ants who belonged to "certain peasant strata owning property,"[42] the murder of many times that number could scarcely
be objected to unless Brecht was willing to impugn the validity
of the original premise.[43]

Brecht's writing is dotted with words like *coercion* (*Zwang*)
and *violence* (*Gewalt*) when he speaks of the Soviet Union. Passages with these expressions uniformly underscore the need for
such practices as long as the right side resorts to them. He explained the dialectic in *Me-ti*, addressing the question of "Unfreiheit unter Me-en-leh [Lenin] und Ni-en" and comparing the
accomplishments of the Bolsheviks with the actions of the old
rulers. The Bolsheviks had liberated the land from all types of
coercive violence that retarded progress. Of course they knew
that they, unlike the past rulers, could not be economically free
as individuals, only collectively. "So they organized their liberation, and thus coercion came into being; coercion is employed
against all currents that threaten the large-scale production of
goods for all."[44] The repression of "well-to-do" peasants for the
betterment of the country was, said Brecht, "a violent business,"[45] and the abolition of classes required "a violent impetus."[46] Killing was acceptable and regarded as a necessary evil if
it occurred as part of a regulated revolutionary process. The
"classics"—Marx and Engels—had given their blessing to selective killing, after all, because it would take place in order to
do away with killing: "The classics established no statutes that
forbade killing. They were the most compassionate of human
beings, but they saw enemies of humanity before them who
could not be overcome through persuasion. All that the classics
strived for was directed at creating the kind of conditions in
which killing no longer benefited anyone. They fought against
the kind of violence that attacks and against violence that
retards movements. They did not hesitate to pit violence
against violence."[47] As Brecht put it in *Die heilige Johanna der
Schlachthöfe*, "Only violence helps where violence governs."
Or even more crassly in *Die Massnahme*:

What base act would you not commit to
Abolish baseness?
If you could finally change the world,
Would you think too highly of yourself?

Who are you?
Sink down in filth
Embrace the butcher, but
Change the world: it needs it![48]

Revolutionary necessity called for the plowshares to be beaten into swords for use against enemies of the people. But even assuming for the moment that those ordering the repression were genuinely committed to what they perceived to be historically necessary revolutionary action, what happened to innocent people who got in the way? Or did innocence perhaps cease being a consideration under these circumstances? What exactly constituted guilt? Brecht's variation of "when wood is chopped, chips fly" sounded something like this: "The bread is hurled at the people with such force that it slays many."[49] But who was charged with "hurling" the historically necessary bread and why? "The most beneficial organizations are created by scoundrels," he said, "and more than a few virtuous people stand in the way of progress."[50] Accepting the surface rationale of "socialist construction" apparently made the need for some sort of special treatment of persons unintentionally but objectively inhibiting progress clear. Except where does Brecht ever allow for the early morning NKVD knock at the door because someone wanted a bigger apartment and denounced the previous inhabitant to the police as the head of the Moscow central of the Gestapo (or because the NKVD happened to have fallen behind in filling its weekly quota of arrests)? In other words, where does Brecht betray the slightest awareness that millions of those arrested impeded the progress of the "revolution" neither objectively nor subjectively? Did Brecht really believe in some way or another that the more innocent some people were, the more they deserved to die?[51]

How exactly were "the most beneficial organizations" capable of being created by scoundrels? Maybe he thought that such men were active in lower-level positions and kept in check by decent superiors, who called upon the scoundrels to fulfill unpleasant but necessary tasks in pursuit of some greater good. If so, who were the good men at the top directing it all, say, in 1937? Notwithstanding the presence of honest superiors, were the scoundrels—for instance, in the police force—not certain to get out of hand anyway? Brecht recognized that the type of police work necessary in a revolutionary situation was not for the tenderhearted. Being a policeman was not a full-time or lifelong occupation; "it can be a brief mission," Brecht said, adding that certain "jobs" were sure to undermine a policeman's humanity. "There are tasks that can only be carried out for a brief time. Among these is police work."[52] The state had no right, he elaborated elsewhere, to expect a man to perform police chores permanently.[53] Brecht had the Soviet Union in mind here; he certainly knew about the Cheka or NKVD and perceived the dangers inherent in its very existence. "What the Cheka can become may be seen in the Gestapo," he said as early as 1934.[54] But he viewed the danger as a potentiality, not as an overriding fact of daily life in the Soviet Union. On the other hand, he had a curious confidence in the power of "good posts" to exert a sort of magical control over the scoundrels: "Do not call for good people, rather create good posts. A good post is a post that does not require a good person."[55] Did such positions in the party and state apparatus already exist? Evidently not, according to Brecht, who remarked to Benjamin in 1938: "There can be no doubt, on the other hand, that certain criminal cliques are active in Russia herself. That is evident from time to time from their crimes."[56]

In what areas were these "criminal cliques" active? In the police? In the courts?[57] Were there scoundrels in the upper echelons of the Soviet government as well? Brecht seemed to believe that mediocre and even disreputable men possibly present at the top found themselves similarly held in check by sound institutions administered "by the people." He wrote: "A country in which the people govern themselves has no need of an especially brilliant leadership. . . . If the institutions are good, the individual man does not need to be especially good."[58] But there is some point in wondering how Brecht imagined that such a system functioned if it was infested by scoundrels at various levels of the state apparatus whose "posts" or jobs pressed them willy-nilly into formation of the most blessed institutions, and this in spite of their best efforts to subvert the system. Perhaps Brecht thought of these men in terms of their being part of some quasi-Mephisophelean power, holdovers of capitalism, that constantly willed evil but under socialism somehow always did good.

Even so, the question still remains: who designed "good posts" in the first place, jobs that caused men out to derail the locomotive of history to divert it involuntarily onto tracks actually leading in the direction of socialism? And if these posts had yet to be created, how could Brecht sustain the hope that they ever would be, given the machinations and intrigues of all the wreckers active within the party and secret police apparatus? Would some great personality eventually drive these scoundrels out of the temple? There is at least some reason to think that Brecht recognized such a savior in Stalin, and it was surely not difficult for him to imagine that the *vozhd*, who was "generally so useful," might have been betrayed by scoundrels in the police and the judiciary who had been arresting innocent millions unbeknownst to the leader. "Ah, si le roi le savait," Georg Lukács admits to have thought of Stalin occasionally in the early thirties.[59] And when Stalin had Ezhov and Jagoda, the two former NKVD chiefs, dispatched in the same way they had done away with millions of their victims, such actions could certainly be taken as graphic evidence of Stalin's own goodheartedness. What never shows up in Brecht's published or unpublished writings in these years is the slightest glimmer of understanding such as the kind that led to the arrest of Osip Mandelshtam:

His cockroach whiskers leer
And his boots gleam.
Around him a rabble of thin-necked
    leaders—
Fawning half-men for him to play
    with.
They whinny, purr or whine
As he prates and points a finger,
One by one forging his laws, to be
    flung
Like horseshoes at the head, the eye
    or the groin.

And every killing is a treat
For the broad-chested Ossete.[60]

THE GREAT DRIVER OF THE LOCOMOTIVE OF HISTORY, OR, WHAT IF HE IS INNOCENT?

Brecht never protested publicly about the arrest of his friends in the USSR, nor was he very prompt to place these incidents in the category of "crimes." In 1939 he drew up this balance sheet: "now koltsov arrested in moscow. my last russian connection over there. no one knows anything about tretjakov, who is supposedly a 'japanese spy.' no one knows anything about neher, who is said to have been engaged in trotskyist activities at the instigation of her husband. reich and lazis have stopped writing me, and grete gets no answer from her acquaintances in the caucasus and in leningrad. bela kun has also been arrested, the only of the political figures I saw. Meyerhold lost his theater, but is supposedly being allowed to produce opera."[61]

News of this sort reached him quickly, too. Rumors about the fate of Carola Neher were circulating in the West shortly after she and Erich Mühsam's widow Zensi were taken in by the NKVD. Brecht tried to help her, too, within limits. He asked Lion Feuchtwanger (who had visited Moscow in December 1936 and January 1937) to find out what he could about her whereabouts.[62] Brecht heard about Ernst Ottwalt's arrest at approximately the same time. He had been picked up in November 1936, and in February 1937 Brecht received a bizarre letter from Bernard von Brentano, who told him that "bourgeois newspapers" had accused him, Brentano, of denouncing Ottwalt to the Soviet government for writing him letters "friendly to Hitler." Brecht had already heard the news about Ottwalt's arrest, he told Brentano, but no additional details had reached him.[63] As for some of the others whom Brecht mentioned in his journal, Tretjakov disappeared in July 1937. Brecht had information about his arrest by summer 1938 at the very latest,[64] but by then he already assumed that Tretjakov was dead. Finally, Brecht received the news of Koltsov's disappearance directly from Maria Osten. He had been picked up in December 1938.

Did Brecht regard his vanished friends as innocent or were they "virtuous people" who accidently stepped in front of the locomotive of history? Perhaps Brecht reasoned along the lines of Kaganovich, who said in 1939 that it had been of the utmost importance at the start to keep this locomotive "on the socialist tracks." The task of keeping it there "had to be carried out amidst the struggle against the avowed and masked Trotskyite and Bukharinite traitors to socialism." In their attacks on the locomotive of history, these traitors had aimed their poisoned shafts primarily at the driver. "But what distinguishes the locomotive driver, Comrade Stalin, is the fact that the more furiously the enemy attacks him, the more crushing is his rebuff." Kaganovich went on: "Stalin drove the locomotive of history down and up steep inclines and over sharp turns and curves; he left in the firebox only what was valuable as fuel to create driving power and promptly threw out the slag, without, however, littering the track. He precisely calculated, theoretically and practically, the moment to apply the brakes so as to avoid smashing the train." And utilizing every ounce of power of the locomotive of history, Comrade Stalin had chosen the proper moments to put on speed and promptly opened the throttle whenever it was necessary to accelerate speed towards socialism.[65]

Was it right for a revolutionary to expect such a locomotive to stop just for a Tretjakov or a Neher? Brecht was reluctant at first even to believe the news about Ottwalt; the information, he told Brentano, seemed to have been disseminated only by bourgeois papers. He himself had been out of touch with Ottwalt for years; besides, he personally still regarded the Bolshevik party as solidly anchored in the Russian proletariat, and, in his opinion, the Russian economy was developing as part of a profound revolutionary process.[66] "Small and blind, indeed," Brecht may have been telling himself, "are the people who, instead of comprehending the whole of the gigantic task, squandor their time on worry about insignificant details."[67] In any event, he advised Brentano to await some sort of "authentic" news. Brecht would then inform the editorial office of *Das*

Wort that Brentano had neither received letters from Ottwalt sympathetic to Hitler nor passed any such information on to the Russians.[68] After several months had passed, the most Brecht could muster in the Ottwalt affair was some black humor. "If he is still capable of sitting [in jail], he's sitting," Brecht replied when Benjamin asked him if Ottwalt was still in prison.[69]

By this time Brecht obviously accepted the authenticity of the rumors about Ottwalt's arrest, but it cannot be ruled out either that he might actually have believed the charges. His reaction to Neher's disappearance illustrates his difficulties imagining that the NKVD was taking in entirely innocent people. Neher, he wrote Feuchtwanger, was said to be in jail in Moscow, though he had no idea why.[70] If Brecht had even an inkling about what was going on in Russia, how could he have asked "why"? But Brecht fished for reasons, and this is the best he could come up with: "Perhaps she was caught up in something because of some sort of woman's affair." In any case he told Feuchtwanger: "It would surely help her if you made some inquiries. I've personally not received an answer to my inquiry from anyone, which I don't appreciate. But maybe you've heard about her over there; if so, I would be grateful if you would write me a few lines. I am incessantly approached for information about her."[71]

Why did Brecht never hit upon senseless terror as the explanation? Perhaps his German experience again narrowed his field of vision; in a perverse way, Hitler had innocent persons carted off in cattle cars to the concentration camps far less frequently, "only" Jews and Communists. If significant numbers of persons in the USSR were vanishing, Brecht may have told himself, there must be an explanation for Neher's arrest somewhere. Either she had indeed been caught up in "treasonous activities" (Brecht did not dismiss the notion as utterly preposterous); or she had fallen victim to an NKVD mistake committed in the act of necessary spy sweeps: "In the course of the completely justified measures taken to counter Goebbels' organizations in the USSR, a mistake can naturally occur, too."[72] Brecht's "overall line" still took precedence over "details," for he urged Feuchtwanger to be discreet about his inquiries in order not to obstruct the work of the judiciary. A simple, private inquiry could underscore her artistic prominence without complicating the work of the judicial authorities. "At any rate, I would appreciate it if you treated my request confidentially because I have no desire either to sew suspicion against the praxis of the [Soviet] Union or to give any people at all the opportunity to claim that I do."[73] Feuchtwanger, who appears to have believed the lie about Neher, later told Brecht: "carola neher was in prison when I was in Moscow. She is said to have been involved in a treasonable conspiracy her husband was behind." Feuchtwanger added a bit too nonchalantly that he had no further details.[74]

Brecht's reaction to Koltsov's arrest exhibits the same helplessness in the face of the simple truth. He wrote Maria Osten (she was in Paris at the time, but soon returned to the USSR to suffer the same fate as Koltsov) that her news about Koltsov had upset him greatly. He had not heard a word, but was now being told that rumors of Koltsov's arrest had been carried in newspapers in Copenhagen. "I so hope that these rumors are not confirmed. Please let me know if you receive more information or anything at all." It was already 1939, and Brecht was still trying to unearth nonexistent "reasons." He simply could not imagine, he said, what Koltsov might have done; he himself only knew Koltsov working tirelessly for the Soviet Union. "Have you any idea what he's been accused of?" Brecht asked Osten.[75] But would Brecht have been satisfied by the explanation that Koltsov, at least according to one account, had been charged with being an agent of Lord Beaverbrook,[76] an explanation that made as much sense as the preposterous charges lodged against Tretjakov?

Tretjakov's fate inspired Brecht to write a poem that discloses none of the astonishment or outrage befitting such an utter absurdity as the accusation that he had been caught spying for Japan. Certainly Brecht's repetition of the line "What if he is innocent?" betrays an element of doubt; but where in the entire poem "Ist das Volk unfehlbar?" is there any sense of sheer incredulity? Brecht struggled to understand:

> One man can destroy what 5000 have built.
> Out of 50 condemned
> One may be innocent.[77]

Brecht trusted the stories of rampant "wrecking" activity, espionage, and sabotage throughout the land; here he suggests merely that one person out of fifty accused of wrecking might possibly be innocent. What about the forty-nine others? Did Brecht ever suspect that even the opposite—forty-nine innocent and one guilty—was still far too high a percentage? Was Tretjakov's arrest, like Neher's, yet another instance of judicial error or was there another explanation hidden somewhere? Maybe Tretjakov's end was attributable to the handiwork of scoundrels in high places (say, in the courts) whose misdeeds had not been restricted by good posts. Brecht wrote:

> To speak of the enemies that may be sitting in the people's courts
> Is dangerous, for the courts need their reputation.[78]

But Brecht undercut the power of his argument by turning it into a suggestion ("may be sitting"), besides which his conclusion reverted to his old dialectic. Even if occasional enemies of the people were sitting on the courts, sending guiltless Soviet citizens like Tretjakov to a miserable death in a forced labor camp, it was dangerous to speak about them—not because you might be picked up yourself before the day was over, but because loose talk undermined the authority of the courts, and "the courts need their reputation." These were, after all, trying times, Brecht may have reasoned; the Soviet Union was on the threshold of a great war, and the crisis called for draconic measures that could not always satisfy the norms of judicial practices appropriate to less unsettled times. The Communist party felt that enemies—spies and saboteurs—were busy hatching plots throughout the land; socialism was flowering, and the class struggle, accordingly, sharpened. Thus, extraordinary circumstances demanded that extraordinary steps be taken to safeguard the Union. Errors were made, it was true, and innocent people suffered; the medicine tasted bitter, but then the patient had been in grave danger:

> Numerous arrests had taken place. . . . Me-ti emphasized extollingly that hardly anyone regarded people as guilty just because they had been arrested. On the other hand, many approved the arrest of those merely under suspicion. It was

seen as an error that the authorities were not in a position to single out the guilty; but it met with approval that, incapable of being certain, they at least made a crude attempt to deal with the evil. The good surgeon separates the cancer from the healthy flesh, the bad ones cut out healthy flesh along with the cancerous portion, it was said. Me-ti regarded the attitude of the people as admirable and said: they treat their police as poor, crude, and stupid servants—that's something, after all.[79]

It evidently spoke well of ordinary Soviet citizens in Brecht's mind that they refused to regard a person as guilty just because he had been arrested and that they demonstrated political maturity by applauding the courage of the NKVD in arresting those merely suspected of having committed crimes. Brecht granted that the authorities' inability to determine guilt with some measure of precision was a "mistake," but squeamishness at the thought of picking up innocent persons had fortunately not caused the NKVD to shy away from taking at least "crude" steps against the evil. It was true that the secret police had not acquitted itself very well from a surgical standpoint; healthy flesh had been destroyed. But Brecht apparently felt confident that the price was not too high a one to pay to rid the patient of cancer.

"PARADE FIGURES"?

In August 1938 Brecht asked if there would also be singing "in the dark times" and replied, "Yes, there will also be singing / About the dark times."[80] But confronted with Tretjakov's arrest, he rephrased his question: "Is it best then to keep silent?"[81] He answered himself by filing his poem away among his unpublished papers. "No voice was raised on his behalf,"[82] he wrote with a tinge of remorse, and Brecht may well have suffered from the pangs of a guilty conscience. In October 1938 he had been taken to task in the Trotskyist journal *Unser Wort* by an outraged Walter Held: "You, Mr. Brecht, knew Karola [sic] Neher. You know that she was neither a terrorist, nor a spy, but an upright person and a highly accomplished artist. Why do you remain silent? Because Stalin pays for your publication 'Das Wort,' this most corrupt and dishonest journal ever published by German intellectuals? How can you still muster the courage to protest against Hitler's murder of Liese Hermann, Edgar André, and Hans Litten?"[83]

Is it fair to accuse Brecht of doing nothing? He tried time and again, wherever he was, to obtain information about Neher's whereabouts.[84] On one particular occasion Brecht and Ruth Berlau visited the Soviet ambassador to Denmark, and Brecht's first question concerned Neher.[85] All to no avail. This must have produced in Brecht an agonizing feeling of helplessness. His poem "Das Waschen" (for "C.N.") reads:

> Now I'm told you're in prison.
> The letters I wrote for you
> Went unanswered. The friends I asked to intervene
> Are silent. I can do nothing for you. . . .[86]

The same emotions may also have prompted similar lines in "An die Nachgeborenen," which Brecht probably wrote in late 1938:

> Is that man there walking along the street
> Perhaps already beyond the reach of his friends
> Who are in need?[87]

But if Brecht was out of reach of friends in trouble, powerless to take action on their behalf, then he must shoulder a fair amount of the responsibility for the limited possibilities at his disposal. He did what he could for Neher, but only within narrowly prescribed bounds; he wrote letters, made inquiries in private, and the results were understandably nil. His own words, uttered in 1935 at the writers' congress in Paris, came back in a way to haunt him: "When the crimes multiply, they become impossible to see. When suffering becomes unbearable, the screams are overheard. A man is beaten and the one watching grows powerless. That is in the natural order of things. When crimes occur like the rain falls, no one cries out 'stop' any longer!"[88] What might have saved Neher and others was a public outcry—if men like Lion Feuchtwanger, Heinrich Mann, and other prominent antifascists known for their sympathies with Soviet Russia had joined with Brecht to insist that the arrests in Russia stop and the innocent be freed. But this was the one step that Brecht, in the interests of antifascism, was unwilling to take. His dialectic presumably caused him to regard his vanished friends as casualties of fascism rather than victims of Stalinism. To change the world Brecht embraced the butcher, bringing Walter Held's scorn down upon him and others who thought like him:

> If Felix Halle, Ernst Ottwald, Karola Neher, Rudolf Haus and so on were sitting in Hitler's dungeons with their lives in immediate danger, would you ever scream, write, and take the poor conscience of the world to task. But when Stalin kills the same people, it does not move you in the least. . . . Then you act surprised when you lose ground, foot by foot, and wonder why fascism continues to expand. Fascism has such an easy time advancing, after all, because you have been beaten beforehand, because you yourselves have already dragged the meager principles that you act as if you are defending against fascism a hundred, a thousand times in the mud; because you are not convinced fighters with character but rather parade figures who have been spiritually and morally undermined by Stalin once and for all. Stalin bought your moral authority in order to lull the conscience of the world to sleep. You presented yourselves for that purpose and then wonder when the conscience of the world turns its back side to you. Your activity can be summed up entirely in one word: betrayal. Betrayal of your books and your morality, betrayal of Hitler's victims and betrayal of Stalin's, betrayal of the masses, and betrayal of yourselves. In all conscience, fascism could find no better allies than such opponents. If you did not exist, Goebbels would have to invent you.[89]

Held, trying to reach the shores of America in 1940 following the same route used soon after by Brecht, was pulled from the trans-Siberian express by the Soviet secret police and disappeared along with his wife and child without a trace.[90]

. . . .

The Dialectician

Such a resilient breed: man
His bad conscience
Enables his existence.
—Brecht, *Gedichte aus dem Nachlass 1*

There is no way of knowing, of course, whether Brecht ever read Held's article. If he did, the public scorn and ridicule that he was held up to must have touched a raw nerve, unless one can imagine that Brecht had not contemplated at least some of these issues during the years when his friends were vanishing in the Soviet Union. That Brecht greeted the news of their disappearance with public silence, however, ought not to be interpreted as a callous disregard for their fate or as a complete lack of reflection about the daily realities of life in the Soviet Union. Whatever he might have thought about the USSR, by 1938 he was certainly not giving in absolutely to the kind of illusions that would have caused the Soviet Union to take on the appearance of a fool's paradise in his mind's eye. Brecht's troubling inability to come to terms with Soviet reality in Stalin's time sprang, rather, from an intricate scheme of interwoven rationalizations. These were his dialectics, and he felt that dialectical thinking had bestowed upon him unique qualifications for untangling the meaning of the historical process. But Brecht's dialectical dogmatics trapped him instead in a web of excuses and justifications that obliged him to regard the imprisonment of innocent persons from the vantage point of the greater historical good and to accept such barbaric features of daily reality in Russia as the obverse of a process of prevailing over the barbarity caused by the capitalist bondage of the past. His thinking along these lines, on the other hand, may have done little to alleviate the pangs of a bad conscience. In the early forties he wrote:

When I, who survived many friends
Hear: the stronger survive
I cry out quickly: It was luck! It was luck!
Otherwise I'd tend to hate myself.[1]

THE GREAT TEACHING

Ironically, Brecht was probably unaware that his own safety
would have been in jeopardy after 1936 if he had spent a prolonged period of time in the USSR. In fact, on two occasions in
mid and late 1936 he had contemplated traveling to Moscow,
and he was also thinking of a trip in late 1937.[2] But as things
developed, these plans fell through, though Brecht evidently
made them ignorant of the fact that his associations with prominent personalities like Kun, Knorin, Koltsov, or Tretjakov could
easily have produced a limitless list of charges against him.
There is a rumor that Brecht narrowly escaped arrest when he
passed through the Soviet Union in 1941, and Reich later made
curious allusions to Brecht's facility for smelling danger and
removing himself from the scene quickly.[3] Of course the terror
in 1941 was not nearly as bad as in 1937 or 1938, but the improvement was only relative, and anyone in the USSR with as
many arrested friends and acquaintances as Brecht must have
had a bulging NKVD file.[4] Certainly factions existed in the secret police; perhaps there was one influenced by upper-echelon
party or NKVD officials who wanted nothing to do with the
embarrassment of having to explain Brecht's arrest after he had
been enticed, like Held, with an entry and transit visa into a
lethal trap; perhaps there was one hoping to act on the "evidence" that had mounted against him. The intense animosity
toward Brecht in certain circles of the German emigration, the
personal vendettas, and the character of some of his most unprincipled enemies makes it unlikely that his arrest would not
have been welcomed or, in a few cases, actively encouraged by
at least a few of his compatriots in Moscow. Whether there is
any truth to the rumor of his narrow escape is, however, impossible to say. Brecht was not arrested, of course, though the
NKVD could have picked him up easily at any time in Moscow

or during his journey from Finland to Vladivostok had it ever come to the issuance of the proper documents.

In the thirties, then, it probably never crossed Brecht's mind that he might well have suffered the same fate as Tretjakov, Neher, or Ottwalt had he settled in the USSR after leaving Germany or had he chanced to be in Moscow at the wrong moment. Later, after Brecht had a chance to talk with Hermann Greid in Sweden, but especially with Bernhard Reich in 1941 in Moscow and with Alexander Granach in the United States, it may finally have dawned on him that arbitrary terror, exacerbated by purposeful denunciations and by the rippling effect of forced confessions incriminating dozens of other innocent persons for every man arrested, lay behind the events in Russia.[5] If so, then the lines of poetry cited above may reflect Brecht's *belated* realization that he had indeed been lucky.[6] But what circumstances blocked the road for Brecht to a balanced assessment of events in the USSR as they happened?

That fascism blinded him to Stalinism is a deceptively simple answer, but a true one nonetheless. His distaste for Hitler and National Socialism was not just cerebral, based on his perception of what fascism denoted historically; his revulsion often bordered on the visceral. He wanted fascism and everything that both produced and went along with it eradicated once and for all, and his exile years were an indefatigable search for the most adequate literary means of contributing to its defeat. "How can we become beastial intellectuals [*Intelligenzbestien*—the phrase is Goebbels'], beastial human beings in the sense that the fascists fear for their power because of them?" Brecht asked. The scum of fascism murdered, but the annihilation of fascism presupposed its own violent death. Therefore, Brecht's central concern was, how could writers write in a "deadly" fashion?[7] The question occurred to Brecht naturally, and many exiled writers were, of course, equally troubled by the frustrating inadequacies of literature and other intellectual means to alter the course of political events. But "vulgarized knowledge characteristically gives birth to a feeling that *everything* is understandable and explained."[8] In Brecht's case, an image of National Socialism that squared with Stalin's vulgarized theory of fascism pushed him off balance; it eliminated any doubt whatever in his mind that fascism could possibly connote something even marginally different from what Stalin and Stalinist Marxism-Leninism said that it was; it fanaticized and obsessed Brecht, placing him at the mercy of a two-edged theory that functioned almost by reflex to channel all forms of antifascism based on that theory in the direction of unequivocal support of the Soviet Union.

The switch from bourgeois democracy to National Socialism was a clear indication that the capitalists could no longer get on with the business of making money "without brutality." A glance in their bank books quickly convinced them of that. Capitalism begat fascism, and any outcry against fascism that failed to take account of the social conditions that gave rise to it with "natural necessity" were unavoidably lacking in sincerity.[9] These were some of Brecht's axiomatic premises, and, having thus defined them, he established a clear-cut task for the writers. The fascist countries had erected an enormous wall of "prattle, scribbling, stale philosophy";[10] behind it they transacted their filthy business. Whereas many writers still spent their time commenting exclusively upon the nonsensical quality of this wall, such an approach to fascism posed no mortal threat to it. It was deadly, on the other hand, to expose the business transactions going on behind the wall.[11] In a word, it was of the utmost importance that the writers see in fascism the historical culmination of capitalism; otherwise, they condemned themselves beforehand to ineffectual resistance and repeated the same mistake committed during the Weimar Republic. In one of his poems Brecht ridiculed intellectuals and writers now in exile for their foolish naiveté with respect to the simple lines of continuity reaching from the Germany that existed before Hitler to the one thriving after his seizure of power:

> And still they extolled the land, incorrigibly,
> In which they had once worked. For them
> It was not the land that had crested in today's,
> Just a first stage and forerunner; rather
> Some throw of the dice from high above
> Had brought about a crude change. Benightedness
> Had descended like seed from another star in the night

Transforming everything. Thus they condemned the natural
  outcome
Of the cause they extolled.[12]

"First stage," "forerunner," "natural outcome"—these were
also the favorite political modalities of Stalin's protégés in the
Comintern. Brecht was clearly immersed in a view of fascism
that excluded the possibility of opposition to it independent
of a parallel allegiance to a different political doctrine. "Only
he who relinquishes the idea of private ownership of the means
of production and whatever belongs to it, and who therefore
wishes to fight along with that class which puts up the stiffest
resistance to private property can fight against fascism."[13] The
only genuine enemy of fascism was therefore communism, and
it was imperative that communism be strengthened.[14] That
Brecht, who once referred to himself as "the enemy of butch-
ers,"[15] was compelled to turn to a butcher for help in transforming "a world in need of change" was the almost natural
consequence of following his own advice in *Die Massnahme*;
and he urged others to do likewise. First, however, they needed
to grasp the "great teaching." Simple, like all great doctrines,[16]
it branded the ownership of property as the root of all evil and
thus also as the cause of fascist atrocities. There was a very real
danger that the writers would continue to regard this planned
violence as inexplicable and unnecessary, even though such ter-
roristic behavior was a functional requisite for the maintenance
of the ruling system of private property.[17]

   The trouble was, there were also atrocities elsewhere in the
world, and because Brecht knew of them, he had to ponder their
implications. Atrocities were a natural if tragic concomitant of
the historical process unfolding in the Soviet Union too, Brecht
implied. Shortly before he died, he came to this conclusion
about the Soviet Union under Stalin: "Breaking out of the barbarity of capitalism can itself reveal barbaric traits. . . . The
revolution unleashes simultaneously marvelous virtues and
anachronistic vices."[18] But Brecht had a habit of uttering categorical pronouncements that often appear to carry the weight
of indisputable truth, whereas, upon closer examination, they
turn out to have glossed over or ignored some of the most es-

sential issues. This was Brecht's dialectic. Just why, for instance, was it not surprising that the revolution devoured its own children?[19] Why did this cannibalism in any sense lay in the realm of historical logicality? Why was it even possible in a society evolving purposefully toward utopia on earth? Executions, concentration camps, and secret police terror were all lawful concomitants of the "brutality" that attended the ownership of private property; once a new social order had been introduced, one making barbarity "superfluous,"[20] these barbaric blights would vanish, or so the thinking went. But the new order existed in the USSR, according to Brecht; the great doctrine was being put into practice in a land—one sixth of the earth's surface—in which the repressed and those who owned nothing had taken over power,[21] and barbarity persisted nevertheless. Why?

Made on the eve of his death in 1956, another of Brecht's seemingly profound utterances disclosed that his understanding of Soviet reality in Stalin's time was still governed by a view of "anachronistic" revolutionary vices that treated barbarity in the USSR as a transitory phenomenon.[22] The terror was presumably understandable, pardonable, because it was not to be avoided under the circumstances; on the other hand, unlike Nazi terror, it was not historically necessary. In search of the hidden nexus between capitalism and fascist atrocities, Brecht asked in 1935: "Why is culture, that last bit of culture remaining to us, jettisoned like ballast; why are the lives of millions of human beings, the vast majority of mankind, so impoverished, destitute, demolished halfway or entirely?"[23] The answer to that question, of course, was clear to Brecht; in the Soviet Union, by stark contrast, there was no destruction of culture.[24] Brecht may have modified his thinking slightly by the late thirties, his laments about Soviet literature and literary criticism being an index of his disillusionment. Literary life in the USSR had lapsed into a state that Brecht characterized as "shitty," which caused him to conclude that literature in the Soviet Union had been "surprised" by the proletarian takeover. But he never inferred that Stalin and the "Bolsheviks" were naturally antagonistic to intellectual endeavors of all kinds or that they made a habit of "destroying" culture. The circumstance that many of Brecht's intellectual and artist friends had disappeared in the Stalinist vortex of dungeons and slave labor camps failed to dent Brecht's confidence in the basic Soviet congeniality with respect to the arts.

Brecht was so sure of the motive forces impelling the historical process forward in its relentless advance toward utopia that he left himself no room for any considerations that departed from a preestablished schema: fascism was a natural stage in the development of advanced capitalism. He did not interpret this lawful development, on the other hand, to mean that the world was necessarily condemned to pass through a period of fascist barbarity, and he assigned all those who accepted either capitalism or fascism as being in the natural order of things to a clearly defined category: "When someone starts talking about necessity, insisting that the very beginning of human activity and the margin of its possibilities are established by insurmountable historical tendencies, contradict him: for his feet are firmly planted on the soil of facts; he is a eulogist of things as they are inasmuch as he supplies the reasons as proof of what he considers necessity. Everything necessarily occurred as it occurred." This person, said Brecht, ought to be branded an apologist.[25] But when Brecht applied his unchallengeable assumptions about capitalism and fascism to communism in its Stalinist form, arguing that communism, nothing else, would follow upon fascism,[26] he fit his own description. For Brecht, it was an epistemological error to look at the capitalist world and succumb to the illusion that things were somehow foreordained—to lose "the power," to quote an analogous passage from Orwell, "of grasping that the world could be other than it is."[27] But Brecht's own dogma caused him to lose this precise power with respect to the Soviet Union. After all, the epistemological outcome described by Orwell was a prime objective of the doctrine that Brecht had embraced in the first place: he forfeited the ability to imagine the Soviet Union in any other than its actually existing Stalinist form.

Brecht's refusal to protest against tyranny and terror in Russia was thus caused by an amalgamation of doubt and rationalization. He simply could not bring himself to believe, on the one hand, that certain happenings in Russia could possibly denote what they appeared to adumbrate. After long conversations with Brecht, Walter Benjamin wrote in his diary: "He follows developments in Russia, likewise Trotsky's writings. They prove that suspicion exists; a justified suspicion that calls for a skeptical treatment of Russian matters. Such skepticism is in keeping with the intent of the [Marxist-Leninist] classics. Should the skepticism be borne out some day, then a struggle against the regime would be called for—a *public* struggle, to be sure. But 'unfortunately' or 'Thank God,' however you wish, this suspicion has not yet become a certainty today."[28] On the other hand, Brecht drew upon a virtually limitless stock of rationalizations to explain away barbarity in Russia as "anachronistic vices."

A particularly ironic side to Brecht's assessment of world events in the thirties and forties is that he periodically defined the cause of his own myopia without realizing it and that he did so in lamenting the inadequacy of the world's response to Hitler. "When we first reported that our friends were being slaughtered, there was a cry of outrage, and many offered assistance. Then a hundred were slaughtered. But when a thousand were slaughtered and the slaughter went on and on, silence took over, and there was no longer much help."[29] People turned away in silence, he explained, because they saw no chance to alter the course of events. In much the same way, Brecht may well have felt that he could do nothing for his friends in Russia; he said as much in the poem that he wrote for Carola Neher and never published. The point, though, is that Brecht did not regard himself as powerless against fascism; his writing was his way of altering events by altering outlooks, and he tried to explain to others how to write in a "deadly" fashion. But the same type of intervention was out of the question for him in the case of the Soviet Union; any public protest, he felt, would be an indirect service to Hitler, besides which he never seems to have regarded the arrest of his friends in the thirties anyway as anything more than isolated occurrences—exceptions or mistakes on the part of the secret police surgeons who cut out more than just the cancerous portion of the flesh. Certainly grounds for suspicion about events in Russia existed, but these remained unconfirmed for the time being. As for the remainder of the arrested, in his possible rationalization of their liquidation Brecht might be characterized as Milosz' Beta, who "could see a new and better order within his grasp. He believed in, and demanded, earthly salvation. He hated the enemies of human happiness and insisted that they must be destroyed. Are they not evil-doers who, when the planet enters a new epoch, dare to maintain that to imprison people, or to terrify them into professions of political faith, is not quite nice? Whom do we imprison? Class enemies, traitors, rabble. And the faith we force on people, is it not true faith? History, History is with us! We can see its living, explosive flame!"[30]

At least a partial cause of Brecht's equivocation on the subject of the terror in Soviet Russia was surely his ignorance about the horrifying scope of the violence. Still, there were any number of inferences that he might reasonably have drawn on the basis of what he did know. Possibly he was thrown off balance by the differences in Nazi and Stalinist methodology. Nazis killed largely in the open, at least as far as Communists and other political opponents of the regime were concerned; the Stalinists preferred to murder in secret. Hitler boasted about Nazi fanaticism and slaughtered in the name of the Master Race; Stalin sought to hide his crimes from the world, arresting "enemies of the people" in the middle of the night and sentencing them *in camera* to quarter-century terms in de facto death camps whose existence Soviet and foreign communists, like Lukács, indignantly denied. The Gestapo tortured to obtain true confessions from political prisoners; the NKVD used the same methods to force its victims to admit to crimes that they had never committed.

The screams of those killed in public squares amplified the inaudible, anonymous scream of those being tortured behind the walls of a Gestapo dungeon, Brecht wrote.[31] But because he accepted the legitimacy of Stalin's show trials, the only real occasion on which innocent men were publicly sentenced to death in the USSR, Brecht was apparently unable to imagine that the condemned Bolsheviks, who had been tortured or coerced into confessions and who thus mostly failed to "scream" in a voice that Brecht could appreciate, might in any way represent only a tiny fraction of those being tortured in out-of-sight NKVD cellars. "What about the unheard screams of fear / Uttered by bleeding Comrades?"[32] Brecht finally asked—in private—in 1956. But by then it was far too late; the bleeding comrades had all bled to death. At least some of these cries, though, had been audible to Brecht at the time they were uttered, and to them he turned a deaf ear so that the following poem is revealed as only a partially true description of Brecht's own writing—valid for Nazi Germany, but tragically unsuited to what Brecht wrote, or failed to write, about Stalinist Russia:

> But shaken with emotion
> Those born later will contemplate the works
> Using the medium of art in the dark times
> To paint unbearable conditions
> And to lend
> Those suffering their powerful voice.[33]

DIFFICULTIES IN WRITING THE TRUTH

Toward the end of the thirties Brecht published an article dealing with "five difficulties in writing the truth." Two of these are particularly useful for what they reveal about the ease with which Brecht "kept silent about the truth," as Manès Sperber put it, and how "*discontinuously*" he overcame the very difficulties that he himself analyzed.[34] Take, for instance, "the courage to write the truth."[35] Courage can be an elusive quality to define, and it is impossible to give a pat answer to whether Brecht's refusal to adopt a meaningful critical posture toward the Soviet Union flowed from an absence of civil or intellectual courage. According to Henry Pachter, Brecht admitted to him about the trials, "it's terrible, but do we have anything besides the Soviet Union?" Pachter urged him to say something publicly about them anyway, but Brecht declined. "In fifty years nothing more will be heard about Stalin, but I want Brecht to be read then, too. That is why I cannot break with the party."[36] But what smacks here of pure opportunism probably sprang from Brecht's overwhelming sense of mission about his own calling, a trait that he shared with Lukács. The historical exclusivity that both men claimed for their political and artistic outlooks is exactly what fostered their inability to challenge the premises that in their minds legitimized their work. Indeed, without the very premises that corrupted their political thinking, it is hard to imagine just what form their art or conception of art could have taken. In fact, one might very well speculate that without these premises, with all their woeful side effects, Brecht would never have become quite the kind of innovative literary genius that he was, a genius of which he himself was particularly aware. Sperber, then, attributes Brecht's "discontinuous" handling of the truth precisely to a "fanatical sense of loyalty to his own work"; not opportunism in the usual sense of the word, but a pervasive feeling of mission about his singular worth as an innovative artist determined Brecht's behavior with respect to Stalinism.[37]

Be that as it may, Brecht's public silence about the Soviet Union and his evasion of the appalling sides of Soviet reality in his writing was at least equally the result of his helplessness in the face of the second difficulty, "the wisdom to recognize the truth."[38] There were all kinds of truths, said Brecht; the key was to discover "*which* truth was worthy of telling."[39] Chairs had seats, for instance, and rain fell from above. The writers who gave themselves over to writing this sort of truth were legion, and they followed the fashion of painters who decorated the walls of sinking ships with still lifes. For them the courage to write the truth never even became a conscious issue, and their consciences were accordingly spotless. "Unperturbed by those in power, and equally unperturbed by the screams of those being raped, they daub at their pictures."[40] Still other writers were peerless as far as their personal hatred and individual defiance of fascism was concerned, and yet the truth escaped them because of their incommensurate understanding of the motive forces behind history. They needed knowledge of materialist dialectics, economics, and history.[41] For without the correct method, the truths worth telling would remain hidden, and those who jotted down ordinary facts in their place forfeited the chance to help render the affairs of the world "manageable." These people could not live up to the demands of writing the truth, and the simple truth that overrode all others in importance was, in Brecht's mind, the essence of fascism as an historical phase of capitalism. "*Fascism can only be combated as capitalism, as the most naked, most insolent, most oppressive, and most deceitful brand of capitalism*," he said, and likened those who opposed fascism while clinging frantically to their illusion about capitalism or who deplored the barbarity engendered by barbarity to persons who wanted their piece of meat without slaughtering the calf. They hoped to devour the calf without seeing the blood.[42]

Brecht's solution to the problem of locating important truths was reminiscent of his entreaty in 1935 to recognize the direct link between fascist barbarity and the ownership of property and to introduce a system of social organization in which barbarity would be superfluous.[43] In defining his five difficulties in writing the truth, Brecht argued that a writer had to expose the avoidable cause of deplorable conditions if he wished to uncover the truth about them. With the avoidable causes finally unveiled, the bad conditions could be combated.[44] But Brecht was poorly equipped to follow his own advice consistently. He shut his eyes to a number of the essential truths of Stalinism. He subordinated unpleasant details to some supposed overall line, resigned himself to the tragic existence of anachronistic faults alongside remarkable qualities, and slipped into the role of an apologist, convinced that his grasp of the dialectic guaranteed his recognition of universal historical truths.

He criticized others mercilessly for stopping short of full disclosure about the truths of capitalism: they refused to recognize it as a disguised brand of bondage. Yet nothing was worse than secret slavery; if slavery was made public, if a condition was recognized and clearly labeled as slavery, then it was at least possible to imagine a different state of affairs—freedom. But as long as actual slavery was constantly talked about as if it were freedom itself, then freedom could no longer even be pictured in the mind. Human progress had always been based upon the discovery of slavery as slavery, and that recognition alone made its abolition possible.[45] In certain respects, Brecht was anticipating Orwell's remark about the ability to imagine the world other than it is, except that Brecht again ended up involuntarily characterizing himself: "Nothing is more pernicious than the attitude of those people who go ahead and sanction certain conditions that are predominant, to be sure, but whose true character has not yet been exposed . . . and who derisively refer to those persons as naive when they take the men in power at their word so as to uncover the discrepancy between their actions and their talk, thereby laying bare the nature of current conditions."[46]

Brecht lived just long enough to hear Khrushchev's confirmation in 1956 of the "justified suspicions" about Russian matters that Brecht had described to Walter Benjamin in 1938. However he may have felt about the German Democratic Republic by then, or even about post-Stalin Russia, he responded to Khrushchev's revelations about the USSR under Stalin by writing several poems that he then withheld from publication.[47] These reveal Brecht's belated understanding of certain truths about life in the Soviet Union in Stalin's time and Stalin's treatment of the people, truths that he now considered worth putting on paper, though not for public consumption:

> The Czar spoke with them
> With weapons and whips
> On bloody Sunday. Then
> They were spoken to with weapons and whips
> Each day of the week and every workday
> By the meritorious murderer of the people.[48]

Other lines, too, suggest that Brecht, in the last months of his life, had revised his view of Stalin in the face of Khrushchev's disclosures at the twentieth party congress. "He who gave all the orders / Was not responsible for all that was done,"[49] Brecht wrote. But there is reason to question whether Brecht actually modified his dialectical assessment of Stalin, whom in the thirties he had called the one generally so useful. For all of Stalin's crimes, Brecht still appears to have clung tenaciously to his system of dialectics, refusing to relativize the historical services that Stalin had rendered the country just because the god had eventually turned out to be "full of maggots."[50] Those who had severed their own ties to the people had chosen to denounce their enemies as "enemies of the people," said Brecht sarcastically, but: "They did not lie about everything."[51] In another poem Brecht wrote in much the same vein: "When the helper appeared, he was / Leprous. But the leper / Helped, after all."[52] Even in 1956, then, Brecht was still just a step away from a rationalization of Stalin's blood purges—as long as he did not lie about everything, helped advance the cause of socialism in the Soviet Union, and could not really be replaced anyway without risking the collapse of the entire system.

Perhaps Brecht had taken the first false step when he convinced himself that there was only one truth, not two, or as many truths as interest groups.[53] For he then became so caught up in the compulsive logic of his closed system of thought that the one truth governing his view of all human society was no longer subject to any certification from outside. All the checks and balances built into his dialectical dogmatics merely served to verify the basic propositions categorized as the embodiment of this one overarching truth. Brecht's mind was thus impervious to any suggestion that the truth emanating from the Soviet Union, which was simply the obverse of the truth about capitalism, might also serve partisan purposes and be as untrustworthy as the "secret slavery" that the West whitewashed as freedom. There is a certain predetermination in Brecht's chain of logic because he consistently disregarded his own advice: in times when delusion was demanded and mistakes promoted, thinking men endeavored to set the record straight about all that they read and heard.[54]

In pursuit of the rule of justice on earth, modeled after his vision of what such an existence should look like, Brecht sought recourse in a method that obliged him to disregard brutality and carnage in that part of the world which he regarded as being the present-day realization of his most cherished dreams about the future. Having embraced a single contorted dogma that lay claim to an exclusive explanation of all beginnings and all ends, Brecht deprived himself of the capacity ever to go back and question the sources—the axiomatic premises. For "over the beginning, no logic, no cogent deduction can have any power, because its chain presupposes, in the form of a premise, the beginning."[55] To understand the world, Brecht mobilized the "self-coercive force of logicality" that then set a compulsory and compulsive process of deduction in motion, investing him with the absolute certainty of being right. Had he heeded the warning of an "old Jew of Galicia" instead, Brecht would have been compelled to rethink his entire political philosophy and, along with it, the aesthetic theory that flowed from the original dogma: "When someone is honestly 55% right, that's very good and there's no use wrangling. And if someone is 60% right, it's wonderful, it's great luck, and let him thank God. But what's to be said about 75% right? Wise people say this is suspicious. Well, and what about 100% right? Whoever says he's 100% right is a fanatic, a thug, and the worst kind of rascal."[56]

N O T E S

. . . .

The following abbreviations have been used in the notes:

BBA   Bertolt-Brecht-Archiv, Berlin (GDR)

GW   Bertolt Brecht, *Gesammelte Werke*. Frankfurt am Main: Suhrkamp Verlag, 1967.

TsGALI   Tsentralnyj gosudarstvennyj arkhiv literatury i iskusstv, Moscow

PREFACE

1. Milosz, *The Captive Mind*, p. 215.
2. See Pike, *German Writers in Soviet Exile*, chapter 10.
3. David Bathrick pursued this very question in Brecht's *Die Rundköpfe und die Spitzköpfe* and *Der aufhaltsame Aufstieg des Arturo Ui*. He demonstrated persuasively the process by which Brecht's economistic approach to National Socialism interfered with his poetic depictions of fascism. For instance, "The historical emplotment of [*Die Rundköpfe und die Spitzköpfe*] profoundly distorts a number of the political realities of the time," and for some of the same reasons *Arturo Ui* is "inadequate in its grasp of Hitler." See Bathrick, "A One-Sided History: Brecht's Hitler Plays," pp. 187 and 194. See also Tauscher's *Brechts Faschismuskritik in Prosaarbeiten und Gedichten der ersten Exiljahre*. Published in the GDR, the book is of limited usefulness, though it does call attention to some of the main issues. Read critically, it actually tends to illustrate my main argument by unintentionally emphasizing the schematic simplicity of Brecht's theory of fascism.
4. Milosz, *The Captive Mind*, p. 48.
5. "Tonbandgespräch mit György Lukács."
6. Lukács, *Gelebtes Denken*, p. 151.
7. Brecht, *Supplementband IV: Gedichte aus dem Nachlass 2*, p. 32.
8. Antonov-Ovseenko, *The Time of Stalin*, p. 320. The Brecht portrait, by the way, does not address the issue of Brecht's attitude toward the Soviet zone of occupation in East Germany from 1945 to 1949 or toward the German Democratic Republic. This ques-

tion needs to be examined in a separate context. Nor, it should
be emphasized, does the following portrait of Lukács deal with
later Soviet or Eastern bloc defamation campaigns against Lukács
(see *Georg Lukács und der Revisionismus* for some of the major
articles published against him in the late fifties) or go into the
events of 1956: Lukács' involvement in the Petöfi circle, his influence on Wolfgang Harich and various anti-Stalinist intellectuals in the GDR, his participation in the ill-fated government of
Imre Nagy, and his eventual banishment to Romania following
the suppression of the Hungarian uprising. In these events
Lukács very much took up an anti-Stalinist position that is keeping with my interpretation of his belated recognition of the
nature of the Stalin regime. This activity does not, however,
change my assessment of Lukács' intellectual development from
1928 to the early fifties and up to Stalin's death.

CHAPTER I

1. Lukács, *Gelebtes Denken*, p. 171.
2. Lukács, "Parteidichtung," in *Schriften zur Ideologie und Politik*,
   p. 401.
3. Cf. Lukács, *Gelebtes Denken*, p. 29.
4. Cf. Lukács, *Geschichte und Klassenbewusstsein*, p. 34. In an
   interview published posthumously in the *New Left Review*,
   Lukács emphasized: "An effective fight against fascism was only
   possible within the ranks of the Communist movement. I still
   adhere to this opinion." Quoted from Lukács, *Gelebtes Denken*,
   p. 10.
5. "Tonbandgespräch." Lukács presumably had the essay "Kunst
   und objektive Wahrheit" in mind. It appeared first in Russian
   translation (*Literaturnyj kritik* 9 [1935]: 5–23), but not in German until well after the war.
6. Ibid.
7. To his credit, Lukács never later "emended" any of those essays
   first published in the thirties, at least not to my knowledge.
8. Lukács, *Gelebtes Denken*, p. 185.
9. The complete quote runs as follows: "Opposition against Stalin's
   ideology universal, not limited to aesthetics. (Most [of the writ-
   ings], of course, 'Hegel' for instance, were not publishable at the
   time.)" Ibid., p. 270. Some remarks about *Der junge Hegel*:
   whereas it is true that the book was not published in the Soviet
   Union, Lukács did, after all, receive a Soviet doctorate (*dok-
   torskaja stepen*), his habilitation, from the Academy of Sciences
   for the dissertation. This hardly squares with Lukács' claims

about a book that transgressed the ideological law laid down by Zhdanov: "Don't forget that I wrote my Hegel book in the thirties. It was directed, of course, against the entire official line, for Zhdanov took the position that Hegel was one of the Romantic critics of the French Revolution." Ibid., p. 141; see also p. 166. Lukács spoke as if *Der historische Roman* also offended the "official line." See chapter 6, note 37.

10. "Tonbandgespräch."
11. Kołakowski, *Main Currents of Marxism*, 3: 284.
12. Lukács, *Gelebtes Denken*, p. 267.
13. Ibid.
14. See ibid., p. 132.
15. Ibid., p. 124.
16. Ibid.
17. "Thesen über die politische und wirtschaftliche Lage in Ungarn und über die Aufgaben der Kommunistischen Partei Ungarns (Blum-Thesen)," in *Schriften zur Ideologie und Politik*, p. 307.
18. Ibid., pp. 307–8.
19. Ibid., pp. 311–12.
20. Ibid., p. 312.
21. In his introduction to *Schriften zur Ideologie und Politik*, "Der Begriff der 'demokratischen Diktatur' in der politischen Philosophie von Georg Lukács" (p. lii), Peter Ludz misinterprets the phrase. Apparently not spotting it as a key Comintern slogan, Ludz argues that the phrase was understood in the Comintern, not coined there, to be a plaidoyer "for a common battle of all proletarian masses (social democratic, too) against feudalism as well as fascism." The Comintern's slogan that helped hinder a united front in these years comes across in Ludz' interpretation as a plea in favor of joint action and thus an index of Lukács' antisectarianism in the Blum theses.
22. "Offener Brief des Exekutivkomitees der Kommunistischen Internationale an die Mitglieder der Kommunistischen Partei Ungarns," in *Schriften zur Ideologie und Politik*, pp. 733–34.
23. Of course, Stalin first began referring to fascism and social fascism as "twin brothers" much earlier, in 1924, not "around" 1928.
24. Lukács, *Geschichte und Klassenbewusstsein*, p. 32.
25. Lukács, *Gelebtes Denken*, p. 130. See also "Diskussion über die Blum-Thesen (1956)," in *Schriften zur Ideologie und Politik*, p. 770.
26. See especially chapters 6 and 7 of this study.
27. Lukács, *Geschichte und Klassenbewusstsein*, p. 35.
28. Lukács, *Gelebtes Denken*, p. 132; Lukács, *Geschichte und Klassenbewusstsein*, p. 42.
29. Lukács, *Geschichte und Klassenbewusstsein*, pp. 42–43.

CHAPTER 2

1. Lukács, "Znachenie 'Materializma i èmpiriokrititsizma' dlja bol-shevizatsii kommunisticheskikh partij," p. 147.
2. See Oskar Negt's introduction, "Marxismus als Legitima-tionswissenschaft: Zur Genese der stalinistischen Philosophie," in the volume *Kontroversen über dialektischen und mecha-nistischen Materialismus*, pp. 7–48.
3. Lukács, "Der grosse Oktober 1917 und die heutige Literatur," p. 97.
4. Lukács, *Gelebtes Denken*, p. 143. The phrase was David Rjazanov's, uttered when Lukács presented himself to Rjazanov in the Marx-Engels Institute. Now these kinds of journeys to Moscow were obviously not made without consultation with the party; often enough, being sent to Moscow was a form of banish-ment or discipline for some infraction or other. Whether this first stay in Moscow was, for the time being, the final round of the scandal produced by Lukács' Blum theses has never been estab-lished, though there are some circumstances to support that as-sumption. Lukács' first article in the *Moskauer Rundschau* did not appear until September 1930, but he had been in Moscow since early in the year: Lukács evidently attended the second congress of the Hungarian Communist party in Moscow in February–March 1930 and remained in the Soviet capital after-wards. *Gelebtes Denken*, p. 139. Lukács' trip to Moscow in 1930 can easily be explained as the fulfillment of his obligation to attend that congress: he was, of course, a member of the Hun-garian central committee. But, as Lukács later put it laconically, the Hungarian party did not "reelect" him to the central com-mittee at this congress. "Autobiographie." It would seem sensible to argue, then, that the Blum theses were first officially discussed in the presence of all the principals involved at this particular congress, the result being Lukács' de facto expulsion from the central committee. If so, the fact that Lukács remained behind in Moscow after the congress might very well point to the disciplin-ary or punitive quality of his "Cominternment." One additional argument: in *Gelebtes Denken*, p. 159, Lukács said, "The time of the Blum theses was 1930." Yet he wrote the theses in 1928, and the Comintern first reacted to them in print in 1929. His refer-ence to the year 1930 perhaps means that the theses were in fact not discussed at any length until the second Hungarian party congress meeting that year, for which, after all, Lukács had origi-nally written them.
5. See Kołakowski, *Main Currents of Marxism*, 3: 63.
6. Ibid., p. 64.
7. Ibid., p. 76.
8. See Ermolaev, *Soviet Literary Theories*, p. 89.

9. Mitin, "Ocherednye zadachi raboty na filosofskom fronte v svjazi s itogami diskussii," p. 17.

10. "Ob itogakh diskussii i ocherednykh zadachakh marksistsko-leninskoj filosofii," in *Pravda*, 26 January 1931.

11. Shurygin, "Itogi obsuzhdenija pisma tov. Stalina v partorganizatsii IKP filosofii," p. 242; Mitin, "Ocherednye zadachi raboty na filosofskom fronte v svjazi s itogami diskussii," p. 13.

12. Mitin, "Über die Ergebnisse der philosophischen Diskussion," p. 384.

13. "Ob itogakh diskussii i ocherednykh zadachakh marksistsko-leninskoj filosofii," in *Pravda*, 26 January 1931.

14. Shurygin, "Itogi obsuzhdenija pisma tov. Stalina v partorganizatsii IKP filosofii," p. 242.

15. Mitin, "Ocherednye zadachi raboty na filosofskom fronte v svjazi s itogami diskussii," pp. 22–23.

16. Mitin, "Über die Ergebnisse der philosophischen Diskussion," p. 349.

17. Ibid.

18. Ibid., p. 353.

19. Ibid., p. 357.

20. Mitin, "Ocherednye zadachi raboty na filosofskom fronte v svjazi s itogami diskussii," p. 12.

21. Ibid., pp. 12–13.

22. Ibid., p. 17.

23. Stalin, "O nekotorykh voprosakh istorii bolshevizma," p. 6.

24. Shurygin, "Itogi obsuzhdenija pisma tov. Stalina v partorganizatsii IKP filosofii," p. 240. The translation fails to do justice to the original.

25. Mitin, "Über die Ergebnisse der philosophischen Diskussion," p. 363.

26. Ibid.

27. See, for instance, Utis, "Stalin and the Art of Government."

28. See ibid., p. 210, for a discussion of the workings of this artificial dialectic.

29. Arendt, *The Origins of Totalitarianism*, pp. 467–68.

30. Ibid., p. 468.

CHAPTER 3

1. Mitin, "Ocherednye zadachi raboty na filosofskom fronte v svjazi s itogami diskussii," pp. 20–21. The italics are in the original.

2. Lukács, "Der grosse Oktober 1917 und die heutige Literatur," p. 96.

3. Ibid., p. 99.

4. Orwell, *1984*, p. 178.

5. Even a poet like Osip Mandelshtam was not entirely immune.

See, for instance, Freidin, "Mandel'shtam's 'Ode to Stalin': History and Myth."

6. Alexander Weissberg tells the following story, which illustrates some of the points made about Stalin's artificial dialectic in the preceding chapter and perhaps has at least a remote relevance to Georg Lukács' intellectual and spiritual evolution: "Yagoda asks Stalin, 'Which would you prefer, Comrade Stalin: that Party members should be loyal to you from conviction or from fear?' And Stalin is alleged to have replied: 'From fear.' Whereupon Yagoda asked, 'Why?' To which Stalin replied: 'Because convictions can change: fear remains.'" Quoted from Dallin and Breslauer, *Political Terror in Communist Systems*, p. 42. The story is probably apocryphal, but the principle that it expresses is valid nevertheless.

7. See chapter 8, note 123.

8. Brown, *The Proletarian Episode in Russian Literature*, p. 167. These were the years, by the way, in which the prewar intelligentsia was being held responsible for the mistakes of industrialization, accused frequently of deliberately sabotaging the First Five-Year Plan. The Shakhty trial, in which bourgeois specialists were charged with various forms of wrecking activity and linked to foreign counterrevolutionary organizations, had already been staged in 1928. Political trials of a "Toiling Peasant party" and an "Industrial party" against well-known technical specialists charged with sabotage and counterrevolutionary activities followed in 1930. The defendants belonging to the mythical Industrial party were also accused of having been involved in preparations for "imperialist intervention." In March 1931, then, the trial of the "union bureau of the central committee of the Menshevik party" was staged, which represented a sort of tangible political pendant to the ideological sides of the philosophy debate. For details, see Medvedev, *Let History Judge*, pp. 110–17. See chapter 4, note 35 for more on the Menshevik trial and the involvement of Rjazanov's Marx-Engels Institute. The following remarks by Stalin in June 1931 convey the paranoid atmosphere of the time: "Two years or so ago things here were such that the most qualified portion of the old technically educated intelligentsia had been infected by the plague of wrecking. What is more, wrecking as a way of bearing was a kind of fashion at the time. Some acted as wreckers, others covered for the wreckers, still others washed their hands in innocence and maintained their neutrality, whereas a fourth group vacillated between Soviet power and the wreckers." Stalin, "Neue Verhältnisse—neue Aufgaben," pp. 415–16. All of this, of course, bordered on being a complete fiction, used in part to feed the encirclement mentality that solidified Stalin's rule at the dangerous time of the First-Five-Year Plan. He explained further: "How did the wreckers' move-

ment originate . . .? As a result of the intensification of the class struggle within the USSR and of Soviet power's policy of the offensive with respect to capitalist elements in the city and the countryside. . . . The activity of the bellicose portion of the wreckers [was] furthered by the interventionist intrigues of the imperialists from capitalist countries . . . present within the land" (416).

9. Brown, *The Proletarian Episode in Russian Literature*, p. 77. The slogan "For the Living Man" was understood to be the expression of dialectical materialism in (literary) practice.

10. Brown, *The Proletarian Episode in Russian Literature*, p. 78.

11. Ibid., pp. 82–83. Lenin had referred to a passage in *Anna Karenina*, in which Tolstoy described the artist Mikhailov and spoke of the act of creating as "removing the coverings" that hide an object from being directly viewed. The artist "removes the coverings" and sees the world as it truly is.

12. Ibid., p. 84.

13. Averbakh, "Proletarian Literature and the Peoples of the Soviet Union," p. 120.

14. Lukács, "Die Fabrik im Walde," *Moskauer Rundschau*, 8 February 1931.

15. This remark is a prime illustration of Lukács' fundamental misunderstanding of the dynamics of the Soviet system under Stalin. What was, of course, a precipitous political decision taken by Stalin to collectivize agriculture forcibly, motivated to a significant degree not by conditions in the countryside at all but by the desiderata of factional struggles going on within the party; what was, moreover, a political action plan not really prescribed by some previously existing ideological or political principle of "pure" bolshevism (see, for instance, Cohen, "Bolshevism and Stalinism," especially pp. 25–27), shows up in Lukács as the expression of the logic of history. As such, one had a perfect right to search for the seeds of the historically lawful, predestined collectivization of agriculture in the works of creative literature. Writers finely attuned to the world of Soviet reality, then, ought to be expected to sense the stirrings of the new policy in Soviet life itself. What Lukács was plainly demanding at this early stage was a fictionalization of fictions about Soviet reality dressed up as a necessity of the historic process. In a word, Lukács was pleading, surely without realizing it, in favor of a Soviet belles-lettres that would act as a fictional illustration of Stalin's politics.

16. In Lukács' praise of Panferov, he was adapting to the recent quasi-official praise of Panferov's work. As Stephan rightly points out, Lukács' appreciation of Panferov followed shortly after the appearance of a number of articles in the Soviet press praising Panferov's work and defending him against attacks by the RAPP leadership. See Stephan, "Georg Lukács' erste Beiträge zur marx-

istischen Literaturtheorie," pp. 101–4. As a result of the initial criticism of RAPP by the Stalinist philosophers (discussed in greater detail in chapter 4), Panferov and "his group," which had originated from inside RAPP, had come out against Averbakh's leadership and were trying to develop a literary method in closer touch with the party's demands for a utilitarian five-year-plan literature. See Brown, *The Proletarian Episode in Russian Literature*, pp. 180–84. The degree of Lukács' adaptation to the official or semi-official position with respect to Panferov ought not to be exaggerated at this stage, however, for it could not have been all that clear to Lukács that the Panferov group had party backing at the time that he praised Panferov; many of the most authoritative articles dealing with the Panferov group appeared after Lukács had left for Berlin. At any rate, none of these considerations changed any of Lukács' basic interpretive categories, which he would abide by throughout his later Soviet exile, especially his obsession with the transition from spontaneity to consciousness. In his discussion of Panferov, he wrote that the "instinctive, spontaneous, eruptive" expression of the class goals of the backward peasants in Panferov's novel, which had come out in the first part of the book only "in a 'human,' a 'natural' form," gave way later to a "more conscious and far-sighted activity and, as a result, a more articulate, clearer, more political language." (I quote here from Stephan, "Georg Lukács' erste Beiträge zur marxistischen Literaturtheorie," p. 103; this particular issue of the *Moskauer Rundschau*, 7 June 1931, was not available to me.) The similarity to Lukács' criticism of Sholokhov with respect to the spontaneity-consciousness dialectic, discussed below, is obvious.

17. For lack of a better term, I translate "Gestaltung" throughout as "representation."

18. Lukács, "Die Fabrik im Walde."

19. Lukács, "Michail Scholochow," *Moskauer Rundschau*, 12 October 1930.

20. Ibid. Curiously, Lukács employs here a more literal translation of the Russian *stikhejnij*, which in a Leninist context translates simply as "spontaneous," as opposed to *soznatelnyj* or "conscious." In Lukács' context, he means a "natural" reaction or form of behavior not governed by conscious awareness of any transcendent purpose (see also note 16 above). Because the tension between consciousness and spontaneity plays such a pivotal role in Lukács' political philosophy and aesthetics, it is important to make the point here that Lukács is speaking of the Cossacks' transformation from a spontaneous, instinctive, visceral reaction to the world around them to a state of conscious awareness. In Lukács' frame of reference, such a transformation

signaled an appreciation of dialectical materialism with all that that entailed.

21. Ibid.

22. Stephan exaggerates the element of "party control" over Lukács and establishes a direct nexus between the party's literary policy and Lukács' theory. He notes that a good deal of Lukács' later ideas on politics and literary theory in his Berlin essays and those articles later written in Soviet exile had already been formulated "under direct party supervision" in Moscow in 1930–31. Stephan, "Georg Lukács' erste Beiträge zur marxistischen Literaturtheorie," p. 80. This oversimplifies the entire process of Lukács' conscious and subconscious adaptation and accommodation to authoritative trends around him.

23. Lukács, "Kunst und objektive Wahrheit," p. 617. Lukács used the German *urwüchsig* (natural, original); the Russian translation of the essay (which only appeared in Russian at the time) employed *stikhejnyj* (spontaneous) for *urwüchsig*. Lukács, "K probleme obektivnosti khudozhestvennoj formy," p. 8.

24. See chapter 8 for more details.

25. The letter was first published in Russian in March 1932 in RAPP's monthly *Na literaturnom postu* and in *Die Linkskurve*, remarkably, the same month. Lukács first mentioned the letter, a copy of which RAPP sent the BPRS, in an article published in June. The point is simply that Lukács had already sketched the outlines of the concept in 1930. It is also important to note, however (especially because this specific issue will later be identified as one that was more exclusively Lukács', not RAPP's), that the RAPP critics never mentioned the letter again after they had initially published it, though four more issues of *Na literaturnom postu* appeared in print before RAPP was formally disbanded. I agree with Ermolaev, who notes: "The RAPP leaders perhaps realized that, contrary to their overemphasis on the role of ideology in the creative process, Engels' letter suggested a considerable independence of literature from ideological bias." Ermolaev, *Soviet Literary Theories*, pp. 113 and 115.

26. Lukács, "Ilja Ehrenburg," *Moskauer Rundschau*, 9 November 1930.

27. Ibid.

28. Lukács, "Neuer Inhalt und alte Form," *Moskauer Rundschau*, 11 January 1931.

29. See, for instance, Stephan, "Georg Lukács' erste Beiträge zur marxistischen Literaturtheorie," pp. 90–92. Stephan is incorrect, on the other hand, when he speaks of RAPP's psychologism "without a socio-historical grounding." Stephan's assessment coincides with the *party*'s description of RAPP's psychological criticism at the time, and Lukács later adopted the same attitude

toward the very organization that he earlier supported. But the real motive behind the criticism of RAPP's emphasis on psychology in literature was not that it lacked a socio-historical foundation but that it pursued the psychological traces of great historical change upon human beings with a mounting disregard for whether the results of such psychological dissection necessarily accorded with the party's understanding of what the inner workings of a "Bolshevik's" mind ought to look like.

30. Lukács, "Neuer Inhalt und alte Form."
31. Lukács did write two articles for the *Moskauer Rundschau* dealing with Tolstoy and Dostoevski, 21 September 1930 and 22 March 1931. In his article on Tolstoy, Lukács again developed the idea of a contradiction between intention and literary outcome, in reliance on Lenin's well-known treatment of Tolstoy's instinctively accurate depiction of the Russian revolution and the disparity between his realistic depiction and his reactionary class background. Dostoevski, on the other hand, reaped only Lukács' scorn: "The contradictory and reactionary element is also the motive artistic principle of his art. That is the reason why his style, too, is not related to the classical traditions of the ascending, revolutionary bourgeois class (as is Tolstoy's); it is indicative, rather, of the most varying Romantic trends in style coming from a lower middle class already vacillating between revolution and reaction."

CHAPTER 4

1. For details see Brown, *The Proletarian Episode in Russian Literature*, chapters 9, 10, and 11; and Ermolaev, *Soviet Literary Theories*, chapters 4 and 5.
2. Ermolaev, *Soviet Literary Theories*, p. 120. See also the article on Litfront in the *Literaturnaja èntsiklopedija*, pp. 506–13.
3. Ermolaev, *Soviet Literary Theories*, pp. 96 and 221. For details on Pereverzev's literary theory and the various attacks on it, see pp. 93–99. See also the summary of Pereverzev's views on literature in Siegel, *Sowjetische Literaturtheorie*, pp. 58–68.
4. Ermolaev, *Soviet Literary Theories*, pp. 98 and 221. See note 35 below for more details concerning the political context.
5. Ibid., p. 120.
6. Ibid., p. 101.
7. Mitin, "Ocherednye zadachi raboty na filosofskom fronte v svjazi s itogami diskussii," p. 19.
8. Ibid.
9. Ibid.
10. For details on Plechanov's influence upon RAPP, see Brown, *The Proletarian Episode in Russian Literature*, pp. 188 and 204.

11. "Za gegemoniju proletarskoj literatury," *Pravda*, 31 August 1931.
12. Mitin, Raltsevich, Judin, and Takser, "Proletarskuju literaturu— na vysshuju stupen!," *Pravda*, 19 November 1931.
13. Ibid.
14. Ibid.
15. Ibid.
16. Lev Mekhlis, "Za perestrojku raboty RAPP," *Pravda*, 24 November 1931.
17. Mitin, "Ocherednye zadachi raboty na filosofskom fronte v svjazi s itogami diskusii," p. 20.
18. See especially Brown, *The Proletarian Episode in Russian Literature*, pp. 200–218, particularly 205–17.
19. Lukács, *Gelebtes Denken*, p. 143. See also chapter 5, note 16.
20. See Gallas, *Marxistische Literaturtheorie*, pp. 60, 199–200, 204, and discussion in Pike, *German Writers in Soviet Exile*, pp. 40–41.
21. See Weber, *Hauptfeind Sozialdemokratie*, pp. 85–93; and Carr, *Twilight of the Comintern*, pp. 45–51.
22. This is not to imply that there were no interventions by party political functionaries, only that these interventions largely mirrored the existence of factional differences within the party concerning cultural and literary policy and that they reflected shifting views and majorities rather than a stable consensus. Moreover, precisely the group that backed Lukács, the men around Neumann, Münzenberg, and Flieg, who were probably behind the first intervention in 1930 by Josef Winternitz (N. Kraus) before Lukács had arrived in Berlin, all lost their party posts after Neumann was removed from the triumvirate of Thälmann, Neumann, and Remmele in late spring 1932. See Bahne, "Die Kommunistische Partei Deutschlands," p. 678. The details of these events will likely never be resolved completely, but enough is known to argue that the differences both in the leadership of the KPD as well as the Comintern in these years preclude any talk of a unified policy for culture. See also note 24 below.
23. See Sziklai's introduction to Lukács, *Wie ist die faschistische Philosophie in Deutschland entstanden?*, p. 13.
24. Stephan offers speculation in place of evidence in this respect. "After a probation of eighteen months in Moscow, Lukács was sent by summer 1931 by the CI to Berlin with the assignment of backing up the party-loyal BPRS leadership around Johannes R. Becher, Andor Gábor, and Otto Biha in the BPRS' factional battles, which were growing more intense." Stephan, "Georg Lukács' erste Beiträge zur marxistischen Literaturtheorie," p. 82. But it was not just a question of the BPRS leadership being "party loyal" and a left-wing faction being somehow antiparty; what occurred was an extension of factional differences over politics that existed within the party and related divergences of opinion on cultural policy.

Stephan makes the same point twice: because Lukács had supported Panferov's group from the outset and demonstrated his "political loyalty" in his reviews for the *Moskauer Rundschau*, "he must have struck the CI in mid 1931 as the right man to swing the disagreements in the BPRS that were reaching a decisive point between the Bund leadership and its left opposition . . . in favor of the party-loyal group" (ibid., p. 100). Stephan's entire interpretation assumes a degree of clarity in "the CI" in questions of literary political policy that simply did not exist at the time, neither there nor, for that matter, in the Soviet Communist party and its approach to literary policy for Soviet writers.

25. See ibid., p. 82.
26. "Tonbandgespräch."
27. "Ob itogakh diskussii i ocherednykh zadachakh marksistsko-leninskoj filosofii," *Pravda*, 26 January 1931.
28. Mitin, "Über die Ergebnisse der philosophischen Diskussion," p. 363.
29. Mitin, "Ocherednye zadachi raboty na filosofskom fronte v svjazi s itogami diskussii," p. 31.
30. For more detailed discussion of the Rjazanov affair, see Medvedev, *Let History Judge*, pp. 132–36. Stalin's hostility toward Rjazanov apparently went back at least to the tenth party congress in 1921. Antonov-Ovseyenko reports this altercation: "After Ryazanov had spoken, Stalin remarked: 'I respect Ryazanov a lot, but I respect Marx more.' Ryazanov parried from his seat: 'Koba, don't embarrass people. Theory is not your strong point." Antonov-Ovseyenko, *The Time of Stalin*, p. 129. I repeat the story merely to underscore the nature of the philosophy debate as an opportunity to settle old scores and to suggest that Lukács, through his association with Rjazanov, may have been in greater political trouble in 1931 than Lukács scholarship has recognized before.
31. "Ob itogakh diskussii i ocherednykh zadachakh marksistsko-leninskij filosofii," *Pravda*, 26 January 1931.
32. Shurygin, "Itogi obsuzhdenija pisma tov. Stalina v partorganizatsii IKP filosofii," p. 243.
33. Ibid. See also by the same author, "Protiv menshevistvujushche-idealisticheskoj falsifikatsii istorii filosofskoj borby Lenina," p. 234.
34. Mitin, "Über die Ergebnisse der philosophischen Diskussion," p. 339.
35. Ibid., pp. 338–39. The "Menshevik trial" took place in March 1931 against a group of former Mensheviks, none of whom had had anything to do with the Menshevik party since the early twenties and who all held posts in Soviet economic and planning agencies at the time of their arrest. The defendants were accused of having rejoined the Menshevik party in the late twenties and then organizing a "center" for it, a "union bureau," within the

Soviet Union. The case was a complete fabrication, but the defendants were charged with economic sabotage and wrecking: in their capacity as planners for the First Five-Year Plan they had premeditatedly lowered the targets of the plan, setting goals less than what they knew the country was capable of meeting. Nor were the charges of conspiracy absent. The "Mensheviks" were said to have joined forces with the "Industrial party" and the "Toiling Peasant party" to make preparations for armed intervention in the Soviet Union from without and for rebellions and revolts from inside the country. See Medvedev, *Let History Judge*, pp. 115–17; and Conquest, *The Great Terror*, pp. 734–40. During the testimony at the trial, David Rjazanov was implicated by a man terrorized into naming him as a contact man for the center at the Marx-Engels Institute. See especially Medvedev, *Let History Judge*, pp. 132–37. According to Antonov-Ovseyenko (*The Time of Stalin*, p. 129), Rjazanov was also charged in effect with having stolen a letter from Darwin to Karl Marx. Rjazanov had obtained the letter from relatives of Darwin, who had stipulated that it not be published, which, as Antonov-Ovseyenko tells the story, Stalin used as the basis for the charge of theft.

36. It is a cruel irony that Jan Stèn, one of the philosophers around Deborin, had directed Stalin's study of Hegelian dialectics from 1925 to 1928. Stèn told a close circle of friends in 1928, "Koba will do things that will put the trials of Dreyfus and of Beilis in the shade." Stèn was first banished to Akmolinsk and then arrested in 1937. He was executed that June. As a way of characterizing Stalin's dialecticians, the following occurrence is also worth relating. When Stèn was arrested, a major article of his entitled "Dialectical Materialism" was scheduled for publication in the relevant volume of the *Great Soviet Encyclopedia*. So the editors reset only that page containing Stèn's signature, changing the author's name to Mark Mitin and thus, as Medvedev puts it, adding to Mitin's list the sole publication that is genuinely interesting. See Medvedev, *Let History Judge*, pp. 224–25. Mitin, by the way, was one of the real authors of the later "authoritative" biography of Stalin (the infamous *Kratkaja biografija*) published by the Marx-Engels Institute after that organization had been swept clean of assorted deviationists.

37. Lukács, *Gelebtes Denken*, pp. 143–44.

38. Lukács, "Autobiographie."

CHAPTER 5

1. "Za gegemoniju proletarskoj literatury," *Pravda*, 31 August 1931.

2. Becher, "Unsere Wendung," p. 8.

3. Ibid.

4. Ibid.
5. During this trip to Germany, incidentally, Tretjakov first met Brecht.
6. Becher, "Unsere Wendung," p. 5.
7. Becher, "Kühnheit und Begeisterung," p. 5.
8. Stalin's letter to *Proletarskaja revoljutsija* as it affected the KPD is dealt with in greater detail in chapter 7.
9. Becher's diction here is strikingly reminiscent of Lukács' political vocabulary. It is perhaps not wrong to assume that Becher and Lukács discussed their programmatic articles before publishing them.
10. Becher, "Kühnheit und Begeisterung," p. 6.
11. Ibid., p. 11.
12. Ibid., p. 11. Becher's remarks elsewhere allow a fairly precise evaluation of the BPRS' familiarity with the mounting Stalinist criticism of RAPP's slogan "For the Removal of Any and All Masks" and the addition of the words "from the class enemy": "The working class puts on no masks whatever in its battle and its dictatorship, and precisely for that reason it demands of our literature that it tear from its enemies any and all masks, the masks of the class enemies, the masks of opportunistic elements, the masks behind which hide vacillating elements" (p. 10).
13. Lukács, "Autobiographie."
14. Lukács, "Postscriptum 1957 zu: 'Mein Weg zu Marx,'" in *Schriften zur Ideologie und Politik*, p. 646.
15. Lukács, *Gelebtes Denken*, p. 158.
16. Lukács' remarks, combined with his answer "I wanted to leave" when asked why he had departed Moscow for Berlin in summer 1931, lend substance to my hypothesis that Lukács' move was an orderly flight to remove himself from an actual or potentially perilous situation. When he adds that he did not return to the Marx-Engels Institute upon his return to Moscow in April 1933 because in the interim Stalin's campaign against RAPP, which was largely an extension of the philosophy debate, had been carried out, the connection is difficult to see at first glance, and Lukács provided no further elucidation. But if Lukács left Moscow in mid-1931 because of the atmosphere created by the philosophy debate and the fear that the attacks on Rjazanov, the Marx-Engels Institute, and, not least of all, on him personally, might have an epilogue, it is justified to conjecture that Lukács perhaps had every reason from his perspective not to set foot in the institute one and a half years later.
17. Lukács, *Gelebtes Denken*, p. 158.
18. Judin was a career denouncer and hatchet man. In 1937 he charged that the "Living Man" slogan of Averbakh and RAPP had been designed to disorientate Soviet writers, and the slogan "Tear Off the Masks" had supposedly meant to Averbakh the unmasking of all of

Soviet reality, the state and its leaders included. For Judin, these were all examples of Trotskyism. Judin also joined in the political denunciations of Averbakh in the aftermath of his arrest. See Brown, *The Proletarian Episode in Russian Literature*, pp. 227–31 and 277. Judin's political-philosophical career, by the way, extended into the postwar era as well. In the late forties, for instance, he established himself as an authority on the interpretation of the "people's democracy," particularly after Dimitrov had proclaimed that such democracy was just a new form of the dictatorship of the proletariat. Following Dimitrov's lead, Judin explained that the people's democracy was one of two historically established kinds of proletarian dictatorship, the other being, of course, the Soviet form. See Brzezinski, *The Soviet Bloc*, p. 74. In 1948 Judin was one of Stalin's personal intrigants kicked out of Yugoslavia by Tito. See ibid., pp. 70–73.

19. "Tonbandgespräch."
20. Becher, "Einen Schritt weiter!," pp. 2–3.
21. "Za gegemoniju proletarskoj literatury," *Pravda*, 31 August 1931.
22. Lukács, "Shaws Bekenntnis zur Sowjetunion," p. 5.
23. Ibid., p. 8.
24. Lukács, "Gerhart Hauptmann," p. 9.
25. Ibid., p. 12.
26. Lukács, *Gelebtes Denken*, p. 159.
27. Averbakh, "Proletarian Literature and the Peoples of the Soviet Union," p. 118.
28. Ibid.
29. Becher, "Kühnheit und Begeisterung," p. 6.
30. Lukács, "Willi Bredels Romane," pp. 24–25. The opening paragraph of Lukács' article followed a brief note signed by Leopold Averbakh, "Zur Programmdiskussion" (pp. 22–23), containing the following remarks: "The reorganization of proletarian writers requires above all lifting the niveau of their Marxist world view. Without raising it energetically, the writer cannot master his material artistically. The lag in proletarian literature, which continues to exist, demonstrated earlier and points up now as well the insufficient Bolshevist cultural niveau of the majority of our writers. This also produces the often emphasized weakness in many of their works. We have explained frequently in the past that the insufficiency of form is only the expression of an insufficiency of content." This passage could be taken for remarks lifted from any of several articles by Lukács dealing with the subject of the writer's "world view," and it is scarcely likely that Lukács' article followed right after an authoritative statement of that sort by sheer coincidence.
31. Lukács, "Willi Bredels Romane," p. 26.
32. Ibid.
33. Ibid., p. 25.

34. Lukács, "Gegen die Spontaneitätstheorie in der Literatur," p. 30.
35. Ibid., pp. 30–31. Gotsche spotted the presumptuousness of Lukács' position immediately and noted that he had held numerous conversations with proletarian readers from the same working-class milieu depicted by Bredel. Their attitude toward Lukács' article was that the "article writer," Lukács, should see if he could do any better than Bredel. Another response to Lukács' criticism was supposedly, "The man ought to write something better, then he can voice his opinion." Gotsche, "Kritik der Anderen," pp. 28–29. Lukács had no intention of accepting the validity of this point, which challenged his entire raison d'être as a party intellectual. His counterargument ran: "A Russian worker would look on in amazement if he were expected to demand first from Comrade Averbakh better novels, short stories, poems, and so on, for example, *before* Averbakh were allowed to come out with his criticism." Lukács, "Gegen die Spontaneitätstheorie in der Literatur," p. 31. Lukács' disputes with Gotsche, by the way, set the pattern for Lukács' behavior in some later polemics. Gotsche told me in 1984 that he had been invited by the BPRS leadership to contribute the article that Lukács then promptly refuted with the voice of authority.
36. Lukács, "Gegen die Spontaneitätstheorie in der Literatur," p. 31.
37. Ibid., p. 32.
38. Ibid.
39. Ibid.
40. "Ein unveröffentlichter Brief Friedrich Engels über Balzac," p. 11. See also chapter 3, note 25. The relevant passages for Lukács (and the emergence of socialist realism) are these: "That Balzac thus was compelled to go against his own class sympathies and political prejudices, that he *saw* the necessity of the downfall of his favourite nobles, and described them as people deserving no better fate; and that he *saw* the real men of the future where, for the time being, they alone were to be found—that I consider one of the greatest triumphs of Realism, and one of the grandest features in old Balzac." Quoted from Ermolaev, *Soviet Literary Theories*, p. 115. Engels' letter was originally written in English.
41. "Ein unveröffentlichter Brief Friedrich Engels über Balzac," p. 12.
42. Lukács, "Tendenz oder Parteilichkeit," p. 18.
43. Lukács, "Tendenz oder Parteilichkeit," p. 19.
44. Ibid., pp. 20–21.
45. Cf. Lukács, "Reportage oder Gestaltung (I)," p. 27.
46. Ibid., p. 28.
47. Ibid., p. 30.
48. Ibid.
49. See Siegel, *Sowjetische Literaturtheorie*, passim, for a discussion of the various schools of sociological criticism from Plechanov to the Soviet critics Fritsche and Pereverzev.

50. Lukács, "Reportage oder Gestaltung (I)," p. 29.
51. Lukács, "Reportage oder Gestaltung (II)," pp. 28–29.
52. Ibid., p. 28.
53. It is interesting to compare Lukács' critical but restrained treatment (by his later standards) of Ilja Ehrenburg in the *Moskauer Rundschau* with his invective in *Die Linkskurve*: "I will not even mention Ehrenburg. In his writing the link between a skeptical and corroded, an intellectualistic and counterrevolutionary world view, and the increasingly conscious avoidance of all methods of literary representation is obvious at first glance." Lukács, "Reportage oder Gestaltung (I)," p. 30. Of particular importance is Lukács' insinuation that Ehrenburg's "avoidance" of a proper creative method as a reflection of his world view was becoming an increasingly premeditated, intentional, and almost sinister act of creative sedition. This kind of suggestion was already outside the perimeters of theoretical differences of opinion and was approaching dangerously close to political denunciation.
54. Lukács, "Reportage oder Gestaltung (II)," pp. 30–31.
55. Ottwalt, "'Tatsachenroman' und Formexperiment."
56. Lukács, "Aus der Not eine Tugend," p. 15.
57. Ibid., p. 16; and Ottwalt, "'Tatsachenroman' und Formexperiment," p. 22.
58. Lukács, "Aus der Not eine Tugend," p. 18.
59. Ibid. Lukács is quoting from Ottwalt, "'Tatsachenroman' und Formexperiment," p. 22. Lukács added the italics.
60. Lukács, "Aus der Not eine Tugend," p. 18.
61. Ibid., p. 19.
62. Ibid.

CHAPTER 6

1. "Der Brief des Genossen Stalin und die KPD," p. 71.
2. Ibid.
3. Lukács, "Der grosse Oktober 1917 und die Literatur," p. 97.
4. Lukács, "Autobiographie."
5. Lukács, "Znachenie 'Materializma i èmpiriokrititsizma' dlja bolshevizatsii kommunisticheskikh partij," p. 147.
6. Lukács, *Gelebtes Denken*, pp. 139–40. Lukács goes on to add: "Stalin maintained that, on the contrary, the Marx-Engels line of Marxism and—unspoken, the Stalin line, too—was the valid one. If one looks at the main purpose pursued here by Stalin, this is naturally a Stalinist concept. But for me, however, it had a very important consequence. Stalin's criticism of Plechanov caused me to formulate a criticism of Mehring, too." Two points: first, I would argue that Lukács did not understand Stalin's motives at the time or identify concepts as "Stalinist," and, second, it is still

noteworthy that he could speak much later of Stalin's cynical intentions and still subordinate that purpose to the validity of what he imagined to be some overriding theoretical truth.

7. See Eörsi's remarks in his introduction to *Gelebtes Denken* (p. 17) about Lukács' rapidly deteriorating state of health.
8. Lukács, "Postscriptum 1957 zu: 'Mein Weg zu Marx,'" in *Schriften zur Ideologie und Politik*, p. 646.
9. Ibid., p. 647.
10. Ibid.
11. Ibid.
12. Ibid., p. 648.
13. Ibid., p. 643.
14. Ibid., p. 648.
15. Ibid.
16. Ibid., p. 643.
17. Lukács, *Geschichte und Klassenbewusstsein*, p. 34.
18. Lukács, *Wie ist die faschistische Philosophie in Deutschland entstanden?*, p. 57.
19. "Der Brief des Genossen Stalin und die KPD," p. 70.
20. Ibid., pp. 71–72.
21. See Thälmann, *Im Kampf gegen die faschistische Diktatur*, pp. 16–17: "In Germany, in the context of the central committee's ideological offensive, we won our correct point against various deviating and vague outlooks with respect to the *Stalin* definition of the twin brothers."
22. For a vivid illustration, see the collection of circular instructions sent by the KPD central committee to the party's regional offices in Weber, *Die Generallinie*. The foreword to this documentation was also published separately under the title *Hauptfeind Sozialdemokratie*.
23. For more detailed discussion, see Pike, "Eine Faschismustheorie der Komintern?"
24. Note Dvorkin's complaints about the absence of any studies of National Socialism, laments he made with no reference to the causes of that absence. See ibid., pp. 66 and 68 (note 46).
25. Gejden, *Istorija germanskogo fashizma*, p. iii.
26. See Pike, *German Writers in Soviet Exile*, pp. 315–17. Ernst Ottwalt was arrested the same day.
27. There is little point in speculating about the reasons why the manuscript never appeared because all such speculation must remain in the realm of conjecture. Only a few points are perhaps worth making: it would be difficult to contend that the radical nature, the "sectarianism," of Lukács' book prevented its appearance at a time when the party was contemplating a change in policy. The manuscript was finished by August 1933, and, assuming that Lukács tried to publish it then, the Comintern was not yet involved in the reexamination of its old policy and articula-

tion of the new. It is at least possible that the manuscript was not published in 1933 or 1934 because there were people within the party who still regarded this type of an ideological exercise as unimportant (even Günther had difficulty getting his volume accepted for publication and into print). But by late 1935, then, Lukács' book was definitely out of line with popular front ideas and ideals, its publication being understandably inappropriate by then.

28. Lukács, *Wie ist die faschistische Philosophie in Deutschland entstanden?* All subsequent page references are given in the text.

29. Lukács, *Gelebtes Denken*, pp. 170–71.

30. Lukács, *Die Zerstörung der Vernunft*, p. 10.

31. *Die Zerstörung der Vernunft* was first published in East Germany in 1954. The greater portion of the manuscript had already been completed, however, during the war years. See Lukács, *Gelebtes Denken*, p. 166.

32. Steiner, "Making a Homeland for the Mind."

33. Kołakowski, *Main Currents of Marxism*, p. 284.

34. Ibid., p. 286.

35. See, for instance, Theodor Adorno's remarks in 1956: "In the book *Die Zerstörung der Vernunft* one finds the most crass manifestation of Lukács' own." Adorno, "Erpresste Versöhnung," in *Gesammelte Schriften*, 2: 251.

36. Lukács, *Gelebtes Denken*, p. 166.

37. Ibid. Lukács also insinuated that *Der historische Roman* was somehow suspect in the eyes of Stalinist officialdom. Its publication was not possible in Russia, he said, explaining: "In the eyes of the publishers I was a suspicious person, suspicious not in the sense of being an enemy but as someone who did not adhere to the prescribed Marxism set down by Fadejev." Ibid., p. 174. This is a half-truth. *Der historische Roman* was in fact published in the Soviet Union in a Russian translation in *Literaturnyj kritik* in 1937 and 1938. It is not inconceivable that one or the other Soviet publisher might have felt uneasy about publishing Lukács; publishing in general in those years was always regarded as a risky proposition because authors kept disappearing without any prior warning, and their publishers were then often held responsible for having brought out the works of an enemy of the people. It is also thinkable that the undeniable antagonism between the Fadejev group and the critics who wrote for *Literaturnyj kritik* played a role. But Lukács seeks to create the impression here that the publication of his work was somehow impossible because it did not fit into the Stalinist scheme of things, and this contention is simply not true. Lukács encountered no difficulty in locating a Soviet publisher in 1937 and again in 1939 for collections of his essays, for instance, which methodologically or theoretically differed not in the least from his study of the historical novel. In

addition, there were firm plans in the early forties to publish *Der historische Roman* in the series "Kleine Bibliothek." TsGALI, Fond 631/12/86/17. The Russian translation, which had already been serialized in *Literaturnyj kritik*, was also scheduled for republication in a single volume by the publishing house Sovetskij pisatel, where it lay "accepted and ready for print." TsGALI, 631/12/86. The few scattered archival documents available to me and pertinent to the subject suggest that its earlier publication in German and Russian was stopped, along with that of a number of other books by German exiles in the Soviet Union, by a combination of paper shortages and the Hitler-Stalin pact (the latter often being the actual cause of the former).

38. Lukács, *Gelebtes Denken*, p. 167.

39. Ibid., pp. 170–71, 173.

40. Lukács, *Die Zerstörung der Vernunft*, p. 10.

41. See especially ibid., pp. 200–201.

42. See especially ibid., p. 246.

43. There is an intriguing similarity between Lukács' theory of fascism and the depiction of National Socialism and its ideology in *Der Herren eigener Geist* by Hans Günther. A wealth of parallels could be easily established: interpretations of specific semifascist or fascistic philosophical and ideological trends are identical; the identical philosophers are treated in much the same way; the categories, especially the overarching idea of the indirect or "critical" apologia, are often identical. It would be interesting, in fact, to conjecture as to why Günther's book was published and Lukács' was not. Lukács may well have shown Günther his manuscript (the two men knew each other), and there is a single vague and undocumented reference in *Der Herren eigener Geist* (p. 132) to Lukács' notion of the "critical apologists," a concept that he developed in these early years only in this particular unpublished manuscript. One wonders, in fact, if there was any direct connection between the appearance of Günther's manuscript and the nonpublication of Lukács'. As just one example of the similarities, compare the following passage in Günther's book to the quotation from Lukács cited above in the text: "The real class content of fascist ideology did not come out on the surface at all, or only in a confusing manner. The class content was covered over and falsified. What was to be achieved had never existed before in history, not in a single one of the earlier states run on violence. The rule of terror *against* the masses was to be erected *with the help* of the masses. . . . *The victims were led astray by a gigantic fraud*" (pp. 54–55). One such passage cannot adequately convey the overall impression of similarity that runs through the entire manuscript and is meant here only to call attention to the problem.

44. Wilhelm Pieck, for instance, spoke of the "parasitic upper stra-

tum of six hundred millionaires" running things in Germany. Pieck, *We Are Fighting for a Soviet Germany*, p. 31.

45. This remark is instructive. If Lukács is capable of speaking about radical, one-hundred-percent fascism, it implies, of course, that in his mind fascism of a sort was already in power in Germany before 1933, just not the unveiled, unrestricted kind. This was a standard outlook in the party, one that was championed prior to 1932 by Heinz Neumann in particular.

46. See, for instance, Weingartner, *Stalin und der Aufstieg Hitlers*, pp. 230–34.

47. See Carr, *Twilight of the Comintern*, pp. 45–51; and Weber, *Hauptfeind Sozialdemokratie*, pp. 86–93.

48. Bahne, "Die Kommunistische Partei Deutschlands," p. 695.

49. Ibid.

50. Pieck, *We Are Fighting for a Soviet Germany*, pp. 35–36.

51. See Weber, *Hauptfeind Sozialdemokratie*, p. 89 (see also chapter 7, note 1). Cf. Gallas, *Marxistische Literaturtheorie*, pp. 60, 199–200, 204, for details concerning Lukács' relations with Neumann, Münzenberg, and Flieg. According to what Lukács told Gallas, he and Flieg were personal friends, and Flieg was in charge of cultural affairs in the party until Neumann's demise in May 1932, when Flieg also lost his influential position in the central committee secretariat.

52. Weingartner, *Stalin und der Aufstieg Hitlers*, pp. 52–53.

53. Weber, *Hauptfeind Sozialdemokratie*, p. 90. See also Carr, *Twilight of the Comintern*, pp. 31–32. Carr quotes a speech by Neumann given in March 1931, in which he proclaimed that a proletarian revolution had become through the course of history an "inescapable necessity"—this being, of course, at least in the context of the later factional disputes, a form of revolutionary radicalism that "underestimated" National Socialism, though the logic had been inherent in the party's, not just Neumann's, entire theory of imperialism and fascism.

54. Quoted from Carr, *Twilight of the Comintern*, p. 90.

55. Pieck, *We Are Fighting for a Soviet Germany*, p. 30.

56. Ibid., p. 25.

57. Thälmann, "Zu unserer Strategie und Taktik im Kampf gegen den Faschismus," p. 289.

58. Thälmann, "Einige Fehler in unserer theoretischen und praktischen Arbeit und der Weg zu ihrer Überwindung," p. 498.

59. See Thälmann's criticism in late 1931 of an article with this passage in a party publication signed "Kr." (presumably Kraus, that is, Josef Winternitz): "A Social Democratic coalition government, standing opposite a paralyzed, splintered, confused proletariat would be a thousand-times greater evil than an *open fascist dictatorship*, which is confronted by a class conscious, resolute, battle-ready, and largely united proletariat." Thälmann,

"Einige Fehler in unserer theoretischen und praktischen Arbeit und der Weg zu ihrer Überwindung," p. 499. Cf. also Remmele's remark in the Reichstag: "The fascist gentlemen do not scare us. They will have demonstrated their inability to govern [werden abgewirtschaftet haben] more quickly than any other government." Quoted in Weber, *Hauptfeind Sozialdemokratie*, pp. 90–91. The important point is, however, that this outlook had a long history, and, though Thälmann later criticized the view during his falling out with Neumann, it was by no means an argument held solely by Neumann and his followers in the party. Ironically, Stalin had noted as early as 1923: "Of course, the Fascists are not asleep. But it is to our advantage to let them attack first; that will rally the whole working class around the communists." In 1930 an article by A. Martynov entitled "Decaying Capitalism and the Fascisization of the Bourgeois State" appeared in the Comintern organ. Martynov argued that the process of decay "breeds ever sharper forces of struggle by the revolutionary proletariat" and was therefore "a necessary condition of its decisive victory." Further, a KPD central committee resolution of mid-1930 held likewise that "the stronger emergence of Fascism in the present period" was "an unavoidable concomitant of the ripening of a revolutionary situation." Carr, *Twilight of the Comintern*, pp. 16, 27–28. The essential similarity with the "automatism" of Lukács' theory of fascism is clear.

60. Thälmann, "Einige Fehler in unserer theoretischen und praktischen Arbeit und der Weg zu ihrer Überwindung," p. 499.
61. "Das XII. Plenum des EKKI. und die KPD.," pp. 386–87.
62. Lukács, *Wie ist die faschistische Philosophie in Deutschland entstanden?*, p. 19.

CHAPTER 7

1. See chapter 6, note 51. There was controversy in the air in any case following the publication of Stalin's letter to *Proletarskaja revoljutsija*, and, though specific details about that controversy are missing, its vague outlines point to a classic instance of the complex of personal rivalry—in this case originally between Neumann and Thälmann—and ideological disputes. Though Neumann had been referred to in the party press as late as August 1931 as the KPD's "actual leader," differences were already emerging then between him and Thälmann. (For this and the following, see Weber, *Hauptfeind Sozialdemokratie*, pp. 86–93.) In October 1931 both men journeyed to Moscow in order to obtain guidelines for future policy. Neumann had hoped to gain Stalin's support for his own policies, but he evidently lost out to Thälmann. On 10 November 1931 the party passed a resolution

against "individual terror" that is usually interpreted as a setback for Neumann (Neumann having been held responsible, for instance, for the slogan "Smash the fascists wherever you meet them!"). In August 1932, in fact, Thälmann accused him of arguing against the classification of that slogan as false and favoring its rejection only as a guide to action that was no longer opportune. Thälmann, "Schlusswort auf dem XII. Plenum des EKKI," p. 273. The differences between Neumann and Thälmann continued behind the scenes, with Neumann and Leo Flieg evidently using Thälmann's defeat in the presidential elections of 1932 to attempt to persuade the Comintern to replace Thälmann as party head. Then, in May 1932, Thälmann and Neumann (along with Remmele and Walter Ulbricht) traveled to Moscow to attend a presidium meeting of the Comintern's executive committee, the ECCI. Stalin backed Thälmann, and Neumann was forced to remain in Moscow working in the ECCI offices. In late August the political secretariat of the presidium of the ECCI removed Neumann from his function as candidate of the politburo of the central committee of the KPD, and a number of men associated with Neumann lost their posts or were given official reprimands (for instance, Leo Flieg and Münzenberg; Josef Winternitz, head of the agitprop division, had been deprived of his position already in December 1931, and Fritz David and Paul Langner had been subjected to harsh criticism. See Bahne, "Die Kommunistische Partei Deutschlands," p. 678. In October Remmele had to leave the secretariat, though he was not relieved of all his duties until December 1933).

As for Stalin's letter to *Proletarskaja revoljutsija*, it too was used as ammunition against Neumann and other KPD functionaries and publicists with outlooks on revolutionary tactics and mass action evidently regarded as too radical, too less subject to the immediate control of the KPD central committee. Thälmann attacked both Winternitz and his deputy, the Russian Alexander Emel (Moissej Lurye), for having "misinterpreted" Stalin's letter. See Thälmann, "Einige Fehler in unserer theoretischen und praktischen Arbeit und der Weg zu ihrer Überwindung," pp. 493–501; and Weber, *Hauptfeind Sozialdemokratie*, p. 85. Thälmann also criticized Paul Langner for his book on mass strikes, in which the latter had supposedly given "an entirely insufficient criticism of the errors of Luxemburgism in this area." Thälmann, "Der revolutionäre Ausweg und die KPD," p. 435. Also, in discussing the significance of Stalin's criticism of Rosa Luxemburg, Thälmann also criticized a book by Fritz David, *Bankrott des Reformismus*, because it similarly contained no criticism of Luxemburg's theory of accumulation, her theory of the economic collapse of capitalism (Luxemburg's version of the "theory of collapse" [*Zusammenbruchstheorie*]), or—an even more dangerous omission—her stance during the Social Democratic debates about mass strikes after 1910. David had contended that strikes were an offensive weapon under the conditions of the general crisis of capitalism, an emphasis, said Thälmann, that oversimplified the revolutionary struggle and ignored the resolutions of the tenth and eleventh ECCI plenums concerning the need to combine the economic and the political struggle. Thälmann, "Der revolutionäre Ausweg und die KPD," pp. 438–39. Thälmann used a different pretext to attack Neumann. On 22 November 1931 the *Rote Fahne*, of which Neumann was the head editor, published Stalin's letter to *Proletarskaja revoljutsija*, preceded by an introduction that, according to Thälmann, was written under the "supervision" of and "sanctioned" by Neumann. Thälmann, "Schlusswort auf dem XII. Plenum des EKKI," p. 274. That introduction was now denounced as "a *serious, inexcusable error*" and as "this *opportunistic blunder*," one that the entire secretariat of the central committee had been forced to correct. Thälmann, "Der revolutionäre Ausweg und die KPD," p. 443. The main charge was that the introduction had spoken of "the 'leftist' draped morass ideology of Trotskyism" ("Stalin über den Kampf gegen Zentrismus," *Die Rote Fahne*, 22 November 1931), whereas, said Thälmann, Stalin had made it clear in his letter that Trotskyism was nothing more than a "counterrevolutionary advance guard of the bourgeoisie." Thus, Neumann had completely misunderstood the essential meaning of the Stalin letter and displayed carelessness in theoretical questions.

These polemics all point to a mixture of personal animosities with political-tactical differences contrived on the basis of Stalin's open letter. Thälmann had also criticized Neumann's "pseudo-revolutionary" assessment of the class struggle, which encouraged the fatalistic reliance on spontaneity (see chapter 6), and it may well be that Thälmann's support from Stalin was associated with an attempt to hold back the KPD's more radical fringe from engaging in adventuresome policies unwelcome in Moscow at the time, in other words, to keep the party as directly responsible as possible to the Stalinist leadership and to stifle grass-roots revolutionary initiatives such as individual terror, mass strikes, etc. Incidentally, Willi Münzenberg was also criticized in connection with the issue of Luxemburgism; in private meetings, Münzenberg had evidently attempted to defend Luxemburg and was forced to confess the error of his ways. Thälmann, "Der revolutionäre Ausweg und die KPD," pp. 459 and 467. One wonders if another of Thälmann's complaints about Neumann in fact reflects the nature of the latter's relationship to his (not quite legal) brother-in-law Münzenberg: "[Neumann] came out in opposition to the justified and absolutely necessary criticism of written works by individual comrades (for instance, Langner) and betrayed his familial narrow-mindedness vis-à-vis his friends." Thälmann, "Schlusswort auf dem XII. Plenum des EKKI," p. 275.

2. Cf., for instance, Luxemburg's well-known remarks regarding proletarian dictatorship: "Public life is gradually lulled to sleep, several dozen party leaders with inexhaustible energy and infinite idealism direct and govern, and among them, in reality, a dozen excellent minds take charge. An elite of the workers is summoned to gatherings now and then in order to clap at the speeches of the leaders, and to agree unanimously to previously formulated resolutions. In effect, then, this is cliquism—a dictatorship, to be sure, not that of the proletariat, however, but of a handful of politicians." Quoted from Leonhard, *Sowjetideologie heute*, p. 178.

3. See Weber, *Die Wandlung des deutschen Kommunismus*, p. 93.

4. Ibid.

5. Ibid., pp. 89–93. See also Nettl, *Rosa Luxemburg*, pp. 748–93, especially p. 776.

6. Cf. Stalin, "Die Oktoberrevolution und die Taktik der russischen Kommunisten," in *Fragen des Leninismus*, p. 109: "What distinguishes this 'theory of permanent revolution' from the well-known theory of menshevism, which denies the dictatorship of the proletariat? Basically nothing. . . . Trotsky's 'permanent revolution' is a species of menshevism."

7. Ibid., p. 117.

8. Stalin, "Über die Grundlagen des Leninismus," pp. 25–26.

9. Stalin, "O nekotorykh voprosakh istorii bolshevizma," p. 6.

10. Ibid., pp. 10–11.

11. Kaganovich, "Für ein bolschewistisches Studium der Geschichte der Partei," p. 2263.

12. Ibid.

13. Ibid., p. 2267.

14. "Der Brief des Genossen Stalin und die KPD," p. 71.

15. "Der Stalinbrief und unser Kampf gegen den Krieg," pp. 136–37.

16. Thälmann, "Der revolutionäre Ausweg und die KPD," p. 440.

17. Ibid., p. 441.

18. Take, for instance, Lukács' following comment about the "left opposition" in prewar German Social Democracy: "This iridescent vacillation, which can be traced in all areas of theory and practice, prevented the left opposition from sharply confronting the increasingly obvious process of an opportunistic infection of the labor movement with the clear-cut line of undistorted Marxism, of dialectical materialism" (p. 182). The point is not that "the unity of theory and practice" was a concept brand new to Lukács after the Soviet philosophy debate; it was, of course, an integral component of his political philosophy from early on. But

the philosophy debate and the Stalinist infection of Lukács' thought contributed to a growing vulgarization and politically motivated manipulation of the notion in his writings.

19. Lukács, *Geschichte und Klassenbewusstsein*, p. 479.
20. Ibid., p. 480.
21. Ibid.
22. Ibid., pp. 480–81.
23. Ibid., p. 482.
24. Ibid.
25. Ibid., pp. 482–83.
26. Ibid., p. 483.
27. Ibid.
28. Ibid., p. 487.
29. Ibid., p. 490.
30. Ibid., pp. 491–92. Ludz contends that Lukács' understanding of the Communist party was not entirely Leninist, that he did not advocate Lenin's theory of the political elite. Ludz, "Der Begriff der 'demokratischen Diktatur' in der politischen Philosophie von Georg Lukács," pp. xliii–xlv. Lichtheim notes that Lukács at first tried to "reconcile Lenin's elitist view of the Communist Party's role with his own residual faith in Rosa Luxemburg and syndicalism"; but later, with Lukács' "elevation of the 'vanguard' to the role of an independent historical entity which alone embodied the true consciousness of the revolution," his version of Leninism became incompatible with Luxemburg's "romantic exaltation of the mass movement." Lichtheim, *Georg Lukács*, pp. 45–47. Kołakowski contends likewise that Lukács "held firmly to Lenin's conception of the party and that his whole theory of class-consciousness formed a logical basis for that conception." In fact, Kołakowski goes on to argue that "Lukács' theory of the unity of theory and practice is logically better suited to Lenin's idea of the party than is Lenin's own philosophy," and that "Lukács provided a better theoretical foundation for belief in the infallibility of the party than anyone before him, Lenin included," which, of course, was reduced under Stalin to the view that "Comrade Stalin is always right." Kołakowski, *Main Currents of Marxism*, 3: 280–82.
31. Lukács, *Lenin*, p. 23.
32. Ibid., p. 27.
33. Ibid., p. 25.
34. Ibid., pp. 25–26.
35. Ibid., pp. 28–29.
36. Ibid., p. 29.
37. Ibid., p. 30.
38. Lukács was not criticized in the 1923 and 1924 controversy over his book for favoring Luxemburg over Lenin; the objections and reservations concentrated almost exclusively on the more philo-

sophical dimensions of *Geschichte und Klassenbewusstsein*. In fact, even Josef Révai referred to Lukács' "polemic" against Rosa Luxemburg in the question of the role of the party and the difference between bourgeois and proletarian revolution, though he did not go into any detail. Révai, "Georg Lukács: *Geschichte und Klassenbewusstsein*," p. 143. Jan Stèn ("Nasha partija i voprosy teorii," p. 99) called Lukács' body of thought "Lukácsism," the "philosophical expression of 'leftwing' communism," which, in the thinking of those years, did place him generally in the company of Luxemburg and the prewar syndicalists, but no specific charge that he differed with Lenin on the role of the party was ever made, though this is the accusation that Lukács was trying to defuse in 1933.

39. For instance, "I entered the Hungarian Communist party in 1918 with a world view that was largely syndicalist and idealistic. In spite of the experience of the Hungarian revolution, I found myself in the backwater of an ultra-left syndicalist opposition against the line of the Comintern (1920–1921). Although after the third world congress I completely understood my previous concrete errors . . ., my book *Geschichte und Klassenbewusstsein*, which I finished in 1922, . . . turned out to be a philosophical summary of these tendencies." Lukács, "Znachenie 'Materializma i èmpiriokrititsizma' dlja bolshevizatsii kommunisticheskikh partij," p. 147. He had said much the same thing in "Mein Weg zu Marx" (1933), except that here he established a link between his "ultra-left subjectivistic activism" and "Luxemburg's theory of accumulation to which I still adhered." Lukács, "Mein Weg zu Marx," in *Schriften zur Ideologie und Politik*, p. 327.

40. Pieck, *We Are Fighting for a Soviet Germany*, p. 16.

CHAPTER 8

1. Quoted from Antonov-Ovseyenko, *The Time of Stalin*, p. 78.
2. See, for instance, Medvedev, *Let History Judge*, p. 148.
3. Stalin, "Rechenschaftsbericht an den XVII. Parteitag über die Arbeit des ZK der KPdSU (B)," p. 563.
4. Ibid.
5. Ibid., p. 514.
6. Antonov-Ovseyenko, *The Time of Stalin*, p. 126. See chapter 12, note 18, in the following portrait of Brecht.
7. "Nashi zadachi," p. 3.
8. Ibid., p. 4.
9. Usievich, "Klassovaja borba v literature," p. 13.
10. "Nashi zadachi," p. 3.
11. Usievich, "Klassovaja borba v literature," p. 13.
12. "Nashi zadachi," p. 5.

13. Usievich, "Klassovaja borba v literature," p. 14.
14. "Nashi zadachi," p. 6.
15. Ibid., p. 9.
16. Usievich, "Za konkretnoe rukovodstvo," p. 4.
17. Ibid.
18. Ibid., p. 13.
19. Ibid., p. 7.
20. Ibid., p. 12.
21. Stalin, "Rechenschaftsbericht an den XVII. Parteitag über die Arbeit des ZK der KPdSU (B)," p. 564.
22. For instance, his article on expressionism came out in July 1933; in the introduction to *Geschichte und Klassenbewusstsein* (p. 40), he claimed that he did not start publishing in *Literaturnyj kritik* until 1934. It is not my purpose here to catch Lukács in minor inconsistencies or memory lapses; but he frequently made statements that are not as accurate as they might be, and one cannot always escape the impression that there was a certain pattern to his forgetfulness. See also note 27 below.
23. Lukács, *Geschichte und Klassenbewusstsein*, p. 40.
24. Usievich, "Za konkretnoe rukovodstvo," p. 12.
25. Lifshitz, in a conversation with this author, noted that *Literaturnyj kritik* had originally lacked a specific direction and that it became "colored" only in the second half of the thirties. But this claim cannot withstand closer scrutiny and probably reflects, like a number of Lukács' comments, Lifshitz' own unawareness of the actual sanctioned nature of certain literary theoretical and literary political concepts that he himself supported.
26. Lukács, "Brief an Alberto Carocci," in *Schriften zur Ideologie und Politik*, p. 671.
27. Lukács, *Gelebtes Denken*, pp. 158–59. Having described the emergence of the journal *Literaturnyj kritik*, which concerned itself with the "revolutionary democratic transformation of Russian literature," Lukács added: "During the last segment of my stay in Russia I participated in that process." It is unclear what Lukács means about his involvement during the last segment of his stay in the USSR in view of the fact that he began writing for the journal in its second issue.
28. Lukács, *Geschichte und Klassenbewusstsein*, p. 40.
29. Lukács, *Gelebtes Denken*, p. 159.
30. See Milosz, *The Captive Mind*, p. 59.
31. Ibid., pp. 54–81.
32. Ibid., p. 55.
33. Lukács, "Brief an Alberto Carocci," p. 676.
34. See chapter 12, note 18, in the following portrait of Brecht.
35. Lukács, "Brief an Alberto Carocci," p. 664.
36. Judin, "Lenin i nekotorye voprosy literaturnoj kritiki," p. 17.
37. Ibid., pp. 23–24.

38. Ibid., p. 12.
39. Ibid., p. 22.
40. Ibid., p. 24.
41. An indication of how little substantial difference there was between Judin and RAPP is Judin's remark that the RAPPists had completely distorted Lenin's comment about "tearing off the masks," which, Judin said, was entirely realistic in the way Tolstoy intended it—as the removal of masks from the police and autocratic stratum, the courts, and bureaucratic institutions. But "the slogan for the removal of any and all masks, entirely correct when interpreted in a concrete manner (which the RAPPists failed to do), merged in Averbakh's tracts with leftwing radical (*levatskij*) Shatskin-Stènist slogans." Ibid., p. 25.
42. None other than Stalin himself, in his diatribe against wreckers among the bourgeois specialists and the old intelligentsia (see chapter 3, note 8), had forecast this development as early as mid-1931. In contrast to the halcyon days of the wreckers, Stalin pointed out, entirely new conditions had now been established. "First of all, it should be pointed out that we beat the capitalist elements in the city and the countryside and are successfully doing away with them." The erstwhile hope of an intervention from abroad was now lost to the bourgeois intelligentsia, and it was self-evident that the effects of these new circumstances would not escape the old technical intelligentsia. "If, now, a significant number of the old . . . intelligentsia that used to sympathize in one way or another with the wreckers has accepted Soviet power, then active wreckers have remained only in limited numbers. . . . But this leads to the conclusion that our policy with respect to the old educated intelligentsia has to be altered accordingly. . . . *To change our attitude toward engineers and technicians of the old school; to demonstrate more attention and to care for them, to draw them more boldly into our work*—that is the task." Stalin, "Neue Verhältnisse—neue Aufgaben," pp. 417–18.
43. Judin, "Lenin i nekotorye voprosy literaturnoj kritiki," p. 26.
44. Ibid., p. 28.
45. Lukács, *Gelebtes Denken*, p. 165.
46. Lukács, "Kunst und objektive Wahrheit," p. 617; "K probleme obektivnosti khudozhestvennoj formy," pp. 8–9. See also the similar phrase on p. 632 and p. 16 respectively, and my comments in chapter 3, note 20.
47. By way of Lev Mekhlis' intervention with Stalin, according to what Lifshitz told me in 1977.
48. See Pike, *German Writers in Soviet Exile*, pp. 259–71.
49. It would be interesting to look more closely at the parallel operation of these two lines; it is at least possible that Stalin allowed the "Fadejev camp," as Lukács called it, to exist as a sort of

counterbalance to tendencies in the other camp (and the other way around). If so, then much of the literary politics of the thirties would disclose examples of Stalin's artificial dialectic, the built-in insecurity that acted to keep both camps as keenly attuned as possible to the slightest fluctuation or possibility of fluctuation of policy hinted at from on high. Curiously, when the group of critics around *Literaturnyj kritik* finally came under intense fire in late 1939 and 1940, leading to the dissolution of the journal and the breakup of Lukács' "New Trend," Lukács took these disputes to be a resurgence of RAPPist and vulgar sociological outlooks that had, so to speak, gone underground since their official condemnation in 1936, only to resurface in 1939 against Lukács with a slight variation of the old argument of a direct identity between world view and creative method. For extended treatment, see Pike, *German Writers in Soviet Exile,* pp. 299–306; see also note 123 below and chapter 12 of the Brecht portrait.

50. The point should be made, though it cannot be pursued here, that there were certainly points of contact between Lukács and the "vulgar sociologists" in terms of their specific attitude toward Soviet writers. It is undeniable, on the other hand, that Lukács and the sociological school of literary criticism had nothing in common in their treatment of past great literature.

51. Lukács, "Kunst und objektive Wahrheit," p. 637.

52. Lukács, "Die intellektuelle Physiognomie des künstlerischen Gestaltens," pp. 183–84.

53. Lukács, "Erzählen oder Beschreiben?," p. 234.

54. Ibid.

55. Ibid.; cf. also Lukács, "Die intellektuelle Physiognomie des künstlerischen Gestaltens," p. 183: "It goes without saying that the role of a world view must be extraordinarily important in the literature of the socialist era, in a literature that reflects the development of a *new type of man.*"

56. Lukács, "Kunst und objektive Wahrheit," p. 643.

57. Lukács, "Die intellektuelle Physiognomie des künstlerischen Gestaltens," p. 186.

58. See Pike, *German Writers in Soviet Exile,* pp. 286–99. See also chapter 11 in the Brecht portrait.

59. Page references from *Wie ist die faschistische Philosophie in Deutschland entstanden?* are given in the text in parentheses.

60. The original manuscript is located in the Lukács Archivum és Könyvtár in Budapest.

61. Lukács, "Das Grand Hotel 'Abgrund,'" pp. 3–4.

62. Ibid., p. 5.

63. Ibid.

64. Ibid.

65. Ibid., pp. 6–7.

66. Ibid., p. 8.
67. Ibid., pp. 9–10.
68. Ibid., pp. 10–11.
69. Ibid., p. 18.
70. Lukács, *Der historische Roman*, pp. 319–21.
71. Ibid.
72. Prior to the popular front Lukács had argued along these very lines: "On the one hand, the tremendous upswing in the socialist economy, the rapid expansion of proletarian democracy, the emergence from amid the masses of many significant personalities with tremendous energy, the growth of proletarian humanism in the praxis of the toiling people and their leaders has a powerful, revolutionary effect upon the consciousness of the best intellectuals in the capitalist world." Lukács, "Erzählen oder Beschreiben?," p. 234. The very first editorial of *Literaturnyj kritik* had made the same point: "It is no accident that the Soviet Union is acquiring ever new, passionate supporters with each passing day, not just from among the toiling masses but also from among the laboring intelligentsia, from among the 'bearers of culture' of the capitalist countries." "Nashi zadachi," p. 3.
73. Lukács, *Der historische Roman*, p. 320. It may be helpful to conjecture about the precise date of Lukács' transition from his and the party's sectarianism of 1933 to the new popular front habits of thought officialized at the seventh world congress, and it is worth reiterating here—because Lukács later claimed the opposite—that he had in no way anticipated this new policy or prepared the way for it. Rather, it seems clear that Lukács restructured his own thinking only after the party itself had reassessed its earlier posture. A selection of Lukács' writings from 1934 and 1935 supports this contention because these statements contain no evidence whatever that Lukács had freed himself at this point, before the Comintern, of his sectarianism. The least liberal of these articles is his abject mea culpa with respect to *Geschichte und Klassenbewusstsein* and his pleas for the bolshevization of the Communist parties made at the Communist Academy in June 1934. In the version published in *Pod znamenem marksizma*, Lukács inveighed against those who counterposed bolshevism with Western European communism. By setting these two political movements in opposition to each other, supporters of this tendency "prepared the way for counterrevolutionary Trotskyism, which replaced the materialistic-dialectic Bolshevist theory and practice with idealistic revolutionary phrases" and expanded the room available for left-wing Social Democracy. The "dangerous demagogic masking of the counterrevolutionary practice of the social fascists accomplished by the left Social Democrats rests essentially on the idealistic revision of Marxism." In all foreign sections of the Comintern, he

went on, the struggle for the world view of Marxism-Leninism needed to be waged with the same seriousness as the battle for the strategic-tactical or organizational line. For it was clear that, "in the realm of ideology, *the front of idealism is the front of the fascist counterrevolution and its accomplices—the social fascists*—and that any concession to idealism, even the most insignificant one, signals *danger* to the proletarian revolution." "Znachenie 'Materializma i èmpiriokrititsizma' dlja bolshevizatsii kommunisticheskikh partii," pp. 147–48.

In an article entitled "Realism in Contemporary German Literature," published in Russian translation in *Literaturnyj kritik* in mid-1934 (and, to my knowledge, never published in German), Lukács characterized contemporary German writers in the following terms: the best and "most conscious" elements were searching and finding the path to the revolutionary working class, though a large number of these writers had fallen under the spell of the national and social demagogy of the fascists. Then there was an intermediate stratum struggling to find their way and "vacillating between fascism and bolshevism." Many of these writers had already "formed a united antifascist front"; many more were nearing that front. Others were courageously fighting against Hitler fascism with the weapons of a writer, though their ideology was often "confused and incorrect." Lukács' own recurrent theory of spontaneity or semispontaneity with respect to Western intellectuals read as follows: once this struggle began to exert a reverse influence upon their world view and their grasp of circumstances in Germany and the driving forces behind them, and once this struggle compelled them to fathom the "global-historical" meaning of the heroic battle of the German proletariat under the guidance of the Communist party, only then would they acquire for themselves the possibility to represent contemporary Germany imaginatively, employing a genuinely realistic creative method. "Realizm v sovremmenoj nemetskoj literature," pp. 52 and 56. Finally, as late as 1935 (and *after* the seventh world congress), in a review of Ernst Bloch's *Die Erbschaft dieser Zeit*, Lukács expressed the hope that Bloch's "honest and brave participation in the fight against fascism will help him to overcome the blatant contradictions present today between his clear political posture against fascism and his philosophical concessions to idealistic and reactionary trends." "*Die Erbschaft dieser Zeit*," p. 20, quoted from the manuscript in the Lukács Archivum és Könyvtár in Budapest. In other words, Lukács was still expressing a kind of maximal program, demanding unconditional "theoretical" backing of Stalinist Marxism-Leninism if an antifascist such as Bloch wished to establish the proper harmony between his theoretical and practical antifascism. He assumed that the process of "self-bolshe-vization" would unfold more or less automatically once this commitment was made.

74. Lukács, *Der historische Roman*, p. 323.
75. Lukács, "Erzählen oder Beschreiben?" p. 234.
76. Stalin, "Über den Entwurf der Verfassung der UdSSR," p. 634.
77. Lukács, "Zum Verfassungsentwurf der UdSSR," p. 53.
78. Lukács, *Der historische Roman*, p. 323.
79. Lukács added, "The revolution in Spain evolving before our eyes reveals this new development most clearly. It shows that a de-mocracy of a new type is in the process of emerging." Ibid., p. 422. It is important to note that Lukács picked up the concept of a "democracy of a new type," which played such an impor-tant role in the postwar Eastern European people's democracies, from José Diaz, head of the Spanish Communist party; from the rhetoric of the Spanish civil war, the notion then found its way into the Comintern and the KPD. Walter Ulbricht, for instance, commented in summer 1937 that it was not enough to propa-gate the slogan of a democratic republic; "rather, it is necessary to explain the *content* of this democratic republic of a new type and to prove why the struggle for a democratic republic is an unavoidable stage in the struggle for the final liberation of the working class, an unavoidable step on the way to socialism." Quoted from Sywottek, *Deutsche Volksdemokratie*, p. 80.
80. Lukács, "Kunst und objektive Wahrheit," pp. 641–42. The origi-nal source of the quotation is from Stalin, "Rechenschaftsbe-richt an den XVII. Parteitag über die Arbeit des ZK der KPdSU (B)," pp. 564–65.
81. Lewin, "The Social Background of Stalinism," p. 132.
82. According to Stalin in a speech given that day at the eighth Soviet congress: "Our Soviet society has managed essentially to realize socialism, to construct a socialist society; that is, it has realized that which Marxists otherwise refer to as the first or lower phase of communism. Thus, the first phase of commu-nism, socialism, has been essentially realized. (Prolonged ap-plause.)" Stalin, "Über den Entwurf der Verfassung der Union der SSR," p. 622.
83. Take these comments, for example, "The dictatorship of the proletariat is an absolutely meaningless expression without Jacobin coercion"; or "the scientific concept of dictatorship means nothing but power based directly on violence, unre-strained by any laws, absolutely unrestricted by any rules." It would be "madness," Lenin said shortly after the revolution, "to renounce coercion." Quoted from Dallin, *Political Terror in Communist Systems*, p. 10.
84. Though the idea had been implicit in many remarks made previ-

ously (for instance, in those at the seventeenth congress in 1934), Stalin only officialized his "motto" in March 1937, after the first two of his three judicial pageants had taken place and in the middle of the terror. In a speech entitled "Shortcomings in Party Work and the Measures to Liquidate Trotskyist and Other Double-Dealers," Stalin said: "It is necessary to destroy the putrid theory that the class struggle dies down increasingly as we achieve more victories. The contention that the class struggle grows less intense is a putrid theory because it lulls the people to sleep; it entices them into a trap. Just the contrary: the more we advance forward and the more success we achieve, the greater the rage of the remnants of the defeated exploiting class, the more its members go over to more harsh forms of militant opposition, the more vile acts they commit against the Soviet state." Quoted from Stalin, "Über die Mängel der Parteiarbeit und die Massnahmen zur Liquidierung der trotzkistischen and sonstigen Doppelzüngler," p. 22. This general axiom, by the way, was not discarded in the USSR (and GDR) until 1956.

85. Friedrich, *Totalitarian Dictatorship*, p. 172.
86. Lukács, "Kunst und objektive Wahrheit," p. 642.
87. Ibid., p. 643.
88. Lukács, "Die intellektuelle Physiognomie des künstlerischen Gestaltens," p. 181.
89. Stalin, "Rede auf der ersten Unionsberatung der Stachanowleute," p. 602.
90. Ibid., pp. 603–4.
91. Lukács, "Die intellektuelle Physiognomie des künstlerischen Gestaltens," p. 183.
92. Ibid. Cf. Lukács' analysis a quarter of a century later: "Whether the class struggle in the country itself, given all the economic difficulties, really intensified decisively—only those experts on the subject doing research can come up with a competent judgment. Stalin, at any rate, quickly found a catchword in an agitational and oversimplified generalization: the unrelenting intensification of class warfare is necessary in the dictatorship of the proletariat. . . . This thesis, which the twentieth party congress already exposed as false, reveals the most fateful consequence of Stalinist methods." Lukács, "Brief an Alberto Carocci," pp. 672–73. This is another striking example of Lukács' accurate retrospective analysis of the essence of Stalinism, combined with his refusal to acknowledge to himself and to his public that he himself had fallen victim to the very Stalinist myths described by him.
93. Quoted from Arendt, *The Origins of Totalitarianism*, p. xxxiii.
94. In 1934 Lukács still called for efforts to persuade those Soviet

writers who were "honestly erring." Lukács, "Kunst und objektive Wahrheit," p. 644.
95. The article appeared first in the January issue of *Literaturnyj kritik*. It must have been written in the last half of 1938.
96. Milosz, *The Captive Mind*, p. 50.
97. Lukács, "Volkstribun oder Bürokrat?" p. 416.
98. Ibid., p. 417.
99. Ibid., p. 419.
100. Ibid., p. 420.
101. Ibid., p. 427.
102. Ibid., p. 443.
103. Ibid., p. 445.
104. Ibid., p. 446.
105. Stalin, "Rechenschaftsbericht an den XVII. Parteitag über die Arbeit des ZK der KPdSU (B)," pp. 579–80.
106. Ibid., p. 583.
107. Lukács, "Brief an Alberto Carocci," pp. 672–73.
108. Lukács, "Volkstribun oder Bürokrat?," p. 447.
109. Ibid. See also Stalin, "Rechenschaftsbericht an den XVII. Parteitag über die Arbeit des ZK der KPdSU (B)," p. 565.
110. Lukács, "Volkstribun oder Bürokrat?," p. 449.
111. Ibid., p. 450.
112. Lukács' choice of words here is chillingly reminiscent of lines in his article "Es geht um den Realismus" to the effect that the decline of expressionism was due in the last analysis to the maturity of the revolutionary masses. Kołakowski may not be unjustified in noting that Lukács ascribed to revolutionary maturity what he well knew to be the work of police repression. *Main Currents of Marxism*, 3: 295. Or was police repression under the circumstances, in Lukács' mind at the time, in the end the same thing as revolutionary maturity? That logic is inherent in his line of reasoning; it is only a matter of following the stringent chain of deductions through to its logical conclusion.
113. Lukács, "Volkstribun oder Bürokrat?," p. 453.
114. Ibid., p. 418. Here in a nutshell is the point where political philosophy intersected with Lukács' theoretical categories: "Overcoming immediate reality"—in politics the elimination of "elemental," "spontaneous," "bureaucratic" reactions to surface reality in favor of conscious self-awareness of the underlying social and historical forces involved—corresponded in Lukács' thinking with the eradication of literary forms that likewise "spontaneously" or "bureaucratically" blocked the road to realism. Such forms had to give way to a creative method based on that "adequate knowledge that only the materialist dialectic, Marxism, makes possible."

115. Ibid., p. 418.
116. *Geschichte der Kommunistischen Partei der Sowjetunion (Bolschewiki)*, p. 419.
117. Ibid., pp. 419–20.
118. Orwell, *1984*, pp. 49 and 229.
119. Ibid., p. 218.
120. Lukács, "Volkstribun oder Bürokrat?," p. 452.
121. Orwell, *1984*, p. 173.
122. Lukács, "Brief an Alberto Carocci," p. 671.
123. Having dealt elsewhere with the controversy of 1939 and 1940 that led to the end of *Literaturnyj kritik*, I can dispense with any further discussion here. (See Pike, *German Writers in Soviet Exile*, pp. 299–305; and chapter 12 in the Brecht portrait). Just one point needs to be made in this context. Some might like to regard this later controversy as an illustration of Lukács' difficulties with the Stalinist establishment in literary affairs. However, though Lukács fought back in the face of harsh criticism and refused to give in to the arguments of those who attacked the journal and his "New Trend," it appears plausible to me that Lukács simply misunderstood what was occurring. He thought these attacks were a resurgence of vulgar sociology and RAPPism, condemned by the party earlier, though it seems thinkable that Lukács, who had always regarded his literary theory as the only acceptable version of dialectical materialism in literature and who loathed the Fadejev group, never grasped the fact that his school of literary criticism had been supported throughout the thirties precisely because it was the literary theoretical expression of Stalin's popular front. His "trend" came to a prompt end when the green light was given to the Fadejev group and other opponents of Lukács to attack him and his ideas after the Hitler-Stalin pact had thrown the last shovelful of dirt over the grave of the popular front. Such was the function, after all, of Stalin's artificial dialectic: at any moment, one group can triumph—be allowed to triumph—over the other, which is never totally annihilated, and the entire process, if the times later call for it, can just as easily be reversed.

CHAPTER 9

1. Chapter 1 of the new manuscript, "Der historische Weg Deutschlands," appeared with minor changes as the chapter "Über einige Eigentümlichkeiten der geschichtlichen Entwicklung Deutschlands" in *Die Zerstörung der Vernunft*. Lukács also intended to publish the 1942 manuscript with a French publisher after the war, but nothing ever came of the plan. See László Sziklai's intro-

duction to *Wie ist Deutschland zum Zentrum der reaktionären Ideologie geworden?*, pp. 7–15.

2. Cf., for instance, Molotov's words spoken on the first day of the war: "This war has been forced upon us not by the German people, not by the German workers, peasants, and intellectuals, whose sufferings we well understand, but by the clique of bloodthirsty fascist rulers." Quoted from Deutscher, *Stalin*, p. 487.

3. The manuscript was evidently written largely in winter 1941/42, though Lukács dated it Tashkent, January 1941, which is impossible. That the book contains some remarks made by Stalin as late as November 1942 indicates that Lukács was still working on the book through the end of the year, after his return to Moscow from Tashkent in summer 1942.

4. Lukács, *Wie ist Deutschland zum Zentrum der reaktionären Ideologie geworden?*, pp. 149–51, 174. Subsequent page references are given in the text in parentheses.

5. The phrase is Milosz' (*The Captive Mind*, p. 206).

6. Cf. Lukács' remarks in his introduction to *Geschichte und Klassenbewusstsein*, p. 32; see also Lukács, "Diskussion über die Blum-Thesen (1956)," in *Schriften zur Ideologie und Politik*, p. 764 as well as "Der Kampf des Fortschritts und der Reaktion in der heutigen Kultur (1956)," in ibid., p. 608: "What Stalin said at the end of the 1920s [sic] about Social Democrats being the twin brothers of fascists and what was then an obstacle for any kind of popular front politics up till the seventh congress of the Comintern belongs here. Stalin's serious error no doubt resulted from his inability to recognize the contradictory nature inherent in these profound strategic problems." Apart from the fact that Lukács failed to recognize these "contradictions" either in the years leading up to the seventh world congress, what is striking about these remarks concerning Stalin in 1956, after the twentieth party congress and Khrushchev's "secret speech," is Lukács' use of the word "mistake" with respect to a major Stalinist policy—a characterization that precludes any serious inquiry into Stalin's decision-making process, the conscious motivation governing it, as well as the effect of his personality upon that process.

7. Lukács, "Aristokratische und demokratische Weltanschauung," in *Schriften zur Ideologie und Politik*, pp. 429–30.

8. Lukács refers here to the speech "Prikaz narodnogo komissara oborony" containing the famous comment about the Hitlers who come and go and the German people who remain; and to "25-ja godovshchina Velikoj oktjabrskoj sotsialisticheskoj revoljutsii," in Stalin, *O velikoj otechestvennoj vojne sovetskogo Sojuza*," pp. 41–48 and 61–77.

9. *Wie ist Deutschland zum Zentrum der reaktionären Ideologie*

geworden?, pp. 23–24; this entire passage was crossed out in Lukács' manuscript, probably after 1945, when Lukács was preparing the manuscript for publication in a French house.

10. There was, it should be mentioned, a built-in artificial dialectic to this policy. Whereas it is true that Stalin, as early as 3 July 1941 (in his first public address to the nation after the German invasion), noted that all the best peoples of Europe, America, Asia, and, "finally, the best people of Germany" roundly condemned the treacherous act of the German fascists and sympathized with the Soviet government, and that in the war against German fascism, the Soviet Union had loyal allies in the peoples of Europe and America, "including the German people who have been enslaved by the Hitlerite ringleaders," it is also a fact that Stalin ended most of his radio addresses, military orders, and communiques with the outburst, "Death to the German aggressors," varying the phrase only occasionally with "Death to the German-fascist aggressors." See Stalin, *O velikoj otechestvennoj vojne*, pp. 12 and 16, and his closing remarks in most of his speeches. This certainly intentional duality in the Soviet German propaganda was most obvious toward the end of the war when Ilja Ehrenburg's celebrated attack on the Germans as an entire people appeared in April 1945 in the daily *Krasnaja zvezda*, the paper of the Red Army, and was roundly denounced only three days later by Georgi Aleksandrov in *Pravda* (Aleksandrov's answer to Ehrenburg was featured prominently in the *Tägliche Rundschau* in the Soviet zone of occupation on 16 May 1945). Considering that, according to Ehrenburg, his article was no different from countless others that he had written throughout the war, and given the promptness of the refutation, the whole affair smacks of a certain amount of orchestration intended to acquaint the German people with the two possible modalities with respect to Soviet policy toward Germany.

11. Of course Lukács had allowed for the factor of gullibility and human weakness in the Germans' susceptibility to illusions and false promises in 1933; the difference between his study in 1933 and in 1942 is more one of degree. In 1933 he had come out far more strongly on the side of pure historical necessity.

12. Lukács added: "Fascist terror then carries this general mistrust, this overall fear in each human being of every other human being not only into the occupational sphere but also into the family. Who can live here, even if he participates in no antifascist movement whatever, safe from denunciation, even by his own family members? (This side of fascist daily reality is depicted with real exactness in Bertold [sic] Brecht's short plays)" (180–81). It is tempting to suggest that in Lukács' view of the daily terror of life under Hitler (a form of repression that was less threatening to citizens more or less willing to go along with things and keep

their mouths shut), he was influenced in his perceptions of fascist reality by his experiences with Soviet life. He had, after all, spent two months himself in an NKVD prison less than a year before he sat down to write his book on fascism. People were arrested in the USSR all the time "for no reason at all," and perhaps Lukács imagined that exactly the same thing was occurring in Nazi Germany, rather than a somewhat more "discriminating" if certainly discriminatory brand of terror aimed not so much at the common people and definitely not at orthodox NSDAP members, but at racial groups and political organizations.

13. Lukács, "Volkstribun oder Bürokrat?," p. 419.

14. For some general thoughts on this subject as they pertain to Trotsky's evaluation of Lenin's singular role in history, see Deutscher, *The Prophet Outcast*, pp. 218–57, passim.

15. Quoted from Cohen, "Bolshevism and Stalinism," p. 19.

16. Kaganovich, "The Great Driver of the Locomotive of History," p. 43.

17. Ibid., p. 54.

18. "Tonbandgespräch."

19. This is another of the passages that Lukács struck from his typescript.

20. Lukács crossed out this passage also. This sort of optimism, based on interrogations of POWs and the examination of documents (letters, diaries, and the like) either captured from the Wehrmacht or taken from the bodies of fallen soldiers, was pervasive among the German exiles. The optimism, in fact, probably contributed to their stilted view of the morale of the Germans both at home and on the front, a confident optimism about the anti-Hitler sentiments of the German masses that also lead to an unjustifiedly optimistic portrayal in their fictional description of circumstances in Germany. These letters and diaries were looked over thoroughly, and *svodki* (reports) were compiled by the main political administration of the Red Army (GlavPURKKA) for use by Soviet and German Communist propagandists. Labeled "secret," they were passed out in limited, numbered copies to various German exiles. These letters, though, were first carefully screened. For instance, report no. 9 for 10 March 1942 was based on 350 letters, from which only 48 were selected for excerpts. Some were from Germany to soldiers in the field, others were addressed home and obviously never arrived. By a close reading of these letters, the GlavPURKKA hoped to establish a clearer picture of Wehrmacht and home morale. As one reads through the excerpts in the *Svodki* preserved in the Friedrich-Wolf-Archiv in the GDR (Mappe 236a/8–18), the impression cannot be avoided that the selectors deluded themselves by picking out mainly those items that illustrated sinking morale and tended to confirm what the propagandists were inclined to believe anyway. Those

who read the excerpts, such as Wolf, were then presented with a distorted picture. Compare the following excerpt: "It is almost impossible to imagine the human and material resources for war that the Russians possess! There is simply no end to it. Every day huge amounts are destroyed, and every day there are new replacements for it." Svodka no. 18, Mappe 236a/18. Or compare the table of contents to Svodka no. 7 from 23 February 1942, Mappe 236a/8: "I. Characteristic individual letters. II. The fighting power of the Red Army. III. The losses of the Hitler army. IV. The situation in the Germany army: dissatisfaction, war weariness, and anti-war feelings among the German soldiers. V. General attitude in Hitler Germany: 1. Supply problems. 2. War weariness, desire for peace vis-à-vis Nazi propaganda, war, and the Hitler regime." Much the same appears to have happened with front diaries taken from the bodies of fallen soldiers. In Wolf's copies he underlined and emphasized precisely those passages that he apparently wanted to believe as typical and widespread, for instance: "We are being lied to so flagrantly and ought not to believe anything anymore. We see a sad Christmas coming up. Morale is sinking, and everyone is starting to brood." "Aus dem Tagebuch des Gefr. Günter Hager F.N. 05001 F," 19 December 1941, Mappe 286. The documents are genuine, of course, but their selective presentation facilitated a selective perception of reality.

Only relatively infrequently do comments like the following appear in the documents: "There are still so many Jews in Brno. They are all wearing yellow stars so that they can already be recognized at some distance, the swine. . . . The German police have already taken up the attack, many [Jews] have been arrested. It would be best to line one up next to the other and shoot them" (20 September 1941). Or: "Have you heard that the Jews have been given a medal—and what a one, a six-edged gold star with the word 'Jew,' which must be worn on the left side of their overcoat! . . . Now one can tell in every case if someone's a Jew, and it doesn't matter if he doesn't look it at first glance. I think that's just great!" (4 October 1941). Or: "Have you heard how the Jews are running around here in Berlin? . . . An Israel star. The Star of Israel. Yellow. 'Jew' is printed on it. Pretty good, isn't it? I think it's great" (3 November 1941). But these horrifying letters were cited among others "from fascist Germany" dealing preponderately with the subjects "Shortage in the labor force" and "food and goods shortages." Thus, Lukács' reference in his 1942 manuscript to what the captured letters told him (either because he was also supplied with the *svodki* or because he discussed their contents with those receiving them) demonstrates one of the ways in which the exiles became captives of their own propaganda.

21. This passage was also eliminated by Lukács.
22. For the history of the political concept of "democracies of a new type" and the "people's democracies," see Skilling, "'People's Democracy' in Soviet Theory." The relevant passage in Dimitrov's speech, delivered in December 1948, reads: "In accordance with the Marxist-Leninist view, the Soviet regime and the people's democratic regime are two forms of one and the same power. . . . These are two forms of the proletarian dictatorship." Ibid., p. 25.
23. See "Márton Horváth über die Lukács-Diskussion (1949)," in *Schriften zur Ideologie und Politik*, pp. 753–62. The actual argument ran that Lukács had spoken of "fundamental" differences between the development of the Soviet Union and that of the people's democracies, thus neglecting the "perspectives" of socialism on a Hungarian and international scale. Ibid., p. 754. As for Révai's judgments, they only evoke a tired sense of déjà vu. What, Révai asked, had given rise to the recent discussion involving Comrade Lukács? "We came to recognize how dangerous our lag in the area of ideology and culture is. So we started to inquire whether there might not be subjective factors next to objective reasons, whether false and pernicious ideas in our own ranks might not be playing a role." Révai, "Die Lukács-Diskussion des Jahres 1949," in *Georg Lukács und der Revisionismus*, pp. 9–10.
24. Lukács, *Gelebtes Denken*, pp. 186–87, 189. Lukács perhaps had these lines by Révai in mind: "Those who are familiar with the history of the Hungarian Communist movement know that the *literary views* espoused by Comrade Lukács from 1945 to 1949 are linked to the *political views* developed by him in the late twenties about political trends in Hungary and the strategy of the Communist party." Révai, "Die Lukács-Diskussion des Jahres 1949," p. 15. Though this accusation would seem to confirm Lukács' contention that a line of continuity stretched from the Blum theses through the thirties and forties, our entire preceding discussion of Lukács' political philosophy and literary theory contradicts that claim. Révai's charges should probably be regarded as nothing more than the standard Stalinist practice of locating evidence of original sin in the form of some past deviation when tracing the cause of the current one.
25. Lukács, *Gelebtes Denken*, p. 188.
26. Lukács, *Wie ist Deutschland zum Zentrum der reaktionären Ideologie geworden?*, p. 189.
27. Lukács, "Freie oder gelenkte Kunst," in *Schriften zur Ideologie und Politik*, p. 432.
28. Ibid.
29. See, for example, Wilhelm Pieck and Otto Grotewohl, "Zehn Jahre Stalinsche Verfassung," *Neues Deutschland*, 5 December 1946.
30. Lukács, "Zum Verfassungsentwurf der UdSSR," p. 53.

31. Lukács, *Gelebtes Denken*, p. 188.
32. On the other hand, the temptation should be resisted to assume that all the sub-Stalins in charge of affairs in the people's democracies regarded the development of their "democracy of a new type" from the outset as a political masquerade. In a speech given to party leaders in spring 1949 and later published in pamphlet form (soon after, reportedly recalled by the government), Josef Révai made the following admissions: "It is obvious that our People's Democracy has not been from the beginning a dictatorship of the proletariat, but became so during the struggle." It had been correct in the early stages of the struggle, "not to show our cards, but often even we forgot that the People's Democracy at this time was more than just a plebeian variety of the bourgeois democracy and that it was a step toward the Socialist transition, which contained even then the elements of development into the dictatorship of the proletariat." Révai also noted that it had been incorrect to emphasize the differences between the development of the Soviet Union and "our development into a People's Democracy, instead of stressing the similarity, the substantial identity, of the two developments." Révai, "The Character of a 'People's Democracy,'" pp. 145 and 148.
33. Orwell, *1984*, p. 178.
34. Lukács, *Gelebtes Denken*, p. 186.

CHAPTER 10

1. Lukács, *Taktik und Ethik*, in *Schriften zur Ideologie und Politik*, p. 27. This essay was later incorporated, in a revised version, into *Geschichte und Klassenbewusstsein* under the title "Was ist orthodoxer Marxismus."
2. Ibid., p. 30. Cf. Kołakowski, *Main Currents of Marxism*, 3: 265.
3. The phrase is Milosz' (*The Captive Mind*, p. 191).
4. For this and the above, cf. Medvedev, *Let History Judge*, pp. 114–17.
5. Lukács, "Shaws Bekenntnis zur Sowjetunion," p. 5.
6. Ibid., p. 6.
7. Lukács, "Zum Verfassungsentwurf der UdSSR," p. 53.
8. Lukács, "Aristokratische und demokratische Weltanschauung," in *Schriften zur Ideologie und Politik*, p. 431.
9. Orwell, *1984*, p. 61.
10. Lukács, "Shaws Bekenntnis zur Sowjetunion," p. 7.
11. See the introductory paragraph to one of Brecht's so-called Stalin poems, in *Supplementband IV*, p. 438.
12. Lukács, *Gelebtes Denken*, pp. 10–11.
13. It may serve some purpose here to refer again to Lukács' own arrest and two-month imprisonment in 1941. Lukács' stepson,

Ferenc Jánossy, spent many years in a camp and was not freed
until after the war. See ibid., p. 184. Lukács, by the way, told
George Steiner the following story (which Steiner related to me):
during the war he was shaken out of bed early one morning by
the dreaded knock on the door; with no further explanations, he
was asked to get dressed and to come along with the uniformed
officers. He was then taken to an airport, where he boarded a
waiting plane that took off and flew for a few hours before land-
ing in some desolate region. In the distance, however, Lukács
spotted floodlights shining down on barbed wire and assumed the
worst. However, he was taken into one of the barracks, which
turned out to be filled with uniformed Wehrmacht officers; there
he delivered an impromptu lecture on Heine. I regard the story as
a complete fabrication. The story that Lukács told Ágnes Heller
about his bridge parties with Lavrentij Berija also strikes me as
apocryphal. But if there is something to it, the story opens up a
whole new dimension to Lukács' activity in Soviet exile. Even if
his account of bridge-playing with Berija is invented, it still casts
an extremely unfavorable light upon Lukács' frivolous attitude
toward events that cost millions of people their lives. In any case,
one searches in vain in Lukács' later writings for any expression
of utter horror at the mass carnage that took place under Stalin.
Eörsi, in fact, speaks in this regard of a certain schizophrenia:
"Lukács represents the intellectually most interesting example
for the schizophrenia of the Communist intelligentsia when he
distinguishes Stalinist death camps qualitatively from other kinds
of death camps. The one kind are, in his eyes, global historical
necessity; the other kind, in contrast, are superfluous pimples on
the shining face of totality." Lukács, *Gelebtes Denken*, p. 24.
14. The concentrated attacks upon Lukács in the Soviet, Hungarian,
and East German press in 1957, 1958, and 1959, following
his return from Romanian exile after the Hungarian uprising,
were unable to induce him to engage in another round of self-
criticism. For some of these critical articles, see *Georg Lukács
und der Revisionismus*. As I remarked in the preface (note 8),
Lukács' actions after 1956 and his run-ins with post-Stalin Stalinists of various nationalities is not at issue in the present study.
15. Conquest, *The Great Terror*, p. 679.
16. Cf. ibid., pp. 679–82.
17. Lukács, *Die Zerstörung der Vernunft*, p. 682. Lukács added:
"[Sartre] dispassionately refutes [Camus'] chain of thought, and
in this point he contents himself with an exposure of the moral
mala fides of Camus and his kind: 'Let's be serious, Camus,' he
explains, 'and tell me please what kind of emotions are evoked in
the heart of an anti-Communist by Rousset's revelations. Despair? Sadness? The disgrace that one is a man? Come on! . . .
The only emotion that such information awakens in him is—it's

hard for me to say it—*joy.* Joy that he finally has his *proof* in hand and that what he sees occurring before him is precisely that which he wanted to see all along." The very fact that Lukács quoted this passage is an indirect admission that the camps existed, though Lukács argued otherwise—passionately—in a manner designed to create the impression that they did not.

18. Ibid., p. 681.
19. Ibid.
20. Ibid., pp. 681–82.
21. Ibid.
22. Ibid., p. 692.
23. Ibid.
24. Ibid., p. 713.
25. Ibid.
26. Ibid., p. 717.
27. Ibid., p. 718.
28. Milosz, *The Captive Mind,* p. 174.
29. Orwell, *1984,* pp. 174–75.
30. Ibid., p. 176.
31. Ibid., p. 32.
32. Lukács, *Gelebtes Denken,* p. 14.
33. Ibid., p. 10.
34. Lukács, *Geschichte und Klassenbewusstsein,* p. 117.
35. For the Brecht comment, see the next portrait, chapter 13. The following utterance attributed to Lukács is instructive in this context. In Ilona Duczynska's paraphrase (Lukács allegedly made the remark to her in 1921), he said: "Communist ethics make it the highest duty to accept the necessity of acting wickedly. . . . The conviction of the true Communist is that evil transforms itself into bliss through the dialectics of historical evolution." Quoted from Congdon, *The Young Lukács,* p. 204.
36. Milosz, *The Captive Mind,* p. 219.

CHAPTER 11

1. *Brecht-Chronik,* pp. 72–73.
2. Brecht, *Arbeitsjournal,* p. 36.
3. Ibid., p. 636; chapter epigraph taken from this page.
4. Brecht, *Arbeitsjournal,* p. 25.
5. Brecht to Becher, 28 June 1933, in Brecht, *Briefe,* pp. 166–67. According to Brecht, "authoritative friends" such as Karl Radek, Mikhail Koltsov, Sergej Tretjakov, and Sergej Dinamov ought to be invited to such a conference, calls for which, he said, had been made independently of him by Kurt Kläber, Ernst Ottwalt, Trude [Richter?], and Otto Biha (Peter Merin).
6. Becher's first known proposal for a writers' conference was made

in his "Bericht über die Tätigkeit während meiner Reise vom 5. Juli bis 17. September 1933," in *Zur Tradition der sozialistischen Literatur in Deutschland*, p. 585.

7. Brecht to Becher, 28 June 1933, *Briefe*, pp. 166—67. Brecht's disparaging remark about "borrowing" names was presumably his way of objecting to Willi Münzenberg's organizational tactics.

8. Brecht to Becher, December 1934, ibid., pp. 227—28.

9. "Eine notwendige Feststellung im Kampf gegen die Barbarei," *GW*, vol. 18, p. 246.

10. Becher, for instance, still sought Brecht's advice in matters relating to cooperation with non-Communist writers and various joint literary-political projects. Cf., e.g., Brecht to Becher, July 1935, *Briefe*, pp. 259—60. Incidentally, Brecht's pronouncements at the congress were later included unabridged in the Russian volume containing the various speeches.

11. See Okljanskij, *Povest o malenkom soldate*, p. 78.

12. Ibid., pp. 52—94. Brecht's private papers, by the way, were confiscated by Soviet border guards when he left the USSR for the West. Ibid., p. 87.

13. Béla Illes, head of the Internationale Vereinigung revolutionärer Schriftsteller (IVRS), had offered Brecht his help in obtaining another entry visa for Steffin as early as summer 1933. Ibid., p. 146.

14. See ibid., p. 145.

15. Steffin apparently went from Denmark to Leningrad first. She had not reached Moscow by early September, but must have arrived there soon after. See Sergej Tretjakov to Brecht, 8 September 1934, BBA, 477/139.

16. Brecht to Steffin, 20—23 September 1934, quoted from Okljanskij, *O malenkom soldate*, pp. 48—49. (The sloppy dating of letters cited from Okljanskij was done by him. Brecht refers here to the page proofs of the first edition of *Der Dreigroschenroman* published by Allert de Lange in Amsterdam.)

17. Brecht to Steffin, 21 October—4 November 1934, ibid., pp. 48—49.

18. Ibid.

19. Cf. ibid., p. 158.

20. Cf. ibid., pp. 153—58.

21. Brecht to Tretjakov, 11 July 1933, *Briefe*, pp. 172—73.

22. Tretjakov to Brecht, 15 July 1933, BBA, 477/147.

23. Tretjakov to Brecht, 16 July 1933, BBA, 477/144.

24. See Reich, *Im Wettlauf mit der Zeit*, p. 371. Incidentally, Tretjakov now began preparations for his edition of *Die heilige Johanna*, *Die Massnahme*, and *Die Mutter*. The volume, *Epicheskie dramy*, which Tretjakov also supplied with an introduction, came out the next year. See Bibliography. "F. Ivanov," in a review of the volume published in *Izvestija*, referred to the

"schematism" of Brecht's plays and expressed his hope that Brecht would one day break free of his "'edifying' asceticism" and write plays in which his characters would not be burdened with the "command to 'instruct.'" Although Ivanov also called Brecht "one of the most significant revolutionary writers of contemporary Germany" (he chose to use the word *literati*), he contrasted Brecht's *Mutter* with Gorky's celebrated novel and noted: "This most talented writer of the German revolution must get away from rhetoric (however gifted and accomplished it may be) and go over to Shakespeareanism, to a theater of great passions, a theater of living, full-blooded personalities who make history." *Izvestija*, 23 July 1934.

25. Béla Illes had issued the invitation back in August 1933; at the time, the congress was scheduled to convene in September 1933. Whether the invitation was extended one year later is not known. Okljanskij, *O malenkom soldate*, p. 146.

26. Tretjakov to Brecht, 8 September 1934, BBA, 477/139–40.

27. Tretjakov to Brecht, 24 June 1935, BBA, 477/131.

28. Tretjakov was ill recurrently in 1936 and early 1937; his last letter to Brecht, dated 3 May 1937 (BBA, 477/120), ought not to be read for signs of changes in Tretjakov's frame of mind caused by his fear of imminent arrest. Cf. also in this vein Herzfelde to Oskar Maria Graf, 16 April and 5 May 1936: "I only saw Tretjakov once. He appears to be going through a crisis" and "I only saw Tretjakov twice and then just briefly. He is suffering from a crisis, his health is probably also not good—in a word, he is not concerned with us. But maybe he really does have too much else on his mind." TsGALI, 631/12/141/323 and 320. Tretjakov's correspondence with Graf (Oskar Maria Graf, *Reise in die Sowjetunion 1934*, pp. 163–90) reveals more about Tretjakov's general attitude toward events in the USSR in 1936 and 1937 than his less frequent letters to Brecht. "I am full of this land," he wrote enthusiastically, for example, on 22 May 1936. Ibid., p. 182.

29. Brecht to Becher, early 1935, *Briefe*, pp. 231–32.

30. Kantorowicz, "Brechts 'Der Dreigroschenroman,'" pp. 61–62.

31. Brecht to Becher, early 1935, *Briefe*, pp. 231–32.

32. See Becher's reply to Brecht of 16 January 1935, *Briefe; Anmerkungen*, p. 958. The article in *Unsere Zeit*, said Becher, reflected Kantorowicz' personal opinion and not any official party attitude toward Brecht's novel. Michael Tschesno also wrote Brecht on behalf of the SDS, telling him that the criticism was, "to put it mildly," absurd; it was Kantorowicz' own "private pleasure" and shared by none of the other members of the SDS.

33. Brecht to Becher, early 1935, *Briefe*, pp. 231–32.

34. Becher to Brecht, *Briefe; Anmerkungen*, p. 958.

35. Bredel to Kantorowicz, 2 February 1935, TsGALI: 631/13/63/3.

36. Uhse, "Zu Brechts 'Dreigroschenroman,'" pp. 65–66.

37. Haland, "Zu Brechts 'Dreigroschenroman,'" pp. 66–67.
38. Ibid.
39. Ibid.
40. Ibid.
41. The one treatment of this episode in East German scholarship is disingenuous. Dieter Schiller mentions the controversy that broke out over Kantorowicz' article and quotes from Uhse's reply. But his conclusion is tendentious nonsense: "It can be assumed that Uhse's counter review did not originate without consultation among the circle of socialist writers in Paris. In any case, Becher's letters to Brecht permit the conclusion that they were intended to help avoid senseless confrontation in the preparatory phase of the Paris congress, to go beyond schematic appraisals of literature, and to do justice to the special characteristics of literary creativity. That was in keeping with Becher's efforts during the time he spent in Paris." Schiller, Pech, Herrmann, and Hahn, *Exil in Frankreich*, p. 543. What about Haland's officious judgment of Brecht, printed—presumably by design—after Uhse's article?
42. Brecht to Steffin, 10–15 February 1935, in Okljanskij, *O malenkom soldate*, p. 44.
43. Brecht to Steffin, 2–6 March 1935, ibid., p. 50. By 20 March Brecht was in Moscow; see Brecht, *Briefe; Anmerkungen*, p. 962. He stayed in the same hotel, the Novaja Moskovskaja, in which Ernst Ottwalt and his wife had been living since their arrival in the USSR. Brecht found his behavior peculiar and wrote Weigel that Ottwalt was everywhere at the same time, but, no matter how he tried, nothing really came of it ("Ottwalt ist wie der Dampf in allen Gassen, verliert viel und hat nichts"). Brecht to Weigel, March–April 1935, *Briefe*, p. 247. See also Okljanskij, *O malenkom soldate*, p. 49. Ottwalt drank heavily and had not cut back after his arrival in Moscow.
44. Brecht to Steffin, 2–6 March 1935, in Okljanskij, *O malenkom soldate*, p. 50. He had been invited by MORT (in German, IRTB), which stood for Internationaler Revolutionärer Theaterbund, headed by Piscator. Reich also played a leading role in the organization until its dissolution in 1936.
45. Brecht to Steffin, 26 February–1 March 1935, ibid., p. 47.
46. Cf. ibid., p. 44.
47. Brecht to Weigel, April 1935, *Briefe*, pp. 248–50.
48. The reception held on 21 April was organized by the Soviet writers' union. Kirsanov read his translation of Brecht's "Ballade vom toten Soldaten," various members of Tairov's Chamber Theater performed selections from the *Dreigroschenoper*, and Carola Neher gave her rendition of ballads and songs from the opera. Wieland Herzfelde discussed Brecht's position within German poetry, and Asja Lazis dealt with the subject of Brecht as a pro-

ducer. "Bert Brekht v Moskve," *Pravda*, 23 April 1935. See also the report on a "Brecht-Abend" published in the *Deutsche Zentral-Zeitung* (10 May 1935).

49. It is interesting to note the frequency with which Brecht's name appears together with other literary figures or (in the case of Kun) politicians who, to put it mildly, did not get along with Georg Lukács. Kun and Lukács, of course, had been archenemies for a number of years, Valdemar Knorin was friends with Tretjakov, and so on. One wonders just how large a factor purely personal matters might have played in Lukács' contempt for Brecht's writing.

50. Brecht to Weigel, April 1935, *Briefe*, pp. 247–48.

51. Brecht to Weigel, March–April 1935, ibid., pp. 247–49.

52. Brecht to Weigel, April 1935, ibid., p. 248.

53. Brecht to Koltsov, late May–early June 1935, ibid., p. 251. Asked later why he had not stayed in Moscow, Brecht replied frivolously, "I could not get enough sugar for my tea and coffee." Quoted in Esslin, *Das Paradox des politischen Dichters*, p. 229.

54. Tretjakov to Brecht, 2 July 1935, BBA, 477/129–130.

55. Tretjakov to Brecht, 19 July 1935, BBA, 477/127–128.

56. Tretjakov to Brecht, 17 September 1936, BBA, 477/121–122.

57. Merin, "Das Werk des Bert Brecht," p. 83.

58. Ibid.

59. Ibid., p. 91.

60. Ibid., p. 96.

61. Ibid., p. 97. Karl Schmückle, one of the editors of *Internationale Literatur*, wrote Merin on 16 May 1935: "Your long article on Bert Brecht is being type-set; it is scheduled to come out in two parts in no. 6 and no. 7. I find the article good and correct in the basic line that it follows. But I do have objections in a number of questions, for example: I think Brecht's specific attitude toward several prominent representatives of the heritage, say, for instance, to Swift—just to mention a single name—could have been handled with greater emphasis and in more depth. As far as Swift is concerned, on the other hand, your article is not yet concerned with 'Spitzköpfe und Rundköpfe.' Then your treatment of the terms 'epic' and 'pedagogy' strikes me as insufficiently convincing. . . . I think this article is especially useful and very profitable for the discussion concerning Brecht's methods and significance. You've surely heard that he is here at the moment. I have had a number of discussions with him." TsGALI: 631/13/69/67.

62. Brustov, "Bertolt Brekht," p. 145.

63. Ibid., p. 146.

64. Ibid., pp. 153–54.

65. Judging by his reference to the "Fight for the Soviet Power of German Workers and Peasants," a slogan that the party had re-

cently scrapped, Brustov was somewhat out of touch with the times.

66. Brustov, "Bertolt Brekht," p. 162.

67. Steffin to Brecht, 20 February 1936, in Okljanskij, *O malenkom soldate*, p. 159. Steffin must have been referring to the version that came out in (the chronically late) *Internationale Literatur* 1 (1936): 25–60.

68. Steffin to Brecht, 4 March 1936, in Okljanskij, *O malenkom soldate*, p. 158. The novel carried a 1935 imprint, but Soviet publications often appeared after their official release date. The novel was favorably reviewed in a well-written article by Hugo Huppert in the Soviet German-language daily *Deutsche Zentral-Zeitung* (29 June 1936). Brecht heard about the review and asked Otto Bork, head of the German section of VEGAAR, to send him a copy. Brecht to Bork, 20 July 1936, *Briefe*, p. 293. He also complimented the work of the press: "The novel is beautifully printed, vastly better than the edition published by the Dutch house." Brecht to Bork, 30 November 1936, ibid., p. 299.

69. Steffin to Brecht, 5 March 1936, in Okljanskij, *O malenkom soldate*, p. 159. Steffin put "soon" into quotation marks. The novel (published by Goslitizdat) was not out in fact until 1937. V. Admoni (see Bibliography) reviewed it well but raised most of the points already made in the previous articles by Kantorowicz, Uhse, Haland, Merin, and Brustov.

70. See Brecht's correspondence with Otto Bork. Brecht to Bork, 20 July and 30 November 1936, *Briefe*, pp. 293–94 and 298–99.

71. See also Brecht's exchange of letters with Piscator about the latter's plans for a film adaptation of "Schweik." Brecht to Piscator, 4 and 21 April, and June 1937, ibid., pp. 321–24. The relationship between Piscator's and Lenfilm's plans is unclear.

72. Steffin to Brecht, 5 March 1936, in Okljanskij, *O malenkom soldate*, p. 159.

73. See Bibliography.

74. See Bibliography. There was apparently some talk of bringing out Tretjakov's book in a German translation. Tretjakov to Graf, 25 February 1936, Graf, *Reise in die Sowjetunion*, p. 179. Most of the individual portraits, by the way, had already appeared in one version or another in various German-language monthlies.

75. See Okljanskij, *O malenkom soldate*, p. 153.

76. See ibid., p. 151, and Tretjakov to Graf, 3 February 1936, in Graf, *Reise in die Sowjetunion*, p. 177. Mikhail Apletin (who later befriended Brecht) was the "shtatnyj zamestitel"—evidently a sort of business manager—acting, together with Tretjakov, as Koltsov's deputy.

77. Becher's brief involvement apparently ended in late February or early March 1936, when Herzfelde (who was in Moscow at the time) and Osten assumed responsibility for preparing the first

issue of the journal. Brecht may also have appeared a logical choice as editor of *Das Wort* because Herzfelde had earlier tried to persuade him to help edit *Die neuen deutschen Blätter.* See Brecht to Becher, July–August 1933, *Briefe*, pp. 176–77. Following the writers' congress in Paris, Brecht wrote Becher on the subject of a monthly: "*It is important that the newly founded association* [that is, the writers' association for the defense of culture, formed at the congress in Paris] *be given an organ and that it begin functioning as a literary society, that is, that it start producing and editing literary works.* . . . In the hard times ahead of us, a publicistic base needs to have been established beforehand." But Brecht also noted, "I regard a journal as less effective because it is always the middle-level people who constantly contribute. A process of *self-clarification among the writers* [*Selbstverständigung der Schriftsteller*] must be begun. The congress is at least a start, but then only a start." Brecht to Becher, July 1935, *Briefe*, pp. 259.

78. Osten to Feuchtwanger, 1 April 1936, TsGALI, 631/13/65/10.
79. Cf. Osten (in Moscow) to Feuchtwanger, 23 May 1936: "I'm leaving here on the 9th or 15th of June." TsGALI, 631/13/65/26.
80. Osten to Ljudmilla Scheinina (in Moscow), 24 July 1936: "How are things; I'm staying with Brecht. The city is hardly bearable. . . . It's almost impossible to breath. Brecht, who constantly wants to abduct me to Denmark, says I wouldn't be able to sleep for eight days in the south, at Feuchtwanger's." TsGALI, 631/12/143/432.
81. Brecht to Piscator, 12 October 1936, *Briefe*, p. 295.
82. Bredel to Herzfelde, 21 December 1936; Herzfelde to Bredel, 28 December 1936, TsGALI, 631/12/143/57 and 55.
83. Bredel to Osten, 17 March 1937, TsGALI: 631/12/143/415.
84. The Lukács circle had regarded Hay early on as a sort of antipode to Brecht. Although Hay was not especially successful as a playwright during his years in Soviet exile (a fact that no doubt rankled him, increasing his hostility toward Brecht and, incidentally, Friedrich Wolf), he was built up by Lukács' backers as a dramatist of genuinely international stature. In unpublished "Gutachten" written by Andor Gábor, one of Lukács' sycophantic followers, Hay's *Haben* was characterized as "the most significant work of central European leftist stage writing during the last half of a decade," "a lasting repertory piece of high value." Gábor later called the play *Kamerad Mimi* "the best product of Comrade Hay" and praised *Der Putenhirt* in similar terms. See Gábors "Gutachten," the one of *Haben* dated 23 July 1937, the others undated, in Gábor's literary estate, Magyar Tudomanyos Akadémia, Budapest, 4481/79 and 80; 4482/87.
85. Cf., e.g., Hay's evaluation of a book submitted to *Das Wort* for review: "Philistine dilletantism without a trace of talent or not

without malicious hostility toward the Soviet Union. There is no reason to review the book or to mention it at all." Dated 28 January 1939, TsGALI, 631/12/154/272.

86. Reich, "Zur Methodik der antifaschistischen Dramatik," p. 71.
87. Brecht to Piscator, March 1937, *Briefe*, p. 316.
88. Brecht to Reich, 11 March 1937, ibid., pp. 312–13.
89. Brecht to Hay, March 1937, ibid., pp. 313–14.
90. Brecht to Becher, 11 March 1937, ibid., pp. 314–15.
91. Cf. Hay's letter to Brecht (7 March 1937, *Briefe; Anmerkungen*, pp. 986–87). Hay's phraseology ("In spite of your good intentions") recalls Lukács' theory about the insufficiency of good intentions when combined with an "incorrect" creative method.
92. Bredel to Benjamin, 28 March 1937, TsGALI, 631/12/141/81.
93. Redaktion "Das Wort" to Benjamin, 27 May 1937, TsGALI, 631/12/ 141/80. I see no reason to believe Erpenbeck when he claims that the rejection resulted from a decision taken by Bredel. Nor is it clear what essay had been received that covered the same material, and why, after all, was Benjamin never asked to shorten the piece?
94. Erpenbeck to Benjamin, 3 July 1937, TsGALI, 631/12/141/79. *Das Wort* regularly published reviews (some by Erpenbeck) of books that had appeared two or three years earlier.
95. Benjamin to Bredel, 20 December 1936; Bredel to Benjamin, 11 March 1937; Benjamin to "Werte Genossen," 14 July 1937, TsGALI, 631/12/141/86, 83, and 77.
96. Erpenbeck to Benjamin, undated, TsGALI, 631/12/141/76.
97. Erpenbeck to Benjamin, 9 December 1937, TsGALI, 631/12/141/70.
98. Aleksandrov, "Obraz materi," p. 44.
99. Ibid., p. 47.
100. For details, see my *German Writers in Soviet Exile*, pp. 286–99.
101. See Kurella to Erpenbeck, 8 June 1938, quoted in ibid., pp. 395–96.
102. Brecht to Kurella, 17 June 1938, *Briefe*, pp. 372–74.
103. Brecht to Bredel, July-August, ibid., pp. 373–74.
104. Cf. *German Writers in Soviet Exile*, pp. 299–306.
105. Hay, "Put k realizmu," p. 34.
106. Ibid., p. 35.
107. Rokotov, "Po puti demokratii" and Rejkh, "Novinki antifashist-skoj dramaturgii."
108. Rokotov to Brecht, 14 August 1939, TsGALI, 631/13/69/171.
109. Ibid.
110. *Furcht und Elend des Dritten Reichs* (Moscow: Mezhdunarod-naja kniga, 1941); *Strakh i otchajanie v III. imperii* (Moscow: "Khudozhestvennaja literatura," 1941); *Ts . . . tishe! ili opasnyj malchik. Pesa v 1. d.* (Moscow: Iskusstvo, 1941); *Der Spitzel. Winterhilfe* (Moscow: Izdatelstvo literatury na inostrannykh

jazykakh, 1944). Various one-act plays also appeared in Soviet periodicals.
111. Kozjura, "Imet," p. 38.
112. Reich, "Uroki literaturnoj diskussii," p. 136.
113. Becher, "Unkenntnis und Aufrichtigkeit," in Becher, *Publizistik*, pp. 19 and 23. The article first appeared in *Literaturnaja gazeta* (26 May 1940).
114. Reich, "Iskazhennaja dejstvitelnost," p. 150.
115. Ibid., p. 152.
116. Ibid., p. 153.
117. Benjamin, *Versuche über Brecht*, p. 132.
118. Brecht, *Arbeitsjournal*, p. 636.

CHAPTER 12

1. Brecht, "The Other Germany," *GW*, vol. 20, pp. 283–84.
2. Antonov-Ovseyenko, *The Time of Stalin*, pp. 210–13, 307.
3. Brecht, "Kraft und Schwäche der Utopie," *GW*, vol. 19, p. 435.
4. Sternberg, *Der Dichter und die Ratio*, p. 24.
5. Brecht, "Kraft und Schwäche der Utopie," pp. 435–36.
6. Ibid. These passages strike me as a more reliable and certainly more elaborate indication of Brecht's attitude toward collectivization than Sternberg's recollections of a 1931 conversation between Brecht, Tretjakov, and some members of the Communist opposition party (the KPO). See Sternberg, *Der Dichter und die Ratio*, p. 23.
7. Brecht, "Über die Diktaturen einzelner Menschen," *GW*, vol. 20, p. 103.
8. Ibid.
9. Stalin, "Questions of Agrarian Policy in the Soviet Union," in Stalin, *Leninism*, pp. 272–73; and Deutscher, *Stalin*, p. 320.
10. Brecht, "Kraft und Schwäche der Utopie," p. 437.
11. Benjamin, *Versuche über Brecht*, p. 130.
12. Sternberg, *Der Dichter und die Ratio*, p. 42.
13. Brecht, "Kraft und Schwäche der Utopie," p. 438.
14. Ibid.
15. Stalin, "Dizzy with Success," in *Leninism*, p. 281.
16. Brecht, "Über die Diktaturen einzelner Menschen," pp. 101–2.
17. Ibid. In the late thirties Brecht grew more generally critical of the Soviet Communist party, but he seems never to have attributed its shortcomings to Stalin or to have thought in systemic terms. He told Benjamin in 1938: "In Russia a dictatorship rules *over* the proletariat. A break with it is to be avoided as long as this dictatorship still carries out practical work for the proletariat." Benjamin, *Versuche über Brecht*, p. 135. The devastatingly critical remark that Brecht made in his *Arbeitsjournal* (January 1939,

p. 36) about the general state of affairs in Soviet intellectual life is in a similar vein: his attitude toward the situation remained in spite of everything "critically positive." See also note 66.

18. According to Antonov-Ovseyenko, of the 1,961 voting delegates to the seventeenth party congress in 1934, perhaps two dozen survived Stalin's terror. Antonov-Ovseyenko, *The Time of Stalin*, p. 126. Brecht was not altogether heedless of what was happening to the party; he wrote in *Me-ti* ("Theorie des To-tsi [Trotsky]"): "Twenty years after the takeover of power by the league [Communist party], the prisons were still overflowing, and there were death sentences and trials everywhere in which even old members of the league were involved. Large-scale wars with bourgeois countries were imminent." Brecht, *Me-ti, GW*, vol. 12, p. 524. The passage is worth considering carefully and indicates how difficult it can be at times to pin Brecht down on issues pertaining to the USSR. The comments contain, however, no hint that Brecht regarded the inhabitants of the cells or defendants in the docks as, in the main, entirely innocent. In fact, the reference to imminent war with "bourgeois countries" points in the direction of a rationalization for overflowing prison cells and corresponded with Brecht's general approval of the show trials.

19. Brecht's perceptions must have coincided with Feuchtwanger's. In *Moscow 1937* Feuchtwanger had appeared to be quite critical of the personality cult, but upon closer examination, his criticism deteriorates into meaninglessness. For, calling Stalin a "modest" man, Feuchtwanger supported virtually all of Stalin's policies. Brecht, by the way, found *Moscow 1937* "very interesting" (Brecht to Dudow, July 1937, *Briefe*, p. 331), telling Feuchtwanger: "I find your 'De Russia' to be the best that has yet come out on this subject within European literature. It is such a decisive step to see reason as something so practical and human, something that possesses its own morality and immorality. This is what makes its experimental character manifest, which is of interest to the human race, after all, and which disappears when a rigid morality is set above it, because experimenting itself is of a morally dubious nature. I am very happy that you wrote it." Brecht to Feuchtwanger, August 1937, *Briefe*, p. 334. Much later, by mid-1943, however, Brecht's willingness to believe bad things about Stalin had finally increased, helped along by Souvarine's "depressing book about stalin." *Arbeitsjournal*, p. 589.

20. Brecht, "Ni-ens Ruf," *Me-ti*, p. 467.

21. Ibid. The same kind of thinking concerning the absence of proof surfaces in Brecht's poem "Ist das Volk unfehlbar?," written after Tretjakov's arrest: "To demand papers that prove guilt in black and white / Is senseless, for such papers need not exist. / The criminals have proof of their innocence in hand. / The innocent often have no proof." "Ist das Volk unfehlbar?," p. 743. In other

words, the lack of "documentary evidence" in the case of at least some of those arrested in the USSR did not necessarily prove anything. In the case of Stalin, Brecht implies in *Me-ti*, a dark path was being trod for the first time in history; proof that the road led in the right direction did not exist, therefore, and the people would be more inclined to follow their leader on blind faith if he let himself be enveloped in a shroud of greatness and infallibility.

22. Brecht, "Ansprache des Bauern an seinen Ochsen," *GW*, vol. 9, pp. 683–84.

23. Brecht, "Ni-ens Ruf," *Me-ti*, p. 467.

24. Brecht, "Vorschlag Me-tis, Ni-ens Beinamen betreffend," *Me-ti*, p. 467. See also "Die Verehrung des Ni-en (2)," ibid., p. 536: "Me-ti said: Some know that Ni-en is a useful man in many ways. That means much to them. Some know that he is an ingenious man, the greatest of men, a kind of God. That means not quite as much, perhaps, to them as the other means to the others."

25. Benjamin, *Versuche über Brecht*, p. 131.

26. Brecht, "Über die Freiheit in der Sowjetunion," *GW*, vol. 20, pp. 104–5.

27. Ibid.

28. The fears were understandable (if exaggerated) in the years immediately following the revolution. After the civil war, they were groundless.

29. Brecht, "Über die Moskauer Prozesse," *GW*, vol. 20, p. 115.

30. Brecht, "Über die Diktaturen einzelner Menschen," p. 102.

31. Brecht, "Die Prozesse des Ni-en," *Me-ti*, p. 538.

32. In his analysis of the accusations raised at the trials, Brecht also wrote of one specific point made in the indictment: "On the other hand, the following account is improbable: that agents paid by capitalism, already during the time of the revolution, wormed their way into the Soviet government with the intention of employing all the means at their command to reintroduce capitalism into Russia. This account sounds improbable because it disregards the element of development; it is mechanical, undialectical, rigid." Brecht, "Über die Moskauer Prozesse," p. 115. But this was a major point of the charges leveled against the defendants. If Brecht found it "improbable" (though not utterly absurd), how was it that he could not discern any pattern of improbability in the other charges or any link between Stalin's mysterious combination of the probable and the improbable?

33. Brecht, "Die Prozesse des Ni-en," p. 538.

34. Brecht, "Über die Moskauer Prozesse," p. 111.

35. Ibid., pp. 111 and 113.

36. Ibid., p. 113.

37. Ibid., p. 114.

38. Ibid.
39. Ibid., pp. 114–15.
40. Brecht, *Arbeitsjournal*, p. 589.
41. Fetscher pursues the point in "Brecht und der Kommunismus,"
    pp. 878–79.
42. Brecht, "Über die Unfreiheit unter Ni-en-leh und Ni-en," *Me-ti*,
    p. 438.
43. Brecht was by no means a direct advocate of cruelty or torture,
    but he objected staunchly to any watered-down humanism. He
    explained that Lenin, when he called for the use of terror, had
    spoken out forcefully against a kind of "counterrevolutionary
    humanism" that was out of touch with the requirements of the
    day. "That is not the same as advocating physical torture," Brecht
    explained; "[torture] is never acceptable and does not have to be
    accepted." "Über die Moskauer Prozesse," p. 113. But what about
    the separation of families and mass deportation of "kulaks" to
    uninhabitable regions of arctic Siberia, where they quickly froze
    or starved to death, during the forced collectivization of Soviet
    agriculture? Was that not a form of torture? Did Brecht never
    hear of the NKVD's use of torture to extract confessions from
    innocent prisoners? Such reports circulated widely in the West,
    but perhaps Brecht disqualified them all as unsubstantiated
    rumors. Given his propensity for shutting his eyes to the truth or
    dismissing various Soviet "vices" as historically transitory phe-
    nomena, are there really any grounds for Bormans to believe "un-
    shakably" that Brecht would never have countenanced the in-
    vasion of Czechoslovakia in 1968 or the use of weapons against
    striking Polish workers in 1970 (or in the early eighties)? See
    Bormans, "Brecht und der Stalinismus," p. 73. There is, of course,
    no way of telling for sure, but the dialectic that Brecht resorted to
    as a means of accounting for Stalin's "mistakes" was put into
    service again after 1953 by Brecht and many others.
44. Brecht, "Über die Unfreiheit unter Mi-en-leh und Ni-en," *Me-ti*,
    pp. 438–39.
45. Brecht, "Über die Diktaturen einzelner Menschen," p. 103. Cf.
    also "Theorie des To-tsi [Trotsky]," *Me-ti*, pp. 523–24.
46. Brecht, "Über die Diktaturen einzelner Menschen," p. 101.
47. Brecht, "Über das Töten," *Me-ti*, p. 553.
48. Brecht, *Die heilige Johanna der Schlachthöfe*, GW, vol. 11, p.
    783; *Die Massnahme*, ibid., p. 652. See also the comments in
    "Über die Unfreiheit der Schriftsteller in der Sowjetunion" (*GW*,
    vol. 19, p. 439): "The truth is that bourgeois rule uses different
    forms of coercive violence, quiet kinds in the democracies and
    blatant forms in the fascist states. And the truth is that a stop to
    any kind of violence can only be put by the use of a different kind
    of violence. What happens when one avoids taking a position

with respect to either of these forms of violence being discussed here? Then one lends his support to one of the two kinds of violences that is ruling."

49. Brecht, "Die Widersprüche von Su," *Me-ti*, p. 524.

50. Ibid.

51. These words, of course, were Brecht's celebrated rejoinder to Sidney Hook when the latter asked for his opinion concerning the arrests that followed the assassination of Sergej Kirov. Hook threw Brecht out of his apartment. I do not deal with this apercu elsewhere because, unlike some scholars, I do not regard it as one. Some commentators have been inclined to interpret the utterance as a display of keen insight into the character of totalitarianism. James Lyon, for instance, refers to Henry Pachter's statement in this regard; but Lyon takes no stand of his own and neglects to comment further on the exact nature of this insight. Lyon, *Brecht in America*, p. 302. This interpretation, by the way, appears to go back to Hannah Arendt. Within the context of her exposition of terror and ideology and her view of a totalitarian society in which the distinction between executioner and victim is obliterated, it is easy to see how Brecht's remark fits in. This fails to change the fact, however, that Brecht could scarcely have meant anything of the sort, and those who claim otherwise still bear the burden of proof. Considering the year in which Brecht expressed his opinion, late 1935, and bearing in mind what he then knew of the USSR and how he interpreted it, I can only conclude that Brecht's "apercu" was a frivolous provocation of Hook with no deeper significance to it.

52. Brecht, "Die Polizei von Su," *Me-ti*, p. 547.

53. Brecht, "Über Polizei," ibid., p. 568.

54. Benjamin, *Versuche über Brecht*, p. 124.

55. Brecht, "Die Polizei von Su," p. 547. Cf. also "Über Länder, die besondere Tugenden hervorbringen," *Me-ti*, p. 518, and, in the same vein, in *Galileo*, the comment about the sad plight of countries that need heroes.

56. Benjamin, *Versuche über Brecht*, p. 132. I interpret these lines here to mean that Brecht perceived the existence of Soviet criminal elements arresting the innocent and perverting due process in the USSR, though it might be plausibly argued that he imagined these "criminal elements" to be in the pay of the Gestapo. This latter interpretation, the mass terror as a Gestapo plot to infiltrate the secret police and judiciary and deprive the party of its best cadres through denunciation and false arrest, was not uncommon in the USSR at the time.

57. Cf. Brecht, "Die Verfassung des Ni-en," *Me-ti*, p. 535: "Because [the new system] is being forcibly brought about by small units of men, there is coercion everywhere and no real rule by the people. The freedom of opinion, freedom to assemble, lip-service,

the violent acts of the magistrats [my italics] prove that by no means all basic elements of the *grand order* have been realized and are being developed."
58. Brecht, "Das Land, das keine besonderen Tugenden nötig hat," *Me-ti,* p. 520.
59. See the preceding study of Lukács. Pasternak told Ehrenburg one snowy night, "If only someone would tell Stalin about it!" Cf., similarly, Meyerhold's remarks: "[T]hey conceal it from Stalin." Quoted in Conquest, *The Great Terror,* pp. 112–13.
60. Quoted in Mandelshtam, *Hope against Hope,* p. 13.
61. Brecht, *Arbeitsjournal,* p. 36.
62. One of Brecht's two letters to Feuchtwanger, asking him to press for information about Neher, was, however, probably never sent. Brecht, *Briefe; Anmerkungen,* pp. 992–93.
63. Brentano to Brecht, 23 January 1937, ibid., p. 983.
64. Benjamin, *Versuche über Brecht,* p. 130.
65. Kaganovich, "The Great Driver of the Locomotive of History," pp. 44–45.
66. Brecht to Brentano, early February 1937, *Briefe,* pp. 302–3. There is no denying, on the other hand, that in the late thirties Brecht developed serious doubts about the Soviet Communist party, even if he never came close to breaking with it. He wrote in September 1939: "the talk one hears everywhere to the effect that the bolshevist party has changed itself from the ground up is certainly not correct. the misfortune is precisely that it has not changed itself. . . . the people, the masses, the proletariat are still not deciding things; rather, the government is deciding for the people, the masses, the proletariat. [Stalin] has not brought the people such and such a distance, the people do not 'yet' have this and that interest or do not recognize it 'yet.'" Brecht, *Arbeitsjournal,* p. 67. Comments of this sort make it all the more difficult to understand how Brecht can base so many of his remarks about the USSR on what the ordinary people supposedly thought or desired.
67. The quote is from Milosz, *The Captive Mind,* p. 133.
68. Brecht to Benjamin, early February 1937, *Briefe,* pp. 302–3.
69. Benjamin, *Versuche über Brecht,* p. 130.
70. Brecht to Feuchtwanger, May 1937, *Briefe,* p. 326.
71. Ibid.
72. Brecht to Feuchtwanger, June 1937, ibid., pp. 326–27.
73. Ibid.
74. Feuchtwanger to Brecht, 30 May, BBA, 478/68.
75. Brecht to Osten, undated (late 1938 or early 1939), *Briefe,* pp. 382–83.
76. Conquest, *The Great Terror,* p. 441.
77. Brecht, "Ist das Volk unfehlbar?," *GW,* vol. 9, p. 743.
78. Ibid., pp. 741–43.

79. Brecht, "Besser Fehler zu billigen als Fehler zu rechtfertigen," *Me-ti*, p. 546. Brecht's dialectical explanations appear especially grotesque when compared with the insights of perceptive Soviet intellectuals passed on for one by Nadezhda Mandelshtam: "We never asked, on hearing about the latest arrest, 'What was he arrested for?' but we were exceptional. Most people, crazed by fear, asked this question just to give themselves a little hope: if others were arrested for some reason, then they wouldn't be arrested, because they hadn't done anything wrong. They vied with each other in thinking up ingenious reasons to justify each arrest. . . . Both public opinion and the police kept inventing new and more graphic ones, adding fuel to the fire without which there is no smoke. This was why we had outlawed the question 'What was he arrested for?' '*What for?*' Akhmatova would cry indignantly whenever, infected by the prevailing climate, anyone of our circle asked this question. 'What do you mean, *what for?* It's time you understood that people are arrested *for nothing!*'" Mandelshtam, *Hope against Hope*, p. 11.

80. Brecht, "Motto," *GW*, vol. 9, p. 641.

81. Brecht, "Ist das Volk unfehlbar?," p. 743.

82. Ibid.

83. Held, "Stalins deutsche Opfer und die Volksfront," p. 8.

84. According to what Ruth Berlau told Hans Bunge, she regarded Brecht's concern for Neher as "wonderful"; Neher, after all, "really actually harmed him."

85. "That was very embarrassing for me," Berlau told Bunge.

86. Brecht, "Das Waschen," *GW*, vol. 9, p. 607.

87. Brecht, "An die Nachgeborenen," ibid., pp. 722–25.

88. Brecht, "Eine notwendige Feststellung im Kampf gegen die Barbarei," *GW*, vol. 18, p. 242. See also "Wenn die Untat kommt, wie der Regen fällt," ibid., p. 552.

89. Held, "Stalins deutsche Opfer und die Volksfront," p. 8.

90. See Serge und Sedova, *The Life and Death of Leon Trotsky*, p. 255.

CHAPTER 13

1. *Supplementband IV*, p. 377. See also the poem "Ich, der Überlebende," *GW*, vol. 10, p. 882.

2. See, for instance, Brecht's letter to Wieland Herzfelde, 24 August 1937, *Briefe*, p. 337.

3. Reich, *Im Wettlauf mit der Zeit*, p. 378.

4. On the other hand, there is the curious case of Tretjakov's edition of Brecht's plays, *Epicheskie dramy*. Evidently, this volume was not withdrawn from the library following Tretjakov's arrest; only his introduction was ripped from the front of the book and the

phrase "translated and with an introductory study by S. M. Tretjakov" scratched off the title page. This is the condition of one of the two copies in the Lenin Library today.

5. All three men, especially Reich and Granach, could have given Brecht firsthand impressions of the terror. By the time Brecht passed through Moscow in summer 1941, both Reich and Asja Lazis had been arrested, though Reich was later freed and met with Brecht that May. In the United States, then, Brecht would have had the chance to hear the story of Granach's arrest. In fact, Granach (and Marta Feuchtwanger) had picked up Brecht at San Pedro harbor when he arrived on the ship from Vladivostok. These talks may have changed Brecht's earlier assessment of the terror, though this cannot be deduced from his written statements.

6. Of course, in writing the poem cited above, it is entirely possible that Brecht also or only had friends of his in mind who were either directly or indirectly among Hitler's victims, and Brecht did write several poems about his personal "casualty list," which included names like Margarete Steffin and Walter Benjamin. See *GW*, vol. 10, pp. 826–29. In fact, the published poem "Ich, der Überlebende" was apparently prompted by a German atrocity committed on the Russian front in early 1942 and had nothing directly to do with German victims of Stalinist terror. In a conversation with Brecht, Salka Viertel had expressed her guilt at having survived when so many were dying in the war, the specific event that evoked her sense of guilt being the murder of some 7,000 Russian civilians in Kerch by German occupation troops. The next morning, she found Brecht's poem under her door. Lyon, *Brecht in America*, pp. 37–38. If, when writing the poem on survival cited in the text, Brecht was thinking exclusively of those who had fallen victim to Hitler, and not of his close acquaintances victimized by Stalin's terror, this would lend an ironic dimension to the poem, though the workings of Brecht's mind may well have caused him to regard those who had disappeared in the Soviet Union as being victims of fascism, in a dialectical sense.

7. Brecht, "Gefährlichkeit der Intelligenzbestien," *GW*, vol. 18, p. 253.

8. Milosz, *The Captive Mind*, p. 220.

9. Brecht, "Faschismus und Kapitalismus," *GW*, vol. 20, p. 188.

10. Brecht, "Gefährlichkeit der Intelligenzbestien," p. 253.

11. Ibid.

12. Brecht, *Supplementband IV*, pp. 297–98.

13. Brecht, "Plattform für die linken Intellektuellen," *GW*, vol. 20, p. 239.

14. Ibid., p. 240.

15. Brecht, "Überall Freunde," *GW*, vol. 8, p. 844.

16. Brecht, "Eine notwendige Feststellung im Kampf gegen die Barbarei," *GW*, vol. 18, p. 245.
17. Ibid.
18. Brecht, "Über die Kritik an Stalin," *GW*, vol. 20, p. 325.
19. Ibid.
20. Brecht, "Eine notwendige Feststellung im Kampf gegen die Barbarei," p. 246.
21. Ibid., p. 245.
22. The line reads: "Without knowledge of the dialectic, transitions such as that from Stalin as a motor to Stalin as a break are incomprehensible." "Über die Kritik an Stalin," p. 326.
23. Brecht, "Eine notwendige Feststellung im Kampf gegen die Barbarei," p. 242.
24. Ibid., p. 245.
25. Brecht, "Brechtisierung," *GW*, vol. 20, p. 68.
26. Brecht, "Plattform für die linken Intellektuellen," p. 240.
27. Orwell, *1984*, p. 173.
28. Benjamin, *Versuche über Brecht*, p. 131.
29. Brecht, "Eine notwendige Feststellung im Kampf gegen die Barbarei," p. 242.
30. Milosz, *The Captive Mind*, p. 133.
31. Brecht, "Rede zum II. Internationalen Schriftstellerkongress zur Verteidigung der Kultur," *GW*, vol. 18, p. 248.
32. Brecht, *Supplementband IV*, p. 438.
33. Ibid., p. 348. One might be inclined to interpret the following lines as a plea for understanding: "You who were born later, when you read what I wrote / Remember, friends, the age in which I wrote. / Whatever you may think, do not forget / This age." Brecht, "Bitte an die Nachwelt um Nachsicht," *Supplement IV*, p. 349.
34. Sperber, *Die vergebliche Warnung*, p. 164.
35. Brecht, "Fünf Schwierigkeiten beim Schreiben der Wahrheit," *GW*, vol. 18, p. 222.
36. See Pachter's letter to *The New Republic*, 28 April 1969; the original text of Brecht's remarks is in a private letter from Pachter to Sidney Hook, which the latter made available to me.
37. Sperber, *Die vergebliche Warnung*, p. 164.
38. Brecht, "Fünf Schwierigkeiten beim Schreiben der Wahrheit," p. 224.
39. Ibid.
40. Ibid., p. 225.
41. Ibid.
42. Ibid., pp. 226–27.
43. Brecht, "Eine notwendige Feststellung im Kampf gegen die Barbarei," p. 246.
44. Brecht, "Fünf Schwierigkeiten beim Schreiben der Wahrheit," p. 229.

45. Brecht, "Freiheit der Kunst," *GW*, vol. 20, pp. 54–55.
46. Ibid., p. 55.
47. These are the poems, incidentally, that the Brecht archive (and heirs) claimed for years did not exist.
48. Brecht, *Supplementband IV*, p. 437.
49. Ibid., p. 438.
50. Ibid., p. 437.
51. Ibid., p. 436.
52. Ibid. By way of introduction to one of his Stalin poems, Brecht wrote: "The historical assessment of Stalin is of no interest at the moment and cannot be undertaken due to the absence of facts. But to do away with the damage by his example, his authority must be liquidated." *Supplementband IV*, p. 438. But the lines from the two poems just cited are in their own way, of course, just such an historicized assessment of Stalin.
53. Brecht, "Über Wahrheit," *GW*, vol. 20, p. 190.
54. Brecht, "Über die Wiederherstellung der Wahrheit," *GW*, vol. 20, p. 191.
55. The quotation is from Arendt, *The Origins of Totalitarianism*, p. 473.
56. Quoted from Milosz, *The Captive Mind*, p. iv.

BIBLIOGRAPHY

· ·

LUKÁCS' WRITINGS

"Aus der Not eine Tugend." *Die Linkskurve*, nos. 11–12 (1932): 15–24.

"Autobiographie." Manuscript in Lukács Archivum és Könyvtár, Budapest.

"Die Erbschaft dieser Zeit." Manuscript in Lukács Archivum és Könyvtár, Budapest.

"Erzählen oder Beschreiben?" In *Probleme des Realismus I: Essays über Realismus*, pp. 197–242. Neuwied: Hermann Luchterhand Verlag, 1971.

"Die Fabrik im Walde." *Moskauer Rundschau*, 8 February 1931.

Frühschriften II: Geschichte und Klassenbewusstsein. Neuwied: Hermann Luchterhand Verlag, 1967.

"Gegen die Spontaneitätstheorie in der Literatur," *Die Linkskurve*, no. 4 (1932): 30–33.

Gelebtes Denken: Eine Autobiographie im Dialog. Frankfurt am Main: Suhrkamp Verlag, 1981.

"Gerhart Hauptmann." *Die Linkskurve*, no. 10 (1932): 5–12.

"Das Grand Hotel 'Abgrund.'" Manuscript in Lukács Archivum és Könyvtar, Budapest.

"Der grosse Oktober 1917 und die heutige Literatur." *Kürbiskern*, no. 1 (1968): 89–105.

"Ilja Ehrenburg." *Moskauer Rundschau*, 9 November 1930.

"Die intellektuelle Physiognomie des künstlerischen Gestaltens." In *Probleme des Realismus I: Essays über Realismus*, pp. 151–96. Neuwied: Hermann Luchterhand Verlag, 1971.

"K probleme obektivnosti khudozhestvennoj formy." *Literaturnyj kritik*, no. 9 (1935): 5–23.

"Kunst und objektive Wahrheit." In *Probleme des Realismus I: Essays über Realismus*, pp. 607–50. Neuwied: Hermann Luchterhand Verlag, 1971.

Lenin: Studie über den Zusammenhang seiner Gedanken. Vienna: Malik-Verlag, 1924.

"Michail Scholochow." *Moskauer Rundschau*, 12 October 1931.

"Neuer Inhalt und alte Form." *Moskauer Rundschau*, 11 January 1931.

Probleme des Realismus III: Der historische Roman. Neuwied: Hermann Luchterhand Verlag, 1965.

"Realizm v sovremmenoj nemetskoj literature" (Realism in Contemporary German Literature). *Literaturnyj kritik*, no. 6 (1934): 36–56.

"Reportage oder Gestaltung: Kritische Bemerkungen anlässlich eines Romans von Ottwalt (I. Teil)." *Die Linkskurve*, no. 7 (1932): 23–30.

"Reportage oder Gestaltung: Kritische Bemerkungen anlässlich eines Romans von Ottwalt (II. Teil)." *Die Linkskurve*, no. 8 (1932): pp. 26–31.

Schriften zur Ideologie und Politik. Neuwied: Luchterhand, 1973.

"Shaws Bekenntnis zur Sowjetunion." *Die Linkskurve*, no. 9 (1931): 5–8.

"Tendenz oder Parteilichkeit." *Die Linkskurve*, no. 6 (1932): 13–21.

"Tolstoj in Deutschland." *Moskauer Rundschau*, 21 September 1930.

"Tonbandgespräch mit Prof. György Lukács, geführt von Frau Dr. Siebert am 10.12.1969," Manuscript in Johannes-R.-Becher-Archiv, Akademie der Künste der DDR.

"Über den Dostojewski-Nachlass." *Moskauer Rundschau*, 22 March 1931.

"Volkstribun oder Bürokrat?" In *Probleme des Realismus I: Essays über Realismus*, pp. 413–55. Neuwied: Hermann Luchterhand Verlag, 1971.

Wie ist Deutschland zum Zentrum der reaktionären Ideologie geworden? Budapest: Akadémiai Kiadó, 1982.

Wie ist die faschistische Philosophie in Deutschland entstanden? Budapest: Akadémiai Kiadó, 1982.

"Willi Bredels Romane." *Die Linkskurve*, no. 11 (1931): 22–27.

Die Zerstörung der Vernunft. Neuwied: Hermann Luchterhand Verlag, 1962.

"Znachenie 'Materializma i èmpiriokrititsizma' dlja bolshevizatsii kommunisticheskikh partij" (The Importance of "Materialism and Empirio-Criticism" for the Bolshevization of Communist Parties). *Pod znamenem marksizma*, no. 4 (1934): 143–48.

"Zum Verfassungsentwurf der UdSSR: Die neue Verfassung der UdSSR und das Problem der Persönlichkeit. Aus einem Vortrag." *Internationale Literatur*, no. 9 (1936): 50–53.

BRECHT'S WRITINGS

Arbeitsjournal. Frankfurt am Main: Suhrkamp Verlag, 1973.

Briefe. Frankfurt am Main: Suhrkamp Verlag, 1981.

Briefe; Anmerkungen. Frankfurt am Main: Suhrkamp Verlag, 1981.

Chiki i chuki. Moscow: Gosudarstvennoe izdatelstvo khudozhestvennoj literatury, 1936.

Epicheskie dramy. Perevod s nemetskogo i vvodny ètud S. M. Tretjakova. Moscow-Leningrad: Gosudarstvennoe izdatelstvo khudozhestvennoj literatury, 1934.

Gedichte 1. Vol. 8. Frankfurt am Main: Suhrkamp Verlag, 1967.
Gedichte 2. Vol. 9. Frankfurt am Main: Suhrkamp Verlag, 1967.
Gedichte 3. Vol. 10. Frankfurt am Main: Suhrkamp Verlag, 1967.
Prosa 1. Vol. 11. Frankfurt am Main: Suhrkamp Verlag, 1967.
Prosa 2. Vol. 12. Frankfurt am Main: Suhrkamp Verlag, 1967.
Schriften zur Literatur und Kunst 1. Vol. 18. Frankfurt am Main:
Suhrkamp Verlag, 1967.
Schriften zur Literatur und Kunst 2. Vol. 19. Frankfurt am Main:
Suhrkamp Verlag, 1967.
Schriften zur Politik und Gesellschaft. Vol. 20. Frankfurt am Main:
Suhrkamp Verlag, 1967.
Supplementband III: Gedichte aus dem Nachlass 1. Frankfurt am
Main: Suhrkamp Verlag, 1982.
Supplementband IV: Gedichte aus dem Nachlass 2. Frankfurt am
Main: Suhrkamp Verlag, 1982.

PRIMARY SOURCES

Admoni, V. "Roman Bertolta Brekhta" (A Novel by Bertolt Brecht).
Literaturnyj sovremmenik, no. 3 (1937): 244–50.
Aleksandrov, V. "Obraz materi" (An Image of a Mother). *Literaturnyj
kritik*, no. 6 (1937): 42–62.
Averbakh, Leopold. "Proletarian Literature and the Peoples of the
Soviet Union. For Hegemony of Proletarian Literature." *Litera-
ture of the World Revolution*, no. 5 (1931): 93–125.
———. "Zur Programmdiskussion." *Die Linkskurve*, no. 11 (1931):
22–23.
Becher, Johannes R. "Einen Schritt weiter!" *Die Linkskurve*, no. 1
(1930): 1–5.
———. "Kühnheit und Begeisterung. Der 1. Mai und unsere Literatur-
Revolution." *Die Linkskurve*, no. 5 (1932): 1–11.
———. "Unkenntnis und Aufrichtigkeit." In *Publizistik II 1939–
1945*, pp. 18–23. Berlin-Weimar: Aufbau Verlag, 1978.
———. "Unsere Wendung." *Die Linkskurve*, no. 10 (1931): 1–8.
Benjamin, Walter. *Versuche über Brecht*. Frankfurt am Main: Suhr-
kamp Verlag, 1971.
"Bert Brekht v Moskve" (Bert Brecht in Moscow). *Pravda*, 23 April
1935.
"Brecht-Abend." *Deutsche Zentral-Zeitung*, 10 May 1935.
Bredel, Willi. "Einen Schritt weiter." *Die Linkskurve*, no. 1 (1932):
pp. 20–22.
"Der Brief des Genossen Stalin und die KPD." *Internationale Presse-
Korrespondenz*, no. 3 (12 January 1932): 70–72.
Brustov, A. "Bertolt Brekht." *Zvezda*, no. 9 (1935): 144–62.
Fragen des Leninismus. Berlin: Dietz Verlag, 1951.
Gejden, Konrad. *Istorija germanskogo fashizma* (The History of Ger-

man Fascism). Moscow-Leningrad: Gosudarstvennoe sotsialno-èkonomicheskoe izdatelstvo, 1935.

Georg Lukács und der Revisionismus: Eine Sammlung von Aufsätzen. Berlin: Aufbau Verlag, 1960.

Gotsche, Otto. "Kritik der Anderen—Einige Bemerkungen zur Frage der Qualifikation unserer Literatur." *Die Linkskurve,* no. 4 (1932): 28–30.

Graf, Oskar Maria. *Reise in die Sowjetunion 1934.* Neuwied: Luchterhand Verlag, 1974.

Günther, Hans. *Der Herren eigener Geist: Ideologie des Nationalsozialismus.* Moscow-Leningrad: Verlagsgenossenschaft ausländischer Arbeiter, 1935.

Haland, Paul. "Zu Brechts 'Dreigroschenroman.'" *Unsere Zeit,* no. 8 (2–3 April 1935): 66–67.

Hay, Julius. "Put k realizmu" (The Path to Realism). *Teatr,* no. 2–3 (1939): 32–39.

Held, Walter. "Stalins deutsche Opfer und die Volksfront." *Unser Wort,* no. 4–5 (October 1938): 8.

Huppert, Hugo. "Der Dreigroschenroman." *Deutsche Zentral-Zeitung,* 29 June 1936.

Judin, Pavel. "Lenin i nekotorye voprosy literaturnoj kritiki" (Lenin and Several Problems of Literary Criticism). *Literaturnyj kritik,* no. 1 (1933): 11–31.

Kaganovich, L. M. "Für ein bolschewistisches Studium der Geschichte der Partei. Rede, gehalten am 1. Dezember anlässlich der zehnjährigen Wiederkehr der Gründung des Instituts der Roten Professur." *Internationale Press-Korrespondenz,* no. 117 (15 December 1932): 2661–68.

———. "The Great Driver of the Locomotive of History." In *Stalin,* pp. 41–52. New York: Workers Library Publishers, 1940.

Kantorowicz, Alfred. "Brechts 'Der Dreigroschenroman.'" *Unsere Zeit,* no. 7 (12 December 1934): 61–62.

Kozjura, N. "Imet" (Haben). *Literaturnoe obozrenie,* no. 16 (1940): 36–38.

"Litfront." In *Literaturnaja èntsiklopedija,* pp. 506–13. Moscow: "Sovjetskaja èntsiklopedija," 1934.

Mekhlis, Lev. "Za perestrojku raboty RAPP" (For the Reorganization of RAPP's Work). *Pravda,* 24 November 1931.

Merin, Peter. "Das Werk des Bert Brecht." *Internationale Literatur,* no. 7 (1935): 77–97.

Milosz, Czeslaw. *The Captive Mind.* New York: Vintage Books, 1981.

Mitin, Mark. "Ocherednye zadachi raboty na filosofskom fronte v svjazi s itogami diskussii" (The Primary Goals of our Work on the Philosophical Front in Connection with the Results of the Discussion). *Pod znamenem marksizma,* no. 3 (1931): 12–35.

———. "Über die Ergebnisse der philosophischen Diskussion." In *Kontroversen über dialektischen und mechanistischen Materi-*

alismus, edited by Oskar Negt, pp. 330–91. Frankfurt am Main: Suhrkamp Verlag, 1969.

———, Raltsevich, Pavel Judin, and Takser. "Proletarskuju literaturu—na vysshuju stupen!" (Raise Proletarian Literature to a Higher Level). *Pravda*, 19 November 1931.

"Nashi zadachi" (Our Goals). *Literaturnyj kritik*, no. 1 (1933): 3–10.

Negt, Oskar, ed. *Kontroversen über dialektischen und mechanistischen Materialismus*. Frankfurt am Main: Suhrkamp Verlag, 1969.

"O zhurnale 'Pod znamenem marksizma'" (The Journal "Under the Banner of Marxism"). *Pravda*, 26 January 1931.

"Ob itogakh diskussii i ocherednykh zadachakh marksistsko-leninskoj filosofii" (The Results of the Discussion and the Urgent Tasks of Marxist-Leninist Philosophy). *Pravda*, 26 January 1931.

Orwell, George. *1984*. New York: Signet Classics, 1969.

Ottwalt, Ernst. *Deutschland erwache! Geschichte des Nationalsozialismus*. Vienna-Leipzig: Hess and Co. Verlag, 1932.

———. "'Tatsachenroman' und Formexperiment. Eine Entgegnung an Georg Lukács." *Die Linkskurve*, no. 10 (1932): 21–26.

Pieck, Wilhelm. *We Are Fighting for a Soviet Germany*. Report to the Thirteenth Plenum of the ECCI, December 1933. New York: Workers Library Publishers, 1934.

Pieck, Wilhelm, and Otto Grotewohl. "Zehn Jahre Stalinsche Verfassung." *Neues Deutschland*, 5 December 1946.

Reich, Bernhard. *Im Wettlauf mit der Zeit: Erinnerungen aus fünf Jahrzehnten deutscher Theatergeschichte*. Berlin: Henschelverlag, 1970.

———. "Iskazhennaja dejstvitelnost" (Distorted Reality). *Teatr*, no. 2 (1941): 45–50.

———. "Novinki antifashistskoj dramaturgii" (The Latest in Antifascist Dramaturgy). *Teatr*, no. 2–3 (1939): 57–62.

———. "Uroki literaturnoj diskussii" (The Lessons of the Literary Discussion). *Teatr*, no. 6 (1940): 124–36.

———. "Zur Methodik der antifaschistischen Dramatik." *Das Wort*, no. 1 (1937): 63–72.

Révai, Josef. "The Character of a 'People's Democracy.'" *Foreign Affairs*, no. 10 (1949): 143–52.

———. "Georg Lukács: *Geschichte und Klassenbewusstsein*." In *A "Történelem és Osztálytudat" a 20-as évek vitáiban* (History and Class Consciousness in the Political Debates of the Twenties): *Szöveggyüjtemény IV. Kötet*, edited by T. Krausz and M. Mesterházi, pp. 140–44. Budapest: Lukács Archivum és Könyvtár, 1981.

Rokotov, Timofej. "Po puti demokratii" (On the Road to Democracy). *Teatr*, nos. 2–3 (1939): 51–56.

Shurygin, S. "Itogi obsuzhdenija pisma tov. Stalina v partorganizatsii IKP filosofii" (The Results of the Discussion concerning Comrade Stalin's Letter in the Party Organization of Philosophy Section of the Institute of Red Professors). *Pod znamenen marksizma*, nos. 11/12 (1931): 238–50.

———. "Protiv menshevistvujushche-idealisticheskoj falsifikatsii istorii filosofskoj borby Lenina" (Against the Menshevizing and Idealistic Falsification of the History of Lenin's Philosophical Struggle). *Pod znamenem marksizma*, nos. 11/12 (1931): 230–40.

Stalin, Joseph. *Leninism*. Vol. 1. New York: International Publishers, 1933.

———. "Neue Verhältnisse—neue Aufgaben." In *Fragen des Leninismus*, pp. 402–24. Berlin: Dietz Verlag, 1951.

———. "O nekotorykh voprosakh istorii bolshevizma" (Several Questions regarding the History of Bolshevism). *Proletarskaja revoljutsija*, no. 10 (1931): 3–12.

———. *O velikoj otechestvennoj vojne Sovetskogo Sojuza* (The Great Patriotic War of the Fatherland). Moscow: Voennoe izdatelstvo ministerstva vooruzhennykh sil Sojuza SSR, 1949.

———. "Rechenschaftsbericht an den XVII. Parteitag über die Arbeit des ZK der KPdSU (B)." In *Fragen des Leninismus*, pp. 511–89. Berlin: Dietz Verlag, 1951.

———. "Rede auf der ersten Unionsberatung der Stachanowleute am 17. November 1935." In *Fragen des Leninismus*, pp. 597–612. Berlin: Dietz Verlag, 1951.

———. "Über den Entwurf der Verfassung der UdSSR. Bericht auf dem Ausserordentlichen VIII. Sowjetkongress der UdSSR am 25. November 1936." In *Fragen des Leninismus*, pp. 611–46. Berlin: Dietz Verlag, 1951.

———. "Über die Grundlagen des Leninismus." In *Fragen des Leninismus*, pp. 9–100. Berlin: Dietz Verlag, 1951.

"Stalin über den Kampf gegen Zentrismus: Die Stellung Lenins und der Bolschewiki zu den Strömungen in der Sozialdemokratie der Vorkriegszeit; Wie Lenin gegen Opportunisten und Sumpfpolitiker unversöhnlich kämpfte." *Rote Fahne*, 22 November 1931.

"Der Stalin-Brief und unser Kampf gegen den Krieg." *Die Internationale: Zeitschrift für Praxis und Theorie des Marxismus*, no. 3 (1932): 134–37.

Stèn, Jan. "Nasha partija i voprosy teorii" (Our Party and Questions of Theory). In *A "Történelem és Osztálytudat" a 20-as évek vitáiban* (History and Class Consciousness in the Political Debates of the Twenties): *Szöveggyüjtemény II. Kötet*, edited by T. Krausz and M. Mesterházi, pp. 91–101. Budapest: Lukács Archivum és Könyvtár, 1981.

Thälmann, Ernst. "Einige Fehler in unserer theoretischen und praktischen Arbeit und der Weg zu ihrer Überwindung." *Die Internationale*, no. 11/12 (1931): 481–509.

———. *Im Kampf gegen die faschistische Diktatur. Rede und Schlusswort des Genossen Ernst Thälmann auf der Parteikon-*

ferenz der KPD. im Oktober 1932. Die politische Resolution der Parteikonferenz. Kommunistische Partei Deutschlands, 1932.

——. "Der revolutionäre Ausweg und die KPD: Rede auf der Plenartagung des ZK der KPD am 19. Februar 1932." In *Reden und Aufsätze 1930–1933 (I)*, pp. 358–470. Cologne: Verlag Rote Fahne, 1975.

——. "Schlusswort auf dem XII. Plenum des EKKI." In *Reden und Aufsätze 1930–1933 (II)*, pp. 238–84. Cologne: Verlag Rote Fahne, 1975.

——. "Zu unserer Strategie und Taktik im Kampf gegen den Faschismus." *Die Internationale*, no. 6 (1932): 261–92.

Tretjakov, S. M. *Ljudi odnogo kostra* (Men of the Same Bonfire): *Literaturnye portrety.* Moscow: Gosudarstvennoe izdatelstvo "Khudozhestvennaja literatura," 1936.

Uhse, Bodo. "Zu Brechts 'Dreigroschenroman.'" *Unsere Zeit*, no. 8 (2–3 April 1935): 65–66.

"Ein unveröffentlichter Brief Friedrich Engels über Balzac." *Die Linkskurve*, no. 3 (1932): 11–14.

Usievich, Elena. "Klassovaja borba v literature" (The Class Struggle in Literature). *Literaturnyj kritik*, no. 1 (1934): 13–28.

——. "Za konkretnoe rukovodstvo" (For Concrete Guidance). *Literaturny kritik*, no. 2 (1932): 3–14.

"Das XII. Plenum des EKKI. und die KPD." *Die Internationale*, no. 9 (1932): 373–90.

"Za gegemoniju proletarskoj literatury" (For the Hegemony of Proletarian Literature). *Pravda*, 31 August 1931.

SECONDARY SOURCES

Adorno, Theodor W. *Gesammelte Schriften.* Vol. 2, *Noten zur Literatur.* Frankfurt am Main: Suhrkamp Verlag, 1974.

Antonov-Ovseyenko, Anton. *The Time of Stalin: Portrait of a Tyranny.* New York: Harper & Row, 1981.

Arendt, Hannah. *The Origins of Totalitarianism.* New York and London: Harcourt Brace Jovanovich, 1973.

Bahne, Siegfried. "Die Kommunistische Partei Deutschlands." In *Das Ende der Parteien 1933: Darstellungen und Dokumente*, edited by Erich Matthias and Rudolf Morsey, pp. 655–739. Düsseldorf: Droste Verlag, 1960.

Bathrick, David. "A One-Sided History: Brecht's Hitler Plays." In *Literature and History.* Lanham, Md. and London, 1983.

Bormans, Peter. "Brecht und der Stalinismus." In: *Brecht-Jahrbuch 1974*, pp. 52–76. Frankfurt am Main: Suhrkamp Verlag, 1974.

Brecht-Chronik: Daten zu Leben und Werk. Edited by Klaus Völker. Munich: Carl Hanser Verlag, 1971.

Brown, Edward J. *The Proletarian Episode in Russian Literature 1928–1932*. New York: Columbia University Press, 1950.

Brzezinski, Zbigniew K. *The Soviet Bloc: Unity and Conflict*. Cambridge: Harvard University Press, 1967.

Carr, E. H. *Twilight of the Comintern, 1930–1935*. New York: Pantheon Books, 1982.

Cohen, Stephen F. "Bolshevism and Stalinism." In *Stalinism: Essays in Historical Interpretation*, edited by Robert C. Tucker, pp. 3–29. New York: W. W. Norton & Co., 1977.

Congdon, Lee. *The Young Lukács*. Chapel Hill: University of North Carolina Press, 1983.

Conquest, Robert. *The Great Terror: Stalin's Purge of the Thirties*. New York: Collier Books, 1973.

Dallin, Alexander, and George W. Breslauer. *Political Terror in Communist Systems*. Stanford: Stanford University Press, 1970.

Deutscher, Isaac. *The Prophet Outcast*. Vol. 3, *Trotsky: 1929–1940*. New York: Vintage Books, 1963.

———. *Stalin: A Political Biography*. New York: Vintage Books, 1960.

———. *The Prophet Outcast*. Vol. 3, *Trotsky: 1929–1940*. New York: Vintage Books, 1963.

Ermolaev, Herman. *Soviet Literary Theories, 1917–1934: The Genesis of Socialist Realism*. Berkeley: University of California Press, 1963.

Esslin, Martin. *Das Paradox des politischen Dichters*. Frankfurt am Main: Athenäum Verlag, 1962.

Fetscher, Iring. "Brecht und der Kommunismus." *Merkur*, no. 9 (1973), pp. 872–86.

Freidin, Gregory. "Mandelshtam's 'Ode to Stalin': History and Myth." *Russian Review*, no. 4 (1982): 400–426.

Friedrich, Carl J., and Zbigniew K. Brzezinski. *Totalitarian Dictatorship and Autocracy*. Cambridge: Harvard University Press, 1965.

Gallas, Helga. *Marxistische Literaturtheorie: Kontroversen im Bund proletarisch-revolutionärer Schriftsteller*. Neuwied: Hermann Luchterhand Verlag, 1971.

Geschichte der Kommunistischen Partei der Sowjetunion (Bolschewiki): Kurzer Lehrgang. Berlin: Verlag der sowjetischen Militärverwaltung in Deutschland, 1946.

Kołakowski, Leszek. *Main Currents of Marxism. Its Origin, Growth, and Dissolution*. Vol. 3, *The Breakdown*. Oxford: Oxford University Press, 1978.

Leonhard, Wolfgang. *Sowjetideologie heute: Die politischen Lehren*. Frankfurt am Main: Fischer Bücherei, 1962.

Lewin, Moshe. "The Social Background of Stalinism." In *Stalinism: Essays in Historical Interpretation*, edited by Robert C. Tucker, pp. 111–36. New York: W. W. Norton & Co., 1977.

Lichtheim, George. *George Lukács.* New York: Viking Press, 1970.

Ludz, Peter Christian. "Der Begriff der 'demokratischen Diktatur' in der politischen Philosophie von Georg Lukács." In Georg Lukács, *Schriften zur Ideologie und Politik*, pp. xvii-lv. Neuwied: Hermann Luchterhand Verlag, 1973.

Lyon, James K. *Brecht in America.* Princeton: Princeton University Press, 1980.

Mandelshtam, Nadezhda. *Hope against Hope: A Memoir.* New York: Atheneum, 1976.

Medvedev, Roy A. *Let History Judge: The Origins and Consequences of Stalinism.* New York: Vintage Books, 1973.

Nettl, Peter. *Rosa Luxemburg.* Cologne: Kiepenheuer & Witsch, 1967.

Okljanskij, Jurij. *Povest o malenkom soldate.* Moscow: Izdatelstvo "Sovetskaja Rossija," 1978.

Pike, David. *German Writers in Soviet Exile, 1933–1945.* Chapel Hill: University of North Carolina Press, 1982.

———. "Eine Faschismustheorie der Komintern? Ernst Ottwalts Geschichte des Nationalsozialismus." *Exil: Forschung. Erkenntnisse. Ergebnisse.* no. 1 (1982): 56–68.

Schiller, Dieter, Karlheinz Pech, Regine Herrmann, and Manfred Hahn. *Exil in Frankreich.* Leipzig: Verlag Philipp Reclam jun., 1981.

Serge, Victor and Natalia Sedova. *The Life and Death of Leon Trotsky.* New York: Basic Books, 1975.

Siegel, Holger. *Sowjetische Literaturtheorie (1917–1940): Von der historisch-materialistischen zur marxistisch-leninistischen Literaturtheorie.* Stuttgart: J. B. Metzlersche Verlagsbuchhandlung, 1981.

Skilling, H. Gordon. "'People's Democracy' in Soviet Theory." *Soviet Studies*, no. 6 (1951): 16–33, 131–49.

Steiner, George. "Making a Homeland for the Mind." *Times Literary Supplement*, 22 January 1982.

Stephan, Alexander. "Georg Lukács' erste Beiträge zur marxistischen Literaturtheorie." In *Brecht-Jahrbuch 1975*, pp. 79–111. Frankfurt am Main: Suhrkamp Verlag, 1975.

Sternberg, Fritz. *Der Dichter und die Ratio: Erinnerungen an Bertolt Brecht.* Göttingen: Sache & Pohl Verlag, 1963.

Sywottek, Arnold. *Deutsche Volksdemokratie: Studien zur politischen Konzeption der KPD 1935–1946.* Düsseldorf: Bertelsmann Universitätsverlag, 1971.

Tauscher, Rolf. *Brechts Faschismuskritik in Prosaarbeiten und Gedichten der ersten Exiljahre.* Berlin: Brecht-Zentrum der DDR, 1981.

Utis, O. "Generalissimo Stalin and the Art of Government." *Foreign Affairs*, no. 20 (1952): 197–214.

Weber, Hermann. *Die Generallinie: Rundschreiben des Zentral-
komitees der KPD an die Bezirke, 1929–1933*. Introduction by
Hermann Weber. Düsseldorf: Droste Verlag, 1981.
―――. *Die Wandlung des deutschen Kommunismus*. Vol. 1, *Die
Stalinisierung der KPD in der Weimarer Republik*. Frankfurt am
Main: Europäische Verlagsanstalt, 1969.
―――. *Hauptfeind Sozialdemokratie: Strategie und Taktik der
KPD, 1929–1933*. Düsseldorf: Droste Verlag, 1981.
Weingartner, Thomas. *Stalin und der Aufstieg Hitlers: Die Deutsch-
landpolitik der Sowjetunion und der Kommunistischen Interna-
tionale, 1929–1934*. Berlin: Walter de Gruyter & Co., 1970.
*Zur Tradition der sozialistischen Literatur in Deutschland: Eine
Auswahl von Dokumenten*. Berlin-Weimar: Aufbau Verlag, 1967.

INDEX